MODERNISM AND STILL LIFE

Edinburgh Critical Studies in Modernist Culture
Series Editors: Tim Armstrong and Rebecca Beasley

Available

Modernism and Magic: Experiments with Spiritualism, Theosophy and the Occult
Leigh Wilson

Sonic Modernity: Representing Sound in Literature, Culture and the Arts
Sam Halliday

Modernism and the Frankfurt School
Tyrus Miller

Lesbian Modernism: Censorship, Sexuality and Genre Fiction
Elizabeth English

Modern Print Artefacts: Textual Materiality and Literary Value in British Print Culture, 1890–1930s
Patrick Collier

Cheap Modernism: Expanding Markets, Publishers' Series and the Avant-Garde
Lise Jaillant

Portable Modernisms: The Art of Travelling Light
Emily Ridge

Hieroglyphic Modernisms: Writing and New Media in the Twentieth Century
Jesse Schotter

Modernism, Fiction and Mathematics
Nina Engelhardt

Modernist Life Histories: Biological Theory and the Experimental Bildungsroman
Daniel Aureliano Newman

Modernism, Space and the City: Outsiders and Affect in Paris, Vienna, Berlin, and London
Andrew Thacker

Modernism Edited: Marianne Moore and the Dial *Magazine*
Victoria Bazin

Modernism and Time Machines
Charles Tung

Primordial Modernism: Animals, Ideas, transition (1927–1938)
Cathryn Setz

Modernism and Still Life: Artists, Writers, Dancers
Claudia Tobin

Forthcoming

Slow Modernism
Laura Salisbury

Modernism and the Idea of Everyday Life
Leena Kore-Schröder

Novel Sensations: Modernist Fiction and the Problem of Qualia
Jon Day

Hotel Modernity: Literary Encounters with Corporate Space
Robbie Moore

The Modernist Exoskeleton: Insects, War and Literary Form
Rachel Murray

Modernism and Religion: Poetry and the Rise of Mysticism
Jamie Callison

Abstraction in Modernism and Modernity: Human and Inhuman
Jeff Wallace

www.edinburghuniversitypress.com/series/ecsmc

MODERNISM AND STILL LIFE

Artists, Writers, Dancers

Claudia Tobin

EDINBURGH
University Press

Edinburgh University Press is one of the leading university presses in the UK. We publish academic books and journals in our selected subject areas across the humanities and social sciences, combining cutting-edge scholarship with high editorial and production values to produce academic works of lasting importance. For more information visit our website: edinburghuniversitypress.com

Edinburgh University Press Ltd
The Tun – Holyrood Road, 12(2f) Jackson's Entry, Edinburgh EH8 8PJ

First published in hardback by Edinburgh University Press 2020

Typeset in 10/12.5 Adobe Sabon by
IDSUK (DataConnection) Ltd

A CIP record for this book is available from the British Library

ISBN 978 1 4744 5513 8 (hardback)
ISBN 978 1 4744 5514 5 (paperback)
ISBN 978 1 4744 5515 2 (webready PDF)
ISBN 978 1 4744 5516 9 (epub)

CONTENTS

FIGURES AND PLATES

Figures

Plates

ABBREVIATIONS

AP	Charles Mauron, *Aesthetics and Psychology*, trans. Roger Fry and Katherine John (London: Hogarth Press, 1935).
CPP	Wallace Stevens, *Collected Poetry and Prose*, ed. Frank Kermode and Joan Richardson (New York: Library of America, 1997).
MMD	Margaret Morris and Fred Daniels, *Margaret Morris Dancing: A Book of Pictures* (London: Kegan Paul, 1926).
NR	Wallace Stevens, 'The Noble Rider and the Sound of Words', in *Collected Poetry and Prose*, pp. 643–65.
RF	Virginia Woolf, *Roger Fry: A Biography* (London: Hogarth Press, 1940; repr. 1991).
RPP	Wallace Stevens, 'The Relations Between Poetry and Painting', in *Collected Poetry and Prose*, pp. 740–51.

ACKNOWLEDGEMENTS

I would like to thank the many friends, colleagues and family members who have shaped this book and strengthened it in ways that are hard to measure. I am immensely grateful to Grace Brockington and Stephen Cheeke (my PhD supervisors) for their guidance and enthusiasm at the very outset of this project and throughout its evolution. This book began as a doctoral thesis at the University of Bristol supported by an AHRC doctoral award, for which I am hugely grateful. I found stimulating forums for discussion and inquiry in the English and History of Art departments at the University of Bristol and I am especially grateful to Ralph Pite for his generosity and insights, and for enlarging my sense of the scope of this project. For inspiring conversations in Bristol I thank Michael Malay; and all of my fellow co-founders of the 'Art Writing, Writing Art' research network. I would also like to thank Hester Jones and Alexandra Harris for their wisdom and advice as my PhD examiners – and to express my ongoing appreciation for enlivening discussions and support from Alex.

I am immensely grateful to the Leverhulme Trust for awarding me an Early Career Fellowship at the University of Cambridge, which has enabled me to finish this book while enriching it through my research on colour and the imagination. I thank all my friends, colleagues and students in the Faculty of English and the Department of History of Art at Cambridge, who have been a source of great inspiration. In particular I am grateful to Steven Connor for his advice and guidance, and to Fiona Green for her acute reading and comments on my chapter on Wallace Stevens. For conversation and creative thinking, I especially thank Laura McCormick Kilbride, Sophie Seita and Nicky Kozicharow, and for ever-ready words of encouragement I thank my office mates Rachel Malkin and Diarmuid Hester. Jesus College has provided an inspiring home for me as a Research Associate and I thank Elizabeth Fowden, Preti Taneja, Hjördis Becker-Lindenthal, Rod Mengham, Donal Cooper and Christopher Burlinson, among many other colleagues with whom I have enjoyed enlightening discussions beyond my own discipline.

This project was enriched by working with Frances Spalding on the exhibition *Virginia Woolf: Art, Life and Vision* (2014) at the National Portrait Gallery. I am very grateful to Frances for all that I have learned from her about Woolf, Bloomsbury and beyond, and for her generous spirit, insights and perceptive reading of my manuscript at various stages. The last stage of writing this book was invigorated by my involvement with *Virginia Woolf: An Exhibition Inspired by Her Writings*, and I enjoyed conversations with the circle of artists and researchers it brought together, especially with the curator Laura Smith. Along the way, Philip Goodman has brought a vivid personal element to my research on Bloomsbury. I am grateful to Philip for sharing his memories with me, and to the Goodman and Leigh families for their warmth and generosity.

Many places as well as people have enriched the writing of this book. An IPS award from the AHRC enabled me to conduct research at the Huntington Library, California during my doctoral studies, and to benefit from discussions in the inspiring setting of its botanical gardens. The Paul Mellon Centre for British Art also provided a welcoming and vibrant research community while revising my manuscript some years later as a Postdoctoral Fellow. I thank Sarah Victoria Turner and all of those at the PMC who offered advice and a responsive audience for various iterations of this project. I also thank my colleagues at the universities of the Sorbonne, Paris Diderot, Poitiers and Montpellier, where I have found a warm welcome and receptive audience for my research. My particular thanks go to Catherine Bernard for her interest and hospitality during my visiting fellowship at Paris Diderot.

I am grateful to the institutions and private lenders who have kindly given me permission to reproduce images of works from their collections in this book. Many of them have assisted me immensely with my research. I especially thank Harriet Judd at Pallant House Gallery; Jovan Nicholson; Andrew Nairne, Lucia Hutton and Frieda Midgley at Kettle's Yard; Emily Hill at Charleston; Jonathan Clark Fine Art; and Amy Fairley, Paul Adair and Jenny Kinnear at the Fergusson Gallery, Perth, for their generous assistance in unearthing uncatalogued materials and images. I would also like to thank Peter Khoroche for his responsiveness to my inquiries, and John Hitchens for welcoming me into the home and studio of his father, Ivon Hitchens. I extend my thanks also to the archivists at the British Library, National Art Library and Tate Gallery Archive. I am grateful to the Faculty of English Research Fund for support towards the publication of images in this book.

I would like to acknowledge the following permissions: Excerpt from *The Diary of Virginia Woolf*, Volume I, edited by Anne Olivier Bell. Diary copyright © 1977 by Quentin Bell and Angelica Garnett. Reprinted by permission of Houghton Mifflin Harcourt Publishing Company. All rights reserved. Excerpt from *The Diary of Virginia Woolf*, Volume I, 1915–1919 by Virginia Woolf; ed. by Anne Olivier Bell, assisted by Andrew McNeillie. Published by Hogarth Press. Reprinted by permission of The Random House Group Limited. © 1977. Excerpt from *Roger Fry: A Biography* by Virginia Woolf. Copyright © 1940 by Houghton Mifflin Harcourt Publishing Company, renewed 1968 by Leonard Woolf. Reprinted by permission of Houghton Mifflin Harcourt Publishing Company. All rights reserved. Excerpt from *The Waves* by Virginia Woolf. Copyright © 1931 by Houghton Mifflin Harcourt Publishing Company, renewed 1959 by Leonard Woolf. Reprinted by permission of Houghton Mifflin Harcourt Publishing Company. All rights reserved. I thank The Society of Authors as the Literary Representative of the Estate of Virginia Woolf for permission to reproduce excerpts by Virginia Woolf; Joel Agee for permission to reproduce excerpts from Rainer Maria Rilke, *Letters on Cézanne*, edited by Clara Rilke, translated by Joel Agee (London: Vintage, 1991); Mme Alice Mauron for permission to reproduce excerpts of texts authored by Charles Mauron; and the Margaret Morris Movement International Limited for permission to reproduce material relating to Margaret Morris. Excerpts from Wallace Stevens's annotations in his copy of Charles Mauron's *Aesthetics and Psychology* are reproduced by permission of The Huntington Library, San Marino, California; and quotations from Wallace Stevens's collected poetry are with the kind permission of Faber and Faber Ltd. I thank Clemson University Press for permission to reproduce part of an earlier version of my essay, '"The active and the contemplative": Charles Mauron, Virginia Woolf, and Roger Fry', published in *Virginia Woolf and the World of Books* (Clemson 2018). An earlier version of my discussion of D. H. Lawrence and Cézanne appeared in '"The humbleness of all his objects": Modern Writers, Cézanne, and Still Life', in *The Humble in 19th- to 21st-Century British Literature and Arts,* ed. Jean-Michel Ganteau, Christine Reynier and Isabelle Brasme (Montpellier: PUM, September 2017); and part of Chapter 3 was published as 'Doing a mixed bunch in a *natural* way': Flower Painting and Still Life', *Ivon Hitchens: Space Through Colour* (Pallant House Gallery, 2019). Every effort has been made to trace the copyright holders where necessary, but if any have been inadvertently overlooked, the publisher will be pleased to make the necessary arrangements at the first opportunity.

For their invaluable guidance I thank my editors Rebecca Beasley and Tim Armstrong; and Jackie Jones and Ersev Ersoy at Edinburgh University Press, as well as the anonymous readers of my manuscript. For his attentive reading and copy editing, I am grateful to Tim Clark. Finally, I would like to thank once again all of my friends and family who have nourished and supported me in numerous ways, and whose curiosity has kept my enthusiasm for this project alive. I am hugely grateful to my parents and brother Oliver Tobin for their unstinting good humour and interest; and to all my friends, in particular Hayley Kaimakliotis, Laura Pattison, Clemmie Reynolds, Holly Nicholas and Stella Dilke, for much-needed doses of encouragement along the way. Most of all, I thank Benedict Leigh – my 'still point' – for his thoughtfulness and inquiring spirit, and for never failing to bring a sense of adventure to this (and to any) project. All of the above mentioned will understand when I find myself unexpectedly sympathising with Wyndham Lewis, when he asserts in *Blast*, 2 (1915): 'However musical or vegetarian a [wo]man may be, his [or her] life is not spent exclusively amongst apples and mandolins.' But writing this book has taught me that they can prove the most surprising and communicative of companions.

SERIES EDITORS' PREFACE

This series of monographs on selected topics in modernism is designed to reflect and extend the range of new work in modernist studies. The studies in the series aim for a breadth of scope and for an expanded sense of the canon of modernism, rather than focusing on individual authors. Literary texts will be considered in terms of contexts including recent cultural histories (modernism and magic; sonic modernity; media studies) and topics of theoretical interest (the everyday; postmodernism; the Frankfurt School); but the series will also re-consider more familiar routes into modernism (modernism and gender; sexuality; politics). The works published will be attentive to the various cultural, intellectual and historical contexts of British, American and European modernisms, and to inter-disciplinary possibilities within modernism, including performance and the visual and plastic arts.

Tim Armstrong and Rebecca Beasley

INTRODUCTION: 'NOTHING IS REALLY *STATICALLY* AT REST': CÉZANNE AND MODERN STILL LIFE

> [Cézanne] raised still life to such a point that it ceased to be inanimate.[1]
>
> Wassily Kandinsky

> The apples positively got redder & rounder & greener. I suspect some very mysterious quality of potation [?] in that picture.[2]
>
> Virginia Woolf

> [T]he interior of the picture vibrates, rises and falls back into itself, and does not have a single unmoving part.[3]
>
> Rainer Maria Rilke

> [N]othing is really *statically* at rest – a feeling he seems to have had strongly – as when he watched the lemons shrivel or go mildewed, in his still-life group.[4]
>
> D. H. Lawrence

Still life presents a paradox. The polarities of 'stillness' and 'motion' are thrust into uneasy contact as the 'still' – eternal yet frozen – art object confronts the rhythms and vitality of ephemeral 'life'. Strictly, the term refers to a genre of painting that depicts inanimate objects, yet the implications of 'still life' in the modern world are more complex and enigmatic. Its very designation conjures word play and duality, gesturing toward what the Italian painter Giorgio de

Chirico (1888–1978) described as 'the double life of a still life'.[5] It is this unsettling and mysterious 'doubleness' from which this study takes inspiration.

Still life exists at the borders of private and public space, nature and culture, vitality and mortality. It is, as Bonnie Costello observes, 'a threshold genre'.[6] These dualities and counter-pressures invest still life with fruitful intensity, and sustain its interest for artists despite a critical tradition that regards it as a minor genre. In what follows, I do not intend to present a history of still life or a genre study, but to recover and extend the scope of its meaning across a broad transcultural and disciplinary range.[7] By examining the shifting terms and characteristics ascribed to the genre in painting, I suggest that we can open up a more nuanced discussion of the 'still life' and its significance for modern cultural practices across different media, in literature, painting, sculpture and dance. Further, we can uncover the potential for movement and transformation in the idea of stillness and the ordinary.

Firstly, it will help to briefly trace the rather convoluted etymology of still life as it evolved across European language and culture. Up until the mid-seventeenth century, the Dutch used the term *stilstaende dingen*, meaning 'still-standing things' and indicating living things in a state of rest. In about 1650 the modern term *stilleven* (*stil* meaning 'motionless' and *leven* meaning 'life or nature'), was introduced to connote the painting of 'inanimate objects' or 'immobile nature', rather than living models. The French used related terms, *choses inanimées* and *nature reposée*, meaning 'inanimate things' or 'things at rest'. A rather more morbid inflection was present in the Italian designation, *natura morta*, meaning 'dead nature'. In the mid-eighteenth century, the French also began to use *nature morte*, which has remained the preferred description, despite criticism of its limiting, negative connotations.[8] However, definitions in English directly translated the Dutch term *stilleven* as 'still life'; another interpretation was 'silent life', which departed from its original meaning but established a suggestive alliance between the 'still' and the 'silent'.[9]

As these intermingling trans-linguistic currents make clear, a static quality remains constant across different European cultures even as the term shifts and inflects. The *nature morte*, for instance, is haunted by material decay and in figurative use means 'a person or painting lacking vitality',[10] whereas 'still life' retains the possibility of animation. Nevertheless, the literature on still life and its reception is intertwined with a negative view of the still, which has governed its denigration to a 'minor' position in art-historical hierarchies (below history and religious painting, portraiture and landscape) and elsewhere, because 'stillness' is used adjectively to connote something lacking in life-force and is often associated with a meditative or elegiac mood.

In Percy Wyndham Lewis's polemical critique of modern culture, *Time and Western Man* (1927), he deploys the term *nature morte* as a negative literary attribute, connoting a heavy or sluggish style, lacking in animation, which he saw as symptomatic of early twentieth-century philosophy and literature. In Joyce's *Ulysses*, he finds a constipated narrative in which 'an immense *nature-morte* [. . .] ensues from the method of confining the reader in a circumscribed psychological space into which several encyclopedias have been emptied'.[11] The novel's two main characters, Bloom and Dedalus are, Lewis explains, 'lay-figures' on which a 'mass of dead stuff is hung'.[12] He unleashes a similar critique on Ezra Pound: like 'the *nature mortist*' who 'deals for preference with life-that-is-still, that has not much life, so Ezra for preference consorts with the dead, whose life is preserved for us in books and pictures'.[13] Drawing the 'nature mortists' of literature and art under the same umbrella, Lewis rails against the phenomenon of 'deadness' afflicting Pound, Joyce and those *nature morte* painters of Paris who 'made a fetish of Cézanne's apples'.[14]

Lewis was not alone. The apparent denial of human life imbricated in the subject matter of still life is at the heart of a long tradition that devalues the genre. Still life depicts 'rhopography' – what Norman Bryson describes as 'those things which lack importance, the unassuming material base of life' – typically located in the 'feminine' or domestic sphere.[15] According to Marc Eli Blanchard, the 'tradition of exclusion [. . .] goes from Pliny, who disparaged still life as *riparographia* or "low painting," to [Charles] Lebrun, who advised his students never to take their eyes from the realities of classical history and epic poetry', and continues through Joshua Reynolds' *Discourses on Art* to persist in some contemporary critical discussions, despite recent revisionary efforts.[16] The pejorative view of rhopography is one that Bryson subjects to critique in his important theorisation of the genre, *Looking at the Overlooked: Four Essays on Still Life Painting* (1990), in which he deconstructs the social and ideological codes by which it has been denigrated, showing the categories of 'megalography' ('great things') and rhopography to be intertwined.[17]

However, it is precisely the familiarity and domestic ordinariness of the 'still life' subject that has stimulated the many artists who have employed the genre throughout history. The objects typically depicted in still life include the matter of the table and relate to the domestic sphere: vessels, flowers, game, skulls, *objets d'art*, musical instruments, books, pipe and tobacco, as well as objects such as mirrors, clocks and decaying fruits, which serve as symbols of the transience and ephemerality of life, known as *vanitas* and *memento mori*. The genre can therefore generate multiple oppositions between stillness and movement, nature and culture, morbid and vital, private and public, human and inhuman, which have suggestive aesthetic implications. Indeed, many still life artists have implicitly challenged the premise of immobility. The subtle suggestions of life and human intervention might be signalled, for instance, through the bead of water on the skin of a fruit or a half eaten meal, gesturing toward activities beyond the picture frame. Similarly, while clocks and skulls provide overt symbols of time passing and mortality in some compositions, in others the depiction of insects hovering above flowers or feeding on comestibles (common motifs in seventeenth- and eighteenth-century Dutch *trompe l'œil*) disrupts notions of 'frozen' temporality, intimating an alternative, non-human scale of movement. As Bryson eloquently puts it, 'Besides the rapid, seismically sensitive rhythms set by consumption', the objects of still life 'are also tuned to a slow, almost geological, rhythm that is all their own'.[18]

The dialectic of stasis and motion compressed in 'still life' is central to theories of aesthetics and ekphrasis. A rich ekphrastic tradition plays on the spatial/temporal ambiguities of 'still' from Keats's 'Ode on a Grecian Urn' (1819) to T. S. Eliot's Chinese jar in his poem 'Burnt Norton' in *Four Quartets*, where we encounter: 'The stillness, as a Chinese jar still/ Moves perpetually in its stillness'.[19] What Eliot reveals, two lines later in the poem, as the 'co-existence' as well as the tension between stillness and movement, is central to this study. The self-proclaiming 'stillness' announced by still life appears to substantiate, even to intensify assumptions about painting as atemporal and static, while at the same time asserting its 'living' element. The essential principals or properties of different art forms have of course been debated in such terms since Gotthold Lessing's affirmation of the distinction between the temporal art of poetry and the spatial art of painting in his essay *Laocoön* (1766), and the notion of stillness – as an ideal or limitation – remains embedded in criticism on word and image.[20] Even Murray Krieger, a critic sensitive to these nuances, relegates the still life to a footnote in his essay, '*Ekphrasis* and the Still Movement of Poetry or *Laokoon* Revisited' (1992). He claims that 'the "still" of the genre called still life painting unhappily means only "stilled," inanimate, even in a sense dead'.[21] While recent theorists have shown that the two media can share and exchange qualities, the seemingly essential dualism of the still life might be seen as a microcosm for these continuing debates.[22] The inquiry of this book takes its departure from the semantic slippage and ambiguity that I have noted in cross-cultural translations of still life. I suggest that a re-animation of still life – both as a genre in visual art and as a mode of being – takes place in the first decades of the twentieth century. A concern with 'life', with the possible resuscitation of the inanimate/*morte* subject, is equally embedded within the etymology of still life, and is intensified in its modern re-animation(s).

The very terms of the genre therefore prompt larger aesthetic and ethical questions and a web of connotations, both pejorative and salutary, which coalesce around the troubling and inconclusive notion of stillness. Indeed, we might go so far as to consider still life as an index for the fundamental creative tension in all efforts to create art: how to sustain and represent life in 'still' – permanent and enduring rather than static – forms? *Modernism and Still Life* addresses these questions by exploring still life as a condition in which all arts are implicated, but also as an inter-disciplinary space or mode which has been central to modern cultural practices.[23] It will explore some of the ways in which 'stillness' occupied the creative imagination during the first half of the twentieth century, as well as bringing into relief the modes by which conventional divisions between the 'static' and the 'moving' were interrogated and re-imagined.

Cézanne's Apples

The still lifes of the French Post-Impressionist painter Paul Cézanne (1839–1906) are paradigmatic in my characterisation of modern still life. As we observed in the epigraphs to this Introduction, his works present a mysterious space or mode by which 'moving stillness' – as well as uncanny animation – may be achieved. Widely regarded as the modern master of still life, Cézanne painted nearly two hundred works in which he reinvigorated the genre, offering a model that reconceives the polarities of stillness and movement and demonstrates a revolutionary mode of perception and attention to objects. The artist produced still lifes that are anything but static: they vibrate with a precarious energy. It is this phenomenon, which Wassily Kandinsky, Virginia Woolf, Rainer Maria Rilke and D. H. Lawrence register in their encounters with his works. In their lexicon of responsiveness we detect a 'language' for a spectrum of aesthetic stillness and animation which is important to this inquiry.

Cézanne stimulated a striking number of modern writers to express their feelings for his work in ways that would stretch beyond formal art criticism.[24] In her perceptive essay on Cézanne's late still lifes, Bridget Alsdorf rightly points out that 'the strains of figurative language are necessary to contend with his creative achievement'.[25] As major literary and artistic figures in their own right, the responsiveness of Woolf, Rilke, Kandinsky and Lawrence to Cézanne's still lifes invites closer attention. We begin, therefore, by exploring a collage of their textual responses, which will raise several of the central themes in this study and a constellation of motifs, concerns and desires that amplify our notion of still life.

Lawrence's pronouncement that 'nothing is really *statically* at rest' is at the heart of his idiosyncratic and revisionary essay on the history of art, written in 1929 to accompany a catalogue of his own paintings. In this essay he identifies Cézanne's still lifes as the painter's 'greatest achievement'.[26] Here Cézanne escaped the 'cliché denominator, the intrusion and interference of the ready-made concept', to give 'a complete intuitive interpretation of actual objects'.[27] Cézanne had famously declared that he wanted to 'astonish Paris with an apple', and apples are the subject of a large body of his still life paintings.[28] *The Basket of Apples* c.1893 (plate 1) is an illustrative example: the basket is propped forward, poised to offer a cascade of apples. The fruits themselves seem to hover and shift within their undefined contours; several appear on the brink of rolling off the table amidst the undulating landscape created by the peaks and plunging valleys of the table cloth. The sense of instability is reinforced by the disrupted perspective, which causes the table to tilt forward, its corners out of alignment. Lawrence had already described the effect of Cézanne's 'unsteady apples' in his essay 'Art and Morality' (1925), which concludes, 'Let Cézanne's apples go rolling off the table for ever. They live by their own laws, in their own ambiente.'[29] However, it is in his later essay that this theme receives prolonged attention. In still life 'he gave us a triumphant and rich intuitive vision of a few apples and kitchen pots', Lawrence writes. 'For once his intuitive consciousness triumphed, and broke into utterance. And here he is inimitable. [. . .] It's the real appleyness, and you can't imitate it.'[30] Lawrence's neologism, 'appleyness', seeks to capture the haecceity, or what he calls the 'form and substance and *thereness*', that exudes from Cézanne's representations of apples.[31] He deploys the term 'appleyness' throughout his essay to convey the painter's revolutionary mode of intuitive awareness and recognition of the vital, physical presence of his subjects.

Many have shared Lawrence's attraction toward Cézanne's apples, obtaining creative sustenance from a similar sense of their presence and weighty reality. Woolf's contemplation of Cézanne's *Still Life with Apples* (c.1878) (plate 2), which was purchased by her friend John Maynard Keynes in 1918, borders on the hallucinatory. The small but luminous painting prompted her oft-quoted rhetorical question, 'What can 6 apples *not* be?'[32] The question opens doorways into the signification and expression of modern still life for Bloomsbury, which I pursue in my first chapter.[33] The significance of the genre for the art critic, Roger Fry, will emerge in the same chapter, but his identification of Cézanne's central 'problem' is worth noting here as it illuminates the paradox that I have been developing. According to Fry, for Cézanne the question was how, 'without missing the infinity of nature, the complexity and richness of its vibrations, [. . .] to build that solidly and articulately co-ordinated unity in which the spirit can rest satisfied'.[34] What Fry had observed in his extended analyses of Cézanne's still lifes in his monograph on the painter was the 'infinitely changing quality of the very stuff of the painting which communicates so vivid a sense of life', concluding that, 'In spite of the austerity of the forms, all is vibration and movement'.[35] Despite Lawrence's parody of Bloomsbury's formalist aesthetics elsewhere in his own commentary on Cézanne (a parody which was based on his fundamental misunderstanding of Fry's aesthetics as disembodied), the pair share a sense of the vibrant, vibrational stillness underlying the painter's encounter with the apple.[36] As we have seen, Lawrence's concept of 'appleyness' is intimately related to something that he defines as Cézanne's 'intuitive feeling that nothing is really *statically* at rest'. In the passage that follows, Lawrence directly identifies this feeling with still life:

> – he seems to have had [it] strongly – as when he watched the lemons shrivel or go mildewed, in his still-life group, which he left lying there so long so that he *could* see that gradual flux of change: and partly to

> fight the cliché, which says that the inanimate world *is* static, and that walls *are* still. In his fight with the cliché he denied that walls are still and chairs are static.[37]

Lawrence troubles the implicit question of temporality in still life. By evoking Cézanne's mode of intense, long looking by which he could register the gradual decay of the objects in a composition, he suggests a more complex and subtle temporality in which time is made visible, and matter animate. It could take Cézanne one hundred sessions to produce a still life painting, as he was committed to conveying the gradations of light and colour on an object over time and from multiple perspectives; and his brush could remain suspended over the canvas for hours before making a single stroke. This prolonged, tentative approach, which constituted a kind of meditative exercise, held a special fascination for Lawrence. He implies that, in dissolving the 'cliché' view of matter as static, the painter opened up a new way of experiencing the world that enlarged the limits of the senses.

Lawrence deploys Cézanne's work in his essay to corroborate his own vitalist aesthetic and visceral receptivity to the 'living' element of matter, but he also signals a tension between vitality and uncanny animation, which is widely expressed in the literature on still life.[38] When he attends to Cézanne's portraits, he finds an even more unsettling elision between human subject and still life object:

> When he makes Madame Cézanne most *still*, most appley, he starts making the universe slip uneasily about her. It was part of his desire: to make the human form, the *life* form, come to rest. Not static – on the contrary. Mobile but come to rest. And at the same time he set the unmoving material world into motion. Walls twitch and slide, chairs bend or rear up a little, cloths curl like burning paper.[39]

The still and the mobile enter into uneasy proximity in this textual re-animation, which is more evocative of a Surrealist rather than a Post-Impressionist vision. Kandinsky was responsive to this sense of the inanimate material world made animate in Cézanne's work when he declared that the painter 'made a living thing out of a teacup, or rather in a teacup he realized the existence of something alive'; he raised still life by recognising 'the inner life in everything'.[40] For Lawrence, Cézanne's objects *are* sentient: in the passage above, the vaguely hostile material world – ostensibly the background of the painting – becomes the animate central subject. This impression of uncanny energy is as palpable in the portraits of Madame Cézanne as in works such as *Still Life: Plate of Peaches* (1879–80) (plate 3), in which the dynamic brush strokes of the background exert a pressure on the left portion of the composition, accentuating the provisional rendering of the table and table cloth, which appear to float in a state of flux, unsupported on the left-hand side. The very wallpaper seems to 'twitch', as in Lawrence's description, and to dislodge the pattern so that it gives the illusion of living foliage unfurling and pressing into the viewer's pictorial space.[41]

The material world within Cézanne's pictures exists in an open temporality, a precarious state of 'rest', which simultaneously indicates repose and prior or potential movement. The boundaries between portrait and still life blur along a spectrum of still movement. From 'appleyness' emerges a new ontology of stillness: the human subject treated, and perhaps even dehumanised, as a still life object. As Lawrence speculates earlier in his essay, 'If the human being is going to be primarily an apple, as for Cézanne it was, then you are going to have a new world of men: a world which has very little to say, men that can sit still and just be physically there, and be truly non-moral.'[42] Through Cézanne, Lawrence reconfigures the perceived limitations of the 'still' and of the still life genre. He highlights one of the bolder claims which I make in this study: that the modern still life is an elastic, absorbent framework within which multiple genres are seen to participate, and that it can function as a mode of being in the world, as well as a mode of attentiveness.

The physicality so admired by Lawrence in Cézanne's still lifes can also prompt discomfort and a sense of reluctant intimacy. David Trotter locates this experience anthropomorphically: the tilted angle of a jug signifies an invitation to look down its 'throat', stimulating a wave of nausea: '[t]he sickness [. . .] from having looked too hard for too long'.[43] My inquiry will explore these visceral responses to still life: from the 'excess' of sensuous pleasure to a sense of disquiet and recoil. For Lawrence, to see the decaying fruit in Cézanne's compositions is, according to Trotter, 'to see a mess or blur, the after-image of movement, and to see death'.[44] Yet to place nausea and death at the limit of the 'form of fascination' Lawrence felt for these paintings is surely to limit his experience.[45] While he certainly registers the decay and morbidity implicit in *nature morte*, we should not overlook that, for him, the intensity of Cézanne's contemplation of still life enacts a way of knowing, of probing the 'hidden', which verges on the mystical. 'Appleyness', Lawrence describes:

> carries with it also the feeling of knowing the other side as well, the side you don't see, the hidden side of the moon. For the intuitive apperception of the apple is so *tangibly* aware of the apple that it is aware of it *all round*, not only just of the front [. . .]. The true imagination is for ever curving round to the other side, to the back of presented appearance.[46]

This lyrically defined imaginative flexing, this 'curving round' of the creative faculty, opens the way for an aesthetic epistemology, which reaches beyond the visual and the tactile. Lawrence envisages the painter's creative process as a detached yet empathetic mode in which his will is subordinated through this exhaustive, renunciatory attitude to everyday objects. 'Cézanne's great effort was [. . .] to shove the apple away from him, and let it live of itself', Lawrence writes.[47] The apple – the painter's habitual still life motif – becomes an index for a particular approach to the world and its representation in art. This struggle for renunciation but also absorption or consummation of the apple is registered as 'a physical correlative', as Anne Fernihough describes it, in the effect of simultaneous stillness and dynamism in Cézanne's still lifes.[48]

If still life paintings can twitch and vibrate, then texts are also still and moving things, 'mobile but come to rest' on the page, to adopt Lawrence's phrase. His textual still lifes play with and dissolve binary characterisations, to show how oppositions, particularly between 'stillness' and 'motion', are misleadingly reified and can be dismantled. He evokes the unstable forces and shifting, disrupted perspectives in Cézanne's paintings, but he also alerts us to their indefinable temporality and the tension between the permanence of objects and their susceptibility to the ravages of time. His essay circles around the terms 'still' and 'static', putting pressure on the terminology of still life. While 'static' takes on a negative, restrictive colouring – the outcome of a 'cliché' mode of perception, which fails to penetrate the 'living' quality of a subject – Lawrence reveals the semantic fertility and ambivalence of the 'still', stretching its connotations and endowing his prose with a corresponding verbal vitality, even vibrational effect. This impression is reinforced typographically where words pertaining to stillness are frequently italicised, creating an effect of leaning forward into motion. The syntax of his verbal still lifes seems to respond to the counter-pressures of Cézanne's compositions and invites analogy with the painter's positioning of objects, which often appear on the very brink of motion, or precariously balanced. We recall, for instance the painting of peaches (plate 3), where two fruits appear ready to tip over the wave-like crests of the table cloth and plunge to the floor.

Cézanne seems to have carefully constructed these internal movements in his still lifes. An acquaintance recorded that the painter 'set out the peaches in such a way as to make the complementary colors vibrate, grays next to reds, yellows to blues, leaning, tilting, balancing the fruit at the angles he wanted, sometimes pushing a one-sou or two-sous piece under them'.[49] The German poet, Rainer Maria Rilke, marvelled at the chromatic conversations engendered by these compositions of objects, and he chronicled his sensations in a series of letters to his wife following visits to Cézanne's memorial exhibition in Paris in 1907. Noting the use of 'pure chrome yellow and burning lacquer red in his lemons and apples', Rilke suggests that the painter 'knows how to contain their loudness within the picture: cast into a listening blue, as if into an ear, it receives a silent response from within'.[50] He renders this chromatic dialogue in a lush prose ekphrasis of Cézanne's *The Black Marble Clock* (c. 1870) (plate 4):

> Brightly confronting each other on the white cloth are a coffee cup with a heavy dark-blue stripe on the edge, a fresh, ripe lemon, a cut crystal chalice with a sharply scalloped edge, and, way over on the left, a large, baroque triton's shell [. . .]. Its inward carmine bulging out into brightness provokes the wall behind it to a kind of thunderstorm blue, which is then repeated, more deeply and spaciously, by the adjoining gold-framed mantelpiece mirror.[51]

Perceived by Rilke with hyper-lucidity, the objects in this composition create an inter-connected, self-contained reality, carving out a space that reverberates with the 'sound' of colour. Even as the black clock announces the stopped time of still life, the interior of the picture 'vibrates' and becomes fluid: the startlingly white cloth seems to pour itself like liquid over the table ledge. In this rather ominous conversation or confrontation (as Rilke has it) between objects, the lip-like opening of the shell hints at utterance. The intimate relationship between sound, colour and vibration highlighted by Rilke, and the influential notion of synaesthesia in cultural discourses of the early twentieth century, informs my own exploration of the multisensory experience of still life. This study is concerned with the 'life' and 'music' of colour, its rhythms and animating effects, and the ways in which it disrupts the silence commonly associated with still life.

'Vibration' – not only the musical term, but also the notion of rhythmic motion from a fixed point – and an associated vocabulary of unstable, barely perceived movement emerges as a suggestive way of describing the internal dynamics of Cézanne's still lifes in appreciations by a range of commentators (including Fry, Lawrence and Rilke). It also has a wider relevance for this inquiry and a philosophical and cultural specificity in the early twentieth century, which I survey later in this Introduction. In an illuminating essay titled 'Cézanne's Doubt' (1945), the phenomenologist philosopher, Maurice Merleau-Ponty, observed that the painter 'did not want to separate the stable things we see and the shifting way in which they appear'.[52] His distinctive approach to chromatic perception was fundamental to this, Merleau-Ponty argued, noting how the painter 'follows the swelling of the object in modulated colors and indicates *several* outlines in blue' so that 'one's glance captures a shape that emerges from among them all, just as it does in perception'.[53] Building on Merleau-Ponty, Paul Smith identifies the role of still life as a colour 'laboratory' in which Cézanne explored how the perception of colour creates the illusion of movement: it 'renders things more quick than still'.[54] Merleau-Ponty would later propose a way of conceiving the vibratory energies of modern painting.

Despite being unable to 'devise things that actually move', painting 'has made for itself a movement without displacement, a movement by vibration or radiation'.[55] This more nuanced model of 'still movement' challenges the boundaries ascribed to the art of painting, and opens up new possibilities in reading the (im)mobility of still life.

The 'Raising' of Still Life

By way of these responses to Cézanne's still lifes, I have introduced several of the key figures in this study and its central themes: the uncanny animation of the object and its implications for the human subject; a form of attention which challenges the limits of sense experience and the fixity of matter; and a shared yet shifting lexicon for stillness and vibrational aesthetics. But what was the particular resonance of still life as it emerged in the twentieth century? The current of animation that I suggested was latent in the genre reveals itself palpably in Cézanne's still lifes and in textual responses to them. This concern with the 'animate inanimate' was a widespread phenomenon in twentieth-century still life, yet it has been little noted in theories of the genre.[56] It is the raising of the status of still life to which Kandinsky refers: embodied in Cézanne's still lifes is his recognition of 'the inner life in everything'.[57] In Charles Sterling's classic study of still life, he identifies the painter's 'complex researches' in this genre as the 'definitive emancipation of a subject hitherto neglected, which at last took its place on an equal footing with other subjects'.[58] The 'inanimate object has cast its spell', Sterling writes, noting the critical consensus that a '"still life spirit" has come over modern painting since Cézanne, impressing on both landscape and the human figure an impassiveness and immobility peculiar to still life'.[59] Indeed, bound up with the broader revision and democratisation of traditional art-historical hierarchies during this period, the still life proved to have the elasticity to absorb and assimilate other genres, producing the hybrid composites we have noted in Cézanne.

To put this more boldly, still life represented an aesthetic battleground in which the major artistic and ethical debates of modern art were played out. Its transformations provide an index for the revolutions of modern art, and more specifically for the approach of individual artists toward the world and its representation. The genre plays a crucial role in the experiments and innovations of Post-Impressionism, Fauvism, Cubism and Surrealism. Georges Braque and Picasso chose still life as the genre through which to address fundamental questions about war, art and the role of the artist in society. The deconstruction and geometric distortion of the objects of Cubist iconography (musical instruments, bottles and glasses, tobacco and playing cards), and Cubism's later synthetic phase, which incorporated *objets trouvés*, extended the still life into three dimensions, thereby renewing attention to everyday objects and their potential for transformation.

We know, then, that still life had a renewed importance for modern artists, but how might it be revealing about the broader context of approaching objects, and about attention to the world more widely? Sterling resists the notion of a specific 'still life approach' but he concedes that '[s]ome artists are prone to feel intensely the serene and static harmonies of the world rather than those harmonies which might be called tense and unstable'. These artists 'readily – but not necessarily – paint inanimate objects'.[60] As the ensuing chapters will demonstrate, however, interplay between the 'serene and static' and the 'tense and unstable' may take place within the space of the modern still life.

Sterling attributes the 'so-called "still life spirit"' during this period to 'a new attitude toward the world and to life: to defend itself against the pressure of the crowd and the tyranny of the machine, the artist has had to stand back from the world'.[61] Alternatively, the still life might be viewed as a permeable structure through which the world makes its presence felt. Costello takes up this stance in *Planets on Tables: Poetry, Still Life, and the Turning World* (2008), a study which explores the domestic, intimate order of still life in the context of the 'expanded and fragmented' spaces of modernity.[62] Focusing on four American writers and one American visual artist, she suggests that, 'For some, attention to intimate objects provides a discrete form of commentary and critique of the public world. For others, the aesthetic arrangement of the domestic world becomes a means of satisfying desire and awakening hope against the threatening forces of external reality.'[63] Whilst the socio-political and historical reasons for the prominence of still life in the twentieth century are not my primary concern, the implicitly political dynamics of passivity and activity, the 'gendering' of space both private and public, and the ethical implications of the 'still', inevitably underlie my own – and indeed any – reading of still life.

The still life genre in painting – and Cézanne's works in particular – remain a touchstone for the vibrating stillness I explore in this study. However, as I have established, I employ the term in a capacious sense, as a broad, inter-aesthetic category, which migrates between the arts in the early to mid twentieth century. In so doing, I necessarily depart from Bryson's assertion that 'still life is the world minus its narratives' or minus the 'capacity for generating narrative interest', which he attributes to its preference for rhopography over the 'great' or 'heroic' subjects of megalography.[64] While this destabilisation of values is persuasive, Bryson's conception of narrative as 'the drama of greatness' is restrictive and denies it the reflective capacity to pause and dwell among overlooked objects.[65] In Blanchard's reading, we are moved by still life precisely because, while 'all still life is a challenge to narrativity', it 'constitutes a praise of the virtues of description'.[66] Narrative is not my central concern, but my inquiry questions the critical consensus that still life precludes narrative movement. My larger project is in agreement here with Cara Lewis's proposition for a 'revised understanding of still life that emphasises not the genre's stasis but rather its malleability and its compatibility with narrative'.[67]

I suggest that reading literary texts in the light of still life offers new ways of thinking about the way time is stilled, paused or re-animated in particular kinds of texts. I build here on attempts over the last two decades to extend the interpretative scope for still life, notably in Rosemary Lloyd's *Shimmering in a Transformed Light: Writing the Still Life* (2005), which explores moments in which narrative pauses to address objects in prose still lifes, primarily in European literatures of the twentieth and twenty-first centuries. Lloyd argues that 'still life, in art and in literature, becomes a means for transferring the anxiety aroused by the contingency of a society in flux and in search of new secular values onto objects whose stubborn thereness is at once a reality and an illusion'.[68] By moving beyond analogies between textual and visual still lifes and taking in further intermedial permutations, my study answers to Lloyd's aim to 'encourage others to explore further possibilities in this fruitful but overlooked area', and to move still life into the foreground.[69]

In what unfolds, I pursue a line of inquiry that the textual meditations on Cézanne have gestured toward: that still life can stimulate a performative attentiveness which circulates around, among and through compositions of objects. Furthermore, while most definitions of the genre describe a group of domestic objects, this occludes more imaginative permutations of an abstract, object-less poetics of stillness, demonstrated in ways quite different from both narrative and description. This book explores diverse manifestations of the 'still life spirit' in prose, painting, sculpture, dance and poetry, to uncover the different ways in which still life can be seen as a renewed mode of vibratory receptivity and an aesthetic of attentiveness. I foreground constellations of artists working across different media, some canonical and some less established in cultural histories of this period, including Virginia Woolf and Roger Fry; J. D. Fergusson, Margaret Morris and Rudolf Steiner; Winifred Nicholson, Ben Nicholson, Ivon Hitchens and David Jones; Wallace Stevens and Charles Mauron; and Aldous Huxley and Mark Gertler.

In so doing, the chapters of this book emphasise the overlapping of national and artistic boundaries. In her introduction to the collection of multi-author essays *The Object as Subject: Studies in the Interpretation of Still Life* (1996), Anne W. Lowenthal observes the tendency for 'nationalist emphases' in surveys and exhibitions on still life in the 1980s, which 'continue to provide a convenient though limiting framework [. . .] often at odds with artists' mobility and fluid national boundaries'.[70] The intervening decades have broadened these frameworks, but I aim to continue this work and to contribute to expanding the plurality of meanings and methods by which still life can be interpreted. The study of material culture and the allure of the 'thing' is important to the inquiries in *The Object as Subject*, which largely focuses on painting.[71] Lowenthal outlines her concern with 'our curiosity about and empathy with objects – the very stuff of everyday life', yet she also acknowledges that 'the methods of material culture are necessary but insufficient for interpreting the work of art as a whole'.[72] This is a view I share. Critical interest in the 'ordinary', the 'everyday' and the material object has increasingly and rightly become part of the critical landscape of modernist studies and furnishes an important background to *Modernism and Still Life*.[73] However, I am interested in still life as a threshold between the material and the immaterial, and in the way it records slippages and journeys between these spheres.

The 'Magic of Things'

The still life asserts the material reality of everyday things and at the same time implies the power to 'enchant' and transfigure objects. Sometimes it appears to invest objects with supersensory potential, as the Frankfurt's Städel Museum acknowledges in the title of its exhibition of 2008: *The Magic of Things: Still Life Painting 1500–1800*. I propose a reading of still life that invites an aesthetics of wonder intimately associated with the prolonged contemplation of commonplace objects; a meditative and sometimes 'spiritual' exercise, enabling entrance into a liminal space in which absence, presence and the 'ordinary' are redefined.[74]

In *The Enchantment of Modern Life* (2001), Jane Bennett suggests that enchantment 'entails a state of wonder' and that it is 'a comportment that can be fostered through deliberate strategies', one of which is 'to hone sensory receptivity to the marvellous specificity of things'.[75] In this study I suggest that the isolation of objects in the stopped or suspended time of still life establishes an aesthetic space that is particularly suited to cultivating this heightened 'sensory receptivity' to things. It corresponds with the 'state of wonder' which Bennett defines by its 'temporary suspension of chronological time and bodily movement'. As in still life, '[t]o be enchanted [. . .] is to participate in a momentarily immobilising encounter; it is to be transfixed, spellbound'.[76] With this formulation in mind, I explore the ways in which still life may be conceived of as a transfixing encounter or heightened state of contemplative 'ec-stasis', which may be secular or 'spiritual' in import.[77] Naturally, the manifestation and character of such still life 'ec-tases' are diverse in the work of the artists I examine, and range from pleasurable delight to the uncanny and pernicious.

The types of sensations and emotions roused by still life are important here. Sterling attributes the still life painter's expression of wonder to the fact that, 'inanimate things, so closely bound up with daily life, represent man's most immediate commerce with matter'; they gave us 'our first contact with the world, and by way of these things the artist revives our maiden sense of wonder and our first dreams'.[78] For Meyer Schapiro, the genre can be identified with 'a sober objectivity', adopted by the artist 'as a calming or redemptive modest task, a means of self-discipline and concentration'.[79] This 'steady looking [. . .] discloses new and elusive aspects of the stable object', so that it may become 'a mystery, a source of metaphysical wonder'.[80] The 'wonder' or 'mystery' of still life represents an inter-linking thread through the chapters of this book, although the assumed stability of the object is often put under pressure. Our excursion into Cézanne's 'unsteady apples' has set the tone for encounters with a more disobedient and autonomous world of the inanimate than can be accommodated in readings of the object-world as subordinate to or wholly manipulated by man.[81]

I propose that still life functions as a contemplative or creative practice (or both), inviting a mode of attentiveness which might serve the poet or writer as much as the painter or observer. For the German philosopher, Arthur Schopenhauer, the ideal of 'pure contemplation' – the loss or merging of consciousness in an object – is demonstrated by the Dutch artists who 'directed such purely objective perception to the most insignificant objects, and set up a lasting monument of their objectivity and spiritual peace in paintings of *still life*'.[82] Schopenhauer goes on to observe that the beholder at once participates in this state and at the same time becomes aware of his own 'restless state of mind' as he is presented with 'the calm, tranquil, will-free frame of mind of the artist' who contemplates 'such insignificant things so objectively, considering them so attentively'.[83]

Still life encounters arguably become more troubled in the context of modernity's crisis of belief in institutional or orthodox religion. However, I will suggest that this does not necessarily preclude the experience of 'spiritual peace'. As I explore the affective exchange between still life, its artists and its auditors, I do not assume (as Sterling does), that the early twentieth-century predilection for the genre registers an increasingly secular or materialist outlook in any straightforward sense.[84] There is a tradition of still life painting, in which we could include Francisco de Zurbarán, Caravaggio, Chardin and Cézanne, for whom the still life functions as an exercise in humbling attention, even as a spiritual discipline. In this tradition, Bryson observes, 'attention itself gains the power to transfigure the commonplace'.[85] Recent studies such as T. J. Gorringe's *Earthly Visions* (2011) go further in establishing still life's concern with 'paying attention' to the overlooked as a crucial element of its 'spiritual intensity'.[86] For Gorringe, a 'sense of grace in the everyday, or of its miraculous nature', is the 'primary [Christian] theological significance of still life painting'.[87] Similarly metaphysical – if not explicitly theological – inflections of attention present themselves in the manifestations of still life I consider in this book.

*

'Still life can hardly avoid quickening attention', Bryson claims, since the 'kind of attention provoked by still life isolates both painter and viewer from the rather hazy, rather lazy visual field the subject normally inhabits'.[88] By probing notions of the tactile, the kinaesthetic and the synesthetic, I seek to enlarge this predominantly perceptual sense of attentiveness. It is my argument that the form of attention prompted by the art of still life acquires a new acuity in the context of the so-called 'culture of distraction' which characterises late nineteenth and early twentieth-century urban modernity.[89] In his influential study, *Suspensions of Perception: Attention, Spectacle, and Modern Culture* (1999), Jonathan Crary suggests that 'it is possible to see one crucial aspect of modernity as an on-going crisis of attentiveness'; and Tim Armstrong similarly highlights 'the dialectic of *attention* and *distraction*' as 'central to turn-of-the-century psychology, and to modernity itself'.[90] Depending on the context, the cultivation of attention was conceived as fundamental as well as antithetical to creativity.[91] Armstrong points out that 'it is a truism that modernism involves a sharpened sense of the speed of change', and narratives of the period often characterise modern artists as preoccupied with the problem of how to represent such experiences.[92] The cult of movement and dynamism expressed in avant-garde movements such as Futurism and Vorticism is often considered in relation to the vertiginous speeds of the machine age, and there have been significant recent efforts to examine the nexus between modernist cultural practice and emerging technologies such as telephony, cinematography and radiography.[93] The focus of this critical interest is exemplified in Enda Duffy's *The Speed Handbook: Velocity, Pleasure, Modernism* (2009), which argues that 'access to new speeds, whether on a roller-coaster, airplane, but especially with the automobile, has been the most empowering and excruciating new experience for people everywhere in twentieth-century modernity'.[94]

Critical characterisations of modernism and modern art emphasise, then, the significance of new modes of travel and technologies of speed which transformed the experience of the body in time and space and lent an increased pace and sense of hyper-stimulation to modern life, especially in the metropolis. The complex and sometimes paradoxical relationship between stillness and movement is therefore at the heart of the problem of attention. Yet this should not eclipse the fact that in representations of modern experience a form of stillness emerges that is not dialectically opposed to movement, but is in fact intimately related to it. Furthermore, interactions between modern cultural practice and new technologies could be part of modernity's re-enchantment.[95] Following Crary, I suggest that stillness and motion (like attention and distraction) are not polarities, but rather exist on a spectrum of more subtle and complex fluctuations. As he points out: 'Attention and distraction were not two essentially different states but existed on a single continuum, and thus attention was [. . .] a dynamic process, intensifying and diminishing, rising and falling, ebbing and flowing.'[96] This corresponds with what I have described as the charged, vibrating stillness set up by the dynamics of the modern still life, and the states of intense affect which it generates. Indeed, Crary provides what could serve as a formulation of the experience of still life when he describes 'the possibility of a fixation, of holding something in wonder or contemplation, in which the attentive subject is both immobile and ungrounded'.[97]

Vibrational Aesthetics

My discussion of Cézanne has highlighted the presence of vibration as a crucial, if overlooked, metaphor for modern aesthetic experience and sensation across different media. There is a case for its widespread significance in multiple discourses of the early twentieth century, bridging the fields of science and technology, art and the spiritual.[98] Modern theories of physics reconceived the material universe in terms of vibrating atoms rather than solid or static matter and provided useful analogues for the vibrational aesthetic in art, while experiments carried out by the Society for Psychical Research, psychic 'transmissions' at spiritualist séances, and theosophical teachings on vibration, invited an alternative (though not necessarily separate) current to these investigations. Many occult groups of the period shared the belief that 'the underlying substance that makes up the universe is more like energy than like matter or mind', and that since all sensation could be conceived as a response to the vibrations of this energy, so all sensory modalities were alike, and thus synaesthesia was 'a real possibility'.[99] Kandinsky was particularly interested in pursuing this idea and his influential conception of colours as 'vibrations of the soul' is a point of reference in several of the chapters in this book.[100]

That the charged interaction between stillness and movement is important to modern art is bolstered by Spyros Papapetros's identification of an 'inorganic form of animation' espoused by much of modernist art and architecture, which he claims 'has less to do with movement than with a form of energy intensified by immobility and stillness'.[101] It is, he suggests, 'an imperceptible vibration, more "spiritual" (*geistig*) than sensory (*sinnlich*)'.[102] The specific examples of Papapetros's study differ from my own, but his argument that 'modern artifacts are radiant and electric; they emanate magnetic powers and vibrate with energy, life, and desire of their own', coincides with my claim for the objects of modern still life.[103]

Vibration can be understood, then, as a figure for the activating interactions between objects, spaces and spectators in the spaces carved out by the modern artist. The modernist interior is often seen as a purified space, emptying the density and profusion of objects that epitomised the Victorian household.[104] Yet within this space, vibrations of colour can register the particular frequency and emotional vector of still life encounters, often situated at the frontiers of experience, or the juncture of the 'material' and the 'immaterial'. In this study, I interpret colour and vibration as 'quickenings' (to use Wallace Stevens's term) or passages between 'art' and 'life', which are significant to the articulation of aesthetic experience.[105]

A fundamental strand in my inquiry is the examination of the development of a vocabulary in which colour, rhythm and vibration (and an associated lexicon of quivering and trembling), became increasingly important in describing experiences of intensified sensitivity and attentiveness in the early twentieth century, in the context of a world understood as perpetually in motion.[106]

Vibration has a primarily twofold signification in *Modernism and Still Life*: corporeal, as a physical sensation and vital force which can traverse the body, and figurative, as a metaphor for the representation of modern experience.[107] It may evoke an intense sensation not visibly manifest, or provide a way of passing between different media and effecting change without imposition (although this might also be pernicious and invasive). Notions of vibration also underwrite my proposition of a more nuanced and complex interaction between stillness and movement, which dissolves polarities while continuing to register their importance for aesthetic thinking, especially in the exchange between different media. Taking the vibrating stillness of the still life as my point of departure, I shall examine the wide-ranging possibilities of a vibrational aesthetics in modern art, which complicates ideas of form in modernism (particularly those received via the Ezra Pound/T. E. Hulme classicist model), as well as offering an alternative to the stream of consciousness and Impressionist approach.

'At the Still Point': Modern Stillness

'Contrary to all expectation, this century may one day be known as the age of stillness, of arrest.'[108] This is Roger Shattuck characterising the art and science of the twentieth century, as he concludes 'The Art of Stillness', the penultimate chapter in his study of the avant-garde in France during the 'Banquet Years', from 1885 to the First World War. 'Simultanism' is the term by which Shattuck defines the 'logic' and 'artistic technique' of this period, signifying 'an approach to immobility and thus an extremely sensitive attunement to the infinite universe'.[109] While he suggests that Baudelaire, Bergson and e. e. cummings describe this state of immobile attunement, one could equally locate a similar phenomenon in the work and thinking of other moderns including T. S. Eliot, Virginia Woolf and Wyndham Lewis. Shattuck perceives in this condition something similar to the paradox of still life that I have elucidated so far. '[E]ven arrest has no final peace', he declares, 'for it continues to be relative motion; nothing can attain absolute stillness in our physical and spiritual system. Yet this remains the goal of the dynamic upheaval in the arts during the Banquet Years.'[110] These ideas give impetus to my own inquiry over a longer chronology. We shall see that what Shattuck describes as 'the ambition of much modern art to be active *and* passive', manifests itself in different ways in each of the ensuing chapters.[111]

Many of the twentieth century's canonical figures and cultural movements, as well as the less prominent, convey an embattled concern with the still and its relationship with movement. Before turning to the specific examples discussed in this study, I would like to sketch out a few more permutations of this dialectic in modern aesthetics. It is played out, as we have seen, in the tension between what Lawrence calls 'shiftiness' and the search for attentive fixity or contemplative stillness encapsulated in Eliot's 'still point of the turning world'.[112] The potent dynamic between the still and the moving was also definitive of the imagery and rhetoric of the Vorticist group of painters, sculptors and poets, including Wyndham Lewis, Henri Gaudier-Brzeska and Ezra Pound. The group maintained a provocative presence in London during 1914–19, expounding an aesthetic that encapsulated the dynamic co-existence of stillness and motion in the image of the Vortex. As Wyndham Lewis proclaimed in the group's magazine *Blast*, 'The Vorticist is at his maximum point of energy when stillest'; and 'This is a great Vorticist age, a great still age of artists.'[113]

The French philosopher, Henri Bergson, whose ideas were 'common currency' among artists and intellectuals in the early twentieth century, embraced a similar tension.[114] As Mary Ann Gillies has argued, the Vorticist conception of a 'maelstrom around a point of stillness' coincided with 'Bergson's claim that life exists fully in every moment of being', meaning that 'each moment is also a still point'.[115] Bergson developed nineteenth-century vitalist philosophy, proposing an understanding of matter infused by a vital force or *élan vital*. In his first work, *Time and Free Will* (1889), he introduced the notion of duration, of man's inner sense of time, which may slow down or speed up in a quite different way from measurable clock time. He posits a re-conception of the construction of reality and of temporality in which the notion of stillness is radically altered. Read through this prism, the 'immobile' objects of still life are indeed never '*statically* at rest'; they reveal the *élan vital* in everyday objects. The implications of Bergson's theories for inter-medial constructions of animate stillness and rhythm in dance and sculpture will come to the fore in my second chapter.

Still life inevitably brings the modern(ist) preoccupation with the 'still moment' into intensified focus. As Lloyd describes, many still life paintings 'have that quality of frozen moments that bring together a particular point in time and a specific place [. . .] in ways that make the objects they highlight universal and timeless'.[116] At its most abstract, still life presents an immobile centre around which parts coalesce, leading us to the variations on the 'still point' that we have encountered thus far. We might think of the invocation to stillness in Mrs Ramsay's command, '"Life stand still here"', which echoes through Woolf's *To the Lighthouse* (1927).[117] Woolf expresses something subtly different, of course, from Eliot's 'still point' or Lewis's sense of the dynamic stillness at the heart of the Vortex, yet she nevertheless articulates a widespread compulsion in modern art: to resist the flux of time and make 'of the moment something permanent' (p. 183). This is not to suggest, then, a cohesive cultural phenomenon or ideological commonality shared by the artists in this study. Rather, it will show that modern art articulates a complex and multifarious relationship with the 'still', which reveals ambivalence as well as fascination, a desire to intensify as well as to disrupt, and an unresolved but often energising tension between movement and stillness.

While specific instances of modernism's quest for the 'still point', 'epiphany' or 'moment of being', are much discussed, little attempt has been made to theorise this phenomenon or to trace the resonance of stillness more widely across the period. The role of the 'still' is largely eclipsed in the story of twentieth-century modernity, which, as I have outlined, is largely told as one of quickening pace, of velocity and mobility, and of rapid social and political change. This tendency remains prevalent in diagnoses of contemporary culture. In *Stillness in a Mobile World* (2011), the editors David Bissell and Gillian Fuller position their collection of essays on 'the conceptual, political and philosophical importance of stillness' within what they identify as 'a world that has increasingly come to be understood through the theoretical and conceptual lens of movement'.[118] My study contributes toward re-balancing the emphasis of much of modernist scholarship, by taking the still life as a lens through which to focus on this overlooked strand in modern culture. There are signs of increasing critical recognition of the complexities of stillness, notably in Louise Hornby's *Still Modernism: Photography, Literature, Film* (2017), which demonstrates how 'photographic stillness – emerges as an indispensable aesthetic category in modernism'.[119] Hornby takes a different focus from my own in examining photographic stillness as a counterpoint to motion and film: a 'difficult' stillness that can nevertheless offer access to that which is usually unseen. The 'moments of stillness' she identifies, however, 'all point to something going awry', to 'car crashes, uneven walks, bad portraiture, total darkness, death'.[120] While acknowledging the shadow side of still life, my exploration focuses largely on a more positive form of stillness in which the artist or viewer might find themselves more intimately connected with and attentive to the local, sensory and vibrantly animate. Nevertheless, I join Hornby in seeking to establish the centrality of stillness in modernist innovation and in questioning the privileging of motion in modernist studies.

My argument is not posited in opposition to studies that emphasise the fascination of modern culture with movement. In fact, this body of scholarship serves to inform and accentuate my point: that stillness and movement are bound up together and energise each other as part of a continuum. The turn to spaces and creative modes of stillness, which I continue to identify over the course of this book, was not disconnected from an engagement with movement, even as it sought in many cases to counterbalance it. Indeed, the rethinking of stillness in the early twentieth century was informed by contemporaneous philosophical and metaphysical ideas about the nature of the self and the role of art in a rapidly changing world.

*

In this Introduction I have argued for the importance of still life as a genre or mode of practice for modern artists, and attempt to offer a corrective to art-historical accounts in which it is marginalised. However, as will have become apparent, I do not propose a defence of still life, but rather to show that stillness has a fertile 'life' in different fields of cultural activity during the early to mid-twentieth century. The spectrum from still life painting to more abstract forms of 'stillness' in modernist aesthetics delineates a large scope for inquiry with potentially endless permutations. This study will naturally not be exhaustive; instead, in each of the ensuing chapters, I take different fields of cultural activity in which encounters between 'stillness' and 'life' are manifested in ways that can be seen to plot the fundamental stages in a narrative about still life and modernism, which uncovers forms of animate stillness at the heart of modern art. The still life will emerge charged with animation, vibration and rhythm, an unstable medium, unexpectedly vital and well suited to the expression of modern concerns. Focusing this inquiry predominantly on art of the first half of the twentieth century allows me to identify the patterns and motifs that characterise the operation of still life and the particular pressures of, and on, the 'still' during this period. For this reason, although still life painting provides a point of entry to these debates, the parameters and definitions of the 'still' and its meaning for modern art remain open. Equally, many of the terms I examine ('rhythm' and 'vibration' in particular) lack a fixed definition in the parlance of the time and often conflate multiple spheres of meaning, but I shall attempt to highlight the historical lineage which shapes their formation and the differences as well as continuities in their usage.

My broad interpretation of still life, and the complex and wide-ranging web of associations and applications generated by it, necessitates my interdisciplinary and transcultural approach. Furthermore, since the history of modern art is one of transnational exchange and inter-medial collaboration, the artists considered here are examined within the overlapping networks in which they operated, revealing a sense of the border-crossing of continental and international modernisms.[121] The progression of chapters is loosely chronological: the parameters are set by the opening exploration of Cézanne and conclude with the textual still lifes of Wallace Stevens and Aldous Huxley. Vibration is an apposite methodological metaphor through which to emphasise resonances and interconnections between the artists explored in each of the chapters and the sites in which they moved, their shared historical or cultural backgrounds, and the common tropes in their creative lexicons. The diverse range of material and archival sources on which I draw sets up new relationships between canonical and overlooked works, which are illuminated by the paradigm of still life and implicitly challenge its marginal status. By revisiting genre hierarchies and characterisations of modern aesthetic forms I therefore aim to pursue Armstrong's claim that '[t]o consider modernism is thus necessarily to engage with culture defined in terms of an interconnected field of activity in which hierarchy and even causality is problematic; in which agreed boundaries are replaced by permeability and relatedness'.[122] As we shall see in what follows, the still life exerts the potency of its 'double life'. It becomes a site of modernity's 'synthetic impulse', but also its 'counter': the 'pursuit of purity and media exclusivity'.[123]

*

When Virginia Woolf sought to evoke Roger Fry's qualities as an art critic, she reached for the image of him as a humming-bird hawk-moth, 'quivering yet still' in his absorbed attention to Post-Impressionist paintings.[124] Such receptive, vibratory states of being and heightened sensory encounters feature widely in her writing. States of 'active' stillness, I argue, were crucial to her experience and representation of art. In my first chapter I trace 'quivering' as a talismanic word across a wide range of Woolf's fiction, non-fiction and autobiographical writing, to show that it is part of a lexicon, as well as a stylistic strategy, through which she attempted to negotiate the dialectic between the shifting and the stable. My exploration of the pervasive figure of the insect in Woolf's writing uncovers the ways in which the sense faculties of the insect aided her in re-imagining the human sensorium and the embodiment of aesthetic experience, with particular focus on 'the violent rapture of colour' in her essay *Walter Sickert: A Conversation* (1934), and the unsettling of associated states of being in her memoir 'Sketch of the Past' (1939).[125]

The second half of this chapter brings Woolf's underexplored biography of Fry into the foreground. It addresses her confrontation with the problem of 'writing' Fry under the imperative not to 'fix' her subject, but rather to register his 'vibratory' non-physical presence. I consider the role of vibration more widely in Woolf's life-writing, and in Fry's art theory, in the context of twentieth-century spiritualism, Quakerism and new communication technologies. Moving away from readings of Fry's formalism as rigid and unrevised, I suggest that his ability to be detached yet receptive – 'quivering yet still' – offers a model through which to explore the particular rhythms of his aesthetic attention and its ambivalent attraction for his biographer. By examining the different functions and meanings of still life (both visual and verbal) in Woolf's and Fry's work, I suggest that we can elucidate a more nuanced sense of their understanding of the relationship between art and life.

The second chapter shifts from embodied quivering in Bloomsbury to forms of 'restless stillness', as the dance theorist André Lepecki terms it, in two European movement practices of the early to mid-twentieth century:[126] the Margaret Morris Movement, established c. 1910 by the British dancer, Margaret Morris (1891–1980) in partnership with the Scottish painter and sculptor, J. D. Fergusson (1874–1961); and eurythmy, the synthetic art form and system of spiritual movement which was instigated in 1912 by the Austrian scientist and philosopher, Rudolf Steiner (1861–1925). This chapter reveals the contribution of movement practitioners to the project of re-imagining aesthetic categories through hybrid sculptural, pictorial and poetic forms that engaged the 'moving stillness' of the body. I suggest that Morris's dance system constituted a vitalist expression of 'still life in motion', which was informed by the pervasive influence of Bergsonian philosophy and the currency of 'rhythm' in the discourses of her immediate circle.

The second section of the chapter investigates a modern aesthetics of sculptural stillness, from its antecedents in the ideas of eighteenth-century art historian Johann Joachim Winckelmann, to the early twentieth-century vogue for re-animating Hellenic and Eastern sculpture in dance. It examines the implications of 'mobilising' sculpture through the living body in Fergusson's understudied sculptural practice and investigates Morris's role as a model who sought to revaluate the gender politics of stasis and movement. The final part of the chapter examines eurythmy as a form of 'moving sculpture' that complicates the relationship between dance and sculpture.[127] Steiner developed his 'new art of movement in space' as an answer to what he defined as the 'spiritual' impulses of modern man and an evolution of sculptural stasis into fluid movement.[128] The role of colour, rhythm and vibration in eurythmy is examined here in relation to Steiner's larger spiritual cosmology, which had strong links to Theosophy, and to his profound engagement with the organicist principles of Johann Wolfgang von Goethe. I argue that eurythmy represents a radical reinterpretation of the seemingly quiescent art of sculpture toward an animating practice with new capacities for synaesthetic experience and performance. By uncovering unexpected interrelations between eurythmy, its practitioners and the Margaret Morris Movement (MMM), this chapter reveals the interweaving of aesthetic, cultural and social connections that underwrite the phenomenon of modern movement practices.

The association of still life and the 'numinous' comes to the foreground in the third chapter in the work of British painters, Winifred Nicholson, Ben Nicholson, David Jones and Ivon Hitchens. I suggest that still life functions in their work as a model through which to explore the relationship between the material and the immaterial, as well as to tease out fundamental aesthetic questions. By contextualising the artists' different commitments to the 'spiritual', from Christian Science to Catholic theology, we gain an enriched understanding of still life as an index to the larger communion between art and life in their work. I draw on correspondence and commentaries by contemporary collectors, Helen Sutherland and H. S. Jim Ede, to argue that still life served as an expression of the spiritually inflected aesthetic which was widely manifest in their circle.

A case study of the period in which Hitchens worked alongside the Nicholsons at their home, Bankshead, in Cumberland in 1925, reveals creative exchange between the painters and their shared yet diverse expression of the 'still-life-at-a-window' motif. W. Nicholson's writings and early twentieth-century colour theory provide a context for my readings of her flower paintings, while discourses on the connection between music and colour inform my exploration of Hitchens's still lifes. I build on existing scholarship on modernism and domesticity to explore the different strategies by which these artists attempt to defamiliarise and transform the object world. I suggest the emergence of an 'enchanted' domesticity, which was intimately related to still life and in some cases complicated by direct experience of war. Concluding this chapter, I make an excursion into Ede's art collection at Kettle's Yard, Cambridge, to propose a reading of his domestic space as an extended still life.

In the final chapter of *Modernism and Still Life* we cross the Atlantic to consider the American poet, Wallace Stevens. I argue that his creative project was underpinned by the desire for a transformative attentiveness to the everyday, an 'illumination of the usual' which coincides with the still life aesthetic.[129] My discussion is structured around the poet's annotated personal copy of *Aesthetics and Psychology* (1935), authored by the French aesthetician, Charles Mauron (1899–1966), and now part of the collection of Stevens's books at the Huntington Library, California. Mauron's text, which Stevens read and closely annotated during the 1930s, provides a unique paradigm through which to approach the poet's still life meditations, which become most prominent in *Parts of a World* (1942). I argue that the correlation between Stevens's lyric poetry, criticism and still life is substantiated by exploring the ways in which Mauron's theory of 'inactive' and 'active' contemplation shaped the poet's 'still life aesthetic'.

I read Stevens's 'still life' poems in the light of two traditions in the pictorial representation of the genre: one characterised by sensuous abundance and the other by ascetic abstinence. Such an approach illuminates the poems' internal debates about aestheticism and asceticism, absorption and detachment, contemplation and activity. In light of the poet's self-confessed 'taste' for Georges Braque, I offer a new approach to his long poem *The Man with the Blue Guitar*, which I read as a 'musical still life' alongside Braque's paintings. I argue that in his 'still life poems' Stevens anticipates the model of vibrating modernism that underpins his search for 'unalterable vibration' in 'The Noble Rider and the Sound of Words' (1941),[130] and his understanding of the 'quickenings' between poetry and painting in 'The Relations between Poetry and Painting' (1951). Finally, in a Coda to this chapter, I return to the Bloomsbury circle considered in Chapter 1 to illuminate the nexus between Bloomsbury, Mauron and Stevens.

Following the path of another Atlantic-crossing modernist, Aldous Huxley, and his analysis of still life painters from Mark Gertler to Cézanne, brings my inquiry to its conclusion. Reading Huxley's early art criticism in the light of his later meditation on visionary experience, *The Doors of Perception* (1954), allows me to conclude this study by returning to a series of concerns about still life and its uncanny animate stillness which were raised at the outset in Lawrence's writing on Cézanne.

NOTES

1. Wassily Kandinsky, *Concerning the Spiritual in Art* (1914), trans. M. T. H. Sadler (New York: Dover Publications, 1977), p. 17.
2. Virginia Woolf, *The Diary of Virginia Woolf*, ed. Anne Olivier Bell, assisted by Andrew McNeillie, 5 vols (London: Hogarth Press, 1977–84), I, 18 April 1918, p. 141.
3. Rainer Maria Rilke, *Letters on Cézanne*, ed. Clara Rilke, trans. Joel Agee (London: Vintage, 1991), p. 82.
4. D. H. Lawrence, 'Introduction to his Paintings', in *Selected Essays* (Harmondsworth: Penguin, 1950; repr. from *The Paintings of D. H. Lawrence*, Mandrake Press, 1929), pp. 307–46 (p. 341).
5. Giorgio de Chirico, 'Sull' Arte Metafisica' (1919), quoted by James Thrall Soby, in *Giorgio de Chirico* (New York: Museum of Modern Art, 1966), p. 66.
6. Bonnie Costello, *Planets on Tables: Poetry, Still Life, and the Turning World* (Ithaca: Cornell University Press, 2008), p. 10.
7. For an analysis of the genre's origins in the *xenia* motifs of antiquity and its development through history, see Charles Sterling, *Still Life Painting from Antiquity to the Twentieth Century*, trans. James Emmons, 2nd rev. edn (New York: Harper & Row, 1981 [1959]); for a more recent illustrated history see Sybille Elbert-Schifferer, *Still Life: A History*, trans. Russell Stockman (New York: Harry N. Abrams, 1999).
8. See for instance Camille Mauclair, 'Psychologie de la nature morte', in *Trois Crises de l'Art Actuel* (Paris: Bibliothèque Charpentier, 1906).
9. I draw here on Sterling's discussion of nomenclature, in *Still Life Painting*, pp. 63–4, and Caroline Good's survey in Tim Batchelor, ed., *Dead Standing Things: Still Life Painting in Britain 1660–1740* (London: Tate Gallery, 2012), pp. 13–15.
10. 'nature morte, *n.* and *adj.*', *Oxford English Dictionary* (*OED*) online, http://www.oed.com/view/Entry/125363.
11. Percy Wyndham Lewis, *Time and Western Man* (London: Chatto & Windus, 1927), p. 107.
12. Ibid., p. 119.
13. Ibid., p. 87.
14. Ibid., p. 119.
15. Norman Bryson, *Looking at the Overlooked: Four Essays on Still Life Painting* (London: Reaktion Books, 1990), p. 61.
16. Marc Eli Blanchard, 'On Still Life', *Yale French Studies*, 61 (1981), 276–98 (p. 276).
17. Bryson, *Looking at the Overlooked*, p. 61.
18. Ibid., p. 13.
19. T. S. Eliot, 'Burnt Norton', from *Four Quartets* (first published in 1943), in *The Complete Poems and Plays* (London: Faber & Faber, 1969), pp. 171–98 (p. 175).
20. Gotthold Lessing, *Laocoön: An Essay on the Limits of Painting and Poetry*, trans. Edward Allen McCormick (London: John Hopkins University Press, 1984).

21. Murray Krieger, '*Ekphrasis* and the Still Movement of Poetry; or *Laokoon* Revisited', in *Ekphrasis: The Illusion of the Natural Sign* (Baltimore: John Hopkins Press, 1992), p. 267.
22. This dialectic informs W. J. T. Mitchell's reading of 'the utopian aspirations of ekphrasis – that the mute image be endowed with a voice, or made dynamic and active, or actually come into view, or (conversely) that poetic language might be "stilled," made iconic, or "frozen" into a static, spatial array'. *Picture Theory: Essays on Verbal and Visual Representation* (Chicago: University of Chicago Press, 1999), p. 156.
23. I employ the term 'modern' here, and refer to 'modern artist' and 'modern art' more widely in my study and more frequently than 'modernist', as these are more spacious designations, which can embrace the multiple and sometimes divergent artistic approaches and philosophies that I consider. Similarly, 'arts' and 'artists' are the general terms used to refer to various aesthetic disciplines and their practitioners, and I employ 'artists' in the broadest sense. Further specificity is introduced to examine particular disciplines.
24. These include Émile Zola, Katherine Mansfield, Ernest Hemingway, Gertrude Stein, Samuel Beckett and Wallace Stevens, as well as the writers explored in this introduction. The essays collected in Benedict Leca, ed., *The World is an Apple: The Still Lifes of Paul Cézanne* (London: Giles, 2014), published to accompany the eponymous exhibition at The Barnes Foundation and Art Gallery of Hamilton, offer insights on Cézanne's reception in French literary writing (see Richard Schiff's essay in particular), and affirm the central significance of still life in the critical reception of his work. For a critical reaction to Cézanne's still lifes by his contemporary, the poet-art critic Camille Mauclair, see 'Psychologie de la nature morte' (1906). Unlike the modern writers I discuss, Mauclair laments the lack of life in Cézanne's paintings (see p. 191).
25. Bridget Alsdorf, 'Interior Landscapes: Metaphor and Meaning in Cézanne's Late Still Lifes', *Word & Image*, 26 (2010), 314–23 (p. 315).
26. Lawrence, 'Introduction', p. 337.
27. Ibid., pp. 340–1.
28. Cézanne, quoted by Meyer Schapiro in 'The Apples of Cézanne: An Essay on the Meaning of Still-Life' (1968), in *Modern Art: 19th and 20th Centuries* (London: Chatto & Windus, 1978), pp. 1–33 (p. 30). Schapiro provides an important iconographic and psychoanalytic interpretation of the painter's habitual subject, in which he identifies an expression of latent eroticism. By his own acknowledgement, however, this psychoanalytic reading 'leaves much unexplained' about still life and its objects (pp. 12–13).
29. D. H. Lawrence, 'Art and Morality', in *Study of Thomas Hardy and other Essays,* ed. Bruce Steele (Cambridge: Cambridge University Press, 1985), pp. 161–8 (p. 168). The essay is one of several in which instability becomes central to the vitality of an artwork. In 'Morality and the Novel', written the same year, Lawrence proposes that 'morality is that delicate, forever trembling and changing *balance* between me and my circumambient universe', locating this quality in the novel 'in the trembling instability of the balance'. *Study of Thomas Hardy and Other Essays*, pp. 169–76 (p. 172).
30. Lawrence, 'Introduction', p. 341.

31. Ibid., p. 322. For a discussion of 'appleyness' and 'thereness' in relation to the aesthetics of the philosopher Martin Heidegger, see Anne Fernihough, *D. H. Lawrence: Aesthetics and Ideology* (Oxford: Clarendon Press, 1993), Chapters 8 and 9.
32. *The Diary of Virginia Woolf*, I, 18 April 1918, p. 140.
33. Critics have noted the importance of Cézanne for modern writers but they rarely address the specific implications of still life. Cara Lewis is a notable exception in her attempt to define the role of still life in Virginia Woolf's *To the Lighthouse*, which includes some discussion of Cézanne's paintings. 'Still Life in Motion: Mortal Form in Woolf's *To the Lighthouse*', *Twentieth Century Literature*, 60:4 (Winter 2014), 423–54.
34. Roger Fry, *Characteristics of French Art* (London: Chatto and Windus, 1932), pp. 144–5.
35. Roger Fry, *Cézanne: A Study of his Development* (London: Hogarth Press, 1927), p. 51.
36. Lawrence derides 'the cant phrases like Significant Form and Pure Form' associated with Bloomsbury art criticism ('Introduction', p. 326). In *D. H. Lawrence: Aesthetics and Ideology*, Fernihough offers an important corrective to the view of Bloomsbury art criticism as disconnected from the body – a view perpetuated by Lawrence and many other critics – which misreads Fry's theories and their development over time. I build on Fernihough's argument that an intuitive and physiological response to art was central to both writers, and I develop this reading in my exploration of Fry and Woolf in Chapter 1.
37. Lawrence, 'Introduction', pp. 341–2.
38. I do not deploy Sigmund Freud's theory of the uncanny in this study, but it is worth noting that his conception of *das unheimliche*, which signifies an uncomfortable experience of estrangement within the bounds of the familiar, has parallels with the sense of unease elicited by some still life paintings as they can appear to defamiliarise or remove everyday objects from their usual sphere of reference.
39. Lawrence, 'Introduction', p. 341.
40. Kandinsky, *Concerning the Spiritual in Art*, p. 17.
41. Lawrence develops this vocabulary in his encounters with Cézanne's landscape paintings in the same essay: he is compelled by their 'mysterious shiftiness'. 'Introduction', p. 342.
42. Ibid., p. 339.
43. David Trotter, *Cooking with Mud: The Idea of Mess in Nineteenth-Century Art and Fiction* (Oxford: Oxford University Press, 2000), pp. 217–18.
44. Ibid., p. 219.
45. Ibid., p. 217.
46. Lawrence, 'Introduction', p. 340.
47. Ibid., p. 326.
48. Fernihough, *D. H. Lawrence: Aesthetics and Ideology*, p. 122.
49. Cited by Henri Lallemand in *Cézanne: Visions of a Great Painter* (New York: Todtri, 1994), p. 88.
50. Rilke, *Letters on Cézanne*, p. 87. Fernihough does not pick up on the vibrational quality expressed by Rilke, but she does point to the affinities between his sense of the 'thingness' of Cézanne's apples and Lawrence's writing on this subject, noting 'strong evidence to suggest that Lawrence was reading Rilke in 1924–5'. *D. H. Lawrence: Aesthetics and Ideology*, p. 123.

51. Rilke, *Letters on Cézanne*, p. 88.
52. Maurice Merleau-Ponty, 'Cézanne's Doubt', in *The Merleau-Ponty Aesthetics Reader: Philosophy and Painting*, ed. Galen A. Johnson and Michael B. Smith (Illinois: Northwestern University Press, 1993), pp. 59–75 (p. 63).
53. Ibid., p. 65.
54. Paul Smith, 'Cézanne's Color Lab: Not-So-Still Life', in *The World is an Apple*, pp. 91–143 (p. 138).
55. Maurice Merleau-Ponty, 'Eye and Mind' (1964), in *The Merleau-Ponty Aesthetics Reader*, pp. 121–49 (p. 144).
56. Susan Landauer comes close to addressing this phenomenon when she describes the 'not-so-still life' as the 'most striking incarnation of the genre' in California still life. See Susan Landauer, William H. Gerdts, Patricia Trenton, San Jose Museum of Art, California, eds, *The Not-So-Still Life: A Century of California Painting and Sculpture* (London: University of California Press, 2003), pp. 1–7 (p. 2).
57. Kandinsky, *Concerning the Spiritual in Art*, p. 17.
58. Sterling, *Still Life Painting*, p. 128.
59. Ibid.
60. Ibid., p. 149.
61. Ibid., p. 128.
62. Costello, *Planets on Tables*, p. xvi.
63. Ibid., p. xiii.
64. Bryson, *Looking at the Overlooked*, pp. 60–1.
65. Ibid., p. 61.
66. Blanchard, 'On Still Life', p. 277.
67. Lewis, 'Still Life in Motion', p. 426.
68. Rosemary Lloyd, *Shimmering in a Transformed Light* (London: Cornell University Press, 2005), p. 22. Other suggestive meditations on still life which move between literature and painting include Zbigniew Herbert, *Still Life with a Bridle: Essays and Apocryphas*, trans. John and Bogdana Carpenter (London: Cape, 1993); and Guy Davenport, *Objects on a Table: Harmonious Disarray in Art and Literature* (Washington DC: Counterpoint, 1998).
69. Lloyd, *Shimmering in a Transformed Light*, p. xv.
70. Anne W. Lowenthal, ed., *The Object as Subject: Studies in the Interpretation of Still Life* (Princeton: Princeton University Press, 1996), p. 9.
71. Renewed attention to the object has also been foregrounded in major exhibitions such as *Objects of Desire: The Modern Still Life* at the Museum of Modern Art, New York, 1997.
72. Lowenthal, *The Object as Subject*, pp. 4, 6. For her useful historiography of still life see pp. 6–10.
73. Recent studies include, Liesl Olson, *Modernism and the Ordinary* (Oxford: Oxford University Press, 2009), and Lorraine Sim, *Virginia Woolf: The Patterns of Ordinary Experience* (Farnham: Ashgate, 2010).
74. I employ 'spiritual' as an elastic, umbrella term, which encompasses multiple modes of engagement with the 'non-material' and metaphysical, from orthodox religion to occultism. The term was used freely and often without precise definition by many

of the artists I consider in this study, but I shall attempt to define its specific frame of reference depending on the different contexts in which it is investigated.

75. Jane Bennett, *The Enchantment of Modern Life* (Princeton: Princeton University Press, 2001), pp. 5, 4. Bennett constructs what she calls her 'alter-tale' of enchantment as a counter to the narrative of the 'disenchantment of the world' in modern culture formulated by the German sociologist and philosopher Max Weber. See also Philip Fisher, *Wonder, the Rainbow, and the Aesthetics of Rare Experiences* (Cambridge, MA: Harvard University Press, 1998).
76. Bennett, *The Enchantment of Modern Life*, p. 5.
77. The historical denotations of 'ecstasis' relate to experiences ranging from intensified and rapturous feeling to insensibility, often emerging from sources in mystical writings and related conceptions of ecstasy. My use of the term incorporates both senses in view of the internal paradoxes in still life. See, 'ectasis, *n.*', in *OED* online, http://www.oed.com/view/Entry/59421.
78. Sterling, *Still Life Painting*, p. 158.
79. Schapiro, 'The Apples of Cézanne', pp. 19–20. Vincent van Gogh similarly observed the calming effect ('*pour se calmer*') of still life painting (ibid., p. 15).
80. Ibid., p. 20.
81. Schapiro represents this view of objects as subordinated to man (ibid., p. 14). His description of still life objects as 'instruments of a passion as well as of cool meditation' informs my attempt to reveal the scope and emotional range provoked by these compositions, and the variegated spectrum of forms they might take (p. 20).
82. Arthur Schopenhauer, *The World as Will and Representation*, trans. E. F. J. Payne, 2 vols (New York: Dover Publications: c.1969), I, pp. 196–7.
83. Ibid.
84. My approach is informed by critics who have made the case for 'enchantment' and the role of discourses of the spiritual and occult in modern(ist) experiment, rightly complicating an overly secularised view of the period. See Alex Owen, *The Place of Enchantment: British Occultism and the Culture of the Modern* (Chicago: University of Chicago Press, 2004); Leigh Wilson, *Modernism and Magic: Experiments with Spiritualism, Theosophy and the Occult* (Edinburgh: Edinburgh University Press, 2012); and the research network, 'Enchanted Modernities: Theosophy, Modernism and the Arts, c. 1875–1960', led by Elizabeth Prettejohn and Sarah Turner.
85. Bryson, *Looking at the Overlooked*, p. 64. See Bryson's excellent discussion of this tradition, pp. 60–95.
86. T. J. Gorringe, *Earthly Visions* (New Haven: Yale University Press, 2011), p. 149. Gorringe sees still life painting as a 'paradigm' of the form of attention described by Simone Weil as fundamental to prayer and ethics: an attention to others and to the beauty of the world which 'consists of suspending our thought, leaving it detached, empty and ready to be penetrated by the object' (quoted by Gorringe, pp. 164–5).
87. Ibid., p. 150.
88. Bryson, *Looking at the Overlooked*, p. 89.
89. In *A Sense of Shock: The Impact of Impressionism on Modern British and Irish Writing* (Oxford: Oxford University Press, 2011), Adam Parkes describes the 'flood of impressions', which were 'an unmistakable function of a modern urban environment

that promoted hyperstimulation at the expense of feeling and reflection; [. . .] an inevitable and irresistible consequence of the perpetual shocks and jolts, the jars and collisions, of what later theorists would call the "culture of distraction"' (p. 12).

90. Jonathan Crary, *Suspensions of Perception: Attention, Spectacle, and Modern Culture* (Cambridge, MA: MIT Press, 1999), p. 13; Tim Armstrong, *Modernism, Technology, and the Body: A Cultural Study* (Cambridge: Cambridge University Press, 1998), p. 187.
91. See Armstrong's discussion in ibid., p. 195.
92. Tim Armstrong, *Modernism: A Cultural History* (Cambridge: Polity Press, 2005), p. 3.
93. Recent studies include Sara Danius, *The Senses of Modernism: Technology, Perception, and Aesthetics* (Ithaca: Cornell University Press, 2002); and Andrew Thacker, *Moving through Modernity: Space and Geography in Modernism* (Manchester: Manchester University Press, 2003). There has also been a proliferation of work on moving bodies and dance, including Terri Mester, *Movement and Modernism* (Fayetteville: University of Arkansas Press, 1997), which I explore further in Chapter 2.
94. Enda Duffy, *The Speed Handbook: Velocity, Pleasure, Modernism* (Durham, NC: Duke University Press, 2009), p. 1. This critical interest is also exemplified in David Bradshaw, Laura Marcus and Rebecca Roach, eds, *Moving Modernisms: Motion, Technology, and Modernity* (Oxford: Oxford University Press, 2016). The question of stasis is partly addressed in essays on film (by Paul Saint-Amour, and Garrett Stewart respectively), and on dance (Olga Taxidou), but it has not yet received sustained critical attention.
95. See for instance Ulrika Maude's discussion in 'Modernist Bodies: Coming to Our Senses', in Corinne Saunders, Ulrika Maude and Jane Macnaughton, eds, *The Body and the Arts* (Basingstoke: Macmillan, 2009), pp. 116–30.
96. Crary, *Suspensions of Perception*, p. 47.
97. Ibid., p. 10.
98. Linda Dalrymple Henderson and Tim Armstrong have been foundational in the small but growing body of work on vibrational aesthetics in modernism. See especially Armstrong's chapter, 'Vibrating World: Science, Spiritualism and Technology', in *Modernism: A Cultural History*, pp. 115–34, which shows how scientific ideas regarding energy, quantum physics and radiation were assimilated into modernist literature and became sources for figurations of the creative self. Dalrymple Henderson's essay on 'Vibratory Modernism: Boccioni, Kupka, and the Ether of Space', explores related ideas about vibration in modern science, occultism and art, in Bruce Clarke and Linda Dalrymple Henderson, eds, *From Energy to Information: Representation in Science and Technology, Art, and Literature* (Stanford: Stanford University Press, 2002), pp. 126–49. Shelley Trower has enlarged this field with her study of vibration in the nineteenth century, *Senses of Vibration: A History of the Pleasure and Pain of Sound* (London: Continuum, 2012), and in Shelley Trower and Anthony Enns, eds, *Vibratory Modernism* (Basingstoke: Palgrave Macmillan, 2013). My inquiry shares the cultural and scientific contexts of these studies, yet the fact that there is little overlap in terms of specific examples serves to emphasise the fertile ground generated by considering vibration in the early twentieth century.

99. Bruce Elder, *Harmony and Dissent: Film and Avant-Garde Art Movements in the Early Twentieth Century* (Waterloo, ON: Wilfrid Laurier University Press, 2008), p. 17.
100. Kandinsky, *Concerning the Spiritual in Art*, p. 53.
101. Spyros Papapetros, *On the Animation of the Inorganic: Art, Architecture, and the Extension of Life* (Chicago: University of Chicago Press, 2012), p. xi.
102. Ibid., p. xi.
103. Ibid., p. viii. Papapetros traces the history of animation from the fin-de-siècle to contemporary culture through the work of architects, art historians including Aby Warburg and Wilhelm Worringer, and artists including Fernand Léger and Salvador Dalí.
104. See Alexandra Harris's discussion of the aesthetics of the modern interior and its troublesome relationship with objects, a debate she describes as 'not only about style but also about ways of living', in *Romantic Moderns: English Writers, Artists and the Imagination from Virginia Woolf to John Piper* (London: Thames & Hudson, 2010), pp. 38–58 (p. 54).
105. Wallace Stevens, 'The Relations Between Poetry and Painting' (1951), in *Collected Poetry and Prose*, ed. Frank Kermode and Joan Richardson (New York: Library of America, 1997), pp. 740–51 (p. 747). All further references to this essay are to this edition and will be cited in the body text, as 'RPP' where necessary.
106. The slower mode of being required by still life can be aligned with the project of vibrational aesthetics in the context of 'the numerous attempts to detect, to count and to analyse vibrations' which 'formed part of a struggle against the increasing speeds that characterize modernity, at which things move too fast to be consciously registered' (Trower, *Senses of Vibration*, p. 3).
107. The *OED* provides multiple significations of vibration, of which the following are particularly pertinent to this inquiry: 'An intuitive signal about a person or thing'; 'A supposed movement of this kind in the nerves'; 'a quivering, swaying, or tremulous motion of any kind'; http://www.oed.com/view/Entry/223061.
108. Roger Shattuck, *The Banquet Years: The Origins of the Avant-garde in France, 1885 to World War I*, rev. edn (London: Jonathan Cape: 1969 [1958]), p. 352.
109. Ibid., pp. 349–51.
110. Ibid., p. 351.
111. Ibid., p. 335.
112. Eliot, 'Burnt Norton', *Four Quartets*, p. 173.
113. Wyndham Lewis, 'Our Vortex', *Blast*, 1 (1914), 147–9.
114. Mary Ann Gillies, *Henri Bergson and British Modernism* (Montreal and Kingston: McGill-Queen's University Press, 1996), p. 3.
115. Ibid., pp. 50–1.
116. Lloyd, *Shimmering in a Transformed Light*, 149–50.
117. Virginia Woolf, *To the Lighthouse* (Harmondsworth: Penguin, 1964), p. 183. All further references are to this edition and will be given after quotations in the text.
118. Preface to David Bissell and Gillian Fuller, eds, *Stillness in a Mobile World* (London: Routledge, 2011), no page number.
119. Louise Hornby, *Still Modernism: Photography, Literature, Film* (Oxford: Oxford University Press, 2017), p. 1.

120. Ibid., p. 191.
121. I draw inspiration from approaches to the study of cultural exchange in this period developed by Grace Brockington, in *Above the Battlefield* (New Haven: Yale University Press, 2010), and Grace Brockington, ed., *Internationalism and the Arts in Britain and Europe at the 'Fin de Siècle'* (Oxford: Peter Lang, 2009).
122. Armstrong, *Modernism: A Cultural History*, p. ix.
123. I draw here on Simon Shaw-Miller's useful terms in *Visible Deeds of Music: Art and Music from Wagner to Cage* (New Haven: Yale University Press, 2002), p. 35.
124. Virginia Woolf, *Roger Fry: A Biography* (London: Hogarth Press, 1940; repr. 1991), p. 152. All further references to this essay will be given after quotations in the text, with the abbreviation RF if necessary.
125. Virginia Woolf, *Walter Sickert: A Conversation* (London: Hogarth Press, 1934), p. 12. All further references to this essay will be given after quotations in the text.
126. André Lepecki, 'Still: On the Vibratile Microscopy of Dance', in Gabriele Brandstetter and Hortensia Volckers, eds, *Remembering the Body* (Ostfildern-Ruit: Hatje Cantz, 2000), pp. 334–64 (p. 336).
127. Rudolf Steiner, 'Eurythmy is a Moving Sculpture', introduction to a performance given on 26 December 1923, in *Eurythmy: An Introductory Reader*, original texts compiled and introduced by Beth Usher, translations rev. by Christian von Arnim (Forest Row: Sophia Books, 2006), pp. 270–8 (p. 270).
128. Rudolf Steiner, *A Lecture on Eurythmy: Given at Penmaenmawr on 26th August, 1923* (London: Rudolf Steiner Press, 1967, repr. 1st edn, 1926), pp. 6–9.
129. Wallace Stevens noted this phrase from Edward Sackville-West in his commonplace book; see *Sur Plusieurs Beaux Sujets: Wallace Stevens's Commonplace Book*, ed. Milton J. Bates (Stanford: Stanford University Press, 1989), 'Entry 97', p. 103.
130. Wallace Stevens, 'The Noble Rider and the Sound of Words', in *Collected Poetry and Prose*, pp. 643–65 (p. 663); first delivered as a lecture at Princeton University in 1941 and published in 1942.

I

'QUIVERING YET STILL': VIRGINIA WOOLF, ROGER FRY AND THE AESTHETICS OF ATTENTION

> And there was Roger Fry, gazing at them, plunging his eyes into them as if he were a humming-bird hawk-moth hanging over a flower, quivering yet still. And then drawing a deep breath of satisfaction, he would turn to whoever it might be, eager for sympathy. (RF, p. 152)

With this vivid image, Woolf places us in the midst of what she described as the 'bold, bright, impudent almost' works of modern French art, sharing the excitement of Roger Fry, the art critic and painter, in his encounter with Post-Impressionist paintings (RF, p. 152). Woolf began research for her biography of Fry after his death in 1934 and it was published in 1940, some thirty years after he first introduced the English public to works by Cézanne, Van Gogh and Paul Gauguin at two famously audacious exhibitions, in 1910 and 1912, at the Grafton Gallery, London.[1] Her description of Fry captures the intensity of his engagement with these works of art and constructs a model of aesthetic attention that will become the touchstone in this chapter. I suggest that compressed into this seemingly localised image is a complex of aesthetic and ethical concerns about attention and affect, sympathy and communication, receptivity and rapture, which pivot on the relationship between movement and stillness. Woolf's intimate observation of Fry's physical attitude – his immobile yet responsive state – demonstrates her own attentiveness to the dynamics of aesthetic encounters.[2] The humming-bird hawk-moth at the centre of her vision of Fry has a wider resonance in her work: we shall see that she frequently embodies an aesthetic of attentiveness through the closely observed life of insects. Although the image makes a chronologically late appearance in her writing career, it offers a model through which to examine permutations of the 'quivering yet still', across a range of her fiction and non-fiction.

Woolf's fascination with 'quivering stillness' appears as early as in her second novel, *Night and Day* (1919). Wandering the gardens at Hampton Court, Cassandra experiences a feeling of inexpressible 'bliss', which permeates the 'stillness' and 'brightness' of the bucolic landscape: '[t]he quivering stillness of the butterfly on the half-opened flower, the silent grazing of the deer [. . .], were the sights her eye rested upon and received as the images of her own nature laid open to happiness and trembling in its ecstasy'.[3] In a shift that will become familiar, abstract stillness finds form in the small scale and particular; the trembling 'ec-stasis' of the experiential self is reflected in the anticipatory stasis of the insect.

The permutations of 'quivering' are far-reaching in Woolf's work. They radiate beyond the image of the insect and beyond Post-Impressionism, although these are particularly suggestive contexts for the development of this vocabulary. The etymological root of 'quiver' alerts us to some of the resonances of the word in Woolf's lexicon. In its adjectival form, 'quiver' originates from the Old English 'cwifer', speculatively related to 'cwic', meaning 'alive'.[4] 'Quiver' and 'quivering' may therefore be read as signals – even if barely perceptible – of life and animation, as well as of embryonic or unreleased creative potency. Quivering is central to the sensitised lexicon that Woolf develops in order to describe the vibrating stillness, tension and receptivity associated with moments of intensity and heightened attention such as 'rapture' and 'ecstasy', which I will argue had special claim to her conception of still life. We begin, then, by following the fertile life of this word and its derivatives as it appears across different modes of discourse in Woolf's writing, bringing us into contact not only with the field of the aesthetic but also with the ontological, physiological and psychological.

My central focus in this inquiry is an aesthetic(ised) experience of quivering. This is not to posit a de-historicised or disembodied Woolf, nor to present a portrait of a psychologically unstable figure; rather, I suggest that by examining a culturally and historically inflected vibratory aesthetics in her work, we can register more acutely the ways in which this deeply sensory writer was responsive to the demands of an embodied experience of art. On many occasions in her letters and diaries, she draws on this term to describe states of mind and body generated by the process of making or experiencing art. The Oxford English Dictionary defines 'quiver', in its verbal form, as 'to shake, tremble, or vibrate with a slight rapid motion'; while the phrase 'all of a quiver' signifies 'a state of nervous excitement or anticipation'.[5] The same phrase appears in Woolf's diary on 16 September 1932: 'Now I'm all of a quiver – cant read or write [. . .].

What an ill joined web of nerves – to be kind – my being is! A touch makes the whole thing quiver.'[6] She communicates a paralysing tension inhibitive of creative activity, yet painful conditions of hypersensitivity and nerve-strain are often aligned with creativity in her experience as a writer. In her essay 'On Being Ill', written during a long period of illness in 1925, she challenged what the condition might mean, meditating on the potential for the immobilised body to engage in imaginative flight, and even for illness to initiate 'spiritual change'.[7]

The *OED* illustrates the terms 'quiver' and 'quiveringly' with numerous medical conditions or neurological 'weaknesses', which are often gendered and relate specifically to female experience. However, during the First World War such terms also became part of a vocabulary describing neurological conditions suffered by victims of shell shock whose trauma was physically manifest in their shaking and quivering bodies.[8] Woolf seems both to acknowledge and to subvert the etymology of 'quivering' in another expression of creative agitation recorded in her diary in February 1932, in which she alludes to her feminist project: 'I'm quivering & itching to write my – whats it to be called? – "Men are like that?"'[9] By reconceiving quivering as a potent creative force, she implicitly writes back to the gendering of passivity and sensibility, and the association of women with hypersensitised neurological complaints, which was particularly evident in Victorian literature.[10]

It is significant from a socio-historical perspective that 'quivering' also entered into the lexicon of art criticism in response to the first of Fry's Post-Impressionist exhibitions. In a review entitled 'Post-Illusionism and the Art of the Insane', T. B. Hyslop, a doctor who would later treat Woolf, observed of the artists: '[t]heir efforts are genuine results of physical disease. Nystagmus (or quivering of the eyeball) is responsible for a want of firmness in outline, and affections of the retina for distorted zigzag lines and for defects in the perception of colour.'[11] Hyslop's commentary is indicative of the early reception of Post-Impressionism by the British public and critics alike. Many reviewers of the first exhibition insinuated that nervous disorders and even mental illness had precipitated the stylistic effects that characterised modern French painting. Woolf's use of the word in her description of Fry has a subtly different inflection: it signals dilated attentiveness and physiological sensation. 'Quivering' reveals a visceral reaction more in tune with what Fry described in his account of Post-Impressionism in 1911 as the response to form that arises from 'what in us is rhythmic and vital'.[12] These were qualities Woolf identified in Fry when she travelled with him on an expedition to see Byzantine churches and Greek temples in the spring of 1932. She found her companion 'the best admirer of life and art I've ever travelled with'. He can 'feel his way along a pillar or a carving or a mosaic with a sensibility and vigour' that brings to mind a 'prodigiously fertile spider', she records, moving from tactile acuity to her characteristic sign of perceptual responsiveness: Fry 'quivers his eyes' and pronounces: 'its life, its individuality'.[13] Again, we find that quivering and the perception of vitality form a close association.

The peculiarly active stillness exhibited by Fry at the outset of this discussion is fundamental in this chapter's investigation. 'Quivering yet still' provides a paradigm for a certain kind of aesthetic experience and state of attentive being which brings movement and stasis into proximity. I suggest that this paradigm has correspondences with the approach to making and experiencing art that Woolf developed throughout her career. In her short story 'An Unwritten Novel', published in *Monday or Tuesday* (1921), she frames her reflection on the creation of character through a configuration of quivering suspension reminiscent of the image of Fry. As she endeavours to read the face of 'Minnie Marsh', the embryonic character or 'soul' whom she has not quite yet brought into being, she engages in an act of searching attention:

> in the human eye – how d'you define it? – there's a break – a division – so that when you've grasped the stem the butterfly's off – the moth that hangs in the evening over the yellow flower – move, raise your hand, off, high, away. I won't raise my hand. Hang still, then, quiver, life, soul, spirit, whatever you are of Minnie Marsh – I, too, on my flower – the hawk over the down – alone, or what were the worth of life? To rise; hang still in the evening, in the midday; hang still over the down.[14]

Here, the butterfly and moth provide an analogy for the hesitant perceptions, suspensions and vibratory motions of the unfolding creative process, but also for such phenomena as 'life', 'soul' and 'spirit'. The rhythms of this process are inscribed into the very syntax of this passage. In parallel with the hawk, the prose line hovers, undulates and quivers into motion; the repetition of 'hang still' and scattered dashes creating visual effects of suspension. Despite predatory intent, to 'hang still' expresses a kinship to 'quivering' in its suggestions of indeterminacy, and an ethic of poised restraint underlies these hovering suspensions ('I won't raise my hand'). This passage valorises hovering in suspension as a mode through which to explore hybrid or threshold states. The hawk and the hawk-moth will remain hovering in view as we continue to explore the different visual scales and forms through which Woolf embodies abstract concepts of stillness and suspension.[15]

Spaces, places and states of stillness appear in protean forms in Woolf's work, informing her imaginative and physical geographies.[16] Retaining the quiver of vitality within stillness was crucial to her creative sensibility. In *To the Lighthouse* we witness unease with the fixity of stillness and its relationship to beauty. Meditating on Mrs Ramsay, the painter Lily Briscoe comes to the conclusion that her beauty 'stilled life – froze it. One forgot the little agitations' (pp. 201–2). These 'little agitations' – like quivers – are signs of life's unpredictable intensities and errancies that Woolf seeks to sustain in art. Lily wrestles with this problem at the outset of the novel: 'if it was her [Mrs Ramsay's] beauty merely that one thought of, one must remember the quivering thing, the living thing [. . .] and work it into the picture' (p. 35). Similar preoccupations underlie Woolf's deep-seated ambivalence about the forms that 'stillness' might take in visual art and its apparent indifference to the flux of everyday life. This is evident in 'Pictures and Portraits', a review from 1920 in which she implicitly critiques the opposition between the world outside the National Portrait Gallery and the conditions demanded within it. We witness life's soundscape, 'a stream of sound at once continuous and broken up into a kind of rough music' which inhibits 'think[ing] of pictures. They are too still, too silent.'[17] Stillness and silence are often yoked together in this way in Woolf's writing and we will come back to their troubling qualities later.

Woolf was equally alert to the 'quivering [. . .] living thing' as a reader and critic. In her essay on her contemporary D. H. Lawrence, she identifies '[o]ne of the curious qualities' of his novel, *Sons and Lovers* (1913), as the feeling of 'an unrest, a little quiver and shimmer in his page, as if it were composed of separate gleaming objects, by no means content to stand still and be looked at'.[18] She is sympathetic, then, to Lawrence's conviction that 'nothing is really *statically* at rest'; the conclusion we witnessed him reach in contemplating Cézanne. On the other hand, as a reader of the poet John Donne, Woolf is 'arrested' by the call to attention with which the poet begins his poem, 'A Lecture upon the Shadow': 'Stand still, and I will read to thee'. 'At once we are arrested', she writes in her essay, 'Donne after Three Centuries' (1925), 'Stand still, he commands. [. . .] And stand still we must. With the first words a shock passes through us; perceptions, previously numb and torpid, quiver into being; the nerves of sight and hearing are quickened.'[19] Two years later, Donne's command reverberates through *To the Lighthouse* in Mrs Ramsay's repeated entreaty to her son, James, 'Stand still here', which expands into her metaphysical desire for permanence within flux – '"Life stand still here"'; and finally, at the end of the novel: 'Everything in the whole world seemed to stand still. The Lighthouse became immovable' (pp. 35, 183, 208). 'Standing still' is, I suggest, at the root of the profoundly embodied attention that was vital to Woolf's art.

Nevertheless, many of Woolf's writings express the relationship between fixity and fluidity, or stillness and movement, as a deeply subjective, internal tension. We find an emblematic illustration in her memoir, 'Sketch of the Past' (1939), where she sees herself as 'a fish in a stream; deflected; held in place'.[20] A similarly taut straining against being 'held in place' underlies Jinny's pronouncement in *The Waves* (1931): 'I do not want to be fixed, to be pinioned. I tremble, I quiver, like the leaf in the hedge.'[21] In the very early stages of composition Woolf envisaged her prose-poem, which was originally titled *The Moths*, in a set of images evocative of still life's pattern of movement and stasis: 'The current of the moths flying strongly this way. A lamp & a flower pot in the centre. The flower can always be changing.'[22] *The Waves* is interspersed by 'still life' compositions of domestic objects that hold a peculiar attraction partly for their stabilising, meditative qualities. Rather like a moth to light, Neville is drawn to 'the quiet of ordinary things'.[23] However, the insect metaphor reasserts itself in a different form later in the prose-poem when Bernard declares, as if unfixing himself, 'I have escaped you; I have gone buzzing like a swarm of bees, endlessly vagrant, with none of your power of fixing remorselessly upon a single object.'[24] 'Fixing remorselessly' gives a negative inflection to the intensity and narrow focus of this form of attention on a single object. The year following publication of *The Waves*, Woolf expressed a sense of the nourishment drawn from natural beauty in a similar pattern of images but with a subtly different inflection: 'I can fasten on a beautiful day, as a bee fixes itself on a sunflower', she wrote in her diary: 'It feeds me, rests me, satisfies me, as nothing else does [. . .] This has a holiness. This will go on after I'm dead.'[25] She testifies here to an act of restorative attention that claims contiguity with the sacred and confers on the experience a spiritual charge. As this inquiry unfolds, we shall uncover the affinities and tensions between such forms of attention and their significance for Woolf and Fry in their vision of art and life; and more specifically, as we move toward a closer reading of *Roger Fry* in the second half of this chapter, in their conception of still life.[26] My endeavour, then, is not simply to uncover contested states of stillness and movement in Woolf's writing; rather, I shall reveal a model of vibratory attention (encapsulated by 'quivering') through which she attempts to bridge these states – in a way which gains illumination when read in dialogue with Fry's writings on Cézanne and still life.

'Violent Rapture'

The unstable relations between stillness and movement are evident, then, on a local level in the focused examples I have discussed. Yet these exchanges are also emblematic of Woolf's fundamental epistemological and ontological concerns. 'Now is life very solid or very shifting?' she reflects in a diary entry of 1929, 'I am haunted by the two contradictions. This has gone on for ever: will last for ever; [. . .] this moment I stand on. Also it is transitory, flying, diaphanous.'[27] The bolder claim I would like to make is that this is the axis around which Woolf's creative sensibility turns. The rhythms of the solid and the shifting, of the stable and the moving, inform the texture of her prose and dictate the balance and mass of her syntax. Following the life of the 'quiver' takes us to the heart of these apparent contradictions and the ways in which she mediated between them.

The dialectic between the 'quivering' and the 'still' emerges with different implications in Woolf's memoir, 'Sketch', in which she outlines her 'philosophy' of 'non-being' and 'being'. She had written 'Sketch' concurrently with and as 'a holiday' from her biography of Fry, and the two works invite examination in parallel (p. 87). In *Virginia Woolf: the Patterns of Ordinary Experience* (2010), Lorraine Sim interprets Woolf's 'non-being' and 'being' as 'two phases of daily life', which 'involve contrasting attitudes to the world that are central to her view of ordinary experience'.[28] In this reading, 'non-being' refers to 'a form of perception and a mode of being; the phases of life that are lived automatically and inattentively', rendering one 'blind to the particular and the commonplace', which we remember is the sphere conventionally attributed to still life.[29] On the other hand, 'being' relates 'to the moments in our daily lives that are lived attentively', engaging a 'state of perception' in which pleasure in the everyday is accentuated.[30] Following these distinctions, we can locate a concern with what attention might mean at the heart of Woolf's ontology and aesthetics. However, in taking up Sim's persuasive claim that Woolf's modernism advocates 'a return to small things and daily experience' my inquiry also seeks to go beyond the sphere of the 'ordinary'. Woolf's fascination with the frontiers of sense and supersensuous experience invites us to consider their impact on her model of intense receptivity and how it might reshape perceptions of the object world.[31]

Woolf's 'moments of being' are suggestive in thinking through her aesthetics of attention as they hinge not only on the polarities of stasis and motion, but on closer inspection also contain a series of internal oppositions presenting a complex and unstable spectrum (including states of trance, paralysis, suspension, rapture, and ecstasy). Although by no means homogeneous, they are characterised by suspension or stasis associated with states of shock, and they engender conditions of both pleasure and pain. Woolf describes in 'Sketch' how, in their disquieting, negative manifestations, such moments involve 'a peculiar horror and a physical collapse; they seemed dominant; myself passive' (p. 85). In their more exhilarating or 'positive' forms, these 'exceptional moments' are frequently described using the terminology of 'ecstasy' and 'rapture'. In such instances, they might usefully be read as 'ec-stases'. Merleau-Ponty is helpful in conceiving the temporal corollary to these moments of suspension. We can read them as 'vertical' moments or what he calls 'transversal ecstasis'.[32] Elucidating this concept, Galen A. Johnson writes, '[a]gainst linear seriality, vertical time refers us to a variety of experiences that have as their inner structure losing oneself to the world: joy, euphoria, fascination, infatuation, and artistic creation. The flow of time is stopped up.'[33] This sense of an ecstatic but not always pleasurable atemporal suspension remains a touchstone in this chapter.

*

In Woolf's longest essay on painting, *Walter Sickert: A Conversation* (1934), she locates an erotically charged intermingling of pleasure and pain – a 'violent rapture of colour' – in the space of the picture gallery. Originally printed as a pamphlet by the Hogarth Press, the cover design by her sister Vanessa Bell presents a still life of table wear, grapes and a bottle, which visually introduce the essay's convivial dinner-party setting and conversational tone.[34] It also alerts us to the themes of consumption and nourishment, which are characteristic in Woolf's figurations of the experience of art. The 'hither and thither' of the conversation passing between a group of dinner guests allows her – alighting like a winged insect – to adopt different perspectives in the debate between 'pure' and literary painting and reveals the intricacies of her response to Walter Sickert's paintings (p. 5).[35] However, my concern here is with the body of the insect as a register for the 'violent rapture' of colour experience. Early in the conversation, we witness the bleak prediction that '[w]e shall very soon lose our sense of colour' (p. 5). This is a symptom of life in the modern metropolis where 'days spent in an office' lead to 'atrophy of the eye' (p. 7). The debate shifts when one guest describes a South American insect 'in whom the eye is so developed that they are all eye' (p. 7). These insects absorb the colour of the flowers they feed on in a chameleon-like symbiosis, 'becoming [. . .] the thing they saw' (p. 8).[36] In the ensuing conversation, the insect's dilated sense mechanism – 'all eye' – marks it out as an incarnation of advanced rather than retrograde sensibility. It prompts the speculation: 'were we once insects like that [. . .] all eye? Do we still preserve the capacity for drinking, eating, indeed becoming colour furled up in us, waiting for proper conditions to develop?' (p. 8).

In *Walter Sickert* Woolf presents the picture gallery as a fertile site of 'stillness, warmth and seclusion' like 'the primeval forest'. It invites the visitor to revert to 'the insect stage' of their existence, but rather than an evolutionary regression this 'stage' is characterised by the expansion of ocular sensitivity and represents the healing of modern man's atrophied attention (p. 8). Through this inversion of the capacities of man and insect, Woolf complicates narratives of human progression and evolution, which had been the subject of passionate debate since the publication of Darwin's *On the Origin of Species* (1859).[37] The experience of the gallery visitor is brought directly into parallel with the insect when one guest recounts his physically transformative encounter with Sickert's work: 'Colours went spirally through my body lighting a flare [. . .]. Colour warmed, thrilled, chafed, burnt, soothed, fed and finally exhausted me' (p. 9). The staccato rhythms of Woolf's prose charge the account with an erotic energy: chromatic experience becomes a kind of possession or inhabiting. The trajectory of 'violent rapture' experienced by the gallery visitor has affinities with Roland Barthes' description of the physiological effects of colour in visual art, where it is a 'kind of bliss', 'like a closing eyelid, a tiny fainting spell'.[38] From Woolf's essay emerges a model of sympathetic attention predicated on a dilated sense mechanism and a receptive, even painfully permeable self in which man and insect are brought unexpectedly into close contact.

In his study of rapture and literature, David Punter identifies 'the apparent impossibility of recounting "rapturous states", and of fixing them in words or in time'.[39] According to Punter, rapture indicates both '[th]e act of carrying, or fact of being carried, onwards; force of movement', and a 'transport of mind, mental exaltation or absorption, ecstasy'.[40] It is an experience located within and also beyond the body. This is the tension Woolf confronts in her attempt to write the 'violent rapture of colour' in *Walter Sickert* where the writer finds themselves in 'a region of very strong sensations' but also 'a zone of silence' (p. 12). It is equally a tension manifest in her descriptions of rapturous 'moments of being'. Rapture complicates the polarities and temporalities of movement and stasis, distraction and attention, to reveal experiences in which these states coincide or blur.[41]

Woolf's wider lexicon is peppered with these compound intensities ('violent rapture', 'vibrant rapture', the 'pressure of rapture', 'purest ecstasy').[42] In 'Sketch', these moments are often chromatically illuminated. She recalls the 'colour-and-sound memories' which 'hang together' at her childhood summer home in St Ives, punctuating and even puncturing the 'muffled dulness' or 'cotton wool' of 'non-being' that had closed over the family following the death of her mother (pp. 80, 104). Of the summer garden at St Ives, she writes:

> The buzz, the croon, the smell, all seemed to press voluptuously against some membrane; not to burst it; but to hum round one such a complete rapture of pleasure that I stopped, smelt; looked. But again I cannot describe that rapture. It was rapture rather than ecstasy. (p. 80)

Woolf's intermingled sense experience is predicated on a physically immobile yet dilated self, which vibrates with a rapture shared by the surroundings. Her specification of 'rapture rather than ecstasy' is significant here as it confers a sense of affective transport within '(ec)stasis'. As she probes these 'strong memories' further, she realises that she is 'only the container of the feeling of ecstasy, of the feeling of rapture' (p. 81). Her self-figuration as a porous receptacle recalls the dis-and re-embodiment of colour experience in *Walter Sickert* where viewers in an art gallery absorb the colour they encounter in paintings, becoming shrivelled 'airballs' when deprived of its nourishing life-force.[43] The conception of the self as an absorbent vessel, suspended in a sort of 'ec-stasis' and shaped by the forces that enter it, is significant to the phenomenological attention Woolf gives to aesthetic experience.

I would like to keep her 'moments of being' in mind throughout this inquiry because she harnesses their characteristics – including heightened receptivity, sensory awareness and a suspension of the self – to develop the vibrational model of attention with which I am concerned. Furthermore, Woolf recognises in Fry a reciprocal capacity to be absorbed and transported. In her biography she describes her subject's encounter with Post-Impressionist painting using terminology that recalls her own 'exceptional moments': 'moments of vision when a new force breaks in, and the gropings of the past suddenly seem to have meaning' (RF, p. 161). It becomes increasingly apparent, then, that her two projects in life-writing shared not simply temporal contiguity but also cross-fertilisation of imagery and ideas.

The powerful 'new forces' breaking through everyday perception were not always beneficent; but as she worked through her memories in 'Sketch', Woolf realised that 'the shock-receiving capacity' was what made her a writer (p. 85). Once again she turns to the body of the insect to conjure up a sense of her awkward maturation at the age of fifteen, following the 'second blow of death', that of her half-sister Stella Duckworth, who died only two years after her mother.

> I was thinking; feeling; living; [. . .] with the intensity, the muffled intensity, which a butterfly or moth feels when with its sticky tremulous legs and antennae it pushes out of the chrysalis and emerges and sits quivering beside the broken case for a moment; its wings still creased; its eyes dazzled, incapable of flight. (p. 130)

The quivering pause enacted by the insect signals an immobile yet poised and painfully exposed self; a state of acute receptivity which Woolf elucidates as 'extraordinarily unprotected, unformed, unshielded, apprehensive, receptive, anticipatory' (p. 130). This passage has special interest for its figurative closeness to the entomological image of Fry which appeared during the same period, but I suggest that 'thinking; feeling; living' with 'the intensity' of insects informed her model of creative sensibility throughout her writing career.

Let us return to the image of the moth presented as 'quivering yet still' at the outset of this chapter. It indicates a peculiarly active stillness that has correspondences with the more vulnerable form of 'quivering' Woolf expressed in her entomological image in 'Sketch'. The relationship between passivity and activity was also a question of urgency for Fry. In a recent reappraisal, Adrianne Rubin argues that Fry's aesthetic theory is underpinned by 'the idea that perception is not based on elements being emitted from the work of art to a passive recipient' but rather that 'the spectator plays an active role in seeking sensations from the composition'. She notes his frequent references to a 'state of beholder awareness' described variously as 'attentive passivity', 'alert passivity' or 'passive receptiveness'.[44] Fry's art theory arguably unsettles the polarities of activity and rest, of movement and stillness, that I have examined in relation to 'non-being' and 'being'. He proposes a positive form of passivity, which I suggest coincides with the open receptivity Woolf frequently constructs in her writings about aesthetic experience, and which chimes with her representation of Fry as a humming-bird hawk-moth. The paradox of 'moving' stillness, by which I denote affect as well as motion, is therefore central to her engagement with his thinking and to her own development of a model of vibratory attention. Laura Doyle has suggested that Woolf 'lingered in a tingling, Brownian zone of encounter between self and other; she sought to register the force fields of this "between" where we meet'.[45] In the next section of this chapter, we follow her to linger a little longer in the 'zone' of the insect world and to uncover the sites in which stillness and motion meet in vibrating forms of 'suspension' and 'detachment'.

Artists and Insects

Woolf was peculiarly attuned to insects and she often revealed an eye well trained in entomological observation, as we have seen. But how did insect life offer her a model of aesthetic attention for her writing? The hovering, often fleetingly seen forms of dragonflies, butterflies and moths, as well as the tenacious deliberations of the snail, have a significant presence in her fiction and non-fiction. I suggest that they open up non-human temporalities, while also providing the writer with a vehicle through which to convey unfamiliar perspectives and encounters with the world. Woolf's short story 'Kew Gardens' (1919), for instance, implicitly re-evaluates the nominal hierarchy between man and insect by splicing the narrative between human characters journeying through the garden (with the 'curiously irregular movement' of butterflies), and the slow progress of a snail across a vivid microcosmic landscape.[46]

Crucial for this inquiry, however, is the way in which Woolf's entomological observations informed her approach to the body language of artists and art critics, as well as to representations of art experience. Before examining the figurative potential of insects further, it will therefore be useful to contextualise her interest in entomology. Woolf grew up at the end of an era of great Victorian collectors whose precise observations and classification of insects had swelled the scientific literature. Like many Victorian children, Woolf keenly collected insects as a child, founding an Entomological Society with her siblings. But the twentieth century became 'the age for the study of living insects',[47] and Woolf's interest in the field was sustained in her adult years as she became acquainted with the ideas of pioneering ethologists including Jean-Henri Fabre, W. H. Hudson and Julian Huxley.[48]

Woolf's closely observed renderings of insect life function as analogies for modes of engagement and representation in her writing, which resist the urge to pin down her subject. Christina Alt suggests that, rather than deferring to the 'taxonomic method', Woolf gravitated toward 'disciplines focused on the observation of living organisms as analogies for new methods of seeing and describing life'; methods that might only afford 'fleeting glimpses' of a subject.[49] She was drawn, in other words, to the 'quivering yet still'. Insects were deeply embedded in her image-making consciousness, but they were also, I have argued, important in representing the nuances of aesthetic encounters in visual and verbal art. While commentators have identified a largely negative figuration of insects and of parallels between human and insect societies in Woolf's work and that of her contemporaries, I would argue that the pervasive strand of insect imagery in her writing is not necessarily pejorative, although it often registers ambivalence.[50] In the barely perceptible responsiveness and subtle spectrum of movement peculiar to insects, Woolf found a language for the behaviour and body language specifically manifest in aesthetic experiences.

We might situate her concern with the entomological more directly in relation to still life painting by briefly considering the insect motif, which was part of the traditional iconography of the genre. Painters through history have depicted bees, moths, butterflies, ants and other insects crawling or hovering over arrangements of flowers, fruit and other comestibles. In many still lifes, particularly in Dutch flower paintings of the seventeenth century, one becomes aware through a process of gradual perceptual attunement of a diverse range of insects whose half-hidden existence belies their energetic life.[51] The motif reappears in modern works by Woolf's contemporaries. In Joan Miró's *The Wine Bottle* (1924), a worm gazes up at a fly with bulging eyes; an unsettling flattened form – hovering yet arrested – within a pulsating landscape. Within the interiors of her Bloomsbury circle, Woolf would have experienced the more uplifting motif of the butterfly hovering among flowers, which was frequently employed by Vanessa Bell and Duncan Grant in stylised iterations in their designs for interior decorations and textiles. Woolf would have been familiar, for instance, with Bell's decorative design (plate 5) of butterflies among a vase of flowers painted onto the upper panel of a door at Charleston, her Sussex home, in combination with a lower panel depicting a succulent bowl of fruit. Different insects were traditionally employed as symbolic references and functioned as *vanitas* and *memento mori*. While feasting flies might readily symbolise decay, the moth has a long association in Western art with the soul's 'quest for truth' due to their attraction to light, and butterflies are interpreted as symbols of the transience of life, as well as of the soul's afterlife.[52] Despite being easily overlooked, these seemingly insignificant, diminutive forms gain intimate access to the central subject of still life compositions, while human life is banished. They also import the possibility of movement, registering an animation of the inanimate that unsettles characterisations of 'dead nature' or *nature morte*. Similar pictorial motifs may have fed Woolf's imagination as she constructed the image of Fry in his encounter with Post-Impressionist art. In so far as she introduces connotations of animate intimacy, we can make a visual link between the art critic as a humming-bird hawk-moth feeding on paintings, and the insects of still life hovering over and feasting upon its objects.

An insight from another twentieth-century childhood collector of insects, Walter Benjamin, proves particularly pertinent to Woolf's imagining of aesthetic experience through the figure of the insect. Benjamin observes of Proust that his 'most accurate, most convincing insights fasten on their objects as insects fasten on leaves, blossoms, branches, betraying nothing of their existence until a leap, a beating of wings, a vault, show the startled observer that some incalculable individual life has imperceptibly crept into an alien world'.[53] Benjamin raises questions about forms of attention figured through insect life that I outlined at the outset of this chapter, in particular about the kind of attention implied by 'fastening' on and 'feasting' on aesthetic objects, and about a mode of being in which the unseen or overlooked might play a significant role in presenting new and surprising perspectives.

One of the most striking explorations of such questions in Woolf's fiction appears in the supper party scene in 'The Window' section of *To the Lighthouse*, where we find Mrs Ramsay presiding over a still life arrangement, 'a yellow and purple dish of fruit' (p. 111). She observes with pleasure how Augustus 'feasted his eyes on the same plate of fruit, plunged in, broke off a bloom there, a tassel here, and returned, after feasting, to his hive' (p. 112). Here, still life's 'malleability' is expressed in an arrangement that accommodates different ways of paying attention to objects. The consuming encounter brings with it an appeal for the kind of communal looking and appreciation for which the 'hive' is an index. As Mrs Ramsay acknowledges, 'That was his way of looking, different from hers. But looking together united them' (p. 112).

By foregrounding and implicitly valorising the delicate, sensitive physiology and sensory appendages of insects in her writings, Woolf creates a more complex analogy for the human body. Her sympathetic attention to the vulnerable bodies of invertebrates reveals correspondences with her own acute sense experiences of visual art. Writing to her sister in the spring of 1928 after viewing Bell's recent exhibition with Duncan Grant, she embodies herself as a snail. Praising the painters' 'epic greatness', she then observes that she has 'made myself sufficiently ridiculous in the eyes of two cold blooded creatures who only draw me out to pour salt on my horns and see a little blob of foam (which causes intense pain to the snail) form on the tips'.[54] Her complex relationship with painters is evident in this image of painful exposure coupled with a rather knowing humbleness and self-diminishment in their presence. Indicating the process of osmosis by which salt kills snails by dehydrating them, she identifies the writer as the producer of insignificant, even embarrassing secretions. Nevertheless, we are prompted to wonder what the slow, pondering attentions of the snail might offer, and the image encodes an implicit critique of the 'cold-blooded' artist who cruelly taunts the writer's heightened sensory apparatus.

It is likely that Woolf's imaginative conceptions were fertilised by the considerable interest in and scientific research on insect visual systems during the late nineteenth and early twentieth centuries. Auguste Forel's *The Senses of Insects* (1908) investigated the antennal sense and noted the sensitivity and sensory range of many species, speculating on their capacity to surpass human faculties. He recorded, for instance, the power of ants to perceive ultra-violet light, and the capacity of 'humble-bees' to distinguish colour rather than form.[55] Antennae, or 'horns' in Woolf's image, are readily interpreted as symbols of heightened perception, and they are a familiar feature in her representations of supersensory aesthetic experiences, as we shall see in more detail later. She invites us, through the anatomy of the insect, to enlarge our conception of the sensitive auditor or artist's capacity for intense feeling, and to extend the sensory range of the human body.

On Hovering and Humming-bird Hawk-moths

> 'the silver-grey flickering moth-wing quiver of words'
>
> (Woolf, *The Waves*, p. 184)

Following the publication of her biography of Fry, Woolf wrote with satisfaction, 'I can't help thinking I've caught a good deal of that iridescent man in my oh so laborious butterfly net'.[56] 'Iridescence' endows Fry with a vibrating, chromatic afterlife, as if he absorbed and then emanated the colours of art, like the gallery visitors in *Walter Sickert*. This quality resonates with the paradigm of affective permeability that Woolf employed in writing his biography and, more widely, in her conception of the embodied nature of aesthetic experience. If colour is a mnemonic, associative device in her autobiographical writings, a way to 'bring back' moments of luminosity from the past, it serves a similar purpose in writing about a biographical subject who remained chromatically illuminated in her memory.

The humming-bird hawk-moth imports to Woolf's vision of the art critic a set of visual associations and physiological rhythms peculiar to this insect. But what were the aesthetic and ethical implications of her choice of insect, and what model of encounter does this set up? A brief excursion into the rich store of moth imagery in Woolf's writing reveals her attention to Lepidoptera. Hunting moths was a regular activity during her childhood and she had the post of 'name finder' in her siblings' 'Entomological Society', as she recorded in 'Sketch' (p. 113). Her biographer, Hermione Lee, suggests that this was the 'family ritual' 'which most haunted her imagination'.[57] She was fascinated by the fragile physicality of moths. In a passage from a narrative on night-time moth hunting (written in 1919 but unpublished in her lifetime), Woolf records her intimate observations of a cluster of feeding moths:

> These lumps seemed unspeakably precious, too deeply attached to the liquid to be disturbed. Their probosces were deep plunged, and as they

> drew in the sweetness, their wings quivered slightly as if in ecstasy. Even when the light was full upon them they could not tear themselves away, but sat there, quivering a little more uneasily perhaps.[58]

The insect seems magnetised and ecstatic, yet it also indicates the sense of unease we have observed underlying states of rapture and ecstasy elsewhere in Woolf's writing. A little later in the narrative, the moth hunters come upon a striking specimen displaying '[g]reat underwings of glowing crimson'. 'He was almost still', Woolf writes, 'as if he had alighted with his wing open and had fallen into a trance of pleasure'.[59] The pattern of images in this early essay anticipates Woolf's depiction of Fry's sensuous encounter with visual art. She shared his interest in the natural sciences, which was the subject of his Cambridge degree. She draws on the intensity and precariousness she detected in insect encounters to invest Fry's 'quivering' satisfaction – his own 'trance of pleasure' – with an uneasy undercurrent. The near-stillness of the moth in 'Reading' ('immobile [. . .] drinking deep') prefigures its capture and subsequent death later in the narrative: 'he did not move again'.[60] Her fascination with moths involved ontology as much as entomology; she centres on states in which an insect's relationship to life is at its most intense (imbibing sustenance), or most precarious (close to death or capture).

Woolf spent hours 'hunting up' her catches in Frances Morris's *Butterflies and Moths* (1871), in which the humming-bird hawk-moth is identified with an image and description noting its colour and markings.[61] The moth takes its name from the humming-bird to which it bears a resemblance; it emits a similar humming noise as it hovers, and has a long proboscis with which to drink nectar. Since it is also noted for its sophisticated colour recognition and memory, the insect provides a suggestive body through which to examine the rhythms of attention and affect in Fry's encounter with visual art.

Whether or not Woolf had one of the humming-bird hawk-moth species in her collection, she was evidently aware of its defining characteristics. In her short article, 'Butterflies and Moths: Insects in September', published in *The Times* in 1916, she writes admiringly: 'few sights have a greater enchantment than that of a Hawk moth with its vibrating wings blurred in movement, suspended above a tobacco plant or an evening primrose'.[62] She calls up an echo of this enchantment in constructing the image of Fry's reverential absorption. The moth's capacity to hover suspended in moving stillness, creating the illusion of immobility through the intense activity of its wings, was particularly evocative. Her naturalist contemporaries also commented on the 'rhythmic nature' of insect movement, including H. Eltringham who noted the 'action of the wing mechanism which sets the whole body into vibration'.[63] A final glance at her narrative on moth hunting in 'Reading' reveals her observation of this phenomenon in 'the swift grey moths of the dusk, that only visit flowers for a second, never settling, but hanging an inch or two above the yellow of the Evening Primroses, vibrating to a blur'.[64] When she describes Fry as 'quivering yet still', she recalls this model of vibratory suspension: it comes to signify a mode that negotiates (without eliding) the uncertain time-scape of contemplative detachment and the 'stillness' of visual art.

In her chapter on Post-Impressionism in *Roger Fry*, Woolf observes of her subject:

> That look, that momentary detachment, was so instinctive that it made no break in what he was saying, yet it gave a sense of something held in reserve – things played over the surface and were referred to some hidden centre. There was something stable underneath his mobility. (p. 150)

Woolf alludes here to Fry's instinctive practice of detachment, or 'disinterested contemplation' as he defined it; a contentious concept which was central to his aesthetic theory, and to his early insistence on the separation between aesthetic experience and life.[65] The quivering stillness of his attention as a humming-bird hawk-moth evokes an unfixed, indeterminate mode in which stability and mobility co-exist. He is intimately absorbed, yet somewhat paradoxically, remains detached.

The model of art experience evoked through Woolf's naturalistic metaphor is ethically indeterminate and open to various readings. The exchange appears predatory and implicitly erotic: the traditionally feminised flower, or painting, is rendered passive after being gazed upon, penetrated and consumed. In the extract with which I began this chapter we witness Fry's visceral 'plunging' – or plundering – as he draws the 'nectar' from Post-Impressionist paintings. We might be tempted to interpret this as Woolf's feminist critique of a masculine model of art appreciation, but her playfully ironic characterisation also blurs the roles of prey and predator. We recall the moth's vulnerability to being captured by sharp-eyed entomologists, and its quivering sensibility, which undermines any simple reading in terms of gender. An alternative and more positive reading, albeit one that continues to examine the politics of gender, might find Fry's encounter expressive of an exchange between critic and art object, which is receptive and hesitant, predicated not on mastery but on suspension.[66] Indeed, his instinct for sympathy, his 'turn' to his neighbour, displays a sociability and nourishing intimacy perhaps more readily characterised as feminine. In the next section of this chapter I will argue that such qualities were crucial to Woolf's reading of the 'rhythms' and 'vibrations' in Fry's art and life; and further, that they intersected with models of sympathy and transmission which drew on wider discourses from spiritualism to new communication technologies.

Vibration and Life-writing

In Woolf's essay, 'The Death of the Moth', the fragile life of the moth 'fluttering from side to side', represents a conduit for 'a fibre, very thin but pure, of the enormous energy of the world'.[67] As we have seen, Woolf detects a similarly vibratory energy in Fry. 'Vibration' is particularly pertinent to her life-writing in its signification as 'an intuitive signal about a person or thing'.[68] It offered a mode through which to sense a subject's unseen 'rhythms' of being. In *Roger Fry*, vibration emerges not only as a manifestation of aesthetic affect – a response to a work of art – but also as a peculiar quality or energy with which Fry charged the space around him. Woolf drew on conceptions of vibration from different discourses including the scientific, musical and spiritual, as well as notions of the Fourth Dimension, in her attempt to evoke the less tangible aspects of personhood. The relationship between 'stillness' and 'silence' in the visual and verbal arts became ever more significant in her attempt to 'write' a life without a taxonomic 'pinning down' of her subject. If the insect embodies what Janice Neri calls the 'jarring contrast between life and death' that 'lies at the heart of the paradoxical appeal of still life', then I would propose a similar parallel in the art of biography.[69]

In a diary entry on 20 September 1928, Woolf sketches out ideas for the composition of *Roger Fry*, and simultaneously reveals her struggle to articulate the compelling atmosphere she identifies with his presence. Once again, the hawk-moth is central to this configuration: 'His persuasiveness – a certain density – wished to persuade you to like what he liked. Eagerness, absorption, stir – a kind of vibration like a hawkmoth round him.'[70] The visual and sonic qualities of the humming-bird hawk-moth furnished Woolf with a metaphor through which to express intuitions about Fry that strained against the limits of language. These related as much to energies and intangible experiences as to embodied, physically affective qualities. Woolf's attentiveness to the texture of Fry's presence is evocatively developed in the biography itself. Recalling the 'density' and 'stir' of her diary sketch, she describes one evening in July 1934 two months before Fry's death, when she witnessed him examining a painting: 'His presence seemed to increase the sensation of everything in the room. But at the centre of that vibration was a gravity and a stillness' (RF, pp. 296–7). To enter into his peculiarly charged atmosphere was, Woolf suggests, to feel the vibrations of his excitement, yet simultaneously to be grounded by his underlying stability. Here, she employs vibration as a figure for the non-physical energies that charge and transmit aesthetic experience; but it is also crucial to her conception of receptivity in life-writing. We can situate the term alongside quivering, hovering and suspension in her lexicon of attentiveness.

Woolf's vibrational model of non-physical communion between artist and auditor also functions as a tool for the biographer. In the case of *Roger Fry*

Woolf manifests a special attunement and sensitivity to her subject's non-physical dimensions as she attempts to tap into his 'vibrations'. This form of attention is related to what Kirsty Martin describes as 'feeling for rhythm', a feeling that involves 'deep attention to another person's gestures and movements', and 'imagining the possible energy shaping them'.[71] In the introduction to her sensitive study, *Modernism and the Rhythms of Sympathy* (2013), Martin calls attention to Fry's 'specific attention' to Vanessa Bell and what he describes as '"this miracle of rhythm in you and not in your body only but in everything you do"'.[72] The magnetism Fry feels toward this elusive, diffuse quality in Bell is illustrative, Martin argues, of 'forms of intuitive communion' that are 'at once bodily and intimate transcendence'.[73] As I suggest more widely in this book, vibrations, like 'rhythms', register the energies of less easily defined transmissions between individuals, objects and the communions that constitute aesthetic experience. They are intimately associated elements of the specific form of attention Woolf bestows on Fry.

Woolf's sensitivity to her subject's 'vibrations' and 'rhythms' extends the metaphysical scope of her biography and addresses some of the fundamental questions she posed about life-writing throughout her career. A glance at *Jacob's Room* (1922) illustrates another configuration of vibration and the hawk-moth, which has significance for the art of life-writing. Woolf claimed to have had Fry in her thoughts when she created Jacob, the novel's protagonist, whom she associates with Lepidoptera early in the novel when he momentarily catches a 'red underwing' moth (using Frances Morris's book to identify it).[74] Later, she invokes the same insect to investigate the mysterious enterprise of biography and its attempt to grasp at subtly shifting and unseen facets of character. 'Even the exact words get the wrong accent on them', observes the narrator-biographer,

> But something is always impelling one to hum vibrating, like the hawk moth, at the mouth of the cavern of mystery, endowing Jacob Flanders with all sorts of qualities he had not at all [. . .]; what remains is mostly a matter of guess work. Yet over him we hang vibrating.[75]

Woolf's description of the indefatigable biographer as a hawk-moth, vibrating with anticipation at the threshold of an intriguing but ultimately unknowable 'other', corresponds with her later embodiment of Fry in his habitual posture of contemplative suspension before a work of art. The 'mouth' of the cavern of mystery and the 'mouth' or 'trumpet' of the flower in which the moths quiver, seem associated in a chain of images which suggest but cannot quite render speech (can only 'mouth' it). Crucially, although 'hum'[ming] evokes sonic vibrations, the term also highlights the inadequacy of language and hints at non-verbal communion. Humming is an enigmatic mechanism in insects, but it is also a 'similarly displaced' activity in humans. As Steven Connor points out, it is 'something we do when pleasurably absorbed in something else'. If it can be understood as 'a way of tuning us in to different kinds of activity', and as suggestive of 'some utterance that lies beneath or to the side of speech', humming seems particularly pertinent to both biographer and art critic in their engagement with a subject.[76]

Receptivity to heard yet unseen vibrations aligns the biographer and the art critic, both of whom seek to retain the potency of epistemological uncertainty in their subjects. In *Walter Sickert*, we recall Woolf's ambivalence regarding the capacity of writers to express a powerful response to visual art, which leads her to speculate on the existence of a 'zone of silence in the middle of every art' (p. 12). Turning to the art critics, she finds that they too 'cannot impart what they feel when they go beyond the outskirts' of their medium of words (p. 13). Fry and Woolf were both emphatic about the threshold at which 'explanation' of visual art becomes redundant; when the only authentic response is silence and stillness. As Fry acknowledged in his performative conclusion to *Vision and Design* (1920), which Woolf quotes in her biography: 'Any attempt I might make to explain this would probably land me in the depths of mysticism. On the edge of that gulf I stop' (p. 297).[77] When confronted with the 'the silent kingdom of paint', the chatter of the conversing dinner guests in *Walter Sickert* comes to a similar halt: they reach 'the edge where painting breaks off and takes her way into the silent land' (p. 22). Although Woolf would often challenge the opinions of art critics including Fry, here she defers to their apparent heightened perception and vibrational sensitivity. 'But the critics were still talking with their fingers', she writes, 'They were still bristling and shivering like dogs in dark lanes when something passes that we cannot see' (p. 18). She privileges their silent, visceral attentiveness to the vibrations of a mysterious presence that remains imperceptible to the 'talkers'. While scrutinising body language, she is also alert to intimations of the supersensory, to that which is not yet readable or translatable into words.

'And what is a life? And what was Roger? And if one cant say, whats the good of trying?', Woolf wrote to Vita Sackville-West while at work on her biography in 1938.[78] She reveals the art of biography to be an ambivalent communion, fraught by frustrations and fallings short similar to, but surpassing, those experienced by the art critic. She reminds the reader of *Roger Fry* 'of the perils of trying to guess the secret' behind her subject's 'influence as a human being', invoking his own caution that '"we know too little of the rhythms of man's spiritual life"' (p. 293). However, if the art critic and the biographer both struggle with the essentially unreadable 'otherness' of their subject, Woolf asserts that the biographer has the more difficult challenge. Human beings, she concludes, 'are not consciously creating a book that can be read, or a picture that can be hung upon the wall. The critic of Roger Fry as a man has a far harder task than any that was set him by the pictures of Cézanne' (pp. 293–4).

Woolf translated her problem into that of the portrait painter constrained to compress multiple, shifting impressions of an individual into one static frame. 'What am I to say about you?' she wondered, writing to her sister while embroiled in the 'task': 'Its rather as if you had to paint a portrait using dozens of snapshots in the paint. Either one ought to dash it off freehand, red, green, purple out of ones inner eye; or toil like a fly over a loaf of bread.'[79] The insect metaphor carries the sense of her unresolved negotiation between two models of representation and their vying temporalities: expressionistic spontaneity or the labour of long looking.

In the early stages of planning *Roger Fry*, Woolf had alluded to a more profound sense of the inexpressible dimensions with which she felt compelled to engage in her writing, and which she recognised would have implications for visual art. In a diary entry on 18 November 1935, she marks her awareness of having 'reached a further stage' in her advancement as a writer, by invoking the concept of the fourth dimension:

> I see that there are 4? dimensions; all to be produced; in human life; & that leads to a far richer grouping & proportion: I mean: I: & the not I: & the outer & the inner – no I'm too tired to say: but I see it: & this will affect my book on Roger. Very exciting: to grope on like this. New combinations in psychology & body – rather like painting.[80]

The existence of a fourth dimension had been the subject of extensive investigations, centring on time in the eighteenth century, and on space in the nineteenth, with research intersecting the fields of science and theosophy. By 1910, the 'fourth dimension' had become 'almost a household word', and ideas about the possibility of a parallel, unseen dimension seeped into the popular consciousness and inspired experiments in the visual and literary arts over the following decades.[81] Woolf's numerous references to the term in her writings of the 1930s have various aesthetic implications, but perhaps most pertinent here are her intimations of the ways in which it would shape her book on Fry.[82] In the passage cited above, her prose conveys the feeling of 'groping' toward an enlarged conception of the self for which the fourth dimension offers imaginative potential. As she enumerates the proliferating selves in a permeable syntax of colons, she evokes the 'richer grouping & proportion' which would signify access to unseen spatial and temporal realities, perhaps even signalling a way to penetrate into man's 'spiritual life'. She reveals a thought process behind *Roger Fry* in its embryonic stages, which was more experimental and challenging of convention than its relatively conventional form might suggest.

We might tease out the subtle implications of fourth dimensional thinking for Woolf's writing on Fry by considering the '[n]otions of stillness, silence and process' to which Ian F. Bell calls attention in the translation of fourth dimensional thought into modern literary aesthetics.[83] 'The fourth; the dimension of stillness', is how Ezra Pound concludes the penultimate line of Canto 49, in *The Fifth Decade of Cantos* (1937).[84] Bell provides a gloss on this 'quietude' with a reference to a letter from June 1942, in which the poet writes:

> Stillness – the word is more concrete than IMMOTO [the motionless], for it also suggests silence. What is still is motionless and soundless. But the concept of motionlessness is more important in this line. [. . .] I conceive of a dimension of stillness which compenetrates the Euclidean dimensions.[85]

Pound's close association of silence and stillness is instructive. Without wishing to impose his understanding of the fourth dimension onto Woolf, we are nevertheless reminded of the prominence of silence and stillness in her writings on visual art and can speculate that their co-existence in fourth dimensional thought may have prompted her fascination. Attentiveness to the 'dimensions' of stillness and silence would prove to be important strategies in her development of the art of biography, specifically in the endeavour to access the 'immaterial' dimensions of selfhood yet also in some way to 'bring back' the vibrating presence of an absent – in this case deceased – subject.

The genre of biography, particularly where it addresses a no longer living subject, inherently shares elegiac resonances with still life and its *memento mori* motifs.[86] 'Such a silence', Woolf had written in her diary as she grieved Fry's death, 'Such a poverty. How he reverberated!'[87] *Roger Fry* is an exemplar of the way in which life-writing could attempt to function as a form of 'reverberation' and a way of confronting the silence of death. Tuning into these reverberations in biography was a mode, then, of straining to breach the gap between the living and the dead, and of seeking out the 'invisible presences' Woolf had introduced in 'Sketch' to describe the continuing influence of the deceased on the living (p. 92).

Before we examine the ways in which such ideas readily evoke early twentieth-century experiments in spiritualism, it is worth lingering for a moment on the significance of Woolf's auditory expression of loss. In 1940, she reflected that the affinity between musical form and the structure of her novels had intensified over the course of writing *Roger Fry*. 'You have found out exactly what I was trying to do when you compare it to a piece of music', she observed in a letter to Mrs R. C. Trevelyan, noting the necessity of abstracting the 'mass of detail' in his life into themes, and the 'difficulty of making quotations fit – so many things had to be muted, or only hinted'.[88] The tension between stillness as soundlessness and the vibrational presence that Woolf sought to evoke gains further force in the context of her musical conception for the work.[89]

In 'The Art of Biography' (1939), an essay written during the long gestation of *Roger Fry*, Woolf had compared Victorian biographies to 'the wax figures now preserved in Westminster Abbey, that were carried in funeral processions [. . .] effigies that have only a smooth superficial likeness to the body in the coffin'.[90] Woolf's attention to body language and 'rhythm' in her treatment of Fry presented a challenge to the processes of petrification she saw underlying the Victorian culture of mourning. Indeed, although *Roger Fry* represents an 'act of homage', as Spalding describes it, Woolf resists creating an effigy or 'stilled life' in the pejorative sense of *nature morte*.[91] My reading differs here from Robert Kiely, who invokes the genre as a negative category in his analysis of the biography, lamenting that '[i]nstead of a fleshed-out portrait, what we find more nearly resembles a still life, a painstakingly careful arrangement of objects within a frame'.[92] Leaving to one side for a moment the admiration Fry expressed for still life and his sense that it was the genre most expressive of an artist's personality, Kiely's implication (which is misguided in my opinion), is that a successful portrait or biography requires a quality of fleshiness or definition lacking in Woolf's representation. As I have suggested, however, her concern was to investigate the energies of character untapped by conventional biography; to suggest her subject's 'spiritual' rhythms and vibrations as much as his physicality; or, as she had famously encapsulated the task of the biographer, to weld the 'granite-like solidity' of truth and the 'rainbow-like intangibility' of personality (in this case Fry's 'iridescence').[93] The version of Fry's life that she could relate may have been restricted by his family (who were closely involved in selecting and supplying materials for Woolf to work from), but she could celebrate the 'unfinished' nature of the human being and unsettle fixed images by making using of the 'fertile fact; the fact that suggests and engenders'.[94] In short, although *Roger Fry* received a mixed critical reception and has been somewhat underappreciated by Woolf scholars, it was significant in her project to create a biographical portrait that 'quivers' with life and remains open to the immaterial dimensions of the self.[95]

Vibration, Transmission and a 'Sense of the Unseen'

The relationship between vibration, silence and life-writing can be situated within a nexus of concerns about psychic and scientific research during the fin-de-siècle and the first decades of the twentieth century. As Shelley Trower has shown, pioneers in these fields 'began to understand the connections between internal and external energies – all conceived of as forms of vibration'.[96] Woolf's early essay, 'The Supernatural in Fiction' (1918), characterises the period as one in which the desire to seek the supernatural was bolstered by the 'disputed fact[s]' of psychical research.[97] When she came to describe Fry's formative years after leaving Cambridge in her biography, she evoked a milieu in which the revelations of one 'Mrs Piper', a famous medium, excited 'much discussion', and she records Fry's attendance at meetings of the Society for Psychical Research (a body that undertook scientific investigations of spiritual phenomena), and his interest in unconventional strands of research such as the existence of spirits in 'luminiferous aether' (p. 87).[98] The vibratory model offered by physicists was important in spiritualist conceptions of communications with the dead. If certain frequencies could now be understood to 'extend beyond the sensory thresholds', as in ultrasound and infrared, and the law of the conservation of energy taught that light could continue to exist as radiant heat, such ideas could be harnessed by spiritualists to support conceptions of life as 'a form of vibrant energy that radiates out of the body [. . .] even after death'.[99] One of the founders of the Society for Psychical Research, Edmund Gurney, noted, for instance, that 'it is possible to conceive that vibration-waves [. . .] are a means whereby activity in one brain may evoke a kindred activity in another'.[100]

Woolf evokes a vibrational relationship of a similar kind to Gurney in her essay on the supernatural, referring to a group of writers whose 'sense of the unseen' may stimulate 'quickened perception of the relations existing between men and plants' or 'any one of those innumerable alliances which [. . .] we spin between ourselves and other objects in our passage'.[101] There are multiple allusions to supersensory 'alliances' in her own fiction: in Mrs Dalloway's seemingly telepathic attunement to the shell-shocked soldier, Septimus; or Mrs Ramsay's ability to reach beyond her physical body through an antenna 'trembling out from her [. . .] intercepting certain sentences' (p. 123). The link between insects and 'higher' faculties had been investigated by the entomologist, Auguste Forel, in *Ants and Some Other Insects: An Inquiry Into the Psychic Powers of These Animals* (1904), and the association lingers on in the modernist imagination, as in Pound's famous statement that 'Artists are the antennae of the race'.[102] Similarly, in *Roger Fry* the 'antenna' – that fusion of entomological and mechanical communication apparatus – becomes a metonym for alert, vibratory sensitivity that hints at the supersensory. Echoing her description of Mrs Ramsay, Woolf describes Fry's 'snailhorn sensibility trembling this way and that' in his encounters with visual art, and she embodies his finely tuned critical faculty through a prosthetic extension: '[h]is long wand, trembling like the antenna of some miraculously sensitive insect, settled upon some "rhythmical phrase", some sequence; some diagonal' (p. 262).

Critics have noted telepathic metaphors in Woolf's work, but the bearing that spiritualist notions of communication might have on life-writing and its claim to authenticity has largely been overlooked. The popularity of spiritualism waned in the post-war years, but as Armstrong observes, it 'persists as a secret within modernism, an important way of registering human exchanges in a world rendered strange, super-sensual, technologically connected'.[103] While

Woolf sometimes parodied spiritualism, her attempt to embody Fry's vibratory energy and 'tune in' to his 'reverberations' in the years following his death suggests her absorption of and continuing attraction to contemporary vibrational thought and supersensory notions of communication.[104] In Fry's influential 'An Essay in Aesthetics' (1909), he writes of how in experiencing a work of great art we become conscious of a 'peculiar relation of sympathy' and of a 'special tie' with its creator.[105] *Roger Fry* could be read as an attempt to communicate the author's 'feeling of a special tie' with her subject, but it was also an experiment in giving him agency: 'a gamble' on his 'power to transmit himself', as she described it.[106] The texture of the biography is interwoven with quotations from Fry's writings in a kind of dialogue with the deceased in which she sought to evoke his 'beautiful speaking voice' and conductive power as a lecturer, but also his desire for a shared 'sense of revelation' particularly in relation to Post-Impressionist art (pp. 89, 152).[107] Her opening address for Fry's Memorial Exhibition at Bristol Museum and Art Gallery in July 1935 acclaims him for bringing 'this life and colour, this racket and din into the quiet galleries of ancient art'.[108] For Woolf, the art critic seems to have realised the fantasy of animation that is latent in her critique of the stillness and silence at the National Portrait Gallery, expressed in 'Pictures and Portraits'.

Fundamental to Fry's conception of communion with works of art was the notion of actively cultivating sympathetic attention. In his lecture 'The Meaning of Pictures I – Telling a Story', broadcast by the BBC in 1929, he describes how pictures 'afford the means to us of [. . .] entering into intimate communion with the most sensitive, the most profound, the most passionately contemplative spirits of mankind', as long as we are able to 'vibrate in unison with the special note of each artist'. He goes on to deploy an extended metaphor for the vibrational 'transmission' of art, which resonates with Woolf's account:

> The artist is as it were a transmitting station; we are the receivers when we look at his pictures. But the receivers must be attuned. The study of art is really the tuning of our own special receiving set, so that it can respond in turn to all the great transmitters of past and present times.[109]

Fry's choice of imagery reveals wireless technology as a compelling new model for this disembodied yet 'intimate communion', which would dissolve the boundaries of the public and private. Radio broadcasts had only become readily accessible in around 1928, and as Gillian Beer points out, the 'experience of sound disconnected from its source' was a radically new sense experience.[110] The idea of invisible radio signals communicating across great distances was readily associated with clairvoyance and telepathy. In a lecture at the Quaker Yearly Meeting (later published as *Science and the Unseen World* in 1929), the astronomer and philosopher of science Arthur Eddington described the mind as 'a central receiving station' that 'reads the dots and dashes of incoming nerve-signals'.[111] Fry's paradigm for art appreciation exploits a similar set of images. Tuning one's 'receiving set' to the required 'pitch' or 'frequency' demanded the viewer's sensory exertion and agency as well as his receptive passivity.

As early as his 1911 article on Post-Impressionism, Fry had been conscious of the difficulty of getting people 'to *look* at [. . .] pictures with the same tense passivity and alert receptiveness which the musician can count on from his auditors'. Extending the inter-medial analogy, he somewhat departs from his doctrine of aesthetic purity, explaining that one should look at pictures 'exactly as you would listen to music or poetry'.[112] He demands that the viewer strain toward a state of 'tense passivity' in mind and body: a state of sensory attunement in which he or she becomes, to adapt Woolf's phrase from *Walter Sickert*, 'all ear'. Fry's vision for viewer, artist and work of art, to 'vibrate in unison' – or, as he reaffirmed in his last lectures of 1933–34, to 'set up vibrations in the deeper layers of our consciousness' – reveals his admiration for Kandinsky.[113] We remember that the painter conveyed his influential expressionist theory of art through a vibrational model informed by Theosophy, arguing that 'form-harmony must rest only on a corresponding vibration of the human soul'.[114] While Fry's attitude toward mysticism was ambivalent, his conception of affective transmission in art experience was framed by a sense of its spirituality, if vaguely defined. He introduced the French section of the Post-Impressionist exhibition as an 'attempt to express by pictorial and plastic form certain spiritual experiences', and a (posthumously published) essay of 1928 stated more overtly that a 'work of art' should be 'the medium of a spiritual communication'.[115]

In her biography Woolf draws on Fry's broad denotation of the 'spiritual' as encompassing 'all those human faculties and activities which are over and above our mere existence as living organisms' (p. 236).[116] However, the influence of his Quaker upbringing in shaping his conception of 'spiritual communication' in art should not be overlooked. He grew up in a family which had followed this belief system over seven generations and although he lost his faith in adulthood, the Quaker attitude – in particular the emphasis on ascetic simplicity, devotion and silence as a spiritual practice – continued to inform his way of life. As Woolf noted, it also shaped his 'temperament and tone of mind' (p. 85).[117] She associated his heightened receptivity with his 'spiritual' commitment to art, and his capacity for 'the disinterested life, the life of the spirit' (p. 236). The tenor of the Quaker influence can arguably be felt in his belief, as he expressed it to the poet Robert Bridges, that 'the contemplation of form is a peculiarly important spiritual exercise'.[118] Quakerism, which remains outside British mainstream Christianity, offers an alternative, spiritually inflected understanding of communication. The term 'quaker' derives from the trembling or quaking of a person who undergoes a spiritual experience in which she or he is 'touched' by God.

This powerful idea resonates with Fry's conception of the 'intimate communion' or 'special tie' established between the receptive auditor and a work of art. Art may have replaced God in delivering a spiritual 'quake' to Fry, but his intense 'quivering yet still' responsiveness to it may be read through the Quaker model of spiritual contact.

'Two Rhythms'

'Art and life are two rhythms', Woolf announced in her biography of Fry, calling attention to his well-known insistence on the distinctness of these spheres in his essay 'Art and Life' of 1917 (RF, p. 214). 'Rhythm' joins Woolf's lexicon of 'quivering' and 'vibration' to describe the dialectic between the stillness of contemplative attention and the counter-current of distraction and action, which she considered had dictated Fry's transitions between art and life. Fry had invoked 'rhythm' even earlier in his 'Essay in Aesthetics', where he argued that '[e]motional elements of design are connected with essential conditions of our physical existence', and 'rhythm', as one of these elements, 'appeals to all the sensations which accompany muscular activity'.[119] Woolf laid emphasis on the body as a physical register for the effects of art experience, as we have seen, but when she continues to quote from 'Art and Life' in her biography of Fry, we encounter a rather more ambiguous, disembodied formulation of the 'special spiritual activity of art':

> we find it no doubt open at times to influences from life, but in the main self-contained [. . .] under certain conditions the rhythms of life and of art may coincide with great effect on both; but in the main the two rhythms are distinct, and as often as not play against each other. (p. 214)

Fry's well-known formalist argument hinges on the separation of art and life; but it was not his definitive position. As his more sensitive commentators have shown, to isolate this aspect of his theory is to ignore the ways in which his theories evolved and became less purist, for instance including an increased openness to literature in the post-war period.[120] If Woolf's biography is partly responsible for emphasising the apparent binaries of his theory, she also evokes admiration for his critical approach, which was 'open' to 'revisions and perpetual reorientations' (p. 295).[121] She insists that Fry 'broke the rhythm before it got quite fixed', so that throughout his career '[n]ew rhythms and new themes appear' (p. 296).[122] Rubin suggests that Fry understood rhythm as 'a means through which the artist conveys his conception of life'.[123] Arguably this definition comes closest to Woolf's use of the term in the biography, and indeed to her own conception of rhythm as something that 'goes far deeper than words', and 'style' as 'all rhythm' – a definition which similarly aligns the artist's distinctive but indefinable *élan* or energy and the way in which it informs their expression in any medium.[124]

In the following passage from *Roger Fry*, Woolf harnesses the notion of 'two rhythms' in order to reinterpret Fry's theory of art and thus to 're-read' his life. She detects 'two rhythms in his own life': 'the hurried and distracted life' but also 'the still life'. 'If he survived the war', she goes on to speculate,

> it was perhaps that he kept the two rhythms in being simultaneously. But, it is tempting to ask, were they distinct? It seems as if the aesthetic theory were brought to bear upon the problems of private life. Detachment, as he insisted over and over again, is the supreme necessity for the artist. Was it not equally necessary if the private life were to continue? (p. 214)

According to Woolf, the detached, contemplative attention or 'still life' that Fry advocated in his aesthetic theory engendered its own 'rhythm' in his private life. Drawing on the criteria outlined in 'An Essay in Aesthetics', we can read Woolf's notion of 'still life' as representative of the 'disinterested intensity of contemplation', which Fry ascribed to the 'imaginative life' and which he saw as 'separated from actual life by the absence of responsive action'.[125] Woolf appears to map the distinction between 'actual' and 'imaginative life' onto her biography of Fry, describing how '[t]he quiet painter's life was always being interrupted by demands from the other world, the practical and active world' (p. 124). She elucidates his 'disinterested' and 'detached' mode of aesthetic appreciation in terms that call to mind the practice of meditation – 'One must master detachment' – but she is quick to note that this did not mean 'withdrawal' from the world (p. 295). Indeed, she repeatedly reveals the difficulty of 'cutting off' one 'rhythm' from another.[126] 'Were they distinct?' she wonders, and we recall the whirring wings of the hawk-moth, 'vibrating to a blur'. Was there a way, through this vibratory mode, to keep 'both in being simultaneously'?

Arguably, Fry's vibrational attention aided Woolf in thinking through the manoeuvre between these two states of being. This becomes apparent if we return to the scene mentioned earlier from July 1934, in which she recounts Fry's examination of a friend's painting in order to identify its creator:

> Again his eyes fixed themselves with their very steady and penetrating gaze upon the canvas. Again they seemed to carry on a life of their own as they explored the world of reality. And again as if it helped him in his voyage of discovery he turned and laughed and talked and argued about other things. The two worlds were close together. He could pass from one to the other without impediment. He responded to the whole vibration – the still life and the laughter, the murmur of the traffic in the distance and the voices close at hand. (pp. 296–7)

The anaphoric repetitions of Woolf's prose recreate the rhythms of Fry's intensifying attention, moving toward a state of vibrating stillness. Oscillating between the fixed point of the canvas and the world around him, we note the apparently paradoxical co-existence of steady focus and exploratory movement, which demonstrates 'two rhythms in being simultaneously'. Woolf's depiction of Fry's phantom-like presence passing 'without impediment' is reminiscent of the notions of mediumship and telepathic communions we have explored. She establishes a continuum between the 'two worlds' – the 'still life' and the everyday or 'actual' – which reinforces not only the proximity between 'art' and 'life', but also Fry's capacity to move fluidly between their shifting emotional and aesthetic registers: 'responding to the whole vibration'.

The 'Intoxication' of Still Life

Still life held a central position in Fry's practice and theory. It was bound up with his sense of the importance of detached, contemplative attention, which evidently informed his attraction to the genre in the work of his favourite artists, as well as in his own practice.[127] In 1902, he experienced 'a very intense and vivid sensation' in contemplating a still life by the seventeenth-century Dutch master, Jean-Baptiste-Siméon Chardin, and it prompted him to make the connection between form and feeling that became the basis of his aesthetic theory.[128] 'Just the shapes of those bottles and their mutual relationships gave me the feeling of something immensely grand and impressive', he recalled, before comparing the feeling to his first encounter with Michelangelo's frescoes in the Sistine Chapel.[129]

A similar sense of revelation accompanied his reverential passion for Cézanne. In *Cézanne: A Study of his Development* (1927) Fry wrote of still life as the genre of the greatest depth and spirituality for the painter, wherein he achieved 'the expression of the most exalted feelings and the deepest intuitions of his nature'.[130] In *Roger Fry* Woolf pays oblique tribute to the French painter and to Fry's critical analysis in his monograph, which she pronounced 'a miracle'.[131] *Cézanne* was published by the Hogarth Press with a still life drawing by Fry of fruits and a human skull on the cover in the manner of his subject. Woolf harnesses the lyrical intensity of Fry's encounters with Cézanne's still lifes in a series of 'notional ekphrases' in her biography.[132] In the following passage, a composition of tableware objects favoured by Cézanne functions as an analogy both for Fry's 'revelation and reconstruction' of the painter, and for his compositional method:

> When at last the apple, the kitchen table, and the bread-knife have come together it is felt to be a victory for the human spirit over matter. The milk-jug and the ginger-jar are transformed. These common objects are invested with the majesty of mountains and the melody of music. (RF, p. 285)

Woolf's verbal still life encodes within it what she describes as 'the double story' in *Cézanne*. That is, the unfolding of 'the development of a character or of a picture', which ultimately reveals the interweaving of everyday life and creative transformation (p. 285). Woolf's tone takes its cue from the high register Fry employed in passages on still life in his monograph. He recognised, with some discomfort, that the 'powerful' emotions aroused by such works led him to summon 'fantastic' phrases and figurative language.[133] 'If the words tragic, menacing, noble or lyrical seem out of place before Cézanne's still-lifes', he writes, 'one feels none the less that the emotions they arouse are curiously analogous to these states of mind.' These works are, he concludes, 'dramas deprived of all dramatic incident'.[134] Fry implicitly elevates the status of still life, but his repeated qualifications and apologies in his monograph for the attention he affords the genre reveal a surprising unwillingness to challenge its conventionally 'minor' position.

Fry reaffirmed his claims for Cézanne's still lifes in similarly lofty terms in his lecture, 'The Double Nature of Painting', delivered in 1933.[135] He asserts that the painter 'removes these objects [apples] from our world; they are transposed into a purely spiritual world in which [. . .] they achieve a visual symphony endowed with a deep and inexpressible eloquence. So we wonder if all still-lifes may not be purely plastic works?'[136] Fry endows still life with musical expressivity, a 'spiritual' pitch or vibration which seems to indicate a reappraisal of the genre as a whole. Yet if 'pure plasticity' becomes the ambiguous but defining quality he seeks above all others, then this is in tension with his experience of such works, in which the emotions and states of mind they arouse are deeply entangled with the 'impure' human condition: its tragedy as well as its nobility.

Woolf's revelatory reading of the Cézannian still life described in *Roger Fry* brings to mind the 'exceptional moments' in her own experience, in which 'common objects' are similarly invested with heightened power. However, her fascination with Cézanne departed from (and sometimes gently mocked) Fry's formal considerations. While he had speculated that still life 'raises the question of literary values in a very definite way', it was she who took up this point and considered it as a writer.[137] Cézanne was, as Woolf claims in 'Pictures', 'provocative to the literary sense', and he demonstrated an uncanny ability 'to press on some nerve'.[138] A few months after she first viewed the celebrated painting *Still Life with Apples* (plate 2), which we considered in the Introduction, Woolf expressed a similar sense of stimulus after visiting the National Gallery. 'I see why I like pictures; it's as things that stir me to describe them', she wrote in her diary, 'but then only certain pictures do this; [. . .] only pictures that appeal to my plastic sense of words make me want to have them for still life in my novel'.[139] Like Fry, Woolf was stirred to a mystically inflected yet sensuous reverence for Cézanne's still lifes, but for her there was also a linguistic potency in their malleability or 'plasticity'. We recall her wondering expression, 'What can 6 apples *not* be?' as she relived her encounter with the painting in her diary, and her similarly intriguing observation: 'The apples positively got redder & rounder & greener. I suspect some very mysterious quality of potation [?] in that picture.'[140]

Woolf's response to *Still Life with Apples* has elicited considerable critical attention, but her unusual reference to 'potation' – an archaic word associated with intoxication, potions and alcohol – usually goes unremarked.[141] By employing this term she imports the possibility that the painting exerts a supersensory influence on the viewer. Vanessa Bell similarly admired how 'extraordinarily solid and alive' the painting was, but the sense that the apples take on a life of their own, that they ripen and yet contract is compounded by Woolf's mis-numeration of six apples instead of the seven represented.[142] The mysterious, almost alchemical process she evokes engenders not only intoxicating affect but also temporal excess: the composition seems to strains the stasis on which *nature morte* is predicated. She seems responsive to what Gustave Geffroy (Cézanne's friend) identified as the painter's 'consuming desire to possess the things he sees and admires, [becoming] intoxicated with the spectacle before him', and 'to transfer the sensation of this inebriated state' to the canvas.[143]

The trope of intoxication reappeared when Woolf evoked Fry's experience of viewing the same work in the spring of 1918. He 'very nearly lost his senses. I've never seen such a sight of intoxication', she recorded, adding a characteristically entomological image: 'He was like a bee on a sunflower.'[144] In claiming the experience of excess in words, Woolf seems to subtly appropriate the territory of art writing from the intoxicated Fry. The hawk-moth was also susceptible to such intoxications: Woolf's moth-hunting activities had given her familiarity with the custom of 'sugaring' trees in order to attract the insects, and her article of 1916 on butterflies and moths describes the excitement of finding 'a moth or two with his proboscis deep-plunged in the flood [. . .] often so drunk that a tap sends him helpless to the ground'.[145] Rather than the ekphrastic trope of the writer's inarticulate dumbness when confronted with a work of visual art, Woolf's reaching toward an adequate language for the sensuous impact of Cézanne's apples becomes a verbal performance of heightened receptivity. In place of formal analysis she offers mystery and provocation.

Woolf's writing of still life typically negotiates this shifting threshold between reverence and wry humour. If at times she punctures the authority of art critics, she is equally critical of writers who attempt to paint still life 'in words'. In her essay 'Pictures' we meet these 'victims of the art of painting who paint apples, roses, china, pomegranates, tamarinds, and glass jars as well as words can paint them, which is, of course, not very well'.[146] Nevertheless, she demonstrates the irresistible attraction of still life for writers, which becomes in the following composition an almost gastronomic relish:

> That still life, they [the writers] proceed, pointing to a jar of red-hot pokers, is to us what a beefsteak is to an invalid – an orgy of blood and nourishment, so starved we are on our diet of thin black print. We nestle into its colour, feed and fill ourselves with yellow and red and gold till we drop off, nourished and content.[147]

As Woolf traces the movements of the writers around the gallery, they are revived by the 'orgy' of colour in the representation of red-hot pokers (a flowering plant with long stems and strikingly vibrant blooms, which were a feature of Woolf's and Bell's gardens). Their experience seems to anticipate the 'violent rapture of colour' and chromatic absorption described in *Walter Sickert*, but the passage also evokes the trajectory of Fry's intimate and erotic encounter with Post-Impressionist painting. The life of colour, concentrated in this 'floral' still life with its unconventionally forceful, masculine attributes seems as provocative to the literary sense as Cézanne's paintings. 'Our sense of colour seems miraculously sharpened', Woolf continues, 'We carry those roses and red-hot pokers about with us for days, working them over again in words.'[148] She was perhaps 'working over' her first-hand experience of Bell and Grant's compositions of the same subject painted in the early 1920s (Fry too had painted red-hot pokers c. 1916) – and she singled out Grant's *Red-hot Pokers* as 'a superb picture' in her review of an exhibition at the Mansard Gallery in 1924.[149]

Woolf's fiction and non-fiction is embroidered by compositions of flower arrangements and everyday objects that indicate her attraction to still life, which she shared with her circle of painters. Nevertheless, such compositions also represent sites in which the friction between their respective visions of art and life becomes evident. This is exemplified in 'The Lady and the Looking-Glass: A Reflection' (1929), a short story in which the concentrated form is particularly suited to the focus and intensity of still life.[150] Early in the narrative Woolf sets up a relationship between 'outside' and 'inside' which we might read as a transposition of Fry's 'two rhythms': 'outside, the looking-glass reflected the hall table, the sunflowers, the garden path so accurately and so fixedly that they seemed held there in their reality unescapably. It was a strange contrast – all changing here, all stillness there. One could not help looking from one to the other.'[151] As the speaker's attention intensifies, she perceives the objects (letters) on the table 'all dripping with light and colour at first and crude and unabsorbed', before they undergo transformation:

> drawn in and arranged and composed and made part of the picture and granted that stillness and immortality which the looking-glass conferred. They lay there invested with a new reality and significance and with a greater heaviness, too, as if it would have needed a chisel to dislodge them from the table.[152]

Through this visual oscillation – this vibratory movement between stillness and motion – solidity and fluidity, the objects in Woolf's imaginative world hold their metaphysical and material reality 'in being simultaneously'. The composition might represent the transformation from Impressionist fluidity and flux into the solidity and 'significance' of Post-Impressionism's 'new reality' – its 'significant form'; but she seems to vacillate, looking from 'one to the other', holding both possibilities in tension.[153]

'Immortal Apples' and 'Eternal Eggs'

Let us return, in conclusion, to Fry's studio in Fitzroy Street, London, where Woolf evokes the ubiquitous presence of still life in his everyday life, as well as its significance in his 'spiritual reality':

> It was an untidy room. He cooked there, slept there, painted there and wrote there. There was always a picture on the easel, and on the table an arrangement of flowers or of fruit, of eggs or of onions—some still life that the charwoman was admonished on a placard 'Do not touch'. (RF, p. 201)[154]

The scene evidently left a considerable visual impression as Woolf revisits it later in the same chapter:

> Mrs Filmer had obeyed the command on the placard 'Do not touch'. [. . .] Rows of dusty medicine bottles stood on the mantelpiece; frying pans were mixed with palettes; some plates held salad, others scrapings of congealed paint. The floor was strewn with papers. There were the pots he was making, there were samples of stuffs and designs for the Omega. But on the table, protected by its placard, was the still life—those symbols of detachment, those tokens of a spiritual reality immune from destruction, the immortal apples, the eternal eggs. (p. 215)

This 'frozen' picture of the studio, which has become a still life in itself, performs the function of which Fry himself had written: 'It is in the still-life that we frequently catch the purest self-revelation of the artists.'[155] The 'purest' and seemingly the most impersonal of genres becomes paradoxically a mirror or 'gauge' as Fry describes it of the artist's personality – a way of reading their biography.[156] Woolf's ekphrastic description reveals the artist's studio as a site in which the jostling relations between 'art' and 'life' are played out. The disordered objects subvert their owner's narrative revealing that the spheres of 'art' and 'life' interpenetrate more than Fry's aesthetic theory acknowledges. Different rhythms (cooking, sleeping, painting and writing) not only 'play against each other' but also interact and permeate the same space. In a similar way, when reading Fry's criticism, Woolf described a feeling of contact with his vibrational presence: 'we never feel shut off alone in a studio; morality and conduct, even if they are called by other names, are present; eating and drinking and love-making hum and murmur on the other side of the page' (RF, p. 228). To maintain 'two rhythms in being simultaneously', or to pass between them 'without impediment', is to pursue her vibrational model to its full extension. It is this vibratory attention, this capacity to inhabit seemingly opposite patterns of being, which she seems to appreciate in Fry (even if this sits uneasily with his own theories), as she so vividly emblematises in the quivering suspension of the humming-bird hawk-moth.

*

In the context of the growing political and social destabilisation of the inter-war period, Woolf had expressed greater ambivalence regarding the ethical imperatives of an aesthetic practice symbolised by still life. In an essay originally composed in 1936 for the *Daily Worker* and later published as 'The Artist and Politics', she writes: 'With all these voices crying and conflicting in his ears, how can the artist still remain at peace in his studio, contemplating his model or his apple in the cold light that comes through his studio window?'[157] It seems, then, with a characteristic touch of ironical appreciation, that she describes the elevation of the simple objects of Fry's studio composition into 'immortal apples' and 'eternal eggs'. They exist in a double life: 'protected' by the admonishing placard they are aestheticised, becoming 'still life' rather than simply functional, immobile objects. Woolf implicitly critiques the notion of art's 'immunity' by describing these ordinary comestibles as exposed to the inevitable rhythms of decay and disorder around them. Nevertheless, as 'symbols of detachment' and of 'a spiritual reality immune from destruction', she recognises the role of 'still life' in Fry's effort to cultivate a simple, ordered life in the face of a precarious world-reality. It is, perhaps, the object-world equivalent for his contemplative rhythm.

Woolf's reverse reading of art's 'rhythms' not only challenges Fry's doctrine of aesthetic purity through the example of his own life; it arguably also demonstrates what Christopher Reed speculates is 'an ultra-formalism that seeks to extend its implications beyond the aesthetic realm'.[158] This has all the more poignancy in the historical context of 'The War Years', as the chapter of the biography is titled, in which even the unstable order of Fry's composition functions as a form of endurance, of 'still living'. As Woolf observes in conclusion: 'whatever the connection between the rhythms of life and of art, there could be no doubt about the sensation – he had survived the war' (p. 215). The still life, like the biography, remains an elegiac, if unstable memorial to her subject.

Notes

1. Fry coined the term 'Post-Impressionism' at the first of these exhibitions. The second incorporated British painters such as Duncan Grant, Wyndham Lewis and Vanessa Bell. For a detailed account of the impact and reception of these exhibitions see S. K. Tillyard, *The Impact of Modernism 1900–1920* (London: Routledge, 1988); and J. B. Bullen, ed., *Post-Impressionists in England: The Critical Reception* (London: Routledge, 1988).
2. I situate Woolf's notion of 'quivering' attentiveness within aesthetic debates about Post-Impressionism, but this chapter does not directly trace their impact on her writing since the story of how she and her circle came to regard these exhibitions as a turning point for modern art has been widely discussed. Some of the most stimulating discussions include: Jane Goldman, *The Feminist Aesthetics of Virginia Woolf: Modernism, Post-Impressionism and the Politics of the Visual* (Cambridge: Cambridge University Press, 1998); Ann Banfield, *The Phantom Table: Woolf, Fry, Russell and the Epistemology of Modernism* (Cambridge: Cambridge University Press, 1998); and Parkes, *A Sense of Shock*, pp. 146–77.
3. Virginia Woolf, *Night and Day* (London: Duckworth & Co., 1919), p. 488.
4. 'quiver, *adj.*', in *OED*, http://www.oed.com/view/Entry/156817.
5. 'quiver, *v.*1', in *OED*, http://www.oed.com/view/Entry/156819; 'quiver, n.2', http://www.oed.com/view/Entry/156816.
6. *The Diary of Virginia Woolf*, IV, p. 124. Woolf was upset that a snapshot photograph of her by Leonard Woolf was being published, which she felt was an invasion of her privacy, see n. 4 in the *Diary*.
7. Virginia Woolf, 'On Being Ill' (1930), in Leonard Woolf, ed., *The Moment and other Essays* (London: Hogarth Press, 1947), pp. 14–24 (p. 14).
8. Woolf draws on these characterisations in her portrayal of the shell-shocked Septimus in *Mrs Dalloway* (1925).
9. Virginia Woolf, *A Writer's Diary*: *Being Extracts from the Diary of Virginia Woolf*, ed. Leonard Woolf (London: Hogarth Press, 1953), 16 February 1932, p. 179.
10. Trower notes that '[m]any feminine, "finely strung" characters' in nineteenth-century literature 'tremble and quiver', and 'suffer from the vibratory movements that were increasingly associated with hysterical women' (*Senses of Vibration*, p. 63). It is interesting that George Eliot, the Victorian novelist admired by Woolf, deploys similar language in her novel *Daniel Deronda*, describing her male protagonist who was not 'one of those quiveringly-poised natures that lend themselves to second-sight' (and that this is given as an example of 'quiveringly, *adv.*', in *OED*, http://www.oed.com/view/Entry/156824.
11. T. B. Hyslop, 'Post-Illusionism and the Art of the Insane', *Nineteenth Century* (February 1911), 270–8, repr. in Bullen, *Post-Impressionists in England*, pp. 209–22 (p. 215). See Bullen for further examples of the contemporary press reaction.
12. Roger Fry, 'Post Impressionism', *Fortnightly Review* (1 May 1911), in *A Roger Fry Reader*, ed. Christopher Reed (Chicago: University of Chicago Press, 1996), pp. 99–110 (p. 110).

13. Virginia Woolf, *The Letters of Virginia Woolf*, ed. Nigel Nicholson and Joanne Trautmann, 6 vols (London: Hogarth Press, 1975–80), V (1979), to Ethel Smyth, 4 May 1932, pp. 59–60.
14. 'An Unwritten Novel', in *The Complete Shorter Fiction of Virginia Woolf*, ed. Susan Dick, rev. edn (London: Hogarth Press, 1989), pp. 112–21 (p. 117).
15. Hovering also enters into critical terminology on Woolf. In *The Novels of Virginia Woolf* (London: Methuen, 1977), Hermione Lee repeatedly invokes 'hovering' in her discussion of *To the Lighthouse*, noting '[t]he subtlety with which the figures of speech hover between the inside and the outside of Mr Ramsay's mind' (p. 119). Justin Sausman corroborates my observations on 'quivering' vibratory language in the passage from 'The Unwritten Novel' and his essay makes persuasive connections with 'vibratory occultism', although these do not extend to Woolf or Fry's writing on art. See 'From Vibratory Occultism to Vibratory Modernism: Blackwood, Lawrence, Woolf', in Trower and Enns, eds, *Vibratory Modernism*, pp. 30–52 (p. 44).
16. '[H]ow the quiet lapped me round! & then how dull I got', Woolf writes in her diary at Rodmell, her rural Sussex home; and then, 'how the beauty brimmed over me & steeped my nerves till they quivered'. But this is no easy dichotomy between town and country; as Woolf reminds us later in the same entry, London is a place where 'Faces passing lift up my mind; prevent it from settling, as it does in the stillness at Rodmell.' *Diary of Virginia Woolf 1920–24*, II (1978), 26 May 1924, p. 301.
17. Virginia Woolf, 'Pictures and Portraits', in *The Essays of Virginia Woolf 1919–1924*, ed. Andrew McNeillie, 4 vols (London: Hogarth Press, 1986–1994), III (1988), pp. 163–6 (p. 163). Woolf was reviewing *Personalities: Twenty-four Drawings* (1919) by Edmond X. Kapp (1890–1978).
18. Woolf, 'Notes on D. H. Lawrence', in *The Moment*, pp. 79–82 (pp. 80–1).
19. Woolf, 'Donne after Three Centuries', in *Collected Essays*, ed. Leonard Woolf, 4 vols (London: Hogarth Press, 1966–7), I, pp. 32–45 (p. 32). Woolf's description of quivering as awakening has an affinity with T. S. Eliot's invocation to the stirring spirit in his poem 'Little Gidding', where 'Between melting and freezing / The soul's sap quivers'. *Four Quartets*, p. 191.
20. Virginia Woolf, 'A Sketch of the Past', in *Moments of Being: Autobiographical Writings*, ed. Jeanne Schulkind, rev. Hermione Lee (London: Pimlico, 2002), pp. 78–160 (p. 92). All further references are taken from this edition and will be given after quotations in the text.
21. Virginia Woolf, *The Waves*, new edn (London: Penguin, 1964), p. 46.
22. Woolf, *A Writer's Diary*, 28 May 1929, p. 143.
23. *The Waves*, p. 101. For further discussion in the context of still life painting and women artists, see my essay in 'Virginia Woolf, Still Life and Transformation', in Laura Smith, Enrico Tassi and Eloise Bennett, eds, *Virginia Woolf: An Exhibition Inspired by Her Writings* (London: Tate, 2018), pp. 159–63.
24. Woolf, *The Waves*, p. 73.
25. *The Diary of Virginia Woolf*, IV, 16 September 1932, p. 124.
26. Woolf held Fry's critical faculties in high esteem and they shared a reciprocal interest in each other's work. In this chapter, I am concerned with their paradigms of attention; their friendship has been charted elsewhere, notably in Frances Spalding's

insightful biography, *Roger Fry: Art and Life* (Berkeley: University of California Press, 1980).

27. *The Diary of Virginia Woolf*, III, 4 January 1929, p. 218.
28. Sim, *Virginia Woolf: The Patterns of Ordinary Experience*, p. 14.
29. Ibid., p. 15.
30. Sim, *Virginia Woolf: The Patterns of Ordinary Experience*, p. 16. Woolf's 'moments of being' have been much discussed. Of the many other commentators, Parkes's reading is particularly pertinent to my investigation: he conceives of the 'Woolfian moment' as 'the product of collaboration between two different types of shock – one conscious, material, historical, the other unconscious, traumatic, timeless' (*A Sense of Shock*, p. 147).
31. Sim, *Virginia Woolf: The Patterns of Ordinary Experience*, p. 14. I am in sympathy with Sim's proposition that Woolf's 'moments of being' can be approached as 'empirical' experiences in which 'the body is, if somewhat paradoxically, presented as a conduit to, or vehicle for, a numinous reality' (p. 141), although I would further suggest that foregrounding the body does not preclude processes of disembodiment and spiritualisation.
32. Merleau-Ponty, in *The Visible and the Invisible* (1968), quoted by Galen A. Johnson, in 'Ontology and Painting: "Eye and Mind"', *The Merleau-Ponty Aesthetics Reader*, p. 51.
33. Ibid.
34. Woolf shared an attraction to still life with Bell who frequently painted still lifes and whose compositions of flowers and everyday objects feature in her cover designs for the Hogarth Press. For further discussion see Diana Gillespie, 'Still Lifes in Words and Paint', in *The Sisters' Arts: The Writing and Painting of Virginia Woolf and Vanessa Bell* (New York: University of Syracuse Press, 1988), pp. 225–66.
35. Woolf met Walter Sickert on several occasions during the 1920s and admired his work, declaring it 'all that painting ought to be'. In *Letters of Virginia Woolf*, V, to Quentin Bell, 26 November 1933, pp. 253–54.
36. Woolf does not identify a particular species and evidently employs descriptive license, but her representation could relate to many insects with structurally coloured appearances for camouflage. Works including H. W. Bates's *The Naturalist on the River Amazons* (1863) had recorded the natural phenomena of South America and the region became the setting for Woolf's first novel, *The Voyage Out* (1915).
37. See Gillian Beer on the importance of Darwin's narratives in Woolf's work, and the 'great subtlety' of her responses to them, in *Virginia Woolf: The Common Ground* (Edinburgh: Edinburgh University Press, 1996), p. 13. Goldman calls attention to the affinity between Woolf's notion of the 'insect stage' and a passage from her short story, 'The Sun and the Fish' in which she also (re)writes the evolutionary story. In *The Feminist Aesthetics of Virginia Woolf*, p. 114.
38. Roland Barthes, 'Cy Twombly: Works on Paper' (1979), in David Batchelor, ed., *Colour: Documents of Contemporary Art* (London: Whitechapel, 2008), p. 164.
39. David Punter, *Rapture: Literature, Addiction, Secrecy* (Brighton: Sussex Academic Press, 2009), p. 1.

40. Ibid., p. 1. Woolf's compound term 'violent rapture' also hints at the more disquieting significations attributed to rapture as 'Rape; sexual violation, ravishing', in *OED*, http://www.oed.com/view/Entry/158234.
41. Rapture featured in the terminology of the Bloomsbury art theorist, Clive Bell, in his formalist treatise *Art* (1914). But while Woolf's embodied raptures intermingle everyday experiences with those directly pertaining to art, Bell's are singular to aesthetic experience: 'aesthetic rapture' takes place in a separate sphere from life.
42. Woolf refers to 'vibrant rapture' in *Between the Acts* (1941) (New York: Harcourt Brace, 1969), p. 209; the 'pressure of rapture', in *Mrs Dalloway*, ed., David Bradshaw (Oxford: Oxford University Press, 2009), p. 27; and 'purest ecstasy' in 'Sketch', p. 78.
43. Woolf frequently invokes the unusual term, 'airballs', presumably signifying air bubbles, in *Walter Sickert*, and several times in 'Sketch', where it functions as a metaphor for the body as a suspended, transitory vessel.
44. Adrianne Rubin, *Roger Fry's 'Difficult and Uncertain Science': The Interpretation of Aesthetic Perception* (Oxford: Peter Lang, 2013), p. 20.
45. Laura Doyle, 'Introduction: What's Between Us?', *Modern Fiction Studies*, 50 (2004), 1–7 (p. 1). Doyle's allusion to the 'Brownian zone' refers to the work of the botanist, Robert Brown, who discovered the random motion of particles in 1827, as well as reminding us of Woolf's 1923 essay 'Mr Bennett and Mrs Brown'.
46. Woolf, 'Kew Gardens', in *The Complete Shorter Fiction*, pp. 90–5 (p. 90).
47. Michael A. Salmon, *The Aurelian Legacy: British Butterflies and their Collectors* (Berkeley, CA: University of California Press, 2000), p. 370.
48. Christina Alt, *Virginia Woolf and the Study of Nature* (Cambridge: Cambridge University Press, 2010), p. 54.
49. Ibid., p. 168. On the ethical implications of Woolf's representations of insect life, see also Bonnie Kime Scott, *In the Hollow of the Wave: Virginia Woolf and Modernist Uses of Nature* (Charlottesville: University of Virginia Press, 2012).
50. On the negative figuration of insects see Holly Henry, *Virginia Woolf and the Discourse of Science: The Aesthetics of Astronomy* (Cambridge: Cambridge University Press, 2003), pp. 125–6. Woolf's ambivalence is expressed for instance in 'Pictures', where she wryly characterises writers as 'irresponsible dragon-flies, mere insects, children wantonly destroying works of art by pulling petal from petal'. In *The Moment*, pp. 140–4 (pp. 143–4).
51. A good example of the hidden insect motif can be found in *Flowers in a Vase* by Jan Davidsz de Heem (1606–84), Fitzwilliam Museum, Cambridge.
52. Vincent H. Resh and Ring T. Cardé, eds, *Encyclopaedia of Insects*, 2nd edn (London: Academic Press, 2009), p. 241. Woolf found particular aesthetic potency in the butterfly, famously describing Lily's vision for her painting in *To the Lighthouse* as 'the light of a butterfly's wing upon the arches of a cathedral' (p. 57). At her Sussex home 'Monk's House' she hung a series of butterflies pinned in a frame sent to her by the Argentine writer Victoria Ocampo. She wrote to Ocampo of the butterflies, 'always brilliant; wings stretched, flying, like you: but pinned; unlike you' (7 October 1938, *Letters of Virginia Woolf*, VI, p. 284).

53. Walter Benjamin, 'The Image of Proust', in *Illuminations*, trans. Harry Zohn, ed. Hannah Arendt (New York: Shocken Books, 1968), pp. 201–15 (p. 208). Woolf herself described Proust 'as tough as catgut & as evanescent as a butterfly's bloom' (*The Diary of Virginia Woolf*, III, 8 April 1925, p. 7).
54. *The Letters of Virginia Woolf*, III, 12 May 1928, p. 499.
55. Auguste Forel, *The Senses of Insects*, trans. Macleod Yearsley (London: Methuen, 1908), pp. 25, 29.
56. Woolf, *Writer's Diary*, 9 February 1940, p. 326.
57. Hermione Lee, *Virginia Woolf* (London: Vintage, 1997), p. 31.
58. Woolf, 'Reading', in *Collected Essays*, II, pp. 12–33 (p. 23).
59. Ibid., p. 24.
60. Ibid., p. 25.
61. Woolf, 'Sketch', p. 113. Morris identifies the *Macroglossa Stellatarum* or Humming-bird Hawk-moth, in *A Natural of British Moths*, 4 vols (London: Henry Edward Knox, 1871), I, p. 14–15 (plate V, fig. 2).
62. Woolf, 'Butterflies and Moths: Insects in September', in *The Essays of Virginia Woolf 1933–41*, ed. Stuart N. Clarke (London: Hogarth Press, 2011), VI, pp. 381–3 (p. 382).
63. H. Eltringham, *The Senses of Insects* (London: Methuen, 1933), p. 75.
64. Woolf, 'Reading', p. 22.
65. Later in this chapter I examine Woolf's ambivalence about aspects of Fry's early formalism. For an extended discussion see Christopher Reed, 'Through Formalism: Feminism and Virginia Woolf's Relation to Bloomsbury Aesthetics', *Twentieth Century Literature*, 38 (1992), 20–43; and Julia Briggs, 'Fry, Formalism and Fiction', in *Reading Virginia Woolf* (Edinburgh: Edinburgh University Press, 2006), pp. 96–112.
66. Rubin's gloss on Fry's 'alert passivity' or 'passive receptiveness' supports my reading of Woolf's image: she writes that he 'may simply be suggesting that the viewer need not conquer a work of art through active interpretation, but instead let the work communicate itself to him' (*Roger Fry's 'Difficult and Uncertain Science'*, n. 44, pp. 19–20).
67. Woolf, 'The Death of the Moth' (date unknown), in *The Death of the Moth and Other Essays* (1942), ed., Leonard Woolf (London: Penguin, 1961), pp. 9–12 (pp. 9, 10).
68. 'vibration', in *OED*, http://www.oed.com/view/Entry/223061.
69. Janice Neri, *The Insect and the Image: Visualizing Nature in Early Modern Europe, 1500–1700* (Minneapolis: University of Minnesota Press, 2011), p. 78.
70. *The Diary of Virginia Woolf*, V, p. 172.
71. Kirsty Martin, *Modernism and the Rhythms of Sympathy* (Oxford: Oxford University Press, 2013), p. 27.
72. Fry, quoted in ibid., p. 1. Martin's study is perhaps the most suggestive in recent discussions of 'rhythm' in Woolf and Fry's work; see also Anthony Uhlmann, 'Virginia Woolf and Bloomsbury Aesthetics', in Maggie Humm, ed., *The Edinburgh Companion to Virginia Woolf and the Arts* (Edinburgh: Edinburgh University Press, 2010), pp. 58–73.

73. Martin, *Modernism and the Rhythms of Sympathy*, p. 1. Martin's chapter on Woolf includes persuasive readings of her novels but her focus on sympathy is primarily inter-human and therefore does not take in encounters with visual art or the biography of Fry.
74. Virginia Woolf, *Jacob's Room* (London: Penguin, 1992), p. 17.
75. Ibid., p. 61.
76. Steven Connor, *Beyond Words: Sobs, Hums, Stutters and Other Vocalizations* (London: Reaktion, 2014), pp. 92, 99.
77. A similar expression of restraint made by Fry evidently resonated with Woolf as it is twice cited in the biography: '"It must always be kept in mind that such analysis halts before the ultimate concrete reality of a work of art [. . .] it must leave untouched a greater part of its objective"' (p. 286, and p. 296).
78. Virginia Woolf, *Congenial Spirits: Selected Letters*, ed. Joanne Trautmann Banks (London: Pimlico, 2003), 3 May 1938, p. 400.
79. Ibid., 8 October 1938, p. 413. Woolf's question hints at her difficulty in writing about Bell's romantic relationship with Fry, which goes unmentioned in the biography probably due to constraints set by Fry's family.
80. *The Diary of Virginia Woolf*, IV, p. 353.
81. Linda Henderson, *The Fourth Dimension and Non-Euclidean Geometry in Modern Art* (Princeton: Princeton University Press, 1983), p. 43.
82. Woolf's early reviewers picked up on her interest in the fourth dimension: reviewing *Orlando* for the *New York Times*, Cleveland B. Chase described the author 'set[ting] out to explore still another fourth dimension of writing'. In 'Mrs. Woolf Explores the "Time" Element in Human Relationships', *New York Times*, 21 October 1928, http://www.nytimes.com/books/97/06/08/reviews/woolf-orlando.html. For further discussion of fourth dimensional ideas in Woolf's writing, see Caroline Maclean, *The Vogue for Russia: Modernism and the Unseen in Britain 1900–1930* (Edinburgh: Edinburgh University Press, 2015), pp. 113–16.
83. Ian F. A. Bell, 'Ezra Pound and the Materiality of the Fourth Dimension', in John Holmes, ed., *Science in Modern Poetry: New Directions* (Liverpool: Liverpool University Press, 2012), pp. 130–50 (p. 131).
84. Pound, quoted in ibid., p. 130.
85. Ibid., p. 130.
86. The *memento mori* motif surfaces elsewhere in Woolf's writing. For a reading of *To the Lighthouse* as a novel propelled by this motif, see Lewis, 'Still Life in Motion', p. 444.
87. *The Diary of Virginia Woolf*, IV, 17 October 1934, p. 253.
88. Woolf, *Congenial Spirits*, 4 September 1940, pp. 433–4. Woolf had already expressed her sense of loss sonically in a letter to the composer Ethel Smyth: 'I never minded any death of a friend half as much: its like coming into a room and expecting all the violins and trumpets and hearing a mouse squeak.' *Letters of Virginia Woolf*, V, 6 June 1935, p. 399.
89. In her preface to Adriana L. Varga, ed., *Virginia Woolf and Music* (Bloomington: Indiana University Press, 2014), Varga highlights the connection between Woolf's interest in music and her sensitivity to rhythm but does not explore the musical connotations of vibration.

90. Woolf, 'The Art of Biography', in *The Death of the Moth and other Essays*, pp. 161–9 (p. 162).
91. Frances Spalding, 'Introduction' to Woolf, *Roger Fry*, p. xii. Fry and Woolf both became subjects of elegiac still life paintings: Mark Gertler painted a still life entitled *Homage to Roger Fry* in response to news of his death in 1934, and Duncan Grant produced *Still Life with Bust of Virginia Woolf* (1960). For a reading of Woolf and elegy in the context of photographic stillness see Hornby's chapter, 'Still There: A Theory of Photography', in *Still Modernism*, pp. 145–89.
92. Robert Kiely, '*Jacob's Room* and *Roger Fry:* Two Studies in Still Life', in Robert Kiely, ed., *Modernism Reconsidered* (Cambridge, MA: Harvard University Press, 1983), pp. 147–66 (p. 147). Kiely does not consider the relevance of still life for Fry or his aesthetic theory in any detail, focusing instead on the apparent absence of the protagonists in *Jacob's Room* and *Roger Fry*.
93. Woolf, 'The New Biography' (1927), in *Collected Essays*, IV, pp. 229–35 (p. 229). Other critics have seen these less tangible qualities in a more positive light: Ruth Hoberman views *Roger Fry* as a form of feminist sociobiography in which Woolf creates a portrait of 'a personality in the act of living, rather than a sharply delineated, over materialised figure'. In *Modernizing Lives: Experiments in English Biography, 1918–1939* (Carbondale and Edwardsville: Southern Illinois Press, 1987), p. 185. In an early review, Edward Alden Jewell perhaps obliquely identified Woolf's desire to retain the hidden aspects of her subject when he noted that 'a man's spirit does not rise sharply clear above the sea of strangeness and enigma that encompass it'. 'Virginia Woolf's Life of Roger Fry', *New York Times*, 15 December 1940, http://www.nytimes.com/books/00/12/17/specials/woolf-fry.html.
94. Woolf, 'The Art of Biography', p. 169.
95. For an account of critics who characterise Woolf's biography as 'regressive', see Hoberman's survey, *Modernizing Lives*, p. 182.
96. Trower, *Senses of Vibration*, p. 37.
97. Woolf, 'The Supernatural in Fiction', *Times Literary Supplement*, 31 January 1918, repr. in *Granite and Rainbow* (New York: Harcourt Brace, 1958), pp. 61–4 (p. 63).
98. The founding president of the Society for Psychical Research, Henry Sidgwick, was (like Fry) a member of the Cambridge Apostles. On the alternative spirituality of this circle, see Brockington, *Above the Battlefield*, pp. 40–4.
99. Trower, *Senses of Vibration*, p. 10.
100. Gurney, *Phantasms of the Living* (1886), quoted by Trower, *Senses of Vibration*, p. 51.
101. Woolf, 'The Supernatural in Fiction', p. 64.
102. Ezra Pound, *ABC of Reading* (London: George Routledge and Sons, 1934), p. 57.
103. Armstrong, *Modernism: A Cultural History*, p. 129.
104. See Nicholas Royle's suggestion that Woolf satirises telepathy in 'Kew Gardens'. In *Telepathy and Literature: Essays on the Reading Mind* (Oxford: Basil Blackwell, 1991), pp. 111–20.
105. Roger Fry, 'An Essay in Aesthetics', in *Vision and Design* (London: Chatto & Windus, 1920), pp. 11–25 (p. 20).

106. *Letters of Virginia Woolf*, VI, to Ethel Smyth, 16 August 1940, p. 417.
107. The biography was also polyvocal in the sense that Woolf was obliged to incorporate the comments and suggestions of Fry's family: in 1940 she recorded 'entering 3 different Frys comments into the edges of proofs, and altering my own words to admit theirs' (*Letters of Virginia Woolf*, VI, p. 399). For further discussion see Diane F. Gillespie, 'The Texture of the Text: Editing Roger Fry: A Biography', in *Editing Virginia Woolf: Interpreting the Modernist Text*, ed. James M. Haule and J. H. Stape (Basingstoke: Palgrave, 2001), pp. 91–113.
108. Woolf, 'Roger Fry', published in *The Moment,* pp. 83–8 (p. 83).
109. *The Listener*, 2 October 1929, repr. in *A Roger Fry Reader*, pp. 393–400 (p. 394).
110. Gillian Beer, '"Wireless": Popular Physics, Radio and Modernism', *Cultural Babbage: Technology, Time and Invention*, ed. Francis Spufford and Jenny Uglow (London: Faber & Faber, 1996), pp. 149–66 (pp. 149–50).
111. Eddington quoted by Beer, ibid., p. 153.
112. Fry, 'Post Impressionism' (1911), in *A Roger Fry Reader*, p. 101.
113. Roger Fry, *Last Lectures* (Cambridge: Cambridge University Press, 1939), p. 17.
114. Kandinsky, *Concerning the Spiritual in Art*, p. 29. Fry admired what he described as Kandinsky's 'pure visual music'. In *Letters of Roger Fry*, ed. Denys Sutton, 2 vols (London: Chatto & Windus, 1972), I, p. 49.
115. Fry, quoted by Woolf in *Roger Fry*, p. 177; Fry, 'Reflections on Germany and its Art Collections', quoted by Rubin, *Roger Fry's 'Difficult and Uncertain Science'*, p. 119.
116. Woolf quotes from Fry's *Last Lectures.*
117. Commentators on Fry's aesthetic theory are somewhat quiet about his Quaker heritage, but Spalding's biography of Fry notes the '[d]evout beliefs, ascetic habits' and 'rigorous life-style' that characterized Quakerism (*Roger Fry: Art and Life*, p. 3). Benjamin Harvey discusses the connection between Fry's use of silence in his art criticism and the devotional framework of Quakerism, in 'The Rest is Silence: The Senses of Roger Fry's Endings', *Journal of Art Historiography*, 9 (2013), https://arthistoriography.files.wordpress.com/2013/12/harvey.pdf.
118. Fry, letter of 1924, quoted by Woolf, in *Roger Fry*, p. 230.
119. Fry, 'An Essay in Aesthetics', p. 23.
120. See Reed, 'Through Formalism', p. 23; and on the persistence of a 'problematically narrow version' of formalism, see Sam Rose, 'The Significance of Form', *Nonsite*, 20 (2017), http://nonsite.org/feature/the-significance-of-form#foot_src_12-9852.
121. Reading his books 'one after another' while working on the biography, she came to the conclusion that he was 'the only great critic that ever lived'. *Congenial Spirits*, Letter to Vanessa Bell, 8 October 1938, p. 413.
122. Allen McLaurin argues that Woolf's biography neglects 'the way in which the idea [of rhythm] changes', particularly in Fry's later criticism. In *Virginia Woolf: The Echoes Enslaved* (Cambridge: Cambridge University Press, 1973), pp. 113–20 (p. 114). As my discussion indicates, however, she was alert to the evolving nature of Fry's thought even if she is less interested in tracing specific theoretical shifts.
123. Rubin, *Roger Fry's 'Difficult and Uncertain Science'*, p. 162. For a survey of Fry's denotations of 'rhythm', see ibid., pp. 159–62.

124. *Letters of Virginia Woolf*, III, Letter to Vita Sackville-West, 16 March 1926, p. 247.
125. Fry, 'An Essay in Aesthetics', pp. 21, 14.
126. Fry's phrase, 'cutting off the responsive action', appears in 'An Essay in Aesthetics', p. 19.
127. Among his most significant still life paintings, Spalding calls attention to *Bowl on a Chair, The Blue Bottle, Still-Life with Biscuit Tin and Pots* and *The Madonna Lily* (*Roger Fry: Art and Life*, p. 204).
128. Fry, quoted by Spalding in *Roger Fry: Art and Life*, p. 109. Rubin notes that 'accounts vary' as to whether Fry was inspired by a Chardin still life shown in 1902, or a still life by Cézanne exhibited at the International Society Exhibition in London in 1906 (*Roger Fry's 'Difficult and Uncertain Science'*, p. 44), but in either case, Fry's reaction demonstrates his sense of the peculiar power of still life.
129. Fry, quoted by Spalding in *Roger Fry: Art and Life*, p. 109.
130. Fry, *Cézanne*, p. 38.
131. Woolf, *Congenial Spirits*, Letter to Vanessa Bell, 8 October 1938, p. 413.
132. John Hollander's term for 'the description, often elaborately detailed, of purely fictional painting or sculpture that is indeed brought into being by the poetic language itself'. *The Gazer's Spirit* (Chicago: University of Chicago Press, 1995), p. 4.
133. Fry, *Cézanne*, p. 47.
134. Ibid., p. 42.
135. Fry, 'The Double Nature of Painting', first published in *The Apollo*, May 1969, repr. in *A Roger Fry Reader*, pp. 380–92 (p. 388).
136. Ibid.
137. Ibid.
138. Woolf, 'Pictures' (written in 1925), in *The Moment*, p. 142.
139. *The Diary of Virginia Woolf*, I, 16 July 1918, p. 168.
140. *The Diary of Virginia Woolf*, I, pp. 140–1.
141. The denotations for 'potation' include: 'The action or an act of drinking, esp. the consumption of alcoholic drink; a drink (of alcohol)'; 'A drinking party or drinking bout'; 'A medicinal drink or liquid; a concoction, a potion', in *OED* http://www.oed.com/view/Entry/148763. Critics often glance over the final suggestive line in the diary entry. Goldman omits it from her citation (*Feminist Aesthetics of Virginia Woolf*, p. 139), as does Lloyd (*Shimmering in a Transformed Light*, p. 2). Maggie Humm is one of the few to note that the phrase is indicative of the 'intoxication' Woolf shared with Fry, in 'Virginia Woolf and the Arts', in *The Edinburgh Companion to Virginia Woolf and the Arts*, pp. 1–16 (p. 4).
142. Bell, Letter to Fry, 3 April 1918, *Selected Letters of Vanessa Bell*, ed. Regina Marler (London: Bloomsbury, 1993), p. 213.
143. Quoted by Richard Shiff, 'Morality, Materiality, Apples', in *The World is an Apple*, pp. 147–93 (p. 180).
144. *Letters of Virginia Woolf*, II, to Nicholas Bagenal, 15 April 1918, p. 230.
145. Woolf, 'Butterflies and Moths', p. 382.
146. Woolf, 'Pictures', p. 140.

147. Ibid., p. 143.
148. Ibid.
149. Virginia Woolf, 'It is strange as one enters the Mansard Gallery. . .' (1924), in Andrew McNeillie, ed., *The Essays of Virginia Woolf: 1919–1924*, III, pp. 448–9.
150. Compare also her short stories, 'Solid Objects' (1920), and 'The Mark on the Wall' (1921), both of which enact an intense attention to commonplace things, and invite readings through the paradigm of still life.
151. Virginia Woolf, 'The Lady and the Looking-Glass: A Reflection', in *The Complete Shorter Fiction*, pp. 221–5 (p. 221).
152. Ibid., p. 223.
153. See Parkes's proposal of a reading of the short story in which Woolf chooses and criticises both Impressionism and Post-Impressionism, as well as their adherents Walter Pater and Roger Fry (*A Sense of Shock*, p. 171).
154. Woolf's description of this typical composition invites association with works by Fry such as *Still Life: Jug and Eggs*, 1911, which is now in the Art Gallery of South Australia.
155. Fry, *Cézanne*, p. 41. Woolf presents a similarly revealing portrait of her protagonist in *Jacob's Room* through a still life of the objects in his room (see p. 31), which take on elegiac significance after his death, concluding with the poignant image of his empty shoes.
156. Fry, *Cézanne*, p. 41.
157. Woolf, 'The Artist and Politics', in *The Moment*, pp. 180–2 (p. 182).
158. Reed, 'Through Formalism', p. 38.

2

STILL LIFE IN MOTION

> It has been realized in painting that a still life, of the most ordinary objects, may be (and usually is) a far greater work of art than an enormous painting of some great historic event full of kings and queens! It is time that this was realized in relation to the stage.
>
> Margaret Morris[1]

Movement practices in the early twentieth century reveal a fascination with the relationship between stasis and motion, and the fluidity of these apparent polarities. When the pioneering dancer Margaret Morris sought to define her movement technique in an article of 1917, published in *Arts and Letters* alongside illustrations by Gaudier-Brzeska and J. D. Fergusson, she deployed but also complicated the longstanding binary of visual art and dance. 'I look at dancing from the visual point of view of the artist,' Morris writes, 'seeing movements as combinations of shapes and lines, and ballets as pictures with the possibilities of actual movement added.'[2] She foregrounds the static image as the source of her vision for dance, with gesture and movement as a translation of the drawn line. This intimate alliance between dance and painting was fundamental to her practice and it takes us to the heart of this chapter's inquiry.

Lynda Nead suggests that at the turn of the twentieth century the development of visual technologies rendered the still image 'a conceptual impossibility' at a time when scientific research was proving all bodies to be in a state of relative rest and movement, and psychologists of perception were revealing 'constant muscular activity' in the eye and nervous system. If stillness was 'refuted as a property of the image, the object and the beholder', as Nead suggests, then one might ask what place it could have in movement practices of the period?[3] Through case studies of two European movement practices, this chapter explores the ways in which movement had the potential to encompass subtle scales of motion, including the manifestation of stillness in the body as a performance in its own right. As I suggest more widely in this book, the cultural potency of animation indicated not simply an attraction to speed, but rather to varied forms of motion and arrest – 'diverse velocities' – in Nead's useful phrase, which re-imagined the relationship between the 'static' and 'mobile' arts.[4]

This inquiry begins with the Margaret Morris Movement (MMM) established by the eponymous dancer in 1910, and explores her vision for a 'new and living form of dance' in creative partnership with the Scottish colourist painter and sculptor, J. D. Fergusson.[5] It examines the pair's contribution to the new 'kin-aesthetic modernism' of the early to mid-twentieth century, in which physiological aesthetics scrutinised bodily responses to art, and seemingly static corporeal forms became the object of intensified experiment and rhythmic animation amidst a proliferation of body movement and reform regimes.[6] The second part of the chapter pivots on an investigation of sculptural stillness. It explores 'eurythmy', a synthetic art form and system of movement known as 'moving sculpture', which was initiated by the Austrian scientist and philosopher, Rudolf Steiner in 1912.[7] We shall see that the tension between the static and the mobile in modern movement aesthetics was responsive to the idealisation of stillness as a condition in art reaching back to the eighteenth-century art historian Winckelmann's definition of 'stillness' as 'the state most appropriate to beauty'.[8] However, it was equally responsive to the ancient dream of movement expressed in the myth of the sculptor Pygmalion who falls in love with the beautiful statue he has carved, which Aphrodite eventually brings to life.[9] These impulses were, I suggest, further complicated and contested by emergent technologies of the image.

The creative paradoxes of stilled motion and moving stillness have had a long tradition in the history of dance. As Brigitte Peucker observes, 'dance itself suggests the complementary nature of movement and stasis; it defines motion as emerging from and returning to the "stillness of an ideal pose"'. The dynamic or 'Dionysian' aspect is 'tempered', by 'poses that derive from Apollonian – sculptural – form'.[10] One touchstone for this phenomenon in modernism is the 'still point' conceived by T. S. Eliot in his poem 'Burnt Norton': 'at the still point, there the dance is,/ But neither arrest nor movement'.[11] The Eliotic 'ecstasis' – an experience of stillness grounded in the body yet also generative of spiritual transcendence – is particularly suggestive to theorists of dance. André Lepecki draws directly on the 'non-fixed stillness' conjured by Eliot in order to situate the emergence of modern dance 'gradually along and within this restless stillness'.[12] According to Lepecki, stillness became radical in its re-envisioning, 'no longer as a threat, but as the very source of the dance'.[13] This chapter takes up Lepecki's notion of a 'restless, vibrating' stillness as a way of approaching the peculiar fascination with animate stillness, which I suggest was widely manifest in modern cultural practices, and in particular in Morris and Steiner's ideas of movement.[14] However, Eliot's seemingly paradoxical definition of dance – as 'neither arrest nor movement' – is also important in conjuring an idea of balance. Susan Jones observes that he 'equates the activity of dance with a finely poised equilibrium of physiological and intellectual states' that resemble the 'modernist sublime' which concerns his poetry.[15] A similar ideal for 'finely poised equilibrium' is significant to this discussion as we explore an inter-medial aesthetics of poise and balance in which rhythm and vibration enlarge the category of movement.

'Twin Plasticities'

Margaret Morris harnessed the paradox of moving stillness in dance by mobilising the visual arts in performances ranging from *tableaux vivant* and 'dance poems' to collaborations with photographers and filmmakers. I shall consider three defining areas of experiment during the first two decades of the MMM: first, the techniques by which Morris re-imagined the role of stillness and animation in performance; second, the ways in which these techniques were informed by contemporaneous aesthetic and philosophical ideas in which the loosely defined term 'rhythm' had widespread currency; and finally, the role of sculpture – both ancient and modern – as a touchstone in the staging of corporeal activity and passivity.

These strands of inquiry come into focus in the context of the inter-arts milieu Morris established at her theatre and club, which she founded in 1914 in the bohemian district of Chelsea, London, with Fergusson, who became Art Director of her dance school.[16] A constellation of artists frequented Morris's theatre in its early years, including the painter Augustus John, the Vorticists Jacob Epstein, Wyndham Lewis and Ezra Pound, and the theatre director Edward Gordon Craig, as well as Chelsea neighbours Katherine Mansfield and John Middleton Murry.[17] In 1919, the Arts League of Service recognised Morris's positioning of herself as a 'dancer of the future', by inviting her to give one of four inaugural lectures on the theme of 'Modern Tendencies in Art', alongside T. S. Eliot on poetry, the composer Eugene Goossens on music, and Wyndham Lewis on painting.[18] Morris's belief in the arts 'running together to make one complete work of art' was an aspiration shared by many in her circle, inflected by the influential notion of the *Gesamtkunstwerk*, or total work of art.[19] Many practitioners within the 'Chelsea Group'[20] who gathered at Morris's theatre envisaged theatre in fluid, synthetic terms and emphasised its pictorial qualities. Morris's neighbours, the co-founders of the Greenleaf Players, Maxwell Armfield and Constance Smedley, conceived of their performances as 'a series of pictures – moving pictures', referring to drama as 'a succession of sculptured groups'.[21] Grace Brockington observes that Smedley conceptualised movement as 'a gradient, incorporating stillness as well as dance', while Armfield, informed by his work as a painter, saw theatre as inhabiting a 'scale of movement between the kinetic essence of dance and the inanimate canvas'.[22] For Morris, graphic composition similarly provided a choreographic marker. She applied her understanding of pictorial construction gained from extensive painting practice to choreography, set and costume design, and included the study of modern developments in form, colour, design, music and literature in her school syllabus.[23] Goossens, who became closely involved with the Movement, testified that its practitioners harnessed the 'twin plasticities of paint and body movement' so that they were 'synonymous in theory and practice'.[24]

One framework through which we can examine Morris's pictorialist commitments and experimentation with the interplay between the static picture and moving image is the staged *tableau* or *tableaux vivants*. Situated on the threshold of sculpture, painting and drama, performances of *tableaux vivants* or 'living pictures' (as they were otherwise known), had been a popular pastime in the eighteenth and nineteenth centuries, and typically involved the imitation of painted pictures enacted through posed human bodies often arranged behind wooden frames.[25] Morris did not replicate specific paintings in her performances but she made implicit reference to Pre-Raphaelite art in a *tableau* from a 'dance poem' performed at her theatre in 1917, to Maurice Ravel's setting of 'Sainte' by the French symbolist poet, Stéphane Mallarmé. One photograph from the performance (figure 2.1) reveals Saint Cecilia, 'la sainte pâle' of Mallarmé's poem, with two angels attendant at her feet in a symmetrical composition that evokes the aestheticised religious devotion characteristic of Pre-Raphaelite paintings such as Dante Gabriel Rossetti's stylised group tableau *The Beloved* (1865–6), inspired by the biblical *Song of Solomon*, or the static staged quality of his *Girlhood of Mary Virgin* (1848–9).[26] Morris's tableau is responsive to the formal symmetry of the poem, which is set out in two pairings of verses contrasting the earthly and celestial. The instruments featured in Mallarmé's poem (viola, flute and mandore) are absent; instead, in Morris's musical reproduction, the poet's 'musicienne du silence' breaks her silent meditation and 'comes to life' in a form of dance ekphrasis.[27] The *Lady's Pictorial* periodical readily picked up on the pictorial reference, describing the performance as 'a sort of singing tableau as one might imagine it had [Dante Gabriel] Rossetti been a musician and a producer'.[28]

Throughout the 1920s, Morris held to her belief that '[a]nything presented on the stage is a *picture*, a picture in a very definite frame'; however, the new 'frames' and temporalities of photography offered possibilities beyond the conventions and limitations of the stage.[29] Photographs taken during the first decades of the Margaret Morris Movement by Fred Daniels (1892–1959), a

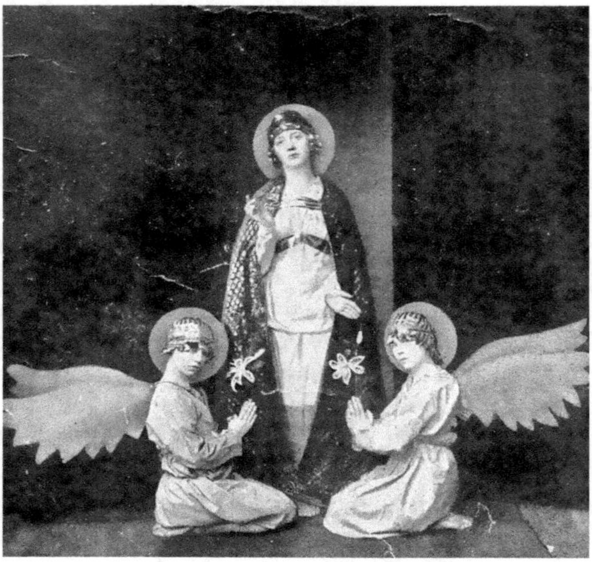

Figure 2.1 Margaret Morris Movement dancers performing 'Sainte'. Published in Reginald R. Buckley, 'Woman of Dreams and Deeds', *Lady's Pictorial*, 17 March 1917. Chelsea Miscellany (CM) 1759, Kensington Central Library. Reproduced with permission of Royal Borough of Kensington and Chelsea

pioneer of British still photography, offer an archive of group *tableaux* and individual poses as well as snapshot pictures and promotional stills, which 'freeze' Morris's otherwise ephemeral stage pictures. Forty of the most visually arresting of these images were published alongside Morris's writings on dance in *Margaret Morris Dancing* (1926). Daniels had studied painting and Morris commended his understanding of line, form and colour in her Preface, attributing the 'vitality' of his compositions to the 'harmony between the point of view of the painter and that of the dancer'.[30] Their collaboration is demonstrative of what the dance historian Judith Alter has described as a relationship of 'mutual support' between the developing arts of photography and modern dance.[31] Daniels' photograph titled *Hymn to the Sun* (figure 2.2) illustrates this collaborative approach: the dancers create a carefully balanced composition under the central archway, which inversely echoes the lines of the dancers' limbs. The sensuality of their bodies and potential for movement is thrown into relief by the rigid classical-style columns which punctuate the framed recesses.

The 'protracted stillness' demanded of participants in *tableau vivant* was, Nead writes, 'always an inevitable assertion of the desire for and possibility for movement'.[32] In Morris's case, if the body posed and aestheticised in 'living pictures' invited comparison with the arts of painting and photography, then her

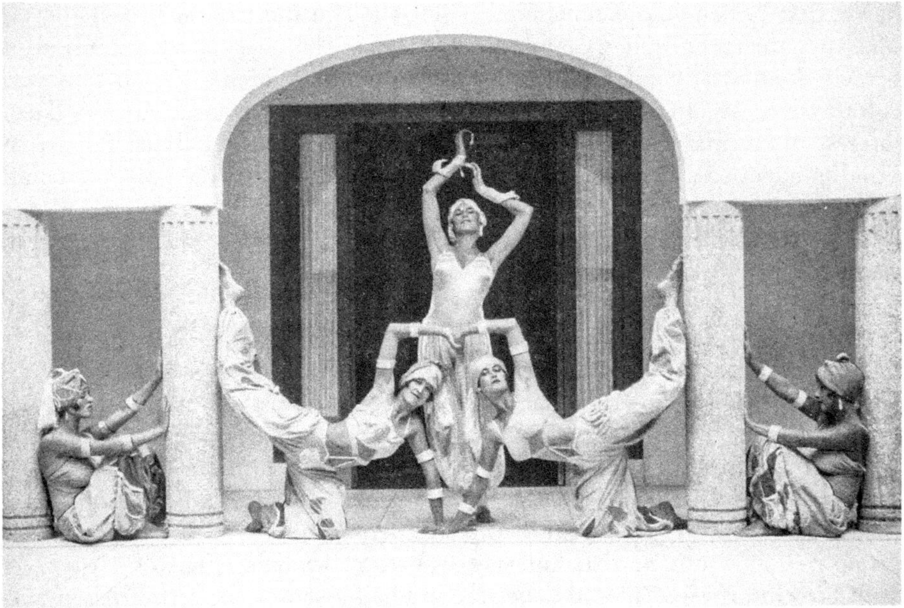

Figure 2.2 Fred Daniels, *Hymn to the Sun*, plate xxxii, in Margaret Morris and Fred Daniels, *Margaret Morris Dancing: A Book of Pictures* (London: Kegan Paul, 1926). Courtesy of The Fergusson Gallery, Perth & Kinross Council/ The Fred Daniels Estate

vision of 'pictures with the possibilities of actual movement added' also conjured a proto-cinematic conception of theatre. *Tableau* had lingering associations with the tastes of the previous century, but cinema transported it 'from the space of its immobility and permanence to the time where it appears and undergoes changes', as the film theoretician Ricciotto Canudo observed in 1911.[33] A short film produced in 1921 featuring Morris and her students dancing in woodland and on a beach in Northern France provides an example of the way in which modern dancers harnessed new technologies of the image.[34] The medium of film allowed even the subtlest motions of the body to be made visible to the viewer. Footage reveals Morris's characteristic exploitation of the tension between the static design of a composition and the potential mobility of the body, although here the emphasis is on metamorphosis. The dancers create a series of symmetrical tableaux organised around a central figure as if posed in a 'pregnant moment' before dissolving into new poses in a fluid sequence of compositions.

The process of realising a 'new and living form of dance' therefore involved positioning the Margaret Morris Movement at the vanguard of technological innovation. Morris's dancers featured in *The Dance of the Moods* (1924), one of the first British colour films made using the Natural Colour process developed by cinematographer Claude Friese-Green. This marked an extension of her vivid chromatic experiments in costume and set design. '[A]nd thus was colour born' declared the *Bystander*, while *Bioscope* affirmed Morris's 'keen interest in cinematography'.[35] The film's screening at the Holborn Empire in London included a live performance by the dancers so that the audience could judge the 'natural' colour quality of the same performance on film,[36] but it would also have emphasised the temporal interplay between the 'living' dancers and their virtual counterparts on screen.

Dance Poetry and 'the Sense of Rhythm'

Morris established rhythm as the basis of her technique in *Margaret Morris Dancing*, where she observes that movement is 'only another form of rhythm'.[37] We can trace her early appreciation for 'rhythm' as a shared quality across different art forms to the modernist magazine, *Rhythm: Art Music Literature*, which was founded in Paris in 1911 by John Middleton Murry with Fergusson acting as arts editor until 1912 (a year before it folded). The 'Rhythmists', as the loose group of contributing artists and writers became known, aligned their project with Post-Impressionism and Fauvism, and had a shared interest in the vitalist philosophy of the French philosopher, Henri Bergson, whose understanding of matter infused by a vital force or *élan vital* exerted a defining influence on their thought and aesthetics.[38]

The arrival of the Ballets Russes in Paris in 1909 played a pivotal role in the coalescence of the group around what Murry described as the indefinable yet 'potent' notion of 'rhythm'.[39] According to Murry, for Fergusson, the term represented 'the essential quality in a painting or sculpture' and 'dancing was obviously linked, by rhythm, with the plastic arts'.[40] In 1913, when Fergusson first introduced Morris to his circle during a visit to Paris with her dance group, it was the Ballets Russes that epitomised these synthetic ideals. Drawing together avant-garde figures across the arts, from Kandinsky and Matisse to Igor Stravinsky, the company were admired for their radical use of colour and movement on the stage – a 'wonderful combination', as Morris described it.[41] The Rhythmist painter, Anne Estelle Rice, identified their achievement in terms that Morris would later invoke in her writings on dance: they created 'life' and made the stage 'a living force', as in the ballet *Le Dieu Bleu*, a 'monumental animated painting'.[42]

The prominence of the theme of dance and the influence of the Ballets Russes has been noted in critical discussions of *Rhythm*, but the implications of its inter-medial Bergsonian aesthetic for modern British dancers such as Morris has not yet been fully explored.[43] As Lisa Tickner rightly points out, '[t]he impact of Diaghilev and the Ballets Russes has been allowed to eclipse the reputations of their contemporaries (many of them women)'.[44] I argue here that Morris conceptualised and promoted her movement practice as a vitalist expression, which was informed by (but not limited to) the influence of Bergsonian philosophy and the model of the Ballets Russes in her immediate circle.

Bergson's conception of an inner rhythm or *élan vital* underlying all life arguably provided a philosophical underpinning for Morris's aspiration to create a 'living art and a real expression of life'.[45] Governed by kinaesthetic awareness of the body's rhythmic life and of the creative tension – as well as the reciprocity – between movement and repose, and between control and free expression, her dance system valorised even the subtlest forms of corporeal animation. She insisted that her pupils learn 'to *feel* the rhythm of the movements' and 'to control the rhythmic contraction and relaxation of the muscles'. This physical register – a 'quick muscular response to all rhythmic forms, whether visual or aural' – was, she maintained, 'essential to the dancer'.[46]

By foregrounding the 'triangle' of rhythmic movement, colour and sound, in her practice and teaching, Morris developed what was arguably a Rhythmist-Fauvist aesthetic in dance.[47] From 1915 onwards, 'dance poems' represented one of the distinctive forms through which she put these principles into practice at her theatre. As the corporeal animation or choreographic translation of poetic texts into dancing, these 'new forms of dramatic work' opened up modes, as she later recognised, in which 'the idea or feeling of the word composition' could be suggested through rhythm rather than gesture. While the components of the visual design or picture (colour, form and line) remained fundamental, they also related to the semantics of a text, so that the dancers could become 'a manifestation of the word composition'.[48]

The art critic and former *Rhythm* contributor, Charles Marriott, testified to the realisation of these synthetic principles in a performance at Morris's theatre in 1917. Crucially, he notices that,

> the distinctions between hearing, seeing and feeling were fused in the sense of rhythm: which it seems to me, is the meaning of dancing. [. . .] In effect one did not hear the words [of the sung music] – one saw them or, better still, felt them by muscular sympathy. The performers did not merely 'illustrate' the words, they danced them.[49]

In Marriott's account, rhythm becomes the unifying element of the composition: it bridges different media and sense faculties so that even the immobile spectator experiences a sort of physiological animation of the text. Marriott's notion of 'muscular sympathy' chimes with Bergson's observations on dance spectatorship in his first book *Time and Free Will* (1889). In the case of performances accompanied by music, he writes that 'the regularity of the rhythm establishes a kind of communication' between the dancer and audience, and it is this feeling of rhythm taking 'complete possession', that produces 'a kind of physical sympathy' in the audience.[50] We recognise in Marriott's account an intuitive model for creativity derived from Bergson's philosophy, which was widely assimilated into the creative rhetoric as well as the performance practice of the artists in Morris's circle. As Smedley described, the shared aim of the Chelsea Little Theatres was 'the restoration of rhythm as the greatest force in art'.[51]

Morris's 'activation' of poetry through physical gesture and movement developed in close collaboration with other pioneers of dance poetry in the Chelsea Group. Her former pupils Hester Sainsbury and Kathleen Dillon became known as the 'Choric School' (formerly the Clarissa Club), along with modernist poet, John Rodker. Their synthetic compositions had affinities with contemporary poetry; as the art and theatre critic Huntly Carter observed, '[e]ach movement was a design as precise as Imagist verse'.[52] Situating their work within the interrelated history of dance and poetry, Ezra Pound wrote a Foreword to a special issue on the Choric School in the poetry magazine *Others* (October, 1915), which similarly expressed a sense of their potential in 'reanimating our verse'.[53] He described the 'curious breaks and pauses, the elaborate system of dots and dashes' by which they translated dance movement into verse.[54] 'The wind wakes up,/ the trees begin to sway,/ and the paper in the street below is blown in circle', begins one of Dillon's 'Poems for Dancing', published in the same issue.[55] The expression of awakening elemental forces suggests the kinetic as well as the visual potential of her verse and its translation into physical movement.

John Rodker offered an ekphrastic reconstruction of a 'cubist dance' produced by Dillon the following year. The performance may have taken place at the Margaret Morris Theatre, which Morris regularly lent to the Choric School since Dillon was her student and assistant. Rodker reported: 'First of all she painted a cubist backcloth. Then she made a cubist dress. Then she tried to transfer the two-dimensioned backcloth into the three dimensions of solid things by dancing out the design.'[56] Dillon was informed by Morris's principles of rhythm and colour derived from modern painting, but here she evidently attempted to reach beyond the aesthetic of the 'living picture' to embody and make mobile the typically flat, deconstructed designs of Cubist painting.[57]

Rodker repeatedly invoked a Bergsonian lexicon in his extended account of the Choric School, drawing attention to a 'conception of movement' which expressed 'pure rhythm – natural and instinctive rhythm', and in Dillon's case, 'spontaneity' and 'élan vital'.[58] Morris's contemporary, the dance historian Cyril Beaumont, defined her technique in a manner consonant with the Bergsonian model when he described it as 'pose in movement' in which '[e]ach pose begets another pose in harmonious sequence'.[59] In this kinaesthetic of transition, the 'immobile' and the 'mobile' function as complementaries and are even simultaneous within a rhythmic continuum. In reading her dance technique we might therefore look to the dialectic that informs Bergson's philosophy, between the static quality of the intellect and the dynamic quality of intuition. As Eiko Nakano points out, these 'apparently opposite factors' are understood as complementary 'rhythms': degrees of tension and relaxation which are 'inseparable in human consciousness'.[60] Morris's early dance teacher, Raymond Duncan (brother of the dancer Isadora Duncan), would have prepared her for the reception of Rhythmist ideas since he understood rhythm to be 'the common denominator of all matter, living and dead', and believed that '"rhythmic motion" connects all matter'.[61] *Rhythm*'s shorter-lived successor, the *Blue Review*, promoted a similar understanding. In the first issue of 1913, W. L. George described rhythm as 'a condition of internal movement within the inanimate, as a suggestion of expanding and retracting life, of phrases (musical, pictorial or literary)'.[62] Part of the appealing flexibility of the term in aesthetic discourses was therefore its capacity to accommodate barely perceptible degrees of movement and vitality across different art forms.

Susan Jones calls attention to the 'very specific reference to physical movement' in Bergson's *Time and Free Will*, which further illuminates the notion of rhythm as a marker for degrees of tension and relaxation. Constructing a metaphor for man's experience of time, Bergson writes: 'We are led to find a superior ease in the movements which can be foreseen, in the present attitudes in which future attitudes are pointed out and, as it were, prefigured.'[63] We can observe a similar phenomenon translated into dance script in a section from Morris's *The Notation of Movement* (1928) on 'Transition Signs', in which she presents the abstract symbol for a leg, or the hyphen-like dashed line or curve to indicate the shift into a subsequent pose in a choreographic sequence.[64] Her notation manifests Bergson's concept of a gesture containing or pointing toward future movement; or, as he alternatively describes it in *Creative Evolution*, 'a duration which is, as it were, a hyphen, a connecting link'.[65] Such examples reaffirm Morris's place in a transnational movement in modern dance, which has been described as Bergsonian in its aspiration 'to make the body into a conduit for such a structured, but nonetheless undivided, continuously flowing movement'.[66] Morris's system of notation aimed to include the 'writing of *all* human movement'; even 'ordinary standing or sitting postures' and almost imperceptible signs of movement such as facial movements, breathing and muscle contractions.[67] She was inscribing the subtlest forms of corporeal animation and kinaesthetic awareness into her movement system.

'Plastic Posing' and the Performativity of Sculpture

Sculpture claims a particularly apposite 'still point' in the middle of this chapter. Morris's interest in the territory of the almost-but-not-quite-still human body is also the territory of sculptural aesthetics and its implicit invitation to animation, to which we now turn. Her movement system intersected in unexpected ways with contemporaneous sculptural aesthetics in Britain, and the complexities of its engagement with stillness and movement. As I noted in the Introduction to this study, the dynamic co-existence of movement and stillness was central to the imagery and rhetoric of the artists known as the 'Vorticists', including Wyndham Lewis, Epstein and Gaudier-Brzeska, who frequented Morris's theatre in the pre- and wartime years.[68] The figure of the dancer – the embodiment of physical dynamism around an immobile axis or 'still point' – was an inspiration for Vorticist painting and sculpture, notably in Gaudier-Brzeska's *Red Stone Dancer* (1913) and Lewis's *Kermesse* (1912).[69] While flowing movement was promoted by the Margaret Morris Movement, the visual aesthetic fashioned in its early years also reveals the influence of Vorticism's hard-edged machine aesthetic. This is evident in the angular, geometric dance figures that characterised the Movement's promotional materials, such as the marching figure, modelled on Morris's pupil Penelope Spencer, set against a rotating vortex of planes (see figure 2.3).

The Vorticists' investment in what Lewis vigorously articulated as the aesthetics of the 'still point' and of 'immobile rhythm' suggests a point of departure from which to pursue the phenomenon of animate stillness in modern sculpture and dance.[70] Firstly, it is worth sketching out the broader context of debates on modern sculpture in this period. Critical narratives have largely asserted an

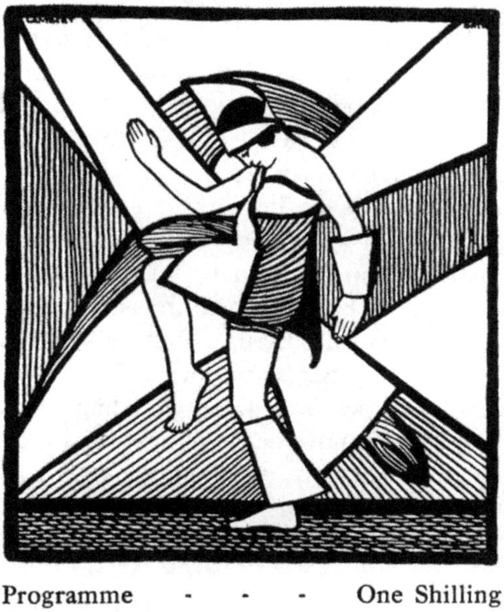

Figure 2.3 Margaret Morris Movement programme design, c. 1914–19. Courtesy of The Fergusson Gallery, Perth & Kinross Council, with permission of Margaret Morris Movement International Limited

opposition between direct carving and modelling; the former associated with modernism and the latter with the 'New Sculpture' of the nineteenth century. However, in an essay titled, 'How Direct Carving Stole the Idea of Modern British Sculpture', Penelope Curtis argues for a more 'plural modernism' in which sculptors such as Gaudier-Brzeska and Epstein, who are typically contextualised as Vorticist carvers, also promoted modelling techniques as 'a way of being modern'.[71] These sculptors extended the 'tradition of statuary' by exploiting the 'inherent potential dynamism' and 'inner tension' of the upright human figure.[72] In their work the statue becomes 'one of the possible forms of the modern'.[73] Curtis also questions the received correlation in sculptural discourses between the static effect produced by works created by direct carving, in contrast to the modelled works by European figurative sculptors who attempted to 'capture movement' so as to invest their sculpture with 'the sense of being held in suspense'.[74] If modern sculptors such as Gaudier-Brzeska were working in a hybridised practice in which they employed direct carving *and* modelling, as Curtis argues, then stillness and motion were consequently both within the purlieu of sculpture, and a transitional position between the two might in itself be a subject for sculptural representation.

Gaudier-Brzeska's slender modelled statuette, *The Dancer* (1913) (figure 2.4) exemplifies this tension for Curtis. It demonstrates an impression of potentiality and dynamism, which can be traced to the sculptor's fascination with Bergson's

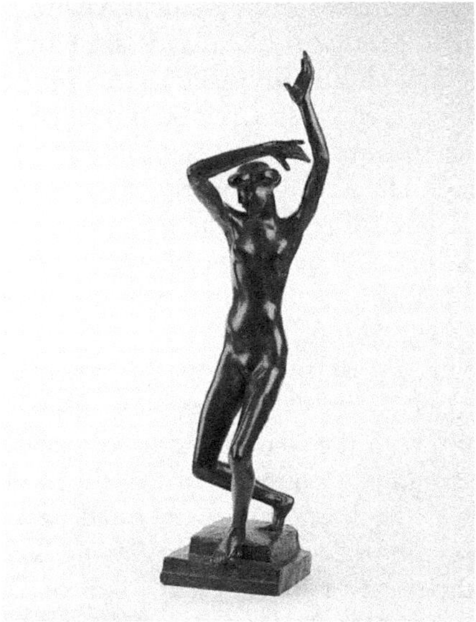

Figure 2.4 Henri Gaudier-Brzeska, *Dancer*, 1913 (posthumous cast, 1967, of the original plaster sculpture), 765 x 220 x 210 mm. Image: Kettle's Yard, Cambridge

theory of creative life-force.[75] Poised as if to descend into the viewer's space the figure's arms are raised in a graceful gesture above her head and her front foot rests lightly on the edge of the pedestal. In this liminal posture, *The Dancer* invites questions about the performativity of the sculptural encounter and the modernist potential of the statue, which also pertain to modern dance performance and specifically to the Margaret Morris Movement.

Drawing on what David Getsy has described as the 'performativity of the act of stillness' in relation to sculpture and the tradition of statuary, we can begin to trace Morris and Fergusson's recognition of a similar potential in their respective art forms.[76] The vogue for statue-posing in the nineteenth century had continued to shape dance experiments in the new century, and it has even been considered as the best representation of 'the modernist kinesthetic'.[77] The performance theorist Francois Delsarte promoted statue-posing and poetic recitation in what became an influential international movement known as Delsartism, 'a philosophy and technique of movement emphasizing a tension between stasis and motion, poses of classical beauty, framed cinematic compositions and speeding bodies', which Carrie J. Preston suggests exerted a largely unrecognised influence on modernist dance.[78] While Morris did not acknowledge direct engagement with Delsartism, it forms part of the broader cultural context in which we can read her sculptural poses and the exploitation of the tension between stasis and motion that characterises her kinaesthetic. The photographic archive of Margaret Morris Movement dancers from the 1920s demonstrates Morris's deployment of the body as a malleable, pliable medium aligned with the plastic arts: an art of 'plastic posing', as Goossens defined it.[79] In photographs such as *Sculpturesque* (figure 2.5), the posed body is explicitly presented as an embodiment of poise and equilibrium, which takes its reference from sculpture. *Sculpturesque* captures a moment of taut suspension between stasis and exuberant motion as a group of dancers circulate around the axis of a tree. In the medium of black and white photography, the dancers' bodies acquire a stone-like quality and in this example the interplay of shadow and light contributes to the 'effect of great sculptural solidity' alluded to in the caption.[80]

Morris's signature solo pose features as the opening image – titled *Poise* (figure 2.6) – in *Margaret Morris Dancing*. It is illustrative of her desire to convey aesthetic affinity with the spatial and ontological liminality of statuary but also the 'internal dynamism' characteristic of the modern statue. Her entire torso and head are thrust back into an exaggerated back bend while her arms strike out in oppositional horizontals and her left leg is raised high so that her whole body weight appears to balance on the ball of one foot. Her costume flows in a circular stream in counter-current to her raised leg, reinforcing the sense of a dynamic, even defiant pose. It exemplifies the emphasis on balance in her dance education system, what one of her leading teachers, Eleanor Elder,

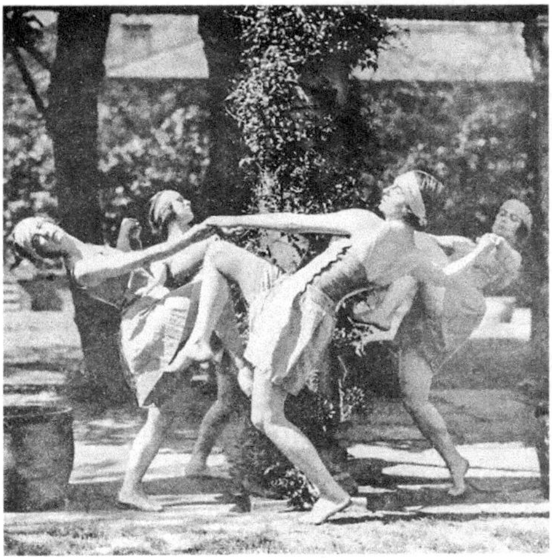

Figure 2.5 Fred Daniels, *Sculpturesque*, plate XI, in Margaret Morris and Fred Daniels, *Margaret Morris Dancing: A Book of Pictures* (London: Kegan Paul, 1926). With the permission of The Fred Daniels Estate. Courtesy of The Fergusson Gallery, Perth & Kinross Council

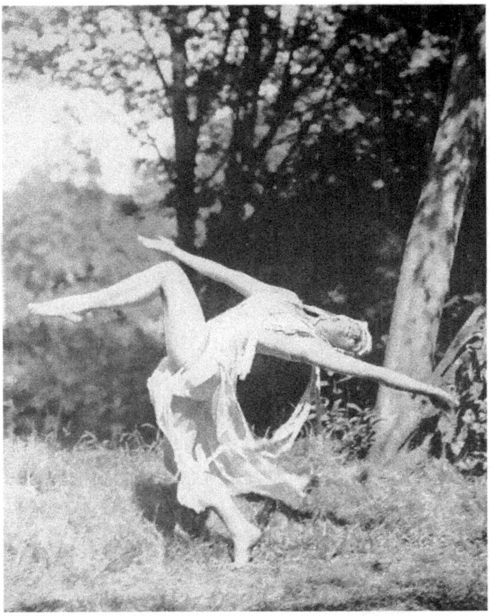

Figure 2.6 Fred Daniels, *Poise*, plate I, in Margaret Morris and Fred Daniels, *Margaret Morris Dancing: A Book of Pictures* (London: Kegan Paul, 1926). With permission of The Fred Daniels Estate. Courtesy of The Fergusson Gallery, Perth & Kinross Council

described as 'the poise of the tight-rope dancer, relaxed, yet alert and confident' which 'brings with it a joy of life'.[81] Simultaneously ecstatic and strenuous, Morris's pose could also serve as a visual emblem for the 'perfection of poise' aspired to by her dancer contemporary, Ruby Ginner: 'Poise is the finest point of balance it is possible to attain, both mentally and physically. [. . .] poise lifts the whole being to a point so delicate that it almost defies definition [. . .] the coordinated mind rises to the same point of serene equilibrium.'[82] The image titled *Poise* functions both as an attempt to align Morris's aesthetic with nature (she poses against a leafy, bucolic background), and also to underscore technological innovation: the photograph's caption informs us that it was 'taken from beneath the tripod of a cinema camera, during the filming of this dance'. The effect of suspension in the posture is of course intensified by the frozen temporality of the film still, which arrests the dancer in what Ginner calls 'that second in infinity when action ceases and there is rest', or Eliot's 'still point'.[83]

Poise was part of a new vocabulary in transatlantic physiological aesthetics that brought kinaesthetic awareness and visual skills into contact. As Robin Veder has noted in the context of American body cultures, its meaning carried over between posture lessons and modern art criticism, making it a 'translation between communities' and 'an exclusive code'.[84] The translation of 'poise' into sculpture can be demonstrated in Fergusson's sculpture of a sideways-inclining female nude, for which *Standing Female Nude (Poise)* (c. 1920) is believed to be a brass cast of the untraced original. It represents one of a series of modestly sized sculptures of stylised, firm-bodied female forms, which he made during the peak of his sculptural activity from 1918–22. Principally known as a painter, he experimented with modelling and direct carving over a period of fifty years, exemplifying the hybrid technique described by Curtis, and exhibiting alongside modern sculptors Jacob Epstein and Frank Dobson in 1925.[85]

Morris and her dancers frequently posed as models for Fergusson, and affinities with her repertoire of postures can be identified in two of his small figurines made c. 1920, *Dancing Nude: Effulgence* and *Female Dancer* (figure 2.7). *Dancing Nude* was cast in shining polished brass expressive of its 'effulgence'; it portrays the supple form of a dancer in a crouched posture reminiscent of Morris's pose in a photograph titled *Sunshine* (published in an article in *Sketch* in 1925), in which she adopts a sensual, theatrical posture of ecstatic receptivity with her arms stretched toward the sky, as if the body has become a channel for what she called 'the power of the sun for health'.[86] *Female Dancer* – a sculpture which was unusually made to be viewed from above, giving full display to its flexed limbs and accentuated plasticity – also has affinities with a pose demonstrated by Morris in a photograph taken on the sands at Harlech in Wales by Vorticist photographer and mystic Alvin Langdon Coburn. In an image from his 'photographic essay' of 1919 documenting Morris and her dancers, her body is framed in a recess in the sand, creating an effect reminiscent of sculptural

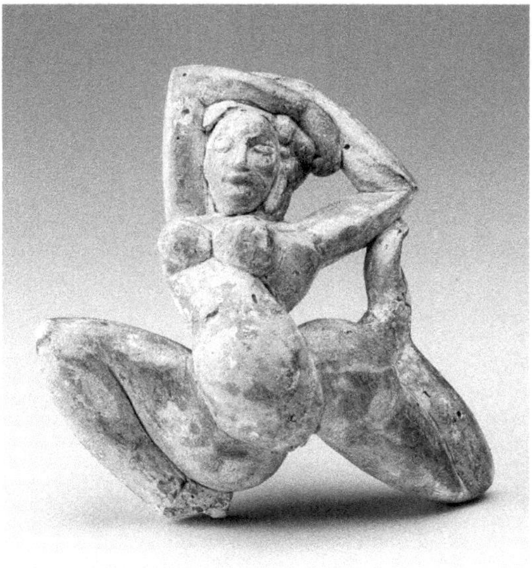

Figure 2.7 J. D. Fergusson, *Female Dancer*, c. 1920. Courtesy of The Fergusson Gallery, Perth & Kinross Council

relief.[87] A few years previously, Coburn had contributed a new visual mode to Vorticism by experimenting with a kaleidoscopic attachment to his camera lens to produce abstract images known as 'vortographs', with a fractured dynamism akin to Vorticist painting. The image of Morris is emphatically static and less experimental in approach, but the angularity of her pose and sharp contrast of shadow and light align it with Coburn's radical technique in his vortographs. On the one hand imbricated in the new rhythms engendered by technologies of photography and film, she was also invested in ways of living and making art that would reconnect the human form with nature.

Trees: A 'Living' Model

The annual Margaret Morris Movement 'Summer Schools of Dancing and Art', which took place from 1917 onwards, mostly in coastal destinations across the UK, Belgium and France, presented opportunities for Morris and Fergusson to experiment with an organic metamorphosis of statuary and statue posing in their respective practices. Natural phenomena, and trees in particular, provided a 'living' model for the interplay of rhythmic movement and fixed form in the body. Fergusson's wooden sculptures, *Dryad* (1924) and *Oak Rhythm* (1925, figure 2.8), are inflected by the idiom of 'primitive' art yet evidently rooted in the dance life and physique of the Margaret Morris Movement. The elongated trunk-body of *Dryad* strains upward with upstretched arms creating a sleek,

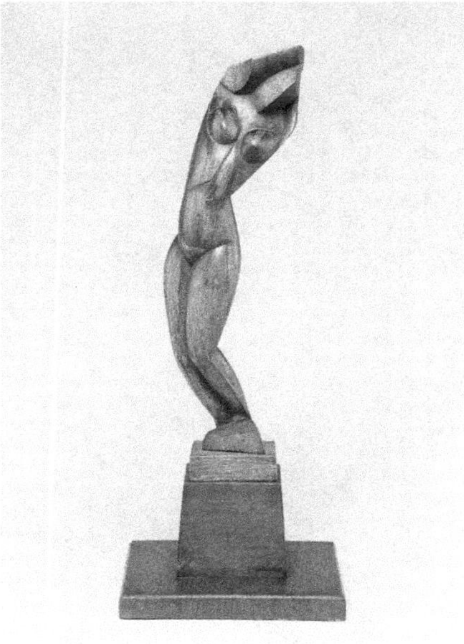

Figure 2.8 J. D. Fergusson, *Oak Rhythm*, 1925, wood, 425 x 127 x 76 mm, Tate. Presented by the Friends of the Tate Gallery, 1964. With permission of The Fergusson Gallery, Perth & Kinross Council. Photo: © Tate, London 2019

taught vertical, while *Oak Rhythm* (1925, figure 2.8) twists sideways with bent knees as if gathering momentum to spring into dance. Exhibiting these works in 1928 at the Lefevre Galleries in London, Fergusson prefaced the catalogue with an extract from the biologist Julian Huxley. Huxley speculates that 'matter is not material', and highlights contemporary scientific investigations including the 'wave-theory of matter', which might precipitate an alternative conception of reality shaped by 'local deformations and vibrations'.[88]

By framing the reception of his work in terms that are on the one hand consonant with modern science and on the other with the 'activation' of materials associated with direct carving, Fergusson encouraged the viewer to experience a 'living' sculptural encounter. Morris gave a similarly vitalist account of *Oak Rhythm*, reporting that Fergusson perceived 'movement and rhythm' in a piece of oak found at Cap d'Antibes (the location of several summer schools), and the figure '"*grew*" out of the form of the wood'; it represented 'the soul of the oak'.[89] Fergusson's essay 'Art and Atavism: the Dryad' (1944) affirms a similar myth of numinous encounter, relating how 'stand[ing] still' and contemplating a tree while staying at Cap d'Antibes led him to apprehend something 'strange' and 'mysterious' beyond its external reality and a sense of it being 'so full of time', which would inform the making of his sculpture.[90]

The desire to cultivate what Fergusson described as 'sympathy' with trees in the midst of a 'mechanical age' can also be located in Morris's embodied practice.[91] A photographic still from *Dryad* (figure 2.9), a dance performed in a garden at Morris's summer school in Brittany, presents the dancer's body as a visual echo of the curved line of the tree trunk and affirms correspondences with Fergusson's wooden sculptures, in particular the slanted form of *Oak Rhythm*.[92] Morris celebrated nature in near pantheistic terms – as 'full of rhythm and life' and even 'spiritual benefit'[93] – and in her practice she sought to emulate 'the life and grace of trees', as one caption to an image of the dancer posing in woodland reminds us.[94] *Palm Tree Rhythm* (figure 2.10) demonstrates what she described as 'harmony of rhythm', as a group of dancers translate the 'internal dynamism' of a large palm tree (instead of a statue) into a rhythmic choreography of reiterated standing 'tree' poses, adapted from *vrksasana* in yoga.[95] The use of natural phenomena, here and in many of Morris's outdoor 'dance pictures', marks an extension of her practice beyond the proscenium arch of conventional theatre – a realisation of 'still life' on and off the stage. It can also be seen as part of the 'return to nature' impulse

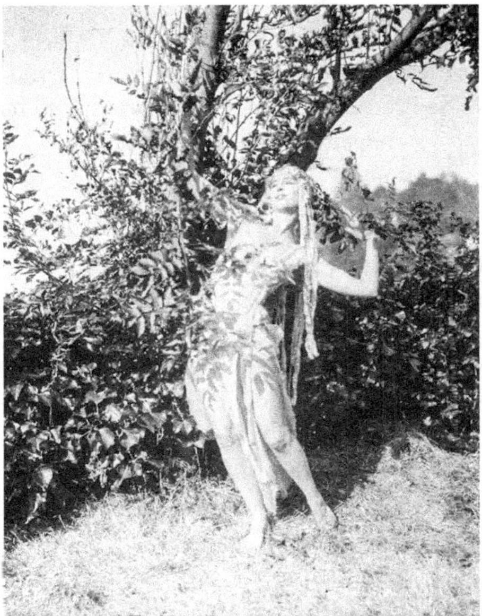

Figure 2.9 Fred Daniels, *Dryad*, plate XXVI, in Margaret Morris and Fred Daniels, *Margaret Morris Dancing: A Book of Pictures* (London: Kegan Paul, 1926). With permission of The Fred Daniels Estate. Courtesy of The Fergusson Gallery, Perth & Kinross Council

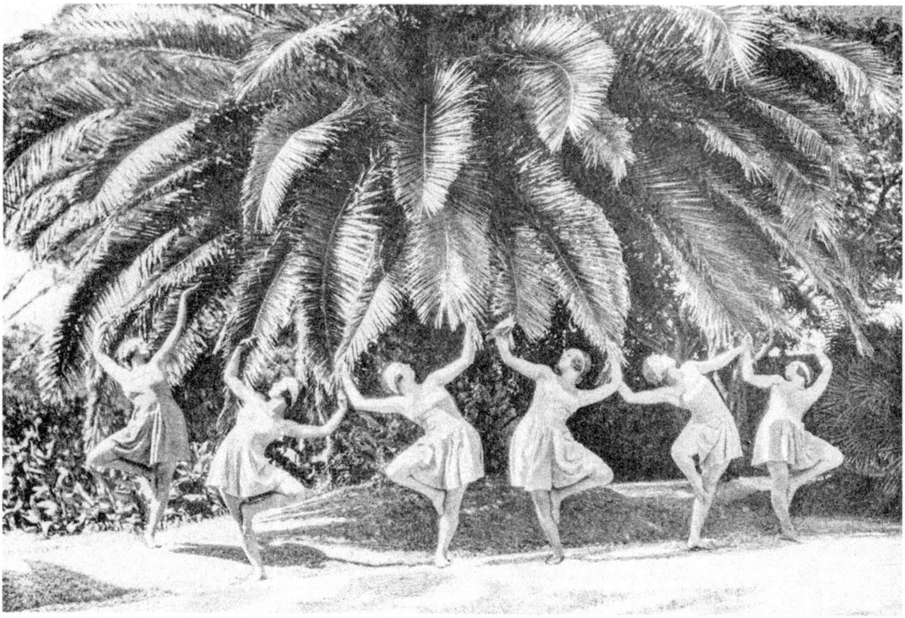

Figure 2.10 Fred Daniels, *Palm Tree Rhythm*, plate XXIII, in Margaret Morris and Fred Daniels, *Margaret Morris Dancing: A Book of Pictures* (London: Kegan Paul, 1926). With permission of The Fred Daniels Estate. Courtesy of The Fergusson Gallery, Perth & Kinross Council

widely apparent in modern dance aesthetics. As J. E. Crawford Flitch commented in 1912, dancers drew on nature's 'multitudinous minor rhythms, each various and distinguishable, merging into a grand rhythm of the whole, the eternal rhythm of life itself'.[96]

If the body was the locus for Morris's communion with the natural world it also provided a paradigm of 'active stillness' that departed from Fergusson's aesthetics. Fergusson's paintings of Morris typically re-imagine her physique as voluptuous and statuesque, exemplified in *In the Patio: Margaret Morris Fergusson* (1925) (plate 6) in which the dancer presides with sculptural immobility over a still life of flowers and fruits, as if she shares the stony insentience of her surroundings.[97] We also note the somewhat laboured eroticism in the placing of the round fruits directly in front of the subject's breasts. Fergusson's pictorial idiom was dominated by stylised representations of women, and he has been charged with rendering his subjects 'impassive and inert, all individuality and capacity for action suppressed', as Sheila McGregor describes it.[98] Nevertheless, Fergusson's posed women do exude power and his nude sculptures in particular convey a muscular tautness and robust vitality, which have more affinity with Morris's aesthetic even if they do not depict her body 'in motion'.

There is a complexity to the gender dynamics of such encounters, which is amplified by the perceived femininity of dance. On the one hand, Morris's belief that art should be based 'on health and excess of vitality' implicitly endorsed the assertion made by *Rhythm*'s first art editor, Michael Sadler, that a work of art 'must be strong, must be alive, and must be rhythmical'.[99] However, Morris sought to achieve this by re-working the 'gendered theory of creativity' advanced by the Rhythmists, in which the female form provided the 'pictorial language' for *élan vital* yet women were believed to have less artistic capacity than men.[100] Morris can be situated in the context of an 'alternative feminist narrative of fertility' which Miranda Hickman has identified in the work of the painter Jessica Dismorr, another contributor to *Rhythm* and subsequently a Vorticist, who represented women as the 'source of aggressive dynamic action'.[101] However, the visual apparatus of the Margaret Morris Movement has a slightly different inflection. As we have seen, Morris promoted the power and strength of held postures and meditative repose as integral (not oppositional) to movement. She shared a sense of the significance of stillness in her practice with the pioneering modern dancer Isadora Duncan. 'For hours I would stand quite still', Duncan recorded, 'my two hands folded between my breasts, covering the solar plexus', in order to discover 'the central spring of all movement'.[102] This idea calls to mind ideas about the *chakra* or energy points in the body and the practice of active stillness in yoga derived from 'Eastern' spirituality, which we will return to. Morris's dance postures did not render her dancers passive or overtly eroticised; rather, they express the 'vital stillness' and 'rhythmic repose always on the edge of action', that Sadler acclaimed in the work of Anne Estelle Rice.[103] In sympathy with several women contemporaries, then, her practice destabilises the ideal of the procreative but immobile female body in a dynamic counterpoint – even a challenge – to the masculine Rhythmist imagination. Similarly, if we return to the sculptural encounter and to Getsy's reading of a 'theater of power relations between active viewers and passive statues', then the dancer's posed body suggests a potential conduit between the active and the passive, which complicates the terms of the 'still' and the 'moving' and the power politics of these encounters.[104]

'Like a Greek Vase Come to Life'

For Morris a fundamental paradigm for the 'greater tranquillity and harmony of rhythm' she sought in her practice could be found in the art of ancient Greece.[105] The vogue for 'Revived Greek Dance' and a wider attraction toward Hellenism flourished in Britain during the late nineteenth and early twentieth centuries.[106] The reinstatement of the Olympic Games in 1896 prompted a 'preoccupation with a Greek ideal of the body', while major archaeological excavations illuminated the ancient history of the region and its artefacts.[107] The dynamic between the reposeful stillness seen to characterise Greek art and the liveliness of its representations of movement presented a peculiar attraction to choreographers. Isadora Duncan is widely recognised as the 'Founding Mother of Greek Dance',[108] but her brother Raymond exerted a formative influence on Morris when he taught her his 'simple and natural technique' in 1909 at the outset of her career.[109] Duncan's repertoire was based on six classical dance positions derived from his studies of depictions of movement in Greek sculpture and ceramics at the British Museum. In a lecture on 'Dance and Gymnastics' (1914), he described the apotheosis of his studies after years of making sketches from Greek vases: 'the day when I had before my eyes a vision of all the movements of these vases synthesized in one single great cinematographic movement. Then I had the vision of ancient Greece in motion.'[110] Duncan's animate vision of ancient Greece – his perception of 'cinematographic movement' – would have influenced Morris's vision of dance as a series of pictures with the movements 'added'.

Classical revival dance sought to unlock kinetic potential in antique forms, or what the film theorist Laura Mulvey has described as the cinematic potential and 'suspended animation' of Greek sculptures: the way they 'convey movement in stillness, images of life in inanimate stone'.[111] To claim the power of the 'pregnant moment' in another medium is a reflex widely noted in ekphrastic literature, but in a sense it also informs the project of classical revival dancers. Ruby Ginner, the founder of the London based 'The Grecian Dancers', asserted the necessity of discovering the 'movements preceding and following this momentary capture by the artist's brush or chisel' in her careful studies of sculpture at the British Museum.[112] She was concerned that technological distractions such as the 'flickering' cinematograph could occlude the 'beauty in the stillness of great hills or sculptured marbles', and she encouraged her students to recover the power of 'repose' in Greek art and to re-adjust the body to its 'centre of gravity' by focusing on the 'stillness and the pauses of Nature'.[113]

In fiction of the period we find endorsement (as well as contestation) of these qualities, which had long been identified with classical sculpture and validated in a tradition of responsive close-looking founded in the eighteenth century by Winckelmann, the leading proponent of neoclassical Hellenism, who argued that the 'repeated contemplation' of a beautiful statue could result in the soul becoming 'more still and the eye more quieter'.[114] When Morris made her first connections with Fergusson and his circle in 1913, their friend John Middleton Murry was writing his novel *Still Life* (published in 1916), in which one of the protagonists, Mrs Craddock, attributes the 'quieting' quality she experiences in front of the Parthenon Marbles at the British Museum to 'a mysterious potency' within them – a quality that another character identifies as 'harmony in the soul'.[115] The continuing attraction of modern artists and dancers to such qualities belies Louise Hornby's suggestion that 'modernism's irksome stillness bears little resemblance to earlier neoclassical associations of stillness with beauty and repose' (although 'irksome' is a good way of describing it).[116] Moreover, the unsettling nature of stillness already lurked at the heart of earlier associations. At the root of Winckelmann's ideal figure was in fact, as Alex Potts has argued, 'a very complex reading' of its formal purity, 'in which a deathly stillness mingles with eruptions of desire and violent conflict'.[117]

Morris's 'Hellenic' dance compositions of the 1920s were avowedly less reverent and historicist than the reconstructions of her contemporaries, as she believed that dance 'must be capable of expressing the ideas and emotions of the twentieth century'.[118] She incorporated the Hellenic frieze into choreography and designs that exploited the tension between the static and the mobile, the harmonious and the irregular. 'A Greek Vase Comes to Life', announced *Eve: the Lady's Pictorial* in August 1921, with an adjoining image of Morris's dancers posing in a classical frieze; and the same month her 'naiads' acquired a double-spread in *Sketch* at the summer school in Normandy, dubbed 'Chelsea-by-the-Sea'. Two years later the same periodical identified in her dancers a sign of 'rhythm in a new form' as they posed in flattened 'living friezes' on a beach in Belgium.

Nevertheless, during and in the aftermath of the First World War there was a renewed cultural urgency in seeking classical models of harmony and equilibrium. Classical revival dancers drew from Graeco-Roman art and architecture to advocate what Ana Carden Coyne describes as the performance of 'peace and sensual harmony' in contrast to the 'masculinity of war'.[119] Morris contributed to this effort when she opened her summer schools to convalescent soldiers during the war and created a technique combining 'Greek' poses and yoga to re-mobilise traumatised bodies.[120] The poignant reciprocity between mobility and stasis that this represented complicates the catchphrase of another British Classical revival dancer, Mary Bagot Stack, who claimed 'Movement is life. Stillness is the attribute of death.'[121] For Morris, the cultivation of stillness in the body could signify positive, progressive ideals linked to social harmony. Her summer schools became alternative sites for the performance of 'positive peace', a form of pacifism that Brockington has shown to have thrived at Morris's Chelsea theatre.[122] Taking classical sculpture as her model was therefore not to aspire to a condition of fixity, but rather to stir 'new and living' rhythms in antique forms: a 'living form of dance for the present and future'.[123]

'Eastern Rhythm'

If Morris achieved 'rhythm in a new form', it was by imagining the performative possibilities of the sculptural body in a hybrid appropriation, which synthesised elements from Hellenic and 'Eastern' art and statuary. Murry's inaugural editorial for *Rhythm* had stated that modernism 'disengages the rhythms that lie at the heart of things, rhythms strange to the eye, unaccustomed to the ear, primitive harmonies of the world'.[124] Like many early twentieth-century artists, Fergusson and Morris were attracted to what they saw as the 'primitive harmonies' of ancient Indian and Cambodian sculptures. Morris acknowledged that many positions in her technique were derived from making close studies of dancing figures from these cultures in the collections of the Trocadéro ethnographic museum in Paris.[125] In one photograph relating to *Le Chant Hindu*, a ballet she produced with Fergusson in 1915, she presents herself as an embodied interpretation of the title, *Eastern Rhythm*, by posing in 'harem'-style costume in a semi-ecstatic posture with closed eyes.[126]

That Morris wanted to position her art of movement in relation to ancient statuary and to stage a relationship between 'Eastern' spirituality and modern dance is exemplified further in a series of unpublished photographs taken during the 1920s, in which she poses next to a votive figure elevated on a pedestal (figure 2.11). Her reverential postures establish a connection with the figure's imperturbable deific expression and centred pose, but by facing toward the spectator she invites a sense of spectacle. Morris's reworking of aesthetic and spiritual rhythms from 'Eastern' art into a new dance vocabulary can be situated within the context of the revived interest in Eastern culture, mysticism and a plethora

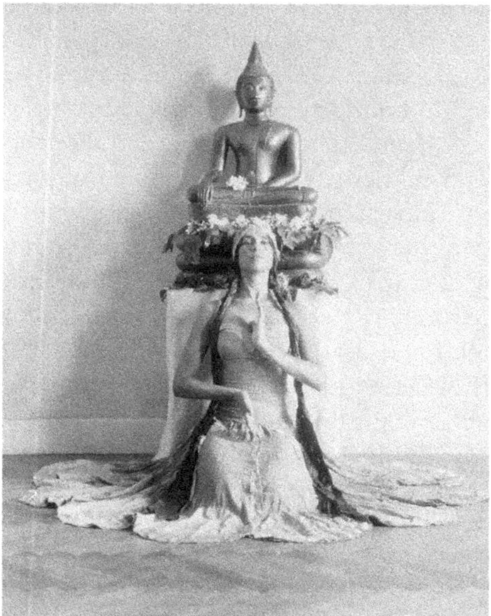

Figure 2.11 Margaret Morris photographed with a statue, c. 1920, unknown photographer (possibly Fred Daniels), Margaret Morris Collection, with permission of the Margaret Morris Movement International Limited. Courtesy of The Fergusson Gallery, Perth & Kinross Council

of unorthodox spiritual teachings during the late nineteenth and early twentieth centuries. Along with many in her close circle, she belonged to the Theosophical Society, which sought to bring together evolutionary science and ancient spiritual wisdom and derived much of its doctrine from Indian mysticism.[127] Hatha yoga, in which the cultivation of 'inner stillness' is fundamental, was popularised in the West during this period and Morris records its 'profound influence' and her integration of its meditative postures into her technique.[128]

Theosophical teachings seem to have infused her dance philosophy, in particular the profound significance placed on cosmic rhythm and vibration, and the notion that thoughts, emotions and even states of the soul could be expressed through corresponding colours and forms.[129] In an article for *Theosophist Magazine* in 1918, the theosophist and MMM teacher Eleanor Elder compared Morris's central directive that a 'definite design' should be traced on stage 'in harmony' with music and movement even if it is 'unseen' or unrealised by the audience, with the theosophical notion of 'thought-forms'.[130] Theosophists argued that 'each definite thought produces a double effect – a radiating vibration and a floating form'.[131] There are strong evocations of this idea in the example Elder gives of 'definite design': Morris's arrangement of a dance to the music of 'The Water Lily' by the American composer Edward MacDowell. The lotus, a symbol of divine beauty in the Eastern traditions and a plant only partly visible as it floats on water, would have been suggestive to Elder in her preoccupation with the seen and unseen. She records how the dancer's arm movements described the petals of a flower and the rippling water, while 'the feet were tracing unseen the shape of a lily lying on a leaf'.[132]

For some spectators in Morris's audience, the dramatic power of celebrated productions such as *The Golden Idol* (1915) (figure 2.12), a solo dance set to music by the French composer, Maurice Debussy, would have derived from a sense of contact with the primal, 'spiritual' potency of votive statues. Morris wore a stylised 'Eastern' costume of golden tissue with a headdress and began the performance by embodying the 'golden idol' in an immobile position reminiscent of Hindu and Buddhist meditation postures. She then gradually unfolded her body through a series of gestures similar to those captured in her and Fergusson's studies of Indian and Cambodian sculptures. Charles Marriott's review of *The Golden Idol* evokes the effect of animate statuary, noting the dancer's 'extreme subtlety and refinement of movements' and observing that the 'static performance' constituted 'what the living picture is to drama'.[133]

If Gaudier-Brzeska's *Dancer* had established an aesthetic encounter that gestured with one pointed foot beyond the conventional space of sculpture, then Morris's *Golden Idol* re-appropriated modes of sculptural display to perform the entire dance within the restricted stage of the pedestal. '[L]imitation of space', she would later write, 'is to the dancer as the canvas to the painter.'[134] The pedestal represented a spatially constrained platform, which would challenge

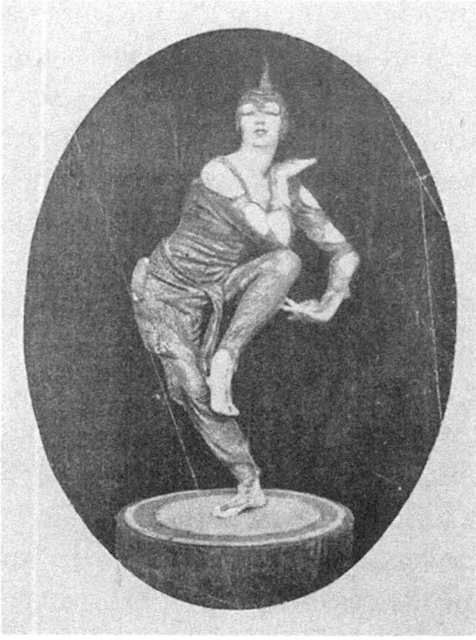

Figure 2.12 Margaret Morris photographed in 'The Golden Idol' (1915), copy of photograph by unknown photographer in the Margaret Morris Collection. With permission of the Margaret Morris Movement International Limited. Courtesy of The Fergusson Gallery, Perth & Kinross Council

the dancer's 'poise' and accentuate her sculptural, three-dimensional aesthetic. Her performance can be seen in the light of the reworking of oriental motifs in the figurines and statuettes that were products of the 'New Sculpture' movement. It invites comparison, for instance, with Edward Onslow Ford's statuette *Applause* (1893) which depicts an Egyptian-style nude clad in a stylised 'eastern' costume, rising clapping from a raised pedestal as if to begin a dance.[135] Morris's production speaks to the reassessment of sculpture's intervention in public and private spheres and to an activating encounter, which was also fundamental to the New Sculpture.[136] By re-imagining the functions of statuary and making sculpture 'dance', she developed a kinaesthetic of moving stillness, which implicitly questioned the perceived boundaries, gender associations and conditions of the arts.

'A Fundamentally New Art': Eurythmy and its Origins

It is one thing to experiment with animating statues in the long tradition stretching back to Pygmalion, but it is another to re-imagine the human body itself as 'sculpture in motion'. Known formally as 'eurythmy', 'sculpture in motion' emerged contemporaneously with the Margaret Morris Movement in 1912, when Rudolf Steiner inaugurated a 'new art of movement in space' which he intended would answer the 'spiritual' impulses of modern man.[137]

He explained that by immersing oneself in 'man's inner life' and following his 'inner mobility', that is by 'entering into his thinking, feeling and willing – into all that can find expression through speech and song – we can create "sculpture in motion"'.[138] Steiner's conception for his movement practice complicates the notion of sculptural stasis by default. While sculptural stillness remains central to the inquiry, in the final sections of this chapter I would like to suggest that eurythmy represents a radical departure from conventional (if contested) definitions of sculpture, and inclines toward an animating, synthetic practice, shaped by spiritually inflected ideas about colour, rhythm and vibration. By tracing the early development of the art form through to the mid-1920s, we can further address the implications of 'mobilising' sculpture through the living body.[139]

The introduction of eurythmy into Britain uncovers unexpected interrelations between the Margaret Morris Movement, theosophical circles and the development of 'dance poetry'. Earlier we saw that theosophy was part of the background to Morris's dance practice; in the ensuing discussion, we will see that Steiner's vision of 'sculpture in motion' was strongly underpinned by his conviction about the spiritual significance of eurythmy and its place in a larger cosmology. From 1902–13 he acted as General Secretary for the German Branch of the Theosophical Society; however, following differences of opinion with members of the Society's 'inner circle' and his concern that it neglected artistic interests, he went on to found Anthroposophy ('anthro' meaning man; 'sophia' meaning wisdom).[140] Christianity was at the centre of his 'anthroposophical science of the spirit', which sought reconciliation between religion, art and science. Encouraged by the Scottish anthroposophist D. N. Dunlop, his closest British colleague, Steiner introduced eurythmy to the attendees of the 'International Summer School of Spiritual Science' held in Penmaenmawr, Wales in 1923. This was followed by further performances in London, and subsequently a small theatre dedicated to eurythmy was built in London's Baker Street.[141] However, we can draw parallels between new experiments in poetry and movement a decade earlier. Crispian Villeneuve notes the roughly coterminous introduction of eurythmy to Steiner's first pupil, Lory Maier-Smits, and the Theosophical Society's International Summer School in Devon in 1912, at which Eleanor Elder (who became Morris's pupil and later taught at her school) performed a dance poem.[142] An account of the summer school reports that Elder accompanied a poet's recital of 'The Dance of Life' with a 'symbolic dance' in which she 'represented "Life"'.[143] It concludes that 'the novelty of dancing to poetry instead of to music' was very well received and 'it is hoped that a repetition will take place in London'.[144] Given the experimentation with 'dance poems' that took place at Morris's Chelsea theatre in the years that followed, this reveals the interweaving of aesthetic, cultural and social connections that underwrite the phenomenon of hybrid movement practices and rhythmic experiments in the early twentieth century.[145] While crucial differences in their practice will become apparent, Steiner and Morris were part of the same pan-European network and in different ways they endeavoured to embody and mobilise the poetic word, and to create new rhythmic forms.[146] Furthermore, as we will see later, eurythmy develops the idea of 'dance poetry' into what Steiner conceived of as 'visible speech'.[147]

The etymology of the term 'eurythmy' complements Steiner's vision of 'sculpture in motion'. 'Eurythmy' derives from a combination of the Greek root *eu*, meaning well-being or beautiful, and 'rhythm', with its multiple significations across different disciplines. The term was employed from the eighteenth to the nineteenth centuries to describe harmonious proportions in architecture, and more widely indicated 'rhythmical order or movement' and 'a graceful proportion and carriage of the body'.[148] This (neo)classical aesthetic suggests the idealised human form portrayed in classical sculpture. Ancient Greek sculpture represents a paradigm for the ideals of harmony and proportion that Steiner invoked in his lectures and writings on eurythmy and sought in its practice.

Eurythmy developed at a moment when, as we have seen, rhythm was at the heart of transnational cultural discourses. According to Michael Cowan, the many associations of 'rhythmus' in German and European culture included 'communal participation, ritual renewal and a connection with nature and the body seemingly lost to modern technological civilization'.[149] In *The Rhythm of Life: Character Building as an Aid to Health* (1907), the theosophist Archibald Keightley addressed 'the rhythm problem', expressing concern for the large numbers of sufferers from 'physical, nervous or mental instability'.[150] Such concerns intensified in the 1920s when Steiner's wife, Marie, acknowledging this desire for slower, 'natural' rhythms to re-balance the velocity of modern life, described the motivation of eurythmy 'to turn our nerves back to earlier states'.[151] Nevertheless, Steiner's own discourses on eurythmy were not 'anti-modern' in tone; like Morris, he positioned his 'fundamentally new' art form as addressing the physiological, mental and spiritual demands of the modern man or woman. By examining Steiner's rhythmic art as a performative attempt to generate not only physical, aesthetic, but also 'spiritual' renewal we can, I suggest, extend Cowan's argument for rhythm as a vehicle of cultural reform and renewal during the early twentieth century.

For the contemporary eurythmist Marjorie Spock, rhythm is understood as 'the interplay between the two opposite poles of contraction and expansion', which are interdependent.[152] Eurythmy was conceived as a 'third, mediating, harmonizing force, acting as a power of balance', which could 'relate these two poles' since in every aspect, 'the life-pulse – a subtle rhythm between the moving and the still – shows itself primal'.[153] What Spock identifies as eurythmy's cultivation of 'subtle rhythm', or 'life-pulse', enabled Steiner's movement practice to realign the borders between stillness and motion, and to synthesise elements of poetry, music, body movement and sculpture within a flexible rhythmic spectrum.

'Moving Sculpture'

In his lecture 'Eurythmy is a Moving Sculpture', which prefaced a recital in Dornach, Switzerland in 1923, Steiner made a direct response to Gotthold Lessing's understanding of 'the limits of the plastic arts'.[154] Following Lessing's characterisation of sculpture as a medium that, in his paraphrase, 'manifests itself as silence, as stillness in the human being', Steiner describes the art form as pertaining to the silent human being 'speaking through his quiescent form'.[155] Here he seems to be continuing a long tradition in thinking about sculpture and the classical ideal for the human body. If we turn back to Getsy's work on statuary and sculpture we find 'the struggle with animation and movement' as the 'central theme' in its history and theory.[156] Steiner similarly delineates sculptural history in terms of its stillness, yet its trajectory is toward animation. He argues that while sculptural representations of the 'human being in a state of rest' were appropriate to earlier epochs (namely the period from ancient Greece to the Renaissance), the importance of the 'will element' in the modern era calls for an attendant shift toward 'the human being in movement' and a 'feeling that form must become fluid'.[157] Furthermore, he proposes that it is impossible to reach an understanding of the human form unless one is aware 'that every motionless form in the human being has meaning only because it is able to pass over into definite movement', or, as he concluded the following year, 'all form in human beings is striving perpetually to become movement'.[158] This statement might appear to privilege a modernist infatuation with motion, but Steiner's endorsement is more complicated in its accommodation of stillness.

Steiner presents the human hand as an illustration of the paradoxical condition of stillness and movement in several introductions to eurythmy performances. 'Even in its motionless state the form of the hand is such as to demand movement', he suggests, and on another occasion he describes how the 'outstretched hand already has within it, in embryo, the pointing hand, the beckoning hand'.[159] We recall a similar logic in Bergson's observations of gesture and the prefiguration of movement perceived by the spectator of dance. There are significant parallels between the two philosophers. Hilary L. Flink draws comparisons between Bergson's desire to unite intellect and intuition as 'interdependent partners in the search for meaning', and Steiner's sense of intuition as the 'third and highest mode of cognition by means of which spiritual reality might be apprehended'.[160] However, Steiner felt there were limitations to Bergson's philosophy: for him the intuition of movement within stillness was the impulse of inner 'spiritual mobility' and could be developed as an organ of spiritual perception.[161]

If the Bergsonian dialectic between the static and the mobile was central to the artistic philosophy of Morris's circle, as well as to the Rhythmist group, Steiner's conception of eurythmy projects this dynamic further, onto the plane of the soul. What he calls the 'spiritual mobility' of the art form[162] is arguably reciprocal with, and even emergent from, the 'discipline' of 'inner stillness', to which he frequently alluded as essential for the development of consciousness and spiritual perception.[163] Steiner's writings on 'spiritual science' often refer to meditative exercises, and one lecture on 'Supersensible Knowledge' (1923) describes the 'negative state' of 'super-stillness' and 'super-quietness' through which one can reach an 'inner stillness of soul', which is at its most intensified during 'the state of wakefulness'.[164] Eurythmy's alliance with 'sculptural stillness' should therefore be situated within this meditative landscape of spiritual thinking and practice.

The relevance of spiritual 'still life' for artistic expression comes into focus in Steiner's lecture on 'The Supersensible Origin of the Arts' (1920). Here, he claims that '[e]urythmy shapes and moves the human organism in a way that furnishes direct external proof of our participation in the supersensory world'.[165] It operates in multiple dimensions simultaneously, as Steiner emphasised in his preface to a recital in the same year, eurythmic gestures affect 'the body, soul and spirit'.[166] This sense of mobility between the 'physical' and the 'spiritual' finds an analogy in the transition between the 'material' and 'ephemeral' art forms: between sculpture and dance. For Steiner, the eurythmic gesture enacted a sort of spiritualisation of the sculptural (but human) body. Pursuing these aesthetic implications further, he described eurythmy as 'an ensouled and spiritualised form of gymnastics', in which the ladder of selves could 'work harmoniously together'.[167]

The roots of Steiner's vitalism can be found in his profound and formative engagement with the work of Goethe, whose scientific writings he edited in 1883–97.[168] In Goethe's 'world of ideas' he recognised the ascension from 'a science of the lifeless' to a 'certain cognition of life', which he aimed to extend through 'spiritual' perception.[169] The Goethean principle of organic metamorphosis and understanding of matter as animate provided the basis for his conception of eurythmy as 'an expression of a Goethean artistic attitude'.[170] In a continuous lineage 'arising naturally out of sculpture' it represented the organic unfolding of artistic development in accordance with the evolution of man.[171] However, as Steiner makes clear in this lecture and elsewhere, this notion of evolution does not necessarily indicate hierarchy or competition: eurythmy simply aspires to its 'rightful position as a younger sister-art'.[172]

Steiner presents an evocative picture of this metamorphic process in the context of the museum of sculpture. From the mid-nineteenth century sculptural encounters increasingly took place in the context of the public museum or 'haunted gallery' as Nead describes it, where the question of stillness and movement was particularly charged. By exercising 'inner vision' cultivated through 'spiritual knowledge', Steiner claimed that the modern visitor could 'see these figures descend from their stands, move about the room [. . .] becoming on all sides filled with movement'.[173] Eurythmy, or 'moving sculpture', was therefore a direct expression of the irresistible 'urge' to 'bring movement' and 'fluidity' into the 'frozen human form'.[174] Not unlike Morris's conception of dance as a 'living art', Steiner envisaged 'living sculpture' as the expression of life-force in its most intimate contact with creation. It could impart 'the feeling of how the universal cosmic life laid hold of the human being'.[175] In the process of establishing these principles, Steiner encouraged his first pupil, Lory Maier-Smits, to make close studies of Greek sculpture and temple dances (although not to imitate them). In her memoirs forty years later, Maier-Smits described her visceral response:

> In the face of this godly beauty – stillness and yet flowing movement were expressed in it – I felt my own body in a new way. There lit up in me a feeling of permitted, god-intended, being-at-home in my own body. [. . .] I felt like a plant which had been standing wilted and limp in the heat [. . .] which now was watered and could fill itself with new life.[176]

The physically transformative experience recorded in these meditations upon sculpture, and the feeling of an unmediated transmission, resonates with Steiner's vision for the practice of eurythmy.[177] Maier-Smits appears to have harnessed this inner vitality in her premiere eurythmic performance given in July 1913 at the summer drama festival of the Theosophical Society in Munich. Drawing on a similar fusion of organic and Hellenic imagery, Margarita Woloschin, a fellow dancer at the event, compared her to a 'Greek *kore* [sculpture]', and observed 'something in her movements like a bud – something physical held back, etherically radiating out into space'. She was like a 'young priestess [. . .] Apollonian and radiant'.[178] The religiosity of language in these aesthetic responses to sculpture – direct in the case of the performer, and mediated in the case of her audience – speaks to a tradition of writing about contemplating classical sculpture as transportative and transcendent but also corporeally affective. Perhaps the most famous illustration is Winckelmann's rapturous ekphrastic description of the Apollo Belvedere in which he feels himself physically transported: his chest 'expand[s] with veneration' and he compares the experience to that of Pygmalion as his image of the statue 'seems to take on life and movement'.[179]

Getsy identifies the 'dream of the moving statue' with its roots in the Pygmalion myth of animation as the 'structuring trope of the aesthetics of sculpture'.[180] In a sense eurythmy – as 'moving sculpture' – can be seen as part of this tradition. However, the view of sculpture as passive or lacking in life, and the 'presumption of stillness' that Getsy detects underlying its discourses through history, finds a more nuanced consideration in Steiner's vision. As we have seen, the intuitive responsiveness conveyed in Maier-Smits' account demonstrates that the sculptural encounter does not by definition preclude movement and can involve vitalising interaction. She appears to have transmitted to her body the plant-like revivification and radiating stillness that she experienced when looking at Greek sculpture. This impulse is subtly different from Pygmalion's because it is participatory. Eurythmy in fact exemplifies Getsy's description of 'the condition of sculptural representation' as 'boundary-less in its physical proximity and real tactility'. We can read it as a radical and performative mode of sculptural encounter in which the viewer's body participates in sculpture's 'corporeal relationality' to the point of metamorphosis.[181] The human body becomes a 'living' sculpture in its own right.

The human form was at the centre of Steiner's vision of visual art; it represented an enlivened 'still point' or nexus between oppositional forces. His lecture on 'Anthroposophy and the Visual Arts' describes 'two poles', one represented by 'the very ancient plastic art' and the other by 'the newly created art of Eurythmy'.[182] He invites us to consider plastic art as a synthesis of the 'wide universe' as it flows together 'in the human form (which is, for the cosmos, a point)'. Eurythmy, on the other hand, expresses the 'human inner life', which 'in darting, oscillating movements, would give rhythmic expression to what has been "compressed" to a point'.[183] Steiner defines this vibrational current in other writings on eurythmy, as the 'flowing-out of forces' of the 'etheric body'.[184] The 'etheric' is essentially rhythmic, he explains, and although it 'dwells' in the physical body it also extends beyond it.[185] Woloschin draws on this idea when she describes Maier-Smits as 'etherically radiating out into space'. The outflowing rhythmic oscillations of the eurythmist were understood to resonate harmoniously with cosmic or spiritual vibrations.

This process can be situated within a broader understanding of reality as essentially vibrating energy, which was shared by contemporaneous artists and occultists alike. We have already encountered Kandinsky, who was influenced by theosophical and anthroposophical ideas, and whose conception of vibratory transmission between the souls of artist and auditor extended to dance.[186] Other contemporary practitioners placed vibration at the centre of their movement theory and practice: Rudolf von Laban understood vibrations as a mode of transmission between dancers and audience, while for his student Mary Wigman, vibration or 'vibrato' itself became a form of movement.[187] Lucia Ruprecht situates both figures in the context of a 'new gestural imaginary' in German movement practices of the period in which the aesthetic of gestural flow promoted by Laban and Wigman mirrored the vitalist belief in 'transhistorical continuities between human and cosmic energy, between the "gestures" of the world and those of the dancer'.[188] She argues that 'the vibrato of a Wigman dancer became part of her gestural idiom', which related 'not to an urge to *see*, but to *sense* more'.[189] In Chapter 1, we saw that embodied quivering – or vibration – could signal heightened sensation in aesthetic experience and responsive looking could be read through body language. In Steiner's work, we find the gestural as the expression of 'inner life' and the workings of a spiritual sense faculty registered in the language of the body.

Returning to Steiner's sense of the relationship between sculpture and eurythmy, we recognise that the two modes of artistic expression were understood as responsive to one another on a vibrational force field. Spock goes as far as to suggest that eurythmy can transcend and reconcile the relationship 'across the threshold that divides the "still" arts from the moving'.[190] The dual spatial-temporal implications of stillness are fundamental here. T. S. Eliot's paradoxical notion – '[i]n the stillness, there the dance is' – provides the backbone for Spock's assertion that eurythmy, while an art of movement, must 'take particular and conscious care to nourish that movement on enlivening stillness'.[191] The 'creative pause' or 'outward coming-to-rest' is essential in eurythmic practice, for it signifies 'the liveliest moment in a rhythm'.[192] This is exemplified in one of the fundamental rhythmic forms in eurythmic choreography: the lemniscate or figure of eight. In the practice of this figure, 'the signature of life', 'both pauses coincide in space [. . .] at the crossing point between the two "spheres of action"'.[193] Steiner seems to gesture toward this pattern in his vision of statues that 'move about the room and meet each other'.[194] In order to convey what Spock calls 'the living breath' expressed by various manifestations of this pattern, the eurythmist must 'live intensively' in the pause 'as the very heart of rhythm'.[195] Thus, the pause becomes symbolic of the 'still life' or 'still point', which is at the very heart of movement.

Steiner's emphasis on the active correlation between cosmic space and the human being – eurythmy's re-presentation of ethereal vibrations as physical gestures – opens up questions about the relationship between internal and external space. Markus Brüderlin and Ulrike Groos allude to something similar in their exhibition catalogue *Rudolf Steiner and Contemporary Art* (Kunstmuseum, 2010), in which they suggest that eurythmy invokes the sculptural principle of 'eversion' (the process of turning inside-out) to 'fluidise' the conventional separation between these fields.[196] This dynamic also manifested itself in the relationship between the art of eurythmy and the space in which it was first performed: the Goetheanum in Dornach, Switzerland. The Goetheanum was a double-domed wooden building, which Steiner intended would evoke a work of 'living' sculpture. It provided a stage orientated toward the new art of movement when it opened in 1920, before the building burnt down two years later. The architecture of the building was said to have coincided with the 'artistic impulse' for eurythmy since work began on the building in 1913, the year after Steiner had introduced eurythmy to his first pupil.[197] Conveying an animate architecture of organic, continuous forms, Steiner intended that the viewer should feel 'a very natural relationship between the moving eurythmists and the stationary forms of the internal architecture and sculpture'. Aspiring toward a total work of art, 'the building and eurythmic movement were meant to grow into one'.[198]

The Danish painter and sculptor Arild Rosenkrantz (1870–1964), who witnessed performances at the Goetheanum and contributed to its decoration, called attention to the peculiar mode of walking practised by eurythmists, a 'slow, stately rhythm' which prompted him to think of the art of ancient Greece: 'It is as if one of the majestic scenes upon a frieze or vase had come to life before us. There is a definite relation in the way the feet meet and leave the ground; a curious lingering, gliding movement.'[199] Rosenkrantz's account evokes the animation of Hellenic depictions of frozen movement, which became a trope in European movement practices of the period. However, his description registers eurythmy's aspiration toward a dematerialised form of movement, one that signalled the spiritual.

'Hidden Eurythmy': Vibration and 'Visible Speech'

The close relationship between stillness and silence in the art of still life came to our attention in Chapter 1. We can now re-invoke these qualities to consider the ways in which eurythmy translates analogies between silence as rest or pause, and speech as movement, into the realm of performance. Steiner draws attention to these correspondences when he states that 'our customary motionless sculpture portrays the silent human soul in all its stillness', whereas a soul 'that is surging and struggling to speak can only be portrayed by bringing the living human form into movement'.[200] Eurythmy seems to express what he viewed as the evolutionary arc from the expression of the silent human being in sculpture, to the performance of speech – the 'cosmic Word' – in gestural movement.[201] From this perspective, we might consider Steiner's 'moving sculpture' within a long ekphrastic tradition which coveted but also sought to unsettle the stillness and quiet equilibrium of the static arts.[202] In 'Movement: The Speech of the Soul' (1924), he declared that eurythmy 'speaks in a definite language of forms', employing the human being as an 'instrument' to produce 'visible song' or, alternatively, 'visible speech'.[203] I would suggest, then, that it represented not only 'moving sculpture' but also 'speaking sculpture': it performed the literal Greek sense of *ekphrasis* as 'speaking out'.

In the same lecture, Steiner made the proposition that 'a kind of hidden eurythmy is already there' in the words of a 'true poet'.[204] He considered speech a sort of immaterial sculpture, which could be rendered visible (and mobile) through the gestures of eurythmy. The 'imaginative, sculpted, coloured use of words' and 'the sculptural principle' in poetry were important stimuli in the development of eurythmy.[205] Steiner encouraged Maier-Smits to immerse herself in the rhythms of ancient Greek poetry, instigating twofold exercises such as the 'peace' and 'energy dance', based on ancient Greek ritual.[206] At the culmination of her training, she performed a pair of poems by Goethe, which illustrate the characteristic alternation between energy and calm, fluidity and stasis, in eurythmy performances. The first poem, 'Ocean Stillness (*Meeresstille*)', evokes the elemental calm alluded to in its title, providing the eurythmist with an opportunity to 'perform' stillness or 'the depiction of a state of trance [. . .] a state which occurs entirely within the soul'.[207] Since it was a representation of an 'inner state', the poem was to be performed with 'vowels only'.[208] The complex relationship between vowels and consonants, which Steiner details in several discourses, governed his sense of the way in which poetic language should be realised in gesture. He described vowel sounds as expressive of the 'inner soul-life of the human being', while the consonant 'paints' external things and gives 'plastic form to what is to be expressed'.[209] This attentiveness to the interplay in language between its plasticity or materiality, and its less tangible quality as a series of signs, inflects the hybridity of eurythmy.

The physiological process through which eurythmy attempted to unfix the frozen forms of speech is also significant here, because it resonates with the cosmic vibrational conception of artistic expression outlined earlier. Steiner explained how in audible speech the 'underlying principles of movement [created internally in the larynx] are arrested as they arise and are transformed into finer vibratory movements', which are carried on air as sound.[210] Eurythmy operates on a similar principle, but the inner vibrations are carried through into external movements by an individual or group to produce 'a living larynx in movement'.[211] The whole body becomes the animating instrument through which speech is released from its arrested form. Furthermore, Steiner implied that a purer form of expression could succeed the referential relationship between word and gesture that occurred in performances of eurythmy accompanied by a poetic recital. His vision for an 'unaccompanied language of Eurythmy' is consonant with a characteristically modernist emphasis on form rather than content. He claimed that the 'plastic-figurative, or musical element' in poetry is where its 'real artistic value' lies, thereby revealing the trajectory of eurythmy's development toward a more purified or abstract expression.[212]

'Living Colour' in Eurythmy Performance

The experience of what Steiner called 'living colour', as opposed to the reductionist view of colour as 'vibrations of the ether', played an enlivening role in his vision for 'living sculpture'.[213] As early as 1914 he observed, 'if you colour a figure you vivify it directly with soul'. The moment a 'restful' 'stationary' form receives colour 'the inner movement of the colour stands out [. . .] and the whirl of spirituality permeates it'.[214] Characteristically, Steiner had taken Goethe's influential, anti-Newtonian theory of colour and optics as a starting point for his investigations into the 'spiritual' perception of colour.[215] 'Colour descends into the surfaces of physical objects', he explained in one of three lectures on the subject in May 1921, 'but it also raises us from the purely material and leads us to the spiritual'.[216]

These perceptions would inform Steiner's sense of the chromatic element in the sculptural shape of eurythmy as it developed in the 1920s. 'Language is truly poetic only in so far as it is used musically, sculpturally, or only in so far as it is filled with colour', he wrote in 1923.[217] In performance, coloured costumes were chosen to reflect the mood of the poem translated into eurythmic gesture, while performers manipulated coloured veils to create subtle circulations of colour around their bodies and to express the 'shades of feeling' in the spoken words.[218] As Rosenkrantz observed of one performance, the 'play of colour seems to have a very definite relationship to the poem which is being recited'.[219] 'Moving sculpture' could therefore be reconceived chromatically through this flowing use of colour, unfixed from matter, which was also crucial in dictating the rhythm, pace and dynamics of a performance.[220] Drawing on Steiner's discourses on the subject, Spock explains that '"Active" colours, will-orientated, move swiftly, vehemently', while '"passive" colours [move] slowly and reflectively'.[221] We experience, for instance, '[t]he stillness of green, the so-called "neutral" colour', which has 'a resting quality that is experienced as harmonious and peaceful'.[222]

Steiner's 'eurythmy figures' initially consisted of a series of pencil sketches of the human form and served as a basic visual index for the metaphysical dimensions on which he claimed that eurythmy could operate, as well as illustrating how chromatics governed the tempo of a performance. Later the figures were carved and coloured in two-dimensional wooden models, each representing a fundamental eurythmic gesture and giving indications on the corresponding use of colour to reflect 'the movement, expressed in the fundamental colour', 'the feeling nuance, expressed by the second colour', and thirdly the 'element of will'.[223] The subtlest expressions of embodied stillness and movement could be directed through the language of colour since the third colour signified the specific area of the body in which the eurythmist should create muscular tension. Steiner noted that even a 'slight contraction' could set 'the tone for the inner character as a whole' as it 'radiates throughout the organism' and is transmitted to the spectator.[224] An area shaded in a particular colour could therefore register the intention for a movement or gesture to 'radiate' beyond the physical form.

The chromatic impact of 'moving sculpture' is revealed in Rosenkrantz's account of productions at the Goetheanum, in which he celebrates the 'vivifying' effects of stage lighting: 'an ever-changing flood of coloured light' in which 'the figures appear like glowing fire-flies', changing to 'greenish-grey embers of light, and then they become bright and dazzling like rubies and sapphires'.[225] It was Steiner's intention that 'the images produced by the movement of people' on stage could be harmonised and continued by the effects of light and colour.[226] Here colour contributes a vibratory element to this synthetic work of art which evokes the painterly as well as the sculptural, underlining eurythmy's contribution to the cultural ideal of the *gesamtkunstwerk*.[227] As Neil Anderson has suggested, 'what was prescient in [contemporaneous European figures such as Gordon] Craig' and his example of total theatre, 'becomes a complete cosmology in Steiner'.[228] The goal of eurythmy, as Rosenkrantz encapsulates it, was to 'make visible as a stage picture *all* the elements which create the true essence of poetry'.[229]

Rosenkrantz's pictorial analogy brings us back to the 'animate pictures' and dance poems we encountered in Morris's movement practice. Through the different examples of 'active' and 'restless' stillness presented in this chapter we have seen that a peculiarly mobile form of 'still life' played a formative role in shaping the arts of movement developed by Morris, Steiner and their associated networks. 'Still life in motion' came to epitomise the modern. The embodiment of still life generated forms of animate stillness and a subtle spectrum of rhythmic movement, underpinned by a web of philosophical and spiritual associations, and informed by the impulse to reveal 'inner life' across different art forms. Whether through enlivening encounters with ancient sources, or through the cultivation of 'poise' and the 'creative pause', these different movement practices demonstrated modes by which 'still life' could be reconceived in corporeal forms, on stage and in daily life. In different ways, then, Steiner and Morris realised the 'dream' of animate painting and 'moving sculpture'.

Notes

1. Margaret Morris and Fred Daniels, *Margaret Morris Dancing: A Book of Pictures* (London: Kegan Paul, 1926), p. 76. (Hereafter abbreviated to MMD.)
2. Margaret Morris, 'Dancing as an Art', *Art and Letters*, October 1917, repr. in Bev Trewhitt and Jim Hastie, ed., *Margaret Morris 1891–1980, Modern Dance Pioneer: A Resource Pack for Teachers and Students of Dance History* (Biggin Hill: International Association of Margaret Morris Movement, 1997), p. 18.
3. Lynda Nead, *The Haunted Gallery: Painting, Photography, Film c.1900* (New Haven: Yale University Press, 2007), pp. 1, 12, 18.
4. Ibid., p. 17.
5. Morris employs the phrase in various formulations across her writings; the citation here is from MMD, p. 85.
6. Robin Veder uses 'kin-aesthetic modernism' to refer to the 'shared strategies and sensibilities' of body cultures and physiological aesthetics, in *The Living Line: Modern Art and the Economy of Energy* (Hanover: Dartmouth College Press, 2015), p. 3. For further discussion of physiological aesthetics see Robert Michael Brain, *The Pulse of Modernism: Physiological Aesthetics in Fin-de-Siècle Europe* (Washington DC: University of Washington Press, 2015), and Michael Cowan, *Technology's Pulse: Essays on Rhythm in German Modernism* (London: Institute of Germanic & Romance Studies, University of London, 2012).

7. Steiner, 'Eurythmy is a Moving Sculpture', p. 271. This translation and others on which I draw in this chapter are based on recorded texts, which were mostly unrevised by Steiner and therefore some errors in transcription must be taken into account.
8. Johann Joachim Winckelmann, *History of the Art of Antiquity*, trans. Harry Francis Mallgrave (Los Angeles: Getty Publications, 2006), p. 204.
9. On the Pygmalion myth see Victor Stoichita, *The Pygmalion Effect: From Ovid to Hitchcock*, trans. A. Anderson (Chicago: Chicago University Press, 2009). For a broad survey of the tendency to treat art works as living beings, see Caroline van Eck, *Art, Agency and Living Presence: From the Animated Image to the Excessive Object* (Boston: De Gruyter, 2015).
10. Brigitte Peucker, *The Material Image: Art and the Real in Film* (Stanford: Stanford University Press, 2007), p. 62.
11. Eliot, *Four Quartets*, p. 173.
12. André Lepecki, 'Still: On the Vibratile Microscopy of Dance', in Gabriele Brandstetter and Hortensia Volckers, eds, *Remembering the Body* (Ostfildern-Ruit: Hatje Cantz, 2000), pp. 334–64 (p. 336).
13. Ibid., p. 338.
14. Accounts of early twentieth-century dance in modernist studies have tended to foreground figures including Isadora Duncan, Louie Fuller, the Ballets Russes and Émile Jaques-Dalcroze. My focus on inter-disciplinary artists who have not yet been fully integrated into genealogies of modernism responds to Kirsten Shepherd-Barr's invitation to examine 'cross-cultural interactions' and the 'richly interdisciplinary nature of modernist theatrical performance'. 'Modernism and Theatrical Performance', *Modernist Cultures*, 1 (2009), 59–68 (pp. 64–5).
15. Susan Jones, '"At the still point": T. S. Eliot, Dance, and Modernism', *Dance Research Journal*, 41 (2009), 31–51 (pp. 31–2).
16. For a detailed account see Margaret Morris, *My Life in Movement* (London: Peter Owen, 1969), p. 68 (hereafter, *MLM*).
17. Margaret Morris, *The Art of J. D. Fergusson: A Biased Biography* (Glasgow: Blackie, 1974), p. 102. For a history of Morris's intersections with other avant-garde dancers, Hélène Vanel and Loïs Hutton, see Richard Emerson, *Rhythm and Colour* (Edinburgh: Golden Hare, 2018).
18. Margaret Morris, 'The Training and Technique of the Dancer of the Future', *Vogue*, July 1923, 19–20.
19. MMD, p. 82. The term was first adopted by the composer Richard Wagner in his essay on 'The Artwork of the Future' (1849) to describe the synthesis of all the arts in theatre, but it was taken up by diverse figures from Kandinsky to Gordon Craig.
20. Brockington's useful term, in *Above the Battlefield*, p. 18. Brockington gives an insightful portrait of the Chelsea artists in the context of the formation of the peace movement in Britain, see esp. pp. 155–211. See also the virtual exhibition which maps these artistic networks, in Grace Brockington and Claudia Tobin, 'London's Little Theatres', *British Art Studies*, 11, https://doi.org/10.17658/issn.2058–5462/issue-11/theatres.
21. Smedley, quoted by Brockington, *Above the Battlefield*, pp. 183, 186.
22. Ibid., pp. 186–7.

23. Morris, 'The Training and Technique', p. 20. Morris's visual art is rarely discussed, but she exhibited at the Eleventh London Salon of the Allied Artists' Association (1919) at the Grafton Galleries, where Fry's Post-Impressionist exhibitions had shaken the art world earlier in the decade. A collection of Morris's visual art is held in the Margaret Morris Collection, Fergusson Gallery, Perth (hereafter MMC). Materials are in the process of being catalogued, therefore my citations follow rudimentary cataloguing.
24. Eugene Goossens, *Overture and Beginners: A Musical Autobiography* (London: Methuen, 1951), p. 139. On Goossens' involvement with the Ballets Russes and with Morris see Emerson, *Rhythm and Colour*, p. 173.
25. See Hillel Schwartz's discussion of *tableau vivant*, in 'Torque: The New Kinaesthetic of the Twentieth Century', in Jonathan Crary and Stanford Kwinter, eds, *Incorporations* (New York: Urzone, 1992), pp. 71–126 (p. 97).
26. Both paintings can be found in the Tate Gallery collection.
27. Stéphane Mallarmé, 'Sainte', in *Poems*, trans. Roger Fry (London: Chatto & Windus, 1936), pp. 126–9.
28. Reginald R. Buckley, 'Woman of Dreams and Deeds', *Lady's Pictorial*, 17 March 1917. In London, Chelsea and Kensington Library, Chelsea Miscellany (CM) 1759.
29. MMD, p. 47.
30. Morris, Preface to MMD.
31. Judith Alter, *Dancing and Mixed Media* (New York: Peter Lang, 1996), p. xi.
32. Nead, *The Haunted Gallery*, p. 72.
33. Ricciotto Canudo, 'The Birth of a Sixth Art' (1911), quoted in Laurent Guido and Olivier Lugon, eds, *Between Still and Moving Images* (Eastleigh: John Libbey, 2012), p. 12.
34. The film is titled, *Looks Very Jolly Doesn't it? Girls and Grace at Miss Margaret Morris' open-air school at Pourville* (1921), by the Topical Budget Film Company, British Film Institute Creative Archive, London.
35. *Bystander*, 9 April 1924. MMC, Newspaper clippings, Green scrapbook (1925).
36. Sarah Street, *Colour Films in Britain: The Negotiation of Innovation 1900–55* (Basingstoke: Palgrave Macmillan, 2012), p. 3.
37. MMD, p. 54.
38. Faith Binckes traces the shifting meanings of 'rhythm' in *Modernism, Magazines, and the British Avant-garde: Reading Rhythm, 1910–1914* (Oxford: Oxford University Press, 2010). Binckes argues that although the term's prevalence in the magazine 'has been most closely connected with Murry's early enthusiasm for Bergson', in fact 'the concept had played a role in the artistic and literary movements of the late nineteenth and early twentieth centuries, of which Bergsonism was only one strand' (p. 62). For a discussion of Fergusson's and Murry's debt to Bergson see Mark Antliff, *Inventing Bergson: Cultural Politics and the Parisian Avant-Garde* (Princeton: Princeton University Press, 1993), esp. pp. 78–83.
39. John Middleton Murry, *Between Two Worlds: An Autobiography* (London: Jonathan Cape, 1935), p. 156.
40. Ibid., p. 156
41. *MLM*, p. 30.

42. Anne Estelle Rice, 'Les Ballets Russes', *Rhythm*, 2:7 (1912), 106–10. Rice was Fergusson's partner prior to Morris and the two women met in Paris in 1913.
43. On the role of dance and the different expressions of 'rhythm' among the Rhythmists, see Peter Brooker, 'Harmony, Discord and Difference: *Rhythm* (1911–13), *The Blue Review* (1913), and *The Signature* (1915)', in Peter Brooker and Andrew Thacker, eds, *The Oxford Critical and Cultural History of Modernist Magazines, Volume I* (Oxford: Oxford University Press, 2009), pp. 314–36. There remains a critical lacuna in considering interpretations of rhythm from Morris's perspective despite the insights of Helen Beale and Angela Smith, in *Outsiders in Paris: John Duncan Fergusson, Katherine Mansfield and their Circles*, no. 9 (Stirling: Stirling French Publications, 2000). John Drummond discusses Fergusson's work in the context of pre-war dance culture but does not pursue the impact of his meeting with Morris, in 'A Creative Crossroads: The Revival of Dance in Fergusson's Paris', in Elizabeth Cumming, ed., *Colour, Rhythm and Dance: Paintings and Drawings by J. D. Fergusson and his Circle in Paris* (Edinburgh: Scottish Arts Council, 1985), pp. 18–23.
44. Lisa Tickner, *Modern Life and Modern Subjects* (New Haven: Yale University Press, 2000), p. 80.
45. Morris, 'Dancing as an Art', p. 17.
46. MMD, pp. 54–5.
47. Ibid., p. 48.
48. Ibid., pp. 62–4.
49. Charles Marriott, 'Some Notes on Dancing', *Art and Letters*, July 1917, repr. in *Margaret Morris: Modern Dance Pioneer*, pp. 10–11.
50. Henri Bergson, *Time and Free Will: An Essay on the Immediate Data of Consciousness* (1889), 3rd edn (New York: Dover Publications, 2001), pp. 12–13.
51. Smedley, in *The Drama in Adult Education*, 6 (1926), Board of Education, pp. 217–18, quoted in Emerson, *Rhythm and Colour*, p. 35.
52. Carter, quoted in Rodker, 'The Choric School', *The Drama*, 23 (1916), 436–46 (p. 441).
53. Ezra Pound, 'Foreword to the Choric School', *Others*, 1:4 (October 1915).
54. Ibid.
55. Dillon, quoted in ibid., p. 60.
56. Rodker, 'The Choric School', p. 443.
57. With former MMM pupils Hélène Vanel and Lois Hutton, Dillon published *Cahiers rythme et couleur*, a collection of essays and poems indebted to Morris's principles. (MMC, Shelf 6, 'MMM in France'). Vanel and Hutton established the École Rythme et Couleur in Vence, France, later known as *Les Six de Rythme et Couleur*. For a detailed discussion see Emerson, *Rhythm and Colour*, esp. chapter 13.
58. Rodker, 'The Choric School', pp. 440–2.
59. MMC, Albums, Cuttings Book 28: Cyril Beaumont, clipping from *Dancing World*, January 1923.
60. Eiko Nakano, 'Katherine Mansfield, *Rhythm* and Henri Bergson', in Janet Wilson, Susan Reid and Gerri Kimber, eds, *Katherine Mansfield and Literary Modernism* (London: Continuum, 2011), pp. 30–41 (p. 31).
61. Alter, *Dancing and Mixed Media*, p. 30.
62. W. L. George, 'The Esperanto of Art', *The Blue Review*, 1 (1913), 28–36 (p. 33).

63. Bergson, quoted in Susan Jones, *Literature, Modernism and Dance* (Oxford: Oxford University Press, 2013), p. 137.
64. Margaret Morris, *The Notation of Movement: Text, Drawings and Diagrams* (London: Kegan Paul, 1928), pp. 85–6.
65. Henri Bergson, *Creative Evolution* (1911), trans. Arthur Mitchell (Lanham: University Press of America, 1983), p. 22.
66. Cowan, *Technology's Pulse*, p. 34.
67. Morris, *Notation*, pp. 8, 10.
68. In her chapter on Lewis and dance in *Modern Life and Modern Subjects*, pp. 79–115, Lisa Tickner describes Lewis's antipathy toward the expressive femininity of Hellenic dance pioneered by Isadora Duncan and Morris, but the considerable social and cultural inter-connections in their circle invite further consideration.
69. David Bomberg, who was also associated with Vorticism, was probably inspired by Morris in making his 'The Dancer' series (1913–14), after witnessing her early summer schools. See Cliff Holden, 'Meeting Bomberg: Tradition and the Dancing Muse' (2004), http://www.cliffholden.co.uk/documents_2004_30.shtml; and Karlien van den Beuckel, 'Torque: Dancers and Sappers in Some Early Bomberg Sketches', exhibition text for *David Bomberg: Objects of Collection* (London: Borough Road Gallery, 2014).
70. Wyndham Lewis, 'Our Vortex', pp. 147–9.
71. Penelope Curtis, 'How Direct Carving Stole the Idea of Modern British Sculpture', in David J. Getsy, ed., *Sculpture and the Pursuit of a Modern Ideal in Britain c. 1880–1920* (Farnham: Ashgate, 2004), pp. 290–318 (p. 292).
72. Ibid., p. 296.
73. Ibid.
74. Ibid., p. 293.
75. See Evelyn Silber, 'Gaudier-Brzeska and Jacob Epstein: Life and Life Force', in Jennifer Powell, ed., *NEW RHYTHMS Henri Gaudier-Brzeska: Art, Dance and Movement in London 1911–1915* (Cambridge: Kettle's Yard, 2015), pp. 50–7.
76. David Getsy, 'Acts of Stillness: Statues, Performativity, and Passive Resistance', *Criticism*, 56 (2014), 1–20 (p. 11).
77. Carrie J. Preston, *Modernism's Mythic Pose: Gender, Genre, Solo Performance* (Oxford: Oxford University Press, 2011), p. 98.
78. Ibid., pp. 5–6.
79. Goossens, *Overture and Beginners*, p. 139.
80. MMD, plate XI.
81. Eleanor Elder, 'Movement, and the Culture of Expression', *The Theosophist*, 39:1 (March 1918), ed. Annie Besant, 616–31 (p. 618).
82. Ruby Ginner, *The Revived Greek Dance* (London: Methuen, 1933), pp. 45–6.
83. Ibid., p. 46.
84. Veder, *Living Line*, p. 178.
85. The Scottish National Gallery of Modern Art's exhibition *J. D. Fergusson* (2013–14) raised the profile of the artist's neglected sculptural output by displaying fifteen sculptures. For a detailed survey see Jonathan Blackwood, 'Sculpture with a Scots Brogue: John Duncan Fergusson, c. 1916–24', in Getsy, ed., *Sculpture and the Pursuit of a Modern Ideal in Britain*, pp. 245–66.

86. MMD, p. 19.
87. The images in his photographic essay are now part of the collection in the George Eastman Museum, New York: https://collections.eastman.org/objects/160921/miss-morris--class?ctx=9690608d-eac7–4128–8ed9–2cca605d50f0&idx=6.
88. Quoted in J. D. Fergusson, *Painting and Sculpture by J. D. Fergusson* (London: Lefevre Galleries, 1928).
89. Margaret Morris, Letter 25 July 1964, repr. in 'Oak Rhythm', J. D. Fergusson: Catalogue entry, Tate, http://www.tate.org.uk/art/artworks/fergusson-oak-rhythm-t00668/text-catalogue-entry.
90. 'Art and Atavism: the Dryad' (1944), repr. in Morris, *The Art of J. D. Fergusson*, pp. 202–10 (p. 205).
91. Ibid.
92. The dryad had potent Celtic associations for Fergusson, but it also became a popular symbol of female physical and sexual liberation appropriated by dancers during this period. See Fiona Macintosh's discussion of the 'maenad' trope in Ginner and Morris: 'Dancing Maenads in Early Twentieth-Century Britain', in Macintosh, ed., *The Ancient Dancer in the Modern World* (Oxford: Oxford University Press, 2010), pp. 188–208.
93. MMC, Correspondence, Letters to Victoria Morris, 2010.718.1.1778.2, 2010.718.1.1778.5.
94. Caption for *Evening Sunlight*, MMD, plate XXII.
95. MMD, p. 53.
96. J. E. Crawford Flitch, *Modern Dancing and Dancers* (London: Grant Richards, 1912), p. 221.
97. Elizabeth Cumming picks up on a similar effect in Fergusson's *La Force* (1910), observing that the figure 'is treated in anonymity as a heavily-outlined element of power almost as a still life object'. 'Colour, Rhythm and Dance: the Paintings and Drawings of J. D. Fergusson and his Circle', in *Colour, Rhythm and Dance*, pp. 6–12 (p. 8).
98. Sheila McGregor, 'L'Esprit Gaulois: Fergusson's Celtic Nationalism', in Alice Strange, Elizabeth Cumming and Sheila McGregor, eds, *J. D. Fergusson* (Edinburgh: National Galleries of Scotland, 2013), pp. 91–102 (p. 97). Fergusson's oeuvre does of course also include sketches and paintings of dancing scenes such as his celebrated *Les Eus* (c. 1913, Hunterian Art Gallery, Glasgow).
99. Morris, quoted in 'Dancing for Cripples: Movement and Health', Educational Supplement, *The Times*, 30 October 1926, MMC, Shelf 8, Books and Publishing. Sadler's declaration appears in 'Fauvism and a Fauve', in *Rhythm*, 1:1 (1911), 14–18 (p. 17).
100. Antliff, *Inventing Bergson*, p. 70.
101. Miranda Hickman, 'The Gender of Vorticism: Jessie Dismorr, Helen Saunders, and Vorticist Feminism', in Mark Antliff and Scott W. Klein, eds, *Vorticism: New Perspectives* (Oxford: Oxford University Press, 2013), pp. 119–36 (p. 133).
102. Isadora Duncan, quoted in Preston, *Modernism's Mythic Pose*, p. 154. On alternative models of motion centering on the 'pathos of repose' and the 'act of standing still, motionless amid the vortex', see Gabriele Brandstetter, *Poetics of Dance: Body, Image, and Space in the Historical Avant-Gardes*, trans. Elena Polzer with Mark Franko (New York: Oxford University Press, 2015), p. 253.

103. Sadler, 'Fauvism and a Fauve', p. 18.
104. Getsy, 'Acts of Stillness', p. 1.
105. MMD, p. 53.
106. For further discussion see Fiona Macintosh, 'The Ancient Greeks and the "Natural"', in Alexandra Carter and Rachel Fensham, eds, *Dancing Naturally: Nature, Neo-classicism and Modernity in Early Twentieth-Century Dance* (Basingstoke: Palgrave Macmillan, 2011), pp. 43–57.
107. Jones, *Literature, Modernism and Dance*, p. 52.
108. Macintosh's description, in 'Dancing Maenads in Early Twentieth-Century Britain', p. 199.
109. MMD, p. 84. Morris emphasised her debt to Duncan in several of her writings, see especially MMD, pp. 84–5. As early as 1910, she began advertising lectures and recitals in Hellenic dancing and she was photographed in Greek style 'statue' poses. Contemporary press and publicity material in the MMC attests to the continued role of reconstructed Greek dance in her productions through the pre- and inter-war years (MMC: Unit 19, Shelf 4, Performing and Publicity; and Shelf 5, Images).
110. Duncan's lecture is reproduced in English translation in Alter, *Dancing and Mixed Media*, pp. 211–17. The extract is from p. 215.
111. Laura Mulvey, *Death 24x a Second: Stillness and the Moving Image* (London: Reaktion Books, 2006), p. 117.
112. Ginner, *The Revived Greek Dance*, p. 16. Macintosh claims that Morris and Ginner 'came to represent the two major strands in the development of Greek dance in Britain in the inter-war years' ('Dancing Maenads in Early Twentieth-Century Britain', p. 299).
113. Ginner, *Revived Greek Dance*, pp. 19, 21, 46.
114. Winckelmann, *History of the Art of Antiquity*, p. 263.
115. Middleton Murry, *Still Life* (New York: E. P. Dutton, 1916), pp. 54, 34. See also Caroline Maclean's discussion of how the novel illustrates Murry's transition from 'rhythm' to 'harmony' as central terms in his aesthetics, in *The Vogue for Russia*, pp. 88–9.
116. Hornby, *Still Modernism*, p. 2.
117. Alex Potts, *Flesh and the Ideal: Winckelmann and the Origins of Art History* (New Haven: Yale University Press, 1994), p. 2. In a further note on this discussion (n. 2, p. 256) Potts points out that when Winckelmann invokes 'still' in the *History* 'the idea of an almost inanimate stillness tends to take precedence over the suggestions of an emotional or moral calm' in the earlier essay *Thoughts on the Imitation of Greek Works* (1755).
118. Margaret Morris, 'Modern Developments in Dancing, A Living Art', *The Yorkshire Post*, 19 June 1922.
119. Ana Carden-Coyne, *Reconstructing the Body: Classicism, Modernism, and the First World War* (Oxford: Oxford University Press, 2009), pp. 281, 283.
120. During the 1920s–30s, Morris developed the therapeutic permutations of her movement practice, working with disabled children, athletes, and in the fields of pre- and post-natal care. See Carden-Coyne's account of her remedial work, ibid., pp. 275–7.
121. Mary Bagot Stack was a British dancer who founded the Women's League of Health and Beauty in 1930. She is quoted by Carden-Coyne, ibid., p. 282.

122. Brockington, *Above the Battlefield*, p. 6.
123. MMD, p. 85.
124. John Middleton Murry, 'Art and Philosophy', *Rhythm*, 1:1 (1911), 9–12 (p. 11).
125. MMD, pp. 85–6 and *MLM*, p. 30.
126. Morris, MMD, plate iii, can be compared with Fergusson's painting, *Margaret Morris dans Le Chant Hindu* (1918). Like many other Western dancers who took inspiration from Asian art, notably Ruth St. Denis and Ted Shawn, whom Morris met in 1922 (*MLM*, p. 100), her performances were aimed at audiences with a taste for exoticism rather than ethnographic accuracy.
127. Numerous works listed in Morris's early reading notebooks investigate esoteric subjects: a notebook dated April 1912 includes Evelyn Underhill's *Practical Mysticism*; Stephen McKenna's *Sixth Sense*; and E. Herman Clark's *The Meaning and Value of Mysticism*, among others (MMC, Unit 20, Shelf 3, Journals, Diaries, Personal Documents). Figures in Morris's circle who shared an interest in unorthodox spirituality, included Raymond Duncan, Coburn, her patron George Davison, and Eleanor Elder, who published *Dance: A National Art* (1918) with the Theosophical Publishing House. In 1919, Krishnamurti, who was believed by the Theosophists to be their long-awaited spiritual teacher, joined Morris's Club (see Emerson, *Rhythm and Colour*, p. 47).
128. Morris studied a book on Hatha yoga with 'great attention'. *MLM*, p. 52.
129. Annie Besant and C. W. Leadbeater addressed these ideas in *Thought Forms* (1901) (London: Theosophical Publishing House, 1925). For a discussion of Theosophical art circles see Sarah Victoria Turner, '"Spiritual Rhythm" and "Material Things": Art, Cultural Networks and Modernity in Britain, c. 1900–1914' (unpublished doctoral thesis, University of London, Courtauld Institute, 2009), and her Enchanted Modernities research network.
130. Elder, 'Movement, and the Culture of Expression', pp. 627–8.
131. Besant and Leadbeater, *Thought Forms*, p. 21.
132. Elder, 'Movement, and the Culture of Expression', p. 628.
133. Marriott, 'Some Notes on Dancing', pp. 10–11
134. MMD, p. 48.
135. The New Sculpture Movement was associated with the late nineteenth century but sustained until the early 1930s. For further analysis of *Applause* see Jason Edwards, ed., *In Focus: The Singer Exhibited 1889 and Applause 1893 by Edward Onslow Ford* (Tate Research Publication, 2015), https://www.tate.org.uk/research/publications/in-focus/the-singer-and-applause-edward-onslow-ford/ancient-egyptian-sources.
136. David Getsy, 'Punks and Professionals: The Identity of the Sculptor 1900–1925', in Penelope Curtis, ed., *Sculpture in 20th-Century Britain: Identity, Infrastructure, Aesthetics, Display, Reception*, 2 vols (Leeds: Henry Moore Institute, 2003), I, pp. 9–20 (p. 11).
137. Rudolf Steiner, *A Lecture on Eurythmy: Given at Penmaenmawr on 26th August, 1923* (London: Rudolf Steiner Press, 1967, repr. 1st edn, 1926), pp. 7–9. Eurythmy differs from 'Eurhythmics', a method of musical training and rhythmical gymnastics formulated by the Swiss composer and musician, Émile Jaques-Dalcroze.

138. Rudolf Steiner, 'Anthroposophy and the Visual Arts' (9 April 1922), lecture trans. from unrevised notes by V. C. Bennie, in Rudolf Steiner Archive and e.Lib (hereafter RSA), http://wn.rsarchive.org/Lectures/19220409p01.html.
139. The charged political and social history of eurythmy and the advancement of its therapeutic and pedagogic applications during the inter-war period are beyond the scope of this discussion. In brief: Steiner's wife Marie and her eurythmy ensemble performed on stages across Europe despite the onset of war in 1914. However, the ideals and practice of eurythmy were opposed to Fascist ideals of corporeality, and the Nazis prohibited eurythmy during the 1930s as part of a wider move to outlaw anthroposophical activities. See Magdalene Siegloch's account in *How the New Art of Eurythmy Began: Lory Maier-Smits, the First Eurythmist* (London: Temple Lodge Publishing, 1997); and Usher's 'Introduction' to *Eurythmy: An Introductory Reader*, pp. 1–9.
140. Steiner relates these events in 'Must I Remain Unable to Speak?', *Autobiography* (London: Anthroposophic Press, 1999), repr. in *Eurythmy: An Introductory Reader*, pp. 11–15. Under the umbrella of anthroposophy, Steiner developed innovative approaches to architecture, education (the Waldorf schools), agriculture (biodynamic farming) and alternative medicine and health (as an advocate of homeopathy).
141. Steiner established a strong connection with Britain, making ten visits to various locations and lecturing across the country from 1902–24. He stayed at Penmaenmawr from 18–31 August 1923, where he gave thirteen lectures. See A. C. H., Introduction to *A Lecture on Eurythmy: Given at Penmaenmawr on 26th August, 1923*, p. 5.
142. Crispian Villeneuve, *Rudolf Steiner in Britain: A Documentation of his Ten Visits*, 2 vols (London: Temple Lodge, 2011), I, p. 358.
143. J. H. Elder, 'The Summer School at Torquay', repr. in ibid., pp. 358–9 (p. 359).
144. Ibid., p. 359.
145. Anne Fernihough notes another example of this interweaving in the 'strong affinities' between eurythmy and 'the dance-philosophy of Isadora Duncan', in *Freewomen and Supermen: Edwardian Radicals and Literary Modernism* (Oxford: Oxford University Press, 2013), p. 70.
146. Usher calls attention to the scope and scale of Steiner's commitment to the art form: 'In addition to the five courses and several hundred introductions to performances, he drew eurythmy choreography, 1300 forms for poems in several languages and for musical selections with a variety of musical instruments'. 'Introduction' to *Eurythmy: An Introductory Reader*, p. 7.
147. Steiner gives an extended discussion on 'Eurythmy as Visible Speech', in a series of lectures under this title (see *Eurythmy: An Introductory Reader*, pp. 112–34).
148. 'eurythmy, n.', in *OED*, http://www.oed.com/view/Entry/65086.
149. Cowan, *Technology's Pulse*, p. 19.
150. Archibald Keightley, quoted in ibid., p. 96.
151. Marie Steiner, quoted in ibid., p. 96.
152. Marjorie Spock, *Eurythmy* (New York: Anthroposophic Press, 1980), p. 17.
153. Ibid., pp. 17–18, 101.
154. Steiner, 'Eurythmy is a Moving Sculpture', p. 271.

155. Ibid., pp. 271–2.
156. Getsy, 'Acts of Stillness', p. 3.
157. Steiner, 'Eurythmy is a Moving Sculpture', pp. 272–3.
158. Ibid., p. 273; Steiner, 'Movement: The Speech of the Soul', an introduction to a performance on 27 April 1924, repr. Anthroposophic Press (New York, 1928), in *Eurythmy: An Introductory Reader*, pp. 51–9 (p. 54).
159. Steiner, 'Eurythmy is a Moving Sculpture', p. 273; 'Movement: The Speech of the Soul', pp. 54–5.
160. Hilary L. Flink, *Bergson and Russian Modernism, 1900–1930* (Illinois: Northwestern University Press, 1999), p. 52.
161. Steiner, 'Eurythmy is a Moving Sculpture', p. 274. He sets out these limitations in *Philosophy, Cosmology, and Religion: Ten Lectures* (delivered in 1922) (London: Anthroposophic Press, 1984), p. 134.
162. Steiner, 'Eurythmy is a Moving Sculpture', p. 274.
163. Steiner employs these terms in 'The Inner Nature of Music and the Experience of Tone', Lecture delivered on 12 November 1906, RSA, http://wn.rsarchive.org/Lectures/GA283/English/AP1983/19061112p01.html.
164. Steiner, 'Supersensible Knowledge: Anthroposophy as a Demand of the Age', Lecture I, 26 September 1923, RSA, https://wn.rsarchive.org/Lectures/GA084/English/AP1943/SupKno_index.html. Steiner outlined exercises for these developments in *Knowledge of the Higher Worlds* (written 1904–5).
165. Steiner, 'The Supersensible Origin of the Arts', 12 September 1920, in *Eurythmy: An Introductory Reader*, pp. 15–20 (p. 17).
166. Steiner, 'Eurythmy', Introductory words at Dornach, 12 December 1920, unknown translator, RSA, http://wn.rsarchive.org/Lectures/EU4313_index.html.
167. Steiner, *A Lecture on Eurythmy: Given at Penmaenmawr on 26th August, 1923*, p. 33.
168. Steiner, 'About the Being of Eurythmy', Introduction to a performance in Berlin, 14 September 1919, in *Eurythmy: An Introductory Reader*, pp. 281–6 (p. 281).
169. Ibid., p. 281. Steiner's first book *Philosophy of Freedom* (1894) outlined how this might be achieved.
170. Steiner, 'About the Being of Eurythmy', p. 281.
171. Steiner, 'Eurythmy is a Moving Sculpture', p. 274.
172. Steiner, 'Eurythmy' (1920).
173. Steiner, 'Eurythmy is a Moving Sculpture', p. 274.
174. Ibid., pp. 274–5
175. Ibid., p. 278.
176. Lory Maier-Smits, quoted by Siegloch, *How the New Art of Eurythmy Began*, p. 47.
177. On Steiner's sense of the curative possibilities and therapeutics of eurythmy see *Eurythmy: An Introductory Reader*, pp. 202–27.
178. Woloschin, quoted in Siegloch, *How the New Art of Eurythmy Began*, p. 75.
179. Winckelmann, *History*, p. 334.
180. Getsy, 'Acts of Stillness', pp. 3–4. Goethe noted that the effect of animation could be achieved if a spectator placed themselves at a certain distance from the Laocoon and alternately opened and shut their eyes: 'we shall see all the marble in motion;

we shall be afraid to find the group changed when we open our eyes again'. 'Observations on the Laocoon' (1798), quoted in Elizabeth Prettejohn, *Beauty and Art 1750–2000* (Oxford: Oxford University Press, 2005), p. 27.

181. Getsy, 'Acts of Stillness', pp. 3–4.
182. Steiner, 'Anthroposophy and the Visual Arts'.
183. Ibid.
184. Steiner, 'Impulses of Transformation for Man's Artistic Evolution', in *Eurythmy: An Introductory Reader*, pp. 20–40 (pp. 22–3).
185. The concept of the 'etheric' was widely employed by occultists and scientists during this period. According to Steiner, '[b]asically everything in the etheric body is rhythm, a cyclical rhythm of movement or activity' (ibid., p. 22).
186. For Kandinsky's comments on the 'search for more subtle expression' in modern dance see *Concerning the Spiritual in Art*, pp. 50–1. Kandinsky was familiar with Steiner's ideas and owned a copy of *Thought Forms* (Owen, *The Place of Enchantment*, p. 230). In *Rudolf Steiner and Contemporary Art*, exh. cat. (Wolfsburg: Kunstmuseum, 2010), Markus Brüderlin and Ulrike Groos describe Kandinsky as part of the 'phenomenon' of 'major artists' who 'regularly occupied themselves with Rudolf Steiner's universal world of ideas, drawing valuable impulses from them for their own work' (p. 10). On the interconnections between abstraction, anthroposophy and theosophy see also Sixteen Ringbom, *The Sounding Cosmos: A Study in the Spiritualism of Kandinsky and the Genesis of Abstract Painting* (Abo: Abo Akademi, 1970).
187. Lucia Ruprecht, 'Gesture, Interruption, Vibration: Rethinking Early Twentieth-Century Gestural Theory and Practice in Walter Benjamin, Rudolf von Laban, and Mary Wigman', *Dance Research Journal*, 47:2 (2015), 23–41 (p. 24).
188. Ibid., p. 24.
189. Ibid., pp. 25, 33.
190. Spock, *Eurythmy*, p. 8.
191. Ibid., p. 6.
192. Ibid., pp. 6, 19.
193. Ibid., pp. 20–1.
194. Steiner, 'Eurythmy is a Moving Sculpture', p. 274.
195. Spock, *Eurythmy*, p. 21.
196. Brüderlin and Groos, *Rudolf Steiner and Contemporary Art*, pp. 26–7.
197. Steiner, quoted by Siegloch, *How the New Art of Eurythmy Began*, p. 62.
198. Ibid.
199. Arild Rosenkrantz, 'Eurythmy: A New Art', illustrated by Rosenkrantz, in 'Eurythmy: The Art of Movement, as inaugurated by Dr. Rudolf Steiner at the Goetheanum, Dornach, Switzerland' (repr. from 'Eve' by The Anthroposophical Publishing Company, London [undated, unpaginated]). London, Rudolf Steiner House Archive: Performing Arts, Eurythmy.
200. Rudolf Steiner, 'Lecture XVI', Dornach, 3 February 1924, in *An Introduction to Eurythmy: Talks Given before Sixteen Eurythmy Performances*, trans. Gladys Hahn (New York: Anthroposophic Press, 1984), pp. 95–100 (p. 100).
201. Steiner, 'Eurythmy is a Moving Sculpture', p. 272.

202. On this tradition see Krieger's '*Ekphrasis* and the Still Movement of Poetry' (1967); and Joseph Frank, 'Spatial Form in Modern Literature: An Essay in Three Parts', *The Sewanee Review*, 53 (1945), 643–53.
203. Steiner, 'Movement: The Speech of the Soul', p. 54; 'Eurythmy as Visible Speech', in *Eurythmy: An Introductory Reader*, pp. 112–34.
204. Steiner, 'Movement: The Speech of the Soul', pp. 56–7.
205. Steiner discusses these ideas in *A Lecture on Eurythmy: Given at Penmaenmawr on 26th August, 1923*, p. 24, and in 'Movement: The Speech of the Soul', p. 57.
206. Siegloch, *How the New Art of Eurythmy Began*, pp. 47–53.
207. Steiner, quoted in ibid., p. 53.
208. Ibid., p. 53. According to Steiner, the complementary poem 'Happy Journey' addressed the experience of the 'outer world' and was therefore to be performed with '*all* the consonants' (p. 53).
209. Steiner, *A Lecture on Eurythmy: Given at Penmaenmawr on 26th August, 1923*, pp. 19, 17.
210. Steiner, 'Eurythmy' (1920).
211. Ibid.
212. Ibid. See Brüderlin and Groos, *Rudolf Steiner and Contemporary Art*, for a survey of Steiner's 'contribution to abstraction and to the overcoming of the artistic concept of mimesis' (p. 22).
213. Rudolf Steiner, 'Lecture 1: 'The Creative World of Colour', 26 July 1914, from The Creative World of Colour: Four Lectures at Dornach, RSA, http://wn.rsarchive.org/Lectures/GA/GA0291/19140726p01.html.
214. Ibid.
215. See ibid., and Rudolf Steiner, *Colour: Three Lectures given in Dornach, 6th–8th May, 1921, with Extracts from his Note-books*, trans. John Salter (London: Rudolf Steiner Press, 1977). Similar in some ways to his theosophist contemporaries, Steiner believed that colour was not only 'living' but could communicate on a supersensory plane.
216. Steiner, 'Lustre and Image', in ibid., pp. 28–41 (p. 41).
217. Steiner, *A Lecture on Eurythmy: Given at Penmaenmawr on 26th August, 1923*, p. 24.
218. Ibid., p. 24.
219. Rosenkrantz, 'Eurythmy: A New Art'.
220. Steiner's chromatic conception of the sculptural body departs from the tradition of Winckelmann and Pater, which had idealised the purity of white marble in classical sculpture although archaeological research began to show that much of ancient sculpture was in fact polychromatic.
221. Spock, *Eurythmy*, p. 100.
222. Ibid.
223. The phrase 'threefold nature of eurythmy' appears in *A Lecture on Eurythmy: Given at Penmaenmawr on 26th August, 1923*, p. 28. Steiner outlines these instructions in 'Boys and Girls at the Waldorf School', Lecture delivered 24 [?] August 1922, in *Eurythmy: An Introductory Reader*, pp. 157–65 (p. 160).
224. Ibid., p. 160.

225. Rosenkrantz, 'Eurythmy: A New Art'.
226. Steiner outlines this vision in 'Light Eurythmy', Dornach, 2 April 1923, in *Eurythmy: An Introductory Reader*, p. 241.
227. Accounts of eurythmy stage performances bear comparison with Kandinsky's vision for theatre as a total work of art. According to Mike Vanden Heuvel, the painter envisaged 'a field of vibrations based in rhythm, color and movement that directly and viscerally resonate within the spectator'. 'Good Vibrations: Avant Garde Theatre and Ethereal Aesthetics from Kandinsky to Futurism', in Trower and Enns, eds, *Vibratory Modernism*, pp. 188–214 (p. 206).
228. Neil Anderson, 'On Rudolf Steiner's Impact on the Training of the Actor', *Literature & Aesthetics*, 21:1 (2011), 158–74 (p. 162).
229. Rosenkrantz, 'Eurythmy: A New Art'.

3

'PAST THE GAP WHERE WE CANNOT SEE': STILL LIFE AND THE 'NUMINOUS' IN BRITISH PAINTING OF THE 1920s–1930s

For the painters considered in this chapter – Winifred Nicholson, Ben Nicholson, Ivon Hitchens and David Jones – still life represented a charged space of experimentation in which the possibilities of heightened and in some cases 'spiritual' vision could be cultivated. It was a way of reaching, in Winifred Nicholson's words, 'past the gap where we cannot see'.[1] Still life was crucial to the development of this loose group of British painters during the 1920s and '30s, several of whom have been marginalised in the larger narratives and geographies of modernism (Winifred Nicholson, Hitchens and Jones), or explored largely for their contribution to abstraction (Ben Nicholson). All were at different times members of the Seven and Five Society, the London-based society of artists established in 1919.[2] The Society played a significant role in promoting and exhibiting modern British art over the next two decades, becoming more progressive from 1926 onwards when Ben Nicholson became chairman. By exploring a fertile period of creative exchange between these artists during the 1920s and early 1930s, we can uncover the different ways in which still life became emblematic of an investigation of reality with numinous as well as aesthetic implications.[3] The term 'numinous' is employed here in the following significations: 'revealing or indicating the presence of a divinity', and 'giving rise to a sense of the spiritually transcendent; (esp. of things in art or the natural world) evoking a heightened sense of the mystical or sublime'.[4] Under this broad umbrella, we shall see a range of different spiritual orientations and vocabularies emerge.[5]

In 1927, the art critic Herbert Furst published a study devoted to still life, which indicates its position in contemporary discourses. He argued that the genre unfairly remained a 'victim' of neglect on three grounds: 'as the lowest form of pictorial art', as a 'dull subject', and in its commercial value.[6] Despite Furst's recognition that still life played 'so prominent a part' in the artistic experiments of the early twentieth century (a recognition he substantiated by exhibiting Ben Nicholson at his London gallery in 1924), he takes us back to the idea of an aesthetic laboratory, defining the genre as 'the ideal *corpus vile* [worthless body] upon which all manner of aesthetical experiments can fitly be conducted'. The objects represented and their 'mundane uses' were of little interest to the artist or viewer.[7] This chapter complicates the characterisation of still life as removed into a purely aesthetic territory and its subject as insignificant, ideas no doubt influenced by Roger Fry's early formalism and reiterated decades later in Charles Harrison's landmark study *English Art and Modernism 1900–1939* (1981). Harrison argues that by the 1920s still life, like landscape, had become 'neutralised', and that these genres functioned as 'aesthetic categories before they were anything else'.[8] The more nuanced possibility of a kind of 'duality' in still life is raised by Furst a little later in his study, with the question of '[h]ow far it is necessary, or even possible to keep the literary tale out of the aesthetic web, or whether, on the contrary, the aesthetic texture should enhance and emphasise associative ideas'. Furst imagines that the 'future will recognise' this duality, and it is one that this chapter pursues.[9] My inquiry demonstrates that a more subtle relationship between art and the everyday object operates in the work of Winifred and Ben Nicholson, Hitchens and Jones. We remember Jane Bennett's formulation which I introduced at the outset of this book: '[t]o be enchanted is to be struck and shaken by the extraordinary that lives amid the familiar and the everyday'.[10] The artists considered here engaged in a mode of attentiveness through which the very notion of the familiar in still life painting was to be re-evaluated and 're-enchanted'. We shall find in their pictures an aesthetic stance that weaves together light, form and the music of colour so as to reconceive the perceived materiality of still life objects.

'Liberation of Colour'

In an article titled 'Liberation of Colour' (1944), published in *World Review*, Winifred Nicholson vividly described her process of composing a floral still life:

> Yesterday I set out to pick a yellow bunch to place as a lamp on my table in dull, rainy weather. I picked Iceland poppies, marigolds, yellow iris; my bunch would not tell yellow. I added sunflowers, canary pansies, buttercups, dandelions; no yellower. I added to my butter-like mass, two everlasting peas, magenta pink, and all my yellows broke into luminosity. Orange and gold and lemon and primrose each singing its note.[11]

Recalling Virginia Woolf's expression of gastronomic relish for 'red-hot pokers' in her essay 'Pictures', Winifred Nicholson demonstrates a mode of still life composition that can be translated into culinary metaphors, rooting it in the sensory domestic world. However, she also makes claims to the 'immaterial': the realm of light and music. Her careful balancing of colour and botanical attentiveness culminates in a sense of exuberance at the 'liberation' of colour and its 'luminosity', demonstrating what she describes earlier in the article as a 'Music of Colour' or 'art of colour' that is 'as scientific as the Theory of Musical Harmony'.[12] That the setting is domestic points to her valorisation of the home as a site for modern art, and of still life as a way of introducing 'spiritual' light and colour into this sphere. Her vision of chromatic emancipation was already nascent in an article titled 'Unknown Colour' published in 1937 in *CIRCLE: An International Survey of Constructive Art*.[13] Here she articulates a theory of colour predicated on its unbounded, animate nature; on her impression that 'colours wish to fly, to merge, to change each other by their juxtapositions' and yet 'for a long time they have been nailed down'.[14] Sharing Woolf's concerns about modern man's diminishing colour sense, Winifred Nicholson envisages cultivating a heightened visual faculty through which to investigate the 'gap of unknown, unseen colour', which she locates between violet and red in the circle of colours.[15] As we shall see, she had already put this idea and much of her colour theory into practice over the previous decade in her flower paintings.[16]

The late nineteenth and first decades of the twentieth centuries had witnessed a 'rediscovery' of colour, to which Winifred Nicholson was responsive. In 'The Role and Modalities of Colour' (1945), Matisse described a trajectory from Delacroix to Cézanne through which he traced the 'rehabilitation of the role of colour, and the restitution of its emotive power'.[17] Winifred Nicholson saw and admired Matisse's paintings on her travels through Paris to Italy in the early 1920s, and his colour theories were a touchstone in several of her published writings as well as in private correspondence. She shared his desire to 'broaden the limits of colour theory' and his intuitive sense that the 'knowledge of colours depends upon instinct and feeling'.[18] Her own passion for painting 'rainbows', or 'the mathematics of colour', as she described it, began in childhood, and a trip to India in late 1919 was pivotal in igniting her receptivity to colour and light.[19] However, her commitment to the liberation of colour was in contrast to the preoccupation with form expressed by her contemporaries in the Seven and Five Society, many of whom (including her husband Ben Nicholson) were influenced by Roger Fry's emphasis on the formal element in painting.[20] Following art-historical precedent, Fry's early writings had demoted colour to a secondary quality in visual art, subordinate to form and to line. A dialectic between form and colour has been seen to characterise the Nicholsons' respective approaches to painting during the 1920s, with Winifred pioneering the blurring of edges and outlines through colour while Ben was attracted to line,[21] although he did acknowledge her influence in the chromatic sphere.[22] The extent to which this dialectic might have a gendered inflection, and the ways in which it became manifest in still life painting, will be explored over the course of this chapter.

The language of colour is often interconnected with spiritual inquiry, particularly among pioneers of abstraction such as Kandinsky and Piet Mondrian, both of whom Winifred Nicholson came to know in Paris in the 1930s. However, her life-long commitment to Christian Science provides the specific background against which the role of colour in her interpretation of still life can be theologically grounded.[23] Christian Science, which was founded in 1879 by Mary Baker Eddy in the United States, 'requires a penetration beyond material appearances to a spiritual order of being that traditional orthodoxy associates with a heaven in the hereafter but that Christian Science considers to be a present fact of scientific demonstrability in human life'.[24] Eddy set out her teachings and practice of spiritual healing in *Science and Health with Key to the Scriptures* (1875), which Winifred Nicholson read closely.[25] In this text Eddy asserts that '[i]mmortal and spiritual facts exist apart from this mortal and material conception' and that '[e]very step towards goodness is a departure from materiality, and is a tendency towards God, Spirit'.[26] One should be cautious about drawing Winifred Nicholson's art and her religious beliefs into a too-simple equation, but by keeping in mind the basic tenets of Christian Science, we can further elucidate the relationship between the 'material' and 'immaterial' in her still life painting.[27] The elevation of what Eddy called 'the spiritual sense' over the 'material' arguably informs her approach to the 'matter' of painting and her attempt to cultivate a heightened perception of light and colour.[28]

'Flowering': The Still Life at Lugano

> Little brown earthenware flowerpots of spring flowers, some in white wrapping paper, all in a row in a window. The delicate but brave texture colour and light, particularly in the flowers, but also throughout the painting, was enchanting. The theme was homely and very simple, but somehow there was transfiguration.
>
> Helen Sutherland[29]

This was the response of Helen Sutherland to Winifred Nicholson's flower paintings, which she had seen at the Mayor Gallery, London in a group exhibition of 1925. Sutherland supported a group of painters, writers and poets who were concerned in different ways with the 'spiritual' in art, and after meeting Ben and Winifred in 1925 she became their friend and patron.[30] In her early years she was influenced by Quakerism but she turned back to the Anglican Church in the late 1920s, although she continued to read and find connections between different theological traditions, and particularly valued the Roman Catholic rites of the Mass.[31] Sutherland sought the 'inward meaning and being' in 'outward things' and resolved to see how she might contribute to its 'rhythme' (*sic*) – an approach which Frances Spalding suggests informed her role as a collector.[32] It certainly informed her language of art appreciation. Following an exhibition of Winifred Nicholson's work at the Beaux Arts Gallery, London a few years later in spring 1927, she observed that the new works 'have a lovely new thing in them, a new mystery and gaiety combined – earthly and unearthly'.[33] Sutherland demonstrates a spiritually inflected lexicon, which was frequently employed in the reception of this group of artists. *The Sunday Times* reviewed the exhibition in similar terms, praising the painter's 'delicate visions, throbbing with light and vibrating with colour [. . .] drenched with the spirit that animates things until the objects become radiantly transfigured'.[34]

The notion of the transfiguration of the everyday and the dynamic between the 'earthly and unearthly', the radiant and the ordinary, was central in what Winifred Nicholson referred to as her period of 'flowering' in Lugano, Italy, where she produced many of the works displayed in her early exhibitions.[35] After their marriage in 1920, the Nicholsons spent each winter up until 1923 at a house situated above Lake Lugano in the Italian Swiss Alps.[36] Winifred Nicholson identified a gift of a pot of lilies of the valley, *mughetti*, from her husband as the catalyst for this 'flowering point':

> [T]his I stood on the window sill – behind was azure blue, Mountain, Lake, Sky, all there – and the tissue paper wrapper held the secret of the universe. [. . .] after that the same theme painted itself on that window sill, in cyclamen, primula, or cineraria – sunlight on leaves, and sunlight shining transparent through lens and through the mystery of tissue paper.[37]

Mughetti (c. 1921–22) (plate 7), and *Cyclamen and Primula* (c. 1922–23) (plate 8), are exemplars of this theme: the painter sets the seemingly 'humble' subject of the flower in conversation with sublime features of the natural world and re-makes both in the exchange. The tissue paper gives the potted plants an altered, somewhat mysterious sculptural form, particularly in *Mughetti* where it is emphasised by pencil markings. Interposed between the flowers and the source of light, the paper wrapping registers as a protective gesture toward the vulnerable life of the flower, a human intervention shielding it from the elemental world. The window sill setting situates these compositions in a threshold position in which the flowers belong neither wholly to the interior world nor the exterior. In *Cyclamen and Primula*, the wrappings create illusory peaks that echo the form of the mountaintops in the landscape behind them and appear to intersect on the horizon line. The predominantly blue-and-white palette used here and in many of the works of this period simultaneously invokes sky, lake

PLATES

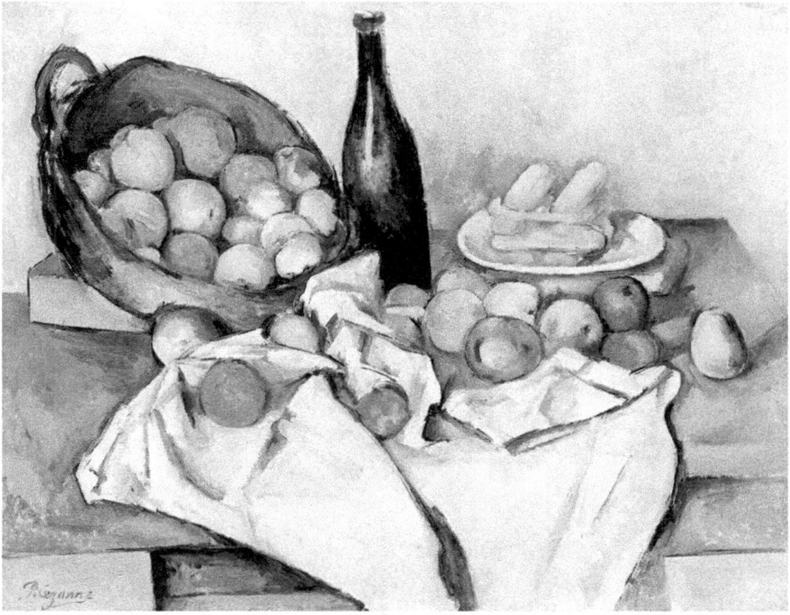

Plate 1 Paul Cézanne, *The Basket of Apples*, c. 1893, Oil on canvas, 25 7/16 x 31½ in. (65 x 80 cm). Chicago, Art Institute of Chicago. Helen Birch Bartlett Memorial Collection, 1926.252. © 2019 The Art Institute of Chicago/Art Resource, NY/Scala, Florence

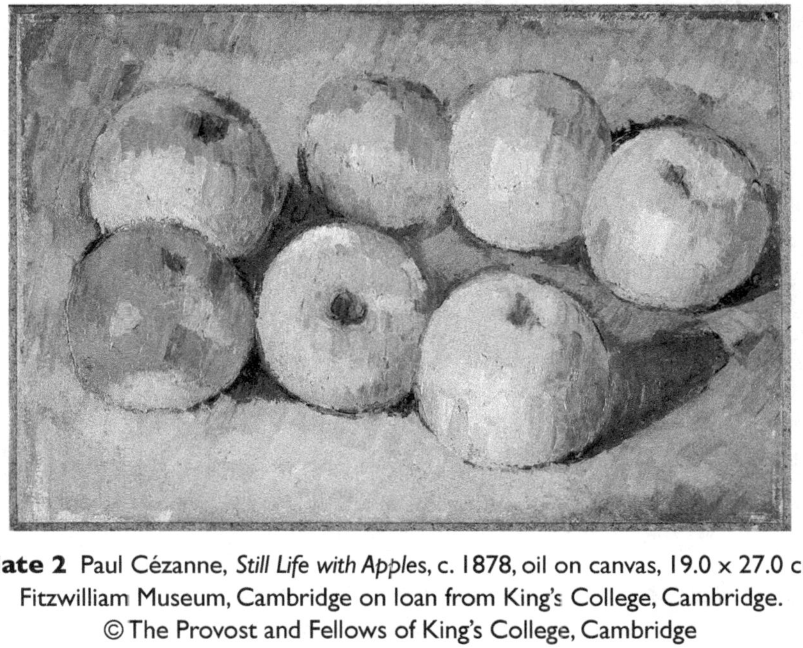

Plate 2 Paul Cézanne, *Still Life with Apples*, c. 1878, oil on canvas, 19.0 x 27.0 cm, Fitzwilliam Museum, Cambridge on loan from King's College, Cambridge. © The Provost and Fellows of King's College, Cambridge

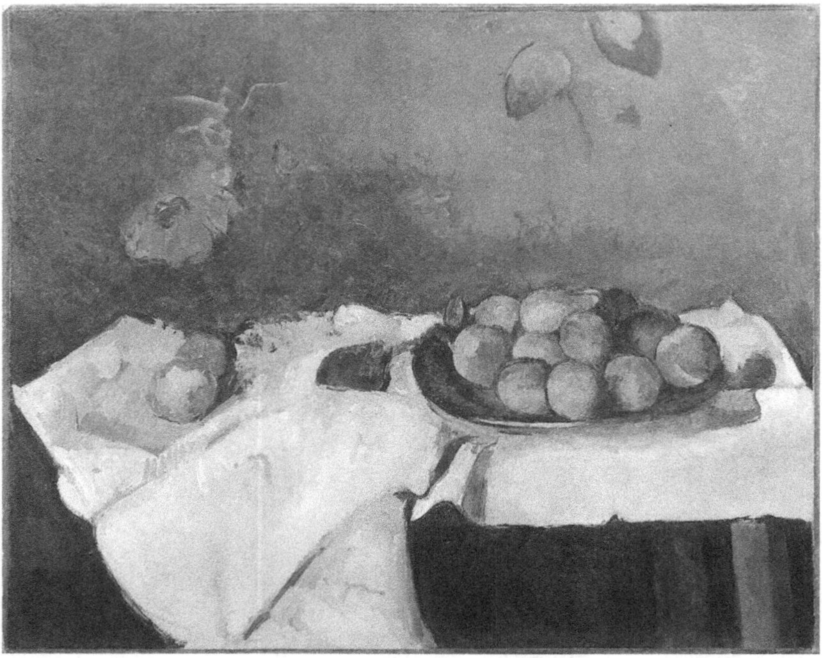

Plate 3 Paul Cézanne, *Still Life: Plate of Peaches*, 1879–80, oil on canvas, 23½ x 28⅞ in. (59.7 x 73.3 cm), Solomon R. Guggenheim Museum, New York Thannhauser Collection, Gift, Justin K. Thannhauser, 1978 78.2514.4

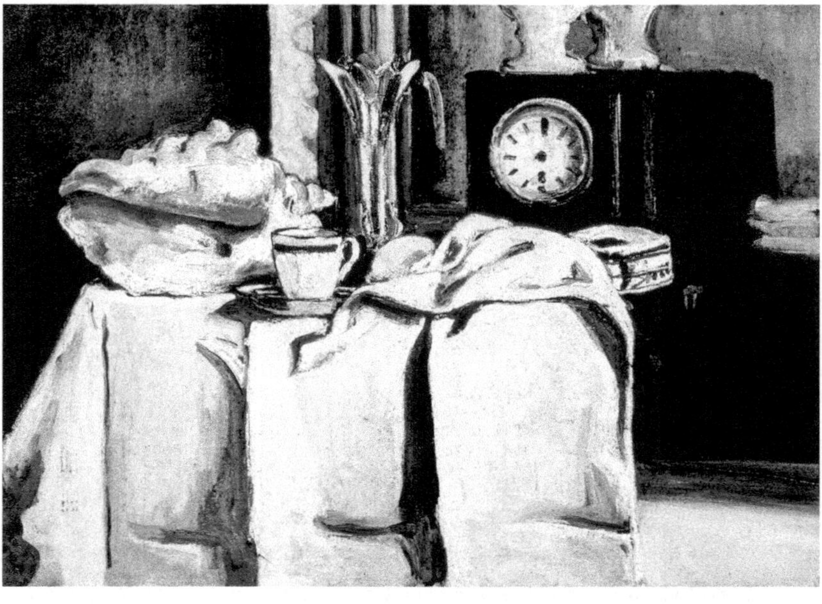

Plate 4 Paul Cézanne, *The Black Marble Clock*, c. 1870, oil on canvas, 55.2 x 74.3 cm, Private Collection/Bridgeman Images

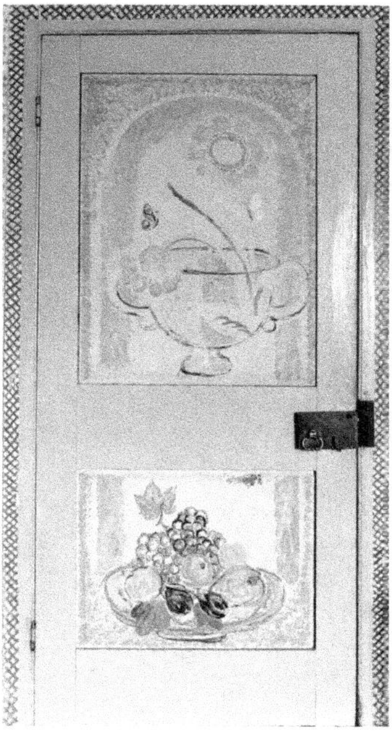

Plate 5 Vanessa Bell, decorative motif on door at Charleston, 1936, oil on wood, 187 x 83 cm. Copyright the estate of Vanessa Bell, courtesy of Henrietta Garnett. Photo © Penelope Fewster for The Charleston Trust

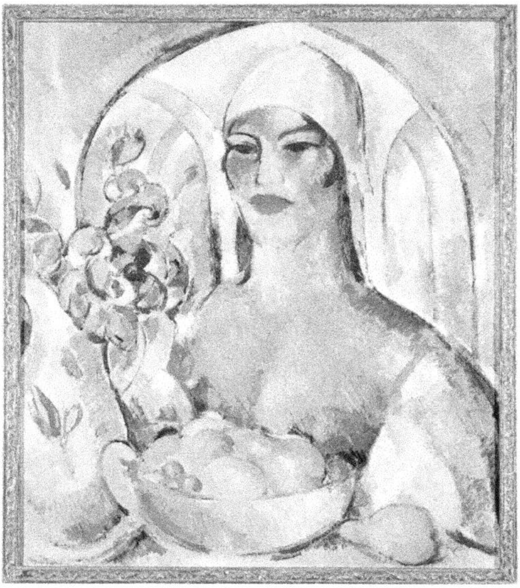

Plate 6 John Duncan Fergusson, *In the Patio: Margaret Morris Fergusson*, 1925, oil on canvas, 71.2 x 61.1 cm, National Galleries of Scotland, bequeathed by Mr and Mrs G. D. Robinson through the Art Fund 1988. © The Fergusson Gallery, Perth & Kinross Council

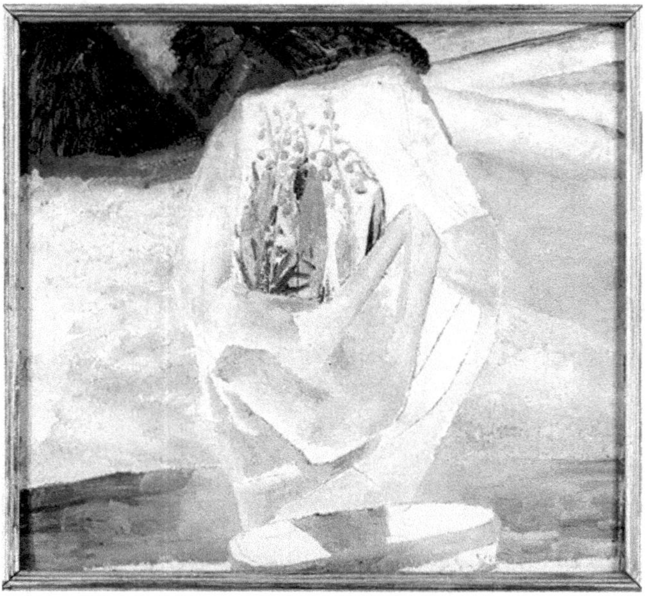

Plate 7 Winifred Nicholson, *Mughetti*, c. 1921–22, oil on board, 53.5 x 56.5 cm, private collection. © Trustees of Winifred Nicholson

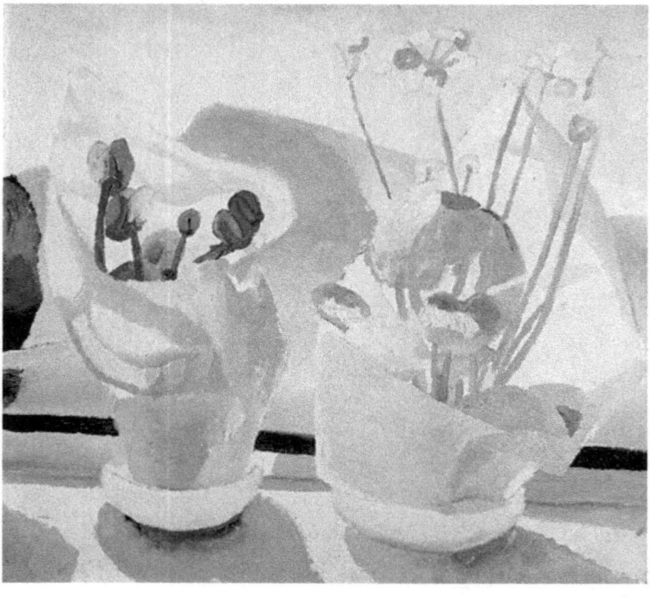

Plate 8 Winifred Nicholson, *Cyclamen and Primula*, c. 1923, oil on board, 500 x 500 mm. Image: Kettle's Yard, Cambridge. © Trustees of Winifred Nicholson

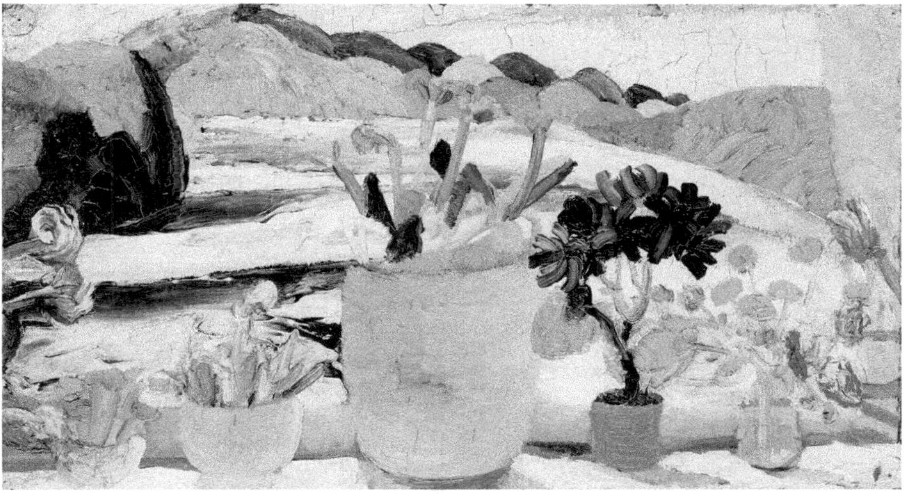

Plate 9 Winifred Nicholson, *Window-Sill, Lugano*, oil on board, 286 x 508 mm, Tate, presented by the Contemporary Art Society, 1940 © Tate. Photo: © Tate, London 2019

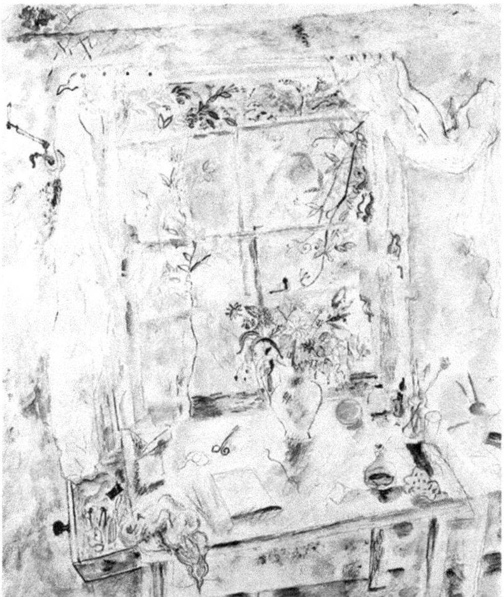

Plate 10 David Jones, *The Artist's Worktable*, 1929, pencil and watercolour, 62.3 x 50.2 cm, private collection. © The Estate of David Jones/Bridgeman Images

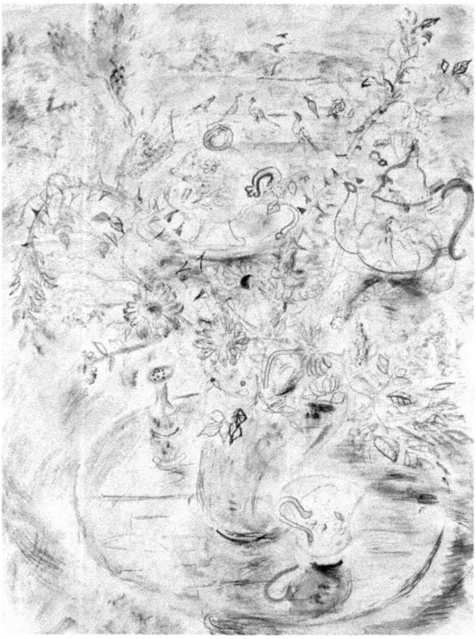

Plate 11 David Jones, *Briar Cup*, 1932, pencil and watercolour, 56.5 x 55.2 cm, private collection. © The Estate of David Jones/Bridgeman Images

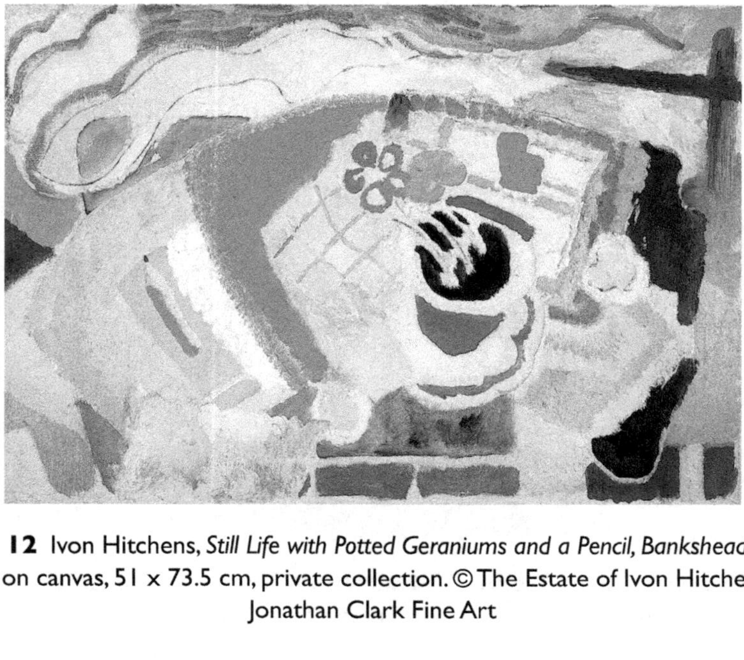

Plate 12 Ivon Hitchens, *Still Life with Potted Geraniums and a Pencil, Bankshead*, 1925, oil on canvas, 51 x 73.5 cm, private collection. © The Estate of Ivon Hitchens/ Jonathan Clark Fine Art

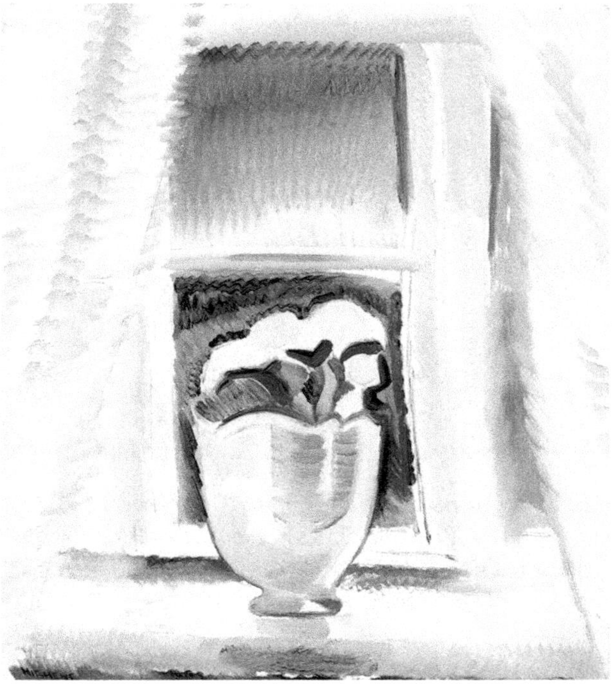

Plate 13 Ivon Hitchens, *Flowers in a Window*, date unknown, oil on canvas, 495 x 445 mm, Salford Museum & Art Gallery.

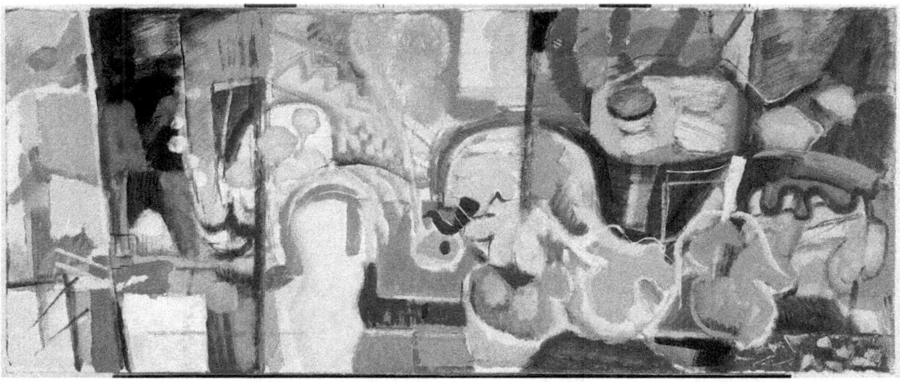

Plate 14 Ivon Hitchens, *The Blackbird Adelaide Road*, 1937, oil on canvas, 85 x 203 cm.

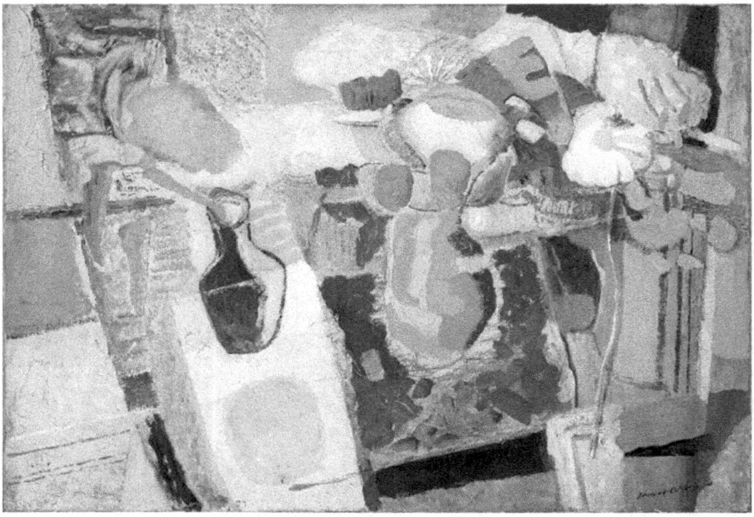

Plate 15 Ivon Hitchens, *Autumn Composition, Flowers on a Table*, 1932, oil on canvas, 781 x 1111 mm, Tate. Presented by Mrs Mary Hitchens, the artist's wife, 1977. © The Estate of Ivon Hitchens. Photo: © Tate, London 2019

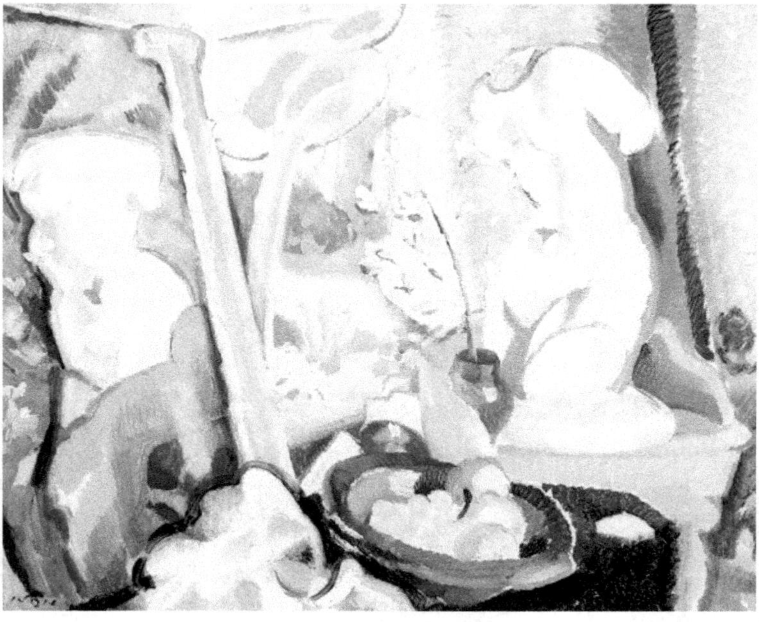

Plate 16 Ivon Hitchens, *Spring in Eden*, oil on canvas, 490 x 595 mm, Swindon Museum & Art Gallery. Image courtesy of Swindon Museum & Art Gallery. © The Estate of Ivon Hitchens

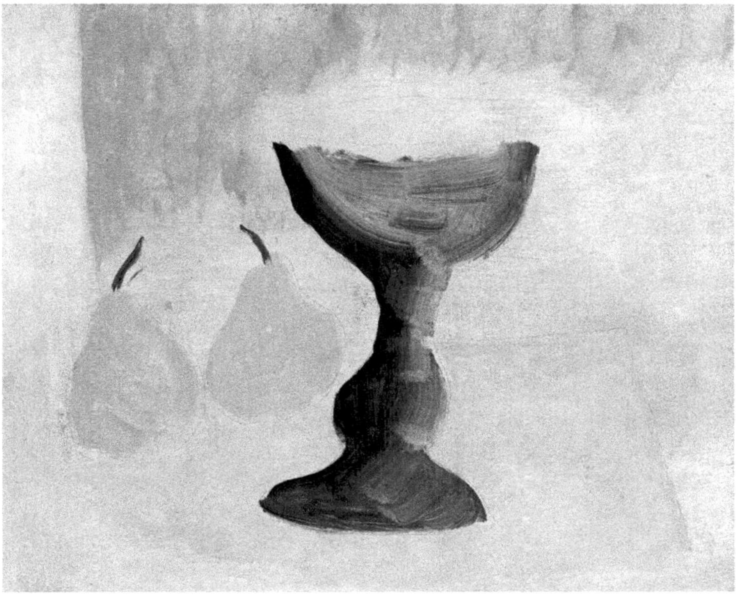

Plate 17 Ben Nicholson *1924 (goblet and two pears)*, oil and graphite on board, 355 x 433 mm. Image: Kettle's Yard, Cambridge. © Angela Verren Taunt. All rights reserved, DACS 2019

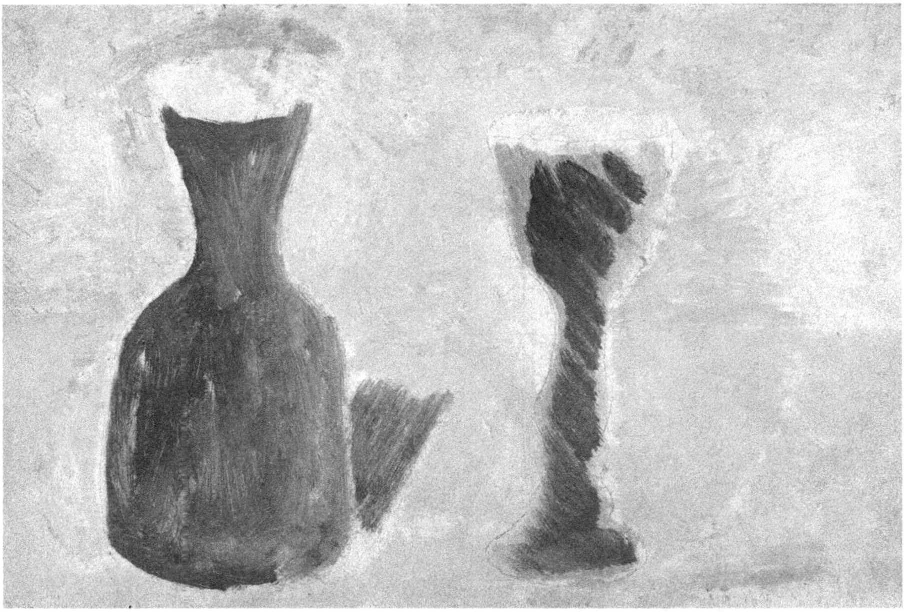

Plate 18 Ben Nicholson, *1925 (jar and goblet)*, oil on composition board, 290 x 450 mm. Image: Kettle's Yard, Cambridge. © Angela Verren Taunt. All rights reserved, DACS 2019

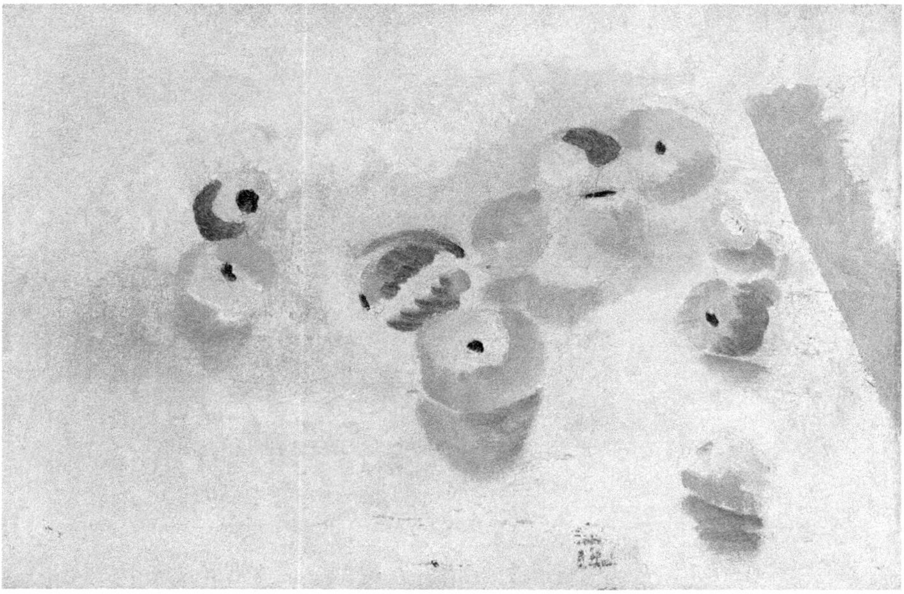

Plate 19 Ben Nicholson, *1927 (apples and pears)*, oil and graphite on canvas, 438 x 678 mm. Image: Kettle's Yard, Cambridge. © Angela Verren Taunt. All rights reserved, DACS 2019

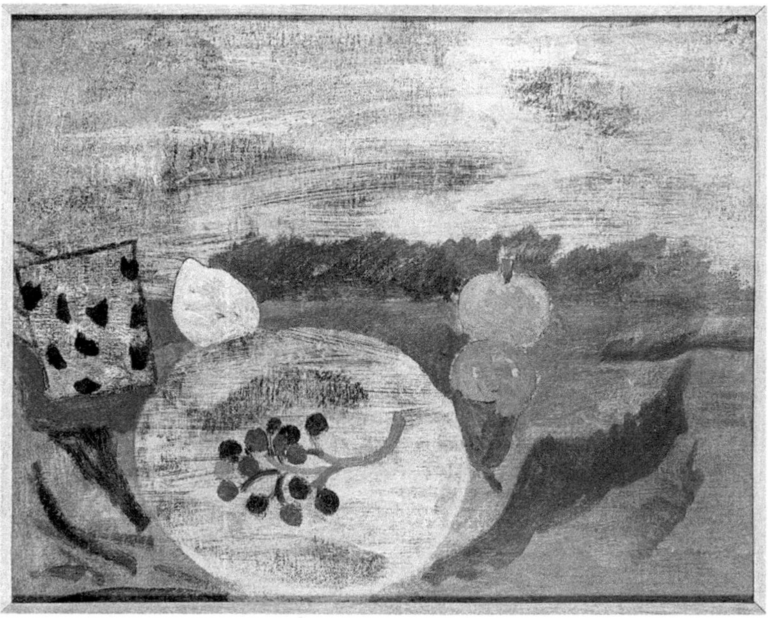

Plate 20 Ben Nicholson, *c. 1926–7 (still life)*, oil on canvas, 56 x 68.5 cm, private collection. © Angela Verren Taunt. All rights reserved, DACS 2019

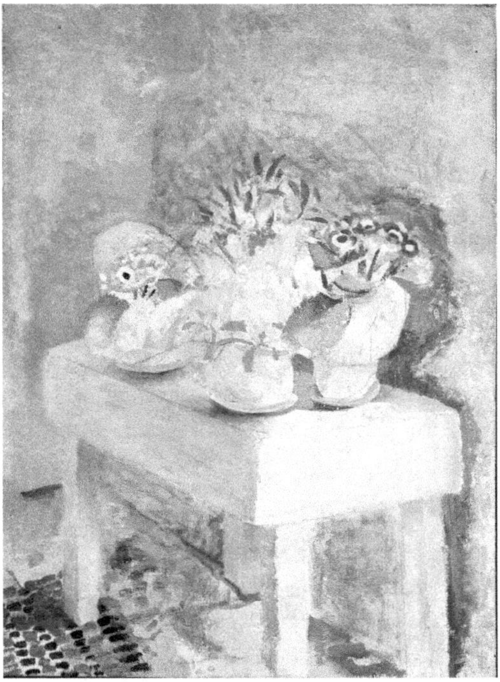

Plate 21 Winifred Nicholson, *Flower Table*, 1928–9, oil on canvas, 1128 x 802 mm, Tate. Purchased with assistance from the Carroll Donner Bequest, 1985. © Trustees of Winifred Nicholson. Photo: © Tate, London 2019

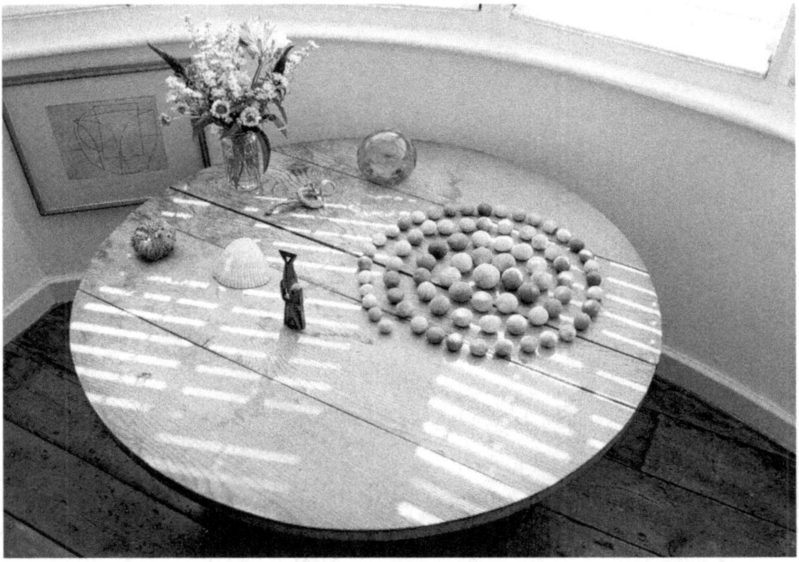

Plate 22 Pebble spiral in Jim Ede's bedroom at Kettle's Yard. Image: Kettle's Yard, University of Cambridge. Photo: Paul Allitt

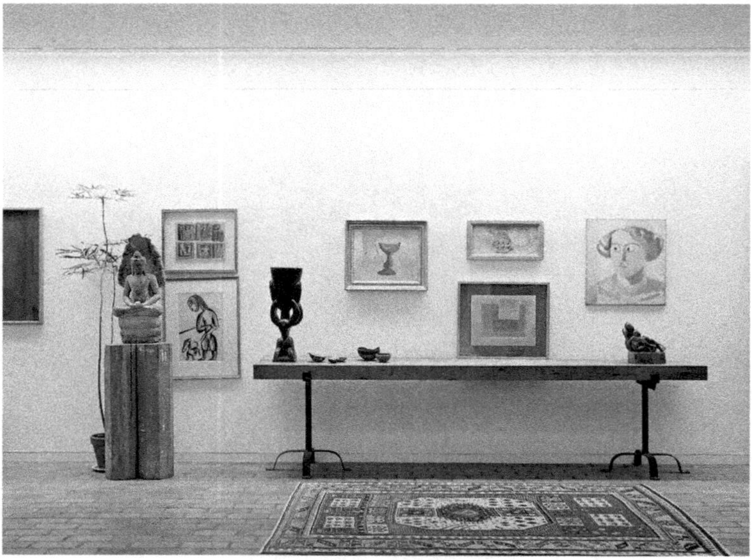

Plate 23 Ground floor extension at Kettle's Yard. Image: Kettle's Yard, University of Cambridge. Photo: Paul Allitt

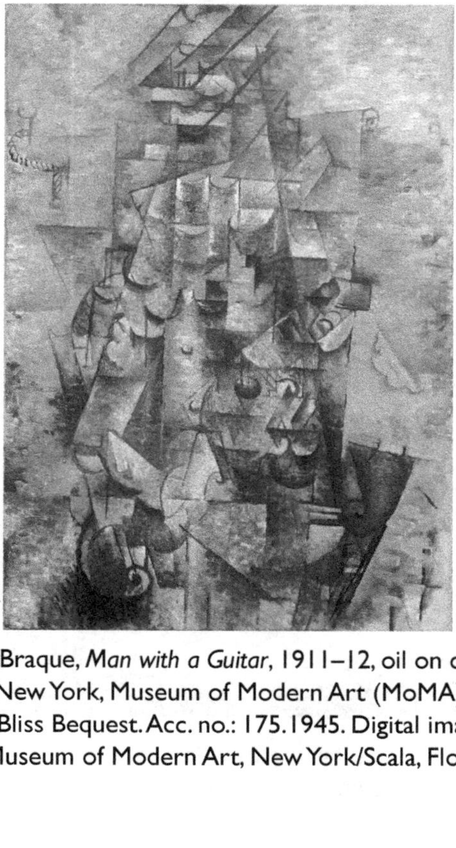

Plate 24 Georges Braque, *Man with a Guitar*, 1911–12, oil on canvas, $45\frac{3}{4} \times 31\frac{7}{8}$ in. (116.2 x 80.9 cm), New York, Museum of Modern Art (MoMA). Acquired through the Lillie P. Bliss Bequest. Acc. no.: 175.1945. Digital image © 2019 The Museum of Modern Art, New York/Scala, Florence

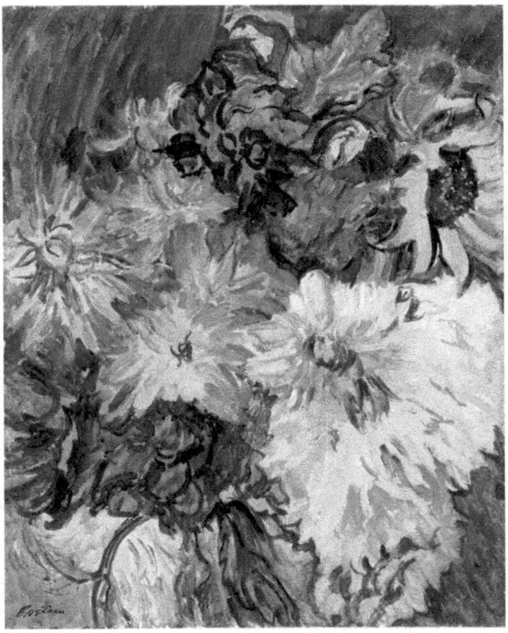

Plate 25 Sir Jacob Epstein, *Dahlias and Sunflower*, c. 1936, watercolour and gouache on paper, support: 558 x 431 mm, Tate. Presented through the Friends of the Tate Gallery, Helena and Kenneth Levy Bequest, 1990. © The estate of Sir Jacob Epstein. Photo: © Tate, London 2019

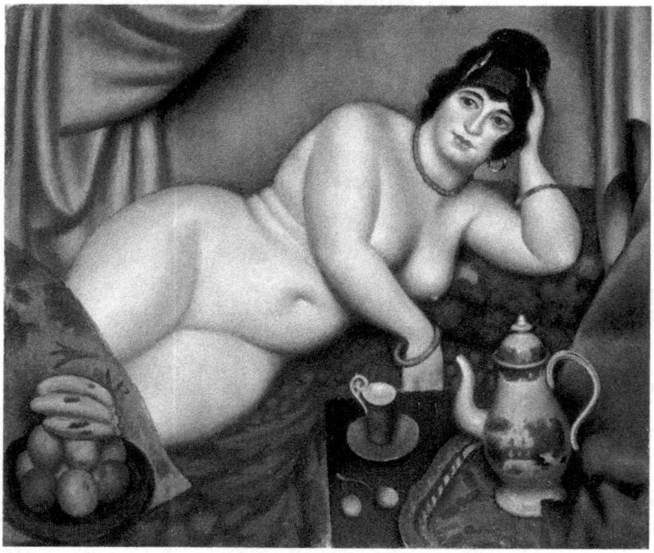

Plate 26 Mark Gertler, *Queen of Sheba*, 1922, oil on canvas, support: 1073 x 940 mm, Tate. Purchased 1963. Photo: © Tate, London 2019

and mountain snow and a sense of elemental fluidity is accentuated by rippling brush strokes.

This theme is reiterated in a warmer palette in *Window-Sill, Lugano* (1923) (plate 9) where the flower pots in the foreground share with the hills edging the lake a palette of glowing terracotta and yellow, and an undulating line of deep indigo blue describes the most distant hills, ripples of lake water, and petals of a flower on the window sill. The profusion of flowers anchored in their pots are disrobed of their usual wrappings and their heads appear to lean into the outer world as if to absorb the warm evening sunlight – several rendered in sensuous impasto strokes applied with the painter's fingers, blending the flower petals with the waves. In this way, she generates colour rhymes that bring the distant landscape and still life, the intangible and the tangible, into contact.

If Matisse was a reference point in dissolving the boundaries between interior and exterior through rich colour harmonies in influential works such as *Open Window at Collioure* (1905), Winifred Nicholson was distinctive in largely eliminating traces of window structures and plunging the viewer into the landscape.[38] On the figurative level this compositional structure (which she would return to throughout her life) suggests a visual metaphor for visionary experience, compelling the viewer to look beyond the spatial coordinates of the home interior and into a sometimes disorientating outer world. She typically exploits the lack of middle ground to evoke an ethereal quality of light-filled space and thin mountain air, which seems to breathe into and around the flowers in these works. 'Azure blue' fuses the elements in her recollections of this period. Blue has a long tradition of association with the intangible and spiritual. Kandinsky's paean to the 'typical heavenly colour' in *Concerning the Spiritual in Art* resonates with the contemplative, luminous blue spaces in Winifred Nicholson's Lugano flower paintings.[39] 'The deeper the blue becomes,' Kandinsky observes, 'the more strongly it calls man toward the infinite, awakening in him a desire for the pure and, finally, for the supernatural.'[40] The quiet, grey-blue tones of *Cyclamen and Primula* also speak to Kandinsky's notion that the brighter blue becomes 'the more it loses its sound, until it turns into silent stillness and becomes white'.[41] The indeterminate 'in between' spaces or pockets of light in these works can be read as 'gap[s] of unknown, unseen colour'; they testify to Winifred Nicholson's belief that all painting is 'painting of air and sky – that holds colours and light – not pictures of objects'.[42] Through her use of colour she introduces a sense of unboundedness into the traditionally enclosed spaces of the still life, exemplifying the 'liberation' of this quality that she would later articulate in her writings.

The painter's memories of Lugano were punctuated by demarcations of light which correspond with her developing aesthetic and spiritual concerns. 'Each day was a miracle of sunlight', she recollected, 'each evening a wonder of stars'.[43] The tissue wrappings in her flower pieces enfold light, creating a striking effect of luminosity in which the flowers appear to glow from within. She was attempting to invoke the 'celestial colour' and light she had encountered on her tour of Italy where she was attracted to the coloured light in the church windows at Ravenna, and in the work of artists such as Piero della Francesca.[44] What she sought was not so much to represent the substantial form of the flower, but the light immanent and emanating from it. H. S. (Jim) Ede, the Tate gallery curator who encountered Christian Science through the Nicholsons after meeting them in 1924, and who shared their belief in the spiritual significance of art, readily associated light with the divine in Winifred Nicholson's work. In *Cyclamen and Primula* he perceived 'the joy of opening windows; not only material ones, into a bright morning'.[45]

Ede drew attention to the paradoxical quality of 'insubstantial substance' in Winifred Nicholson's work, a phrase which captures her compulsion to search beyond the material to encounter 'spiritual reality', yet at the same time to attend to the inherent materiality of her medium.[46] Colour, as pigment and also particles of light, could express itself as a mediator between these spheres. Eddy's association of beauty and colour in *Science and Health* may have informed the painter's aesthetic:

> Beauty is a thing of life, which dwells forever in the eternal Mind and reflects the charms of His goodness in expression, form, outline, and color. It is Love which paints the petal with myriad hues, glances in the warm sunbeam, arches the cloud with the bow of beauty.[47]

Winifred Nicholson frequently invoked the relationship between colour and white light as an analogy for the relationship of all creation to God, envisaging the 'divine' in terms of boundless colour.[48] As she later wrote to a colour scientist, 'spirit, has no line [. . .] – no boundaries, no beginning, no end, no outlines, but colour'.[49] The combination of white tissue and the myriad hues of the potted flowers in her Lugano paintings was, of course, a suggestive framework through which to pursue this analogy in painting. She saw creation as prismatic and interrelated: like a series of mirrors 'the most brilliant things of nature' reflect each other.[50]

The 'spiritual' and the 'material' seem, then, to have been intertwined rather than oppositional in her aesthetic philosophy. As a reviewer from *The Times* remarked of her exhibition at the Lefevre Gallery, London in July 1928, 'She has an uncanny sense of flowers, of what they are behind their shapes and colours, as emanations of earth.'[51] The painter herself addressed this in more searching terms, describing how she could find 'abstract space', 'in the relationship of cloud to flower pot, or mountain peak to nearby shadow'. 'When one does find it,' she explained, 'it is the point where painting touches "spiritual reality" – the fundamental essence of things, beneath, behind, beyond, and before, visual appearance.'[52] The string of prepositions in her last sentence registers the struggle to touch 'spiritual reality' as she grapples to find a language for this undefined, 'unknown' territory. If she sought to represent the 'numinous' in her flower paintings, it was through an intuitive approach which resisted being precisely located or – as she wrote of colour – 'nailed down'.

In the early 1930s when she was living in Paris in a circle of artists including the Dutch constructivist César Domela, Piet Mondrian, Jean Arp and Kandinsky, Winifred Nicholson vigorously pursued the 'liberation of colour' released from form in a series of forty abstract paintings and drawings, which reveal her gradual simplification of the floral still-life-at-a-window motif.[53] One example is *Quarante Huit Quai d'Auteuil* (1935), which can be read as a radical abstraction of flowers in a pot with its composition of two white circular forms, a blue square and yellow geometric shapes emerging from (stem-like) lines.[54] However, pure abstraction did not entirely satisfy her at this stage, and unlike Ben Nicholson, she continued to find more stimulus in representational painting of what she described as 'near things, with hidden things within them'.[55]

Flower and Lamp

The flower represented as a vessel for light remained a central image in Winifred Nicholson's creative lexicon and in her idiom of the sacred within the everyday. 'Any true colour picture gives out light like a lamp', she writes in 'Unknown Colour', returning to this image in an article for the *Christian Science Monitor* in 1954, to imagine the work of art as 'a lamp for delight' and 'a ladder' through which 'translucent thought may travel up and far way' and back down to 'the home hearthfire'.[56] Through such figurations, the work of art is anchored in the domestic sphere where it signifies a potent source of spiritual light as well as a vehicle for imaginative travel. By adapting the tradition of private devotional art – the altarpiece or icon in the home – the painter conceives in the still life a spiritually inflected domestic modernism in which the flower piece and its colour harmonies answer her desire for harmony and 'still order behind the turmoil'.[57]

There are parallels here with the motif of flowers at a window deployed by Virginia Woolf in *The Waves*. We recall that in the early stages of composing her prose-poem, Woolf had imagined 'A lamp & a flower pot in the centre. The flower can always be changing.'[58] In her completed work, she realised this vision in a series of compositions within the elemental preludes to the main narrative, which invite reading as still lifes. In the following example the sun becomes the 'lamp':

> the rising sun came in at the window, touching the red-edged curtain, and began to bring out circles and lines. Now in the growing light its whiteness settled in the plate; the blade condensed its gleam. [. . .] The

> real flower on the window-sill was attended by a phantom flower. Yet the phantom was part of the flower, for when a bud broke free the paler flower in the glass opened a bud too.[59]

Woolf encourages us to read the slow work of the rising sun uncovering the object world and condensing its light into the local colour of material things. The relation between the 'phantom' and the 'real' is reminiscent of Winifred Nicholson's flower paintings where light transforms white tissue into luminous, lamp-like halos. However, what the painter sought beyond visual appearances was not a 'phantom', but the real 'essence' of an object. Her close friend, the poet Kathleen Raine, interpreted her flower paintings as 'a means of stating in visual form an experience of nature as an epiphany'.[60] Raine's theologically inflected language is consonant with what one could call the 'spiritual ecology' of Nicholson's flower paintings: their simultaneous invitation and record of a meditative sensibility toward natural phenomena. In her autobiography Raine records how she would often gaze at the 'luminous smaragdine green' of a bowl of moss and lycopodium and a hyacinth in an amethyst glass, which she kept on the table where she wrote poetry during the Second World War. On one occasion, this practice engendered a mystical experience:

> All was stilled. I was looking at the hyacinth, and as I gazed at the form of its petals and the strength of their curve [. . .] reveal[ing] the mysterious flower-centres with their anthers and eye-like hearts, abruptly I found that I was no longer looking *at* it, but *was* it; a distinct, indescribable, but in no way vague [. . .] shift of consciousness into the plant itself.[61]

Raine goes on to describe her intense identification with the plant, finding herself 'held in a kind of fine attention' in which she could sense 'the very flow of life in the cells', as a 'circulation of a vital current of liquid light'. What she apprehends in the flower's 'dynamic form' seems to her 'of a spiritual not a material order'.[62] The close attention to the physical detail of the flowers, and further, the penetrating vision into their 'liquid light', invites comparison with Winifred Nicholson's representations of living flowers through chromatic vitality. (Raine's description is also reminiscent of the sense of transference and renewed vitality experienced by Steiner's pupil on contemplating Greek sculpture, as we saw in Chapter 2.) Both poet and painter cultivated a 'fine attention' toward flowers and found a language of receptivity in their responsiveness to light. The sense of intimate contact and silent communication evoked in Raine's description is suggested in the conversational juxtapositions and colour rhymes of the flowers in Winifred Nicholson's paintings, which hint at what she referred to as the flowers' 'stories' rather than purely formal arrangements.[63]

Can we read such conjunctions of verbal and visual still life as representative of a private female mysticism in which the sacred space of contemplation is associated with flowers and the creative intimacy of the home? When Winifred Nicholson wrote of the 'shen' quality of flower pieces created by women painting in the courts of Chinese emperors she translated 'shen' as 'wonder, great wonder', and claimed that 'no man artist has painted "shen" that I know of'.[54] If she sought to evoke a contemplative, numinous experience in her floral still lifes, then 'wonder' is the specific state of (feminine) feeling that she cultivated and which she directly associated with colour in numerous writings. The word itself could, she said, 'evoke colour out of blindness'.[65]

The poet and painter David Jones also recognised 'wonder' in her paintings of flowers, identifying the works of the late 1920s and early '30s as her '*most* "wonder-making" painting'.[66] In his interpretation, 'she showed forth the "substance" rather than the "accidents" shining through the apportioned parts of matter that [Thomas] Aquinas said constituted "beauty"'.[67] As we have seen, chromatic sensitivity in painting flowers was Winifred Nicholson's foremost strategy through which to hone, in Bennett's phrase, 'sensory receptivity to the marvellous specificity of things', which fosters 'wonder'.[68]

Flower painting has conventionally been associated with the 'feminine', and regarded as 'minor' or peripheral in its subject matter.[69] Roger Fry, who painted flowers throughout his life despite his reluctance to be associated with the practice, observed that 'Modern European art has always maltreated flowers, dealing with them at best as aids to sentimentality until Van Gogh saw, with a vision that reminds one of Blakes's, the arrogant spirit that inhabits the sunflower, or the proud and delicate soul of the iris.'[70] While Van Gogh famously made sunflowers his radiant subject, Winifred Nicholson was nicknamed 'the female Van Gogh' in British art circles of the late 1920s.[71] Her writings do not express explicit concern with gender politics, but her passionately emancipatory attitude to colour can be aligned with a feminist reclamation of its traditional positioning as a secondary quality, while her quietly revisionist approach to aesthetic hierarchies situated the flower as the central and absorbing subject of her work.[72]

David Jones: The Stillness of War and Peace

The opportunities for metaphysical reflection in still life were of course not limited to women painters. David Jones, who recognised the expression of 'wonder' in Winifred Nicholson's work, employed the still-life-at-a-window composition to numinous effect during a prolific period between 1928 and 1932. He produced a series of still lifes in watercolour and pencil which typically foreground a flower piece or simple objects on a table in front of a window, of which *Artist's Worktable* (1929) (plate 10), and *Briar Cup* (1932) (plate 11) are illustrative examples. Ede noted the 'sense of substance being insubstantial' in Jones's rendering of windows and walls, echoing his description of Winifred Nicholson's work, and thereby drawing the painters together through a shared critical lexicon.[73] Like Winifred Nicholson, Jones used colour as a means through which to evoke the fluidity of matter and the 'spiritual' reality of objects. But the effect is different in his works which are characterised by loosely described forms outlined in pencil, and by a softness and lightness of colour, often applied in washes, which cause the objects to appear ungrounded, to interpenetrate, and sometimes to appear on the threshold of dissolution.

Jones's approach to still life was underpinned by deeply held spiritual convictions. His view of art as essentially sacramental was rooted in Catholicism, to which he had converted in 1921. The French Catholic philosopher, Jacques Maritain (1882–1973), was particularly influential on Jones's thinking, as expressed in his essay 'Art and Sacrament' (1955), which explores the role of the artist as a sacramental maker who parallels the act of divine creation: making 'signs of something other'.[74] Jones frequently invoked an analogy between the Catholic dogma of transubstantiation and the act of 'making' with which the artist is engaged.[75] In Catholic theology, transubstantiation refers to the spiritual change by which the bread and wine used in the sacrament of the Eucharist become Christ's body and blood rather than acting as mere symbols. Jones's implication in applying this belief to art was that a painting 'simply is the scene or whatever it may be, stated in other terms', rather than its re-presentation.[76] This logic enabled Jones to draw parallels with the Post-Impressionist commitment to conveying the solid 'thing' itself rather than fleeting impressions; or as Fry described it: 'not to imitate life, but to find an equivalent for life'.[77]

For Jones, as for Winifred Nicholson, the 'still life at a window' was a motif through which to explore the relationship between the material and the immaterial. Jones articulated his preference for painting from the 'sheltered position' of a window inside a house, often at the home of Helen Sutherland in Northumberland: 'I like the indoors outdoors, contained but limitless feeling of windows and doors.'[78] However, his still lifes do not evoke the clarity of light and spaciousness of Winifred Nicholson's early flower paintings set on windowsills. *Artist's Worktable* hints at the 'indoors outdoors' yet remains firmly within: the sash window is slightly ajar but it reveals little of the outdoor world, although the fronds of a creeper trail down into the room toward the vase of flowers. The delicately rendered translucency of the curtains and the hazy patches of colour that describe the walls create the impression of insubstantial partitions, articulating the slightness of the separation between what Jones frequently referred to as the 'creaturely' world (that of nature), and the space constructed by man for the making of art.[79] The presence of an industrious artist-as-maker is implicit through the depiction of his tools (scissors, rag and paint pots), which are given significance on the work table, accentuated by bold touches of colour, which harmonise with the hues of the flowers. As in Woolf's depiction of Fry's studio, in this sub-genre of the studio-as-still-life we can read a portrait of the artist through his tools. The painting encodes Jones's belief in man as *homo faber*. It enacts what he later described, looking back on the 1930s, as the 'raising' of the homely, handled, commonplace object to the level of the sacramental. Writing of Van Gogh's celebrated still life painting of his chair, Jones acclaims the painter's 'achievement' in giving us 'an abiding image of all "chair-ness"', and at the same time 'rais[ing] that rush-bottomed chair to the status of the *sedes*; one of those thrones which stand before us, with such solid reality, in gleaming Byzantine mosaics'.[80]

The interconnectedness of man and the natural world, which was also fundamental to Jones's theology, is expressed in many of his still lifes of this period. In *July Change* (1930), leaves press up against the windowpanes from outside and the mixed flowers in their vases make the blue air vibrant with colour.[81] The flowers are untamed interlacing profusions of stems and petals, even though the scissors (which also appear in *The Artist's Worktable*) seem to avow that 'change' of whatever sort is in the air. By the time Jones painted *Briar Cup* (1932) (which was bought by Helen Sutherland), he seems almost to have left his 'shelter'. Even the window frame has disappeared, and the thorny flower piece that dominates the composition inhabits a space barely separated from the garden with its strutting birds. The high viewpoint means that the circular table-top appears to rise unsupported, as if floating among but slightly dislocated from the other translucent objects; we look *through* them into the landscape, as if into an image from memory. There are visual cues of Jones's desire to integrate natural and material objects in the bold outlining of the handles of the teapot, cup and tureen, which echo the sinuous lines of the briar stems. The objects in this painting (which is often associated with later compositions of flowers and glassware, notably *Flora in Calix-Light* (1950)), operate variously as symbols of the Eucharist or the Passion through the allusion to the crown of thorns worn by Christ; or as references to the 'chalice' central to the Arthurian myth of the Holy Grail with which the artist was fascinated.

This palimpsest-like layering of meaning was a feature of Jones's densely allusive poetry. His long war poem *In Parenthesis* (1937), which charts the experiences of the soldier John Ball during the First World War (from December 1915 to July 1916), is similarly interwoven with Arthurian legend and allusions to the perilous enchantments of the Grail myth. If Jones's still lifes can be read as struggles to create spaces of security, shelter and harmonious co-existence between natural and man-made objects, they gain further significance in the context of his engagement in and long recovery from the trauma of combat. He began writing *In Parenthesis* in what he described as 'a kind of space between', beginning in 1928 and completing the first draft in 1932, a decade after the end of the First World War and around the same period as the series of still lifes we have discussed.[82]

In his Preface to the poem Jones observed how the imaginations of the soldiers had been profoundly affected by 'the day by day in the Waste Land, the sudden violences and the long stillnesses'. It was 'a place of enchantment' (p. x). In an important passage at the end of Part 2, we witness John Ball just before he experiences his first shell blast. In a kind of fractured textual 'still life', he waits suspended 'in a stillness charged through with some approaching violence'. With his senses 'highly alert' and his body 'incapable of movement or response', he notices 'the exact disposition of small things'. Then this state of strained attention is ruptured as we read,

> Out of the vortex, rifling the air it came – bright, brass-shod, Pandoran; with all-filling screaming the howling crescendo's up-piling snapt. The universal world, breath held, one half second, a bludgeoned stillness. Then the pent violence released a consummation of all burstings out; all sudden up-rendings and rivings-through – all taking out of vents – all barrier-breaking – all unmaking. Pernitric begetting – the dissolving and splitting of solid things. In which unearthing aftermath, John Ball picked up his mess-tin and hurried within; ashen, huddled, waited in the dismal straw. (p. 24)

Jones's still life paintings can be understood as shorings up against this 'bludgeoned stillness'. They re-imagine the terrible ruptured stillness of wartime: the destructive vortex, the 'unmaking' of mechanised warfare, which he saw as a fundamental break with the past. They offer an alternative to this stillness-as-death and stillness-as-waiting-for-death. The structure of the sheltered position at a window to which Jones repeatedly turns in these works contains within it the possibility of peace, shelter and harmony, or at least a bracketing – a 'parenthesis' – of the memory of war. These compositions register the need to 'hurr[y] within', to safety and to gather creative objects. But to bracket is only to put something to one side or set it a little apart within a larger narrative or landscape, rubbing up against its edges. The veins of pencil and watercolour which enmesh the objects in the interwoven surfaces of these works, register as defiant (but also anxious) ripples of life and expressions of nature's continuity and growth.

Despite their light tonality and expression of domestic vitality, Jones's still life compositions speak to the memory of 'dissolving and splitting [. . .] solid things' experienced by John Ball. His state of heightened perception toward the 'exact disposition of small things' seems to be reworked in these compositions, as they worry with reiterated pencil strokes over the outlines of objects – a cup handle or table edge – until they vibrate, as if rendering a sharpened perceptual process.

In the poem much of the action takes place in the woods and undergrowth, where nature bears the brunt of man's destructive force, his 'unearthing'. Yet even in the chaos and horror of the attack in Mametz wood at the end of the poem, the natural world still offers hallowed places of refuge: 'in the very core and navel of the wood there seemed a vacuum, if you stayed quite still, as though you'd come on ancient stillnesses in his most interior place' (p. 181).

In his essay 'Art in Relation to War', written in the early 1940s, Jones wrote that great painting '*is* both peace *and* war'.[83] The physical landscape of war – of wounded trees and wires – reappears, if submerged, in the imagery of thorns, bruise-like smudges of colour and twisting foliage in Jones's still lifes, notably in *Briar Cup*. But these compositions also recall the 'green peace' experienced by the battalion in *In Parenthesis* when they retire from the frontline into a 'sheltering coppice', or snatched moments when a soldier lies on his stomach and looks 'intently into the eye of a buttercup' (pp. 116, 142). In his 'sheltered' still life compositions Jones allows the seemingly solid world to exist in a watery, fluid state of becoming, of repair, for which watercolour is the appropriate medium. Material things are borderless, spilling into each other – connected in their shared creation and in their possibility for metamorphosis. And this, perhaps, is his way out of the destructive 'barrier-breaking' experienced in the heat of battle; a reparative impulse wherein nature and the 'creaturely' world offer some hope of communion and renewal. As he writes in *In Parenthesis*, 'They would make order, for however brief a time, and in whatever wilderness' (p. 22).

In 'Art in Relation to War', Jones described the 'turn' toward still life in modern painting as revealing a much larger political and cultural turn. '[T]his very turning [. . .] from the play of the world-stage, to withdraw to the wings, to seek form quietly in a juxtaposition of small objects [. . .] is of great significance. It throws more light on our culture and its effect upon men than many pages of Charlie Marx.'[84] It was also significant in illuminating the artist's particular outlook. Jones affirms the dignity of humble objects in a way that is characteristic of the still life genre, yet underpinned by his particular spiritual commitments. In his memoir written for Ede in 1935, he elucidated the importance of being 'anthropomorphic': 'to deal through and in the things we understand as men – to be incarnational. To know that a beef-steak is neither more nor less "mystical" than a diaphanous cloud. God loves both.'[85] In the still lifes I have considered here, everyday objects seem vaguely animate and unstable – scissors appear suspended in mid-air, crockery leans at precarious angles – and material things are often barely distinguishable from living phenomena. This animate quality seems expressive of the artist's anthropomorphic impulse, and has the effect of making the apparently familiar object world strange. We find once again that the modern painter of still life seeks enlivened stillness: 'I don't care how static the subject is,' Jones declared, 'but it must be fluid in some way.'[86]

There is, then, a more precarious balance in the painter's rendering of the 'immaterial' and the 'material' than Ede accommodates in his conclusion that these qualities 'fuse' in his work.[87] The eye often feels impeded in its encounter with his still life compositions; it cannot settle, or pass directly through an open window. Rather, it becomes entangled and distracted by the rippling pencil lines and the density of the charged surfaces (as does the reader of Jones's poetry, facing fragmented syntax, compounds of mythical and literary allusions and slippages between past and present). Is this a retracing of the artist's labour as he seeks to pierce beyond the given material world, or the struggle with memory and the spectre of 'unearthing'? Jones's preference for a 'sheltered position' hints at an anxiety about the world outside the window, which the still life at once assuages and disturbs. His restless still lifes pose the question of how far the painter, and indeed the viewer, can transcend material realities, and as such, they hint at what may or may not be a wider struggle in his system of belief.

'A Painters' Place': Still Life at Bankshead and Beyond

The 'still-life-and-landscape' motif as a vehicle for the expression of realities beyond the immediate and material opens up further questions when we consider the conjunction of Winifred Nicholson, Ben Nicholson and Ivon Hitchens painting together at 'Bankshead', the Nicholsons' farmhouse in rural Cumberland in 1925. During the 1920s, Bankshead became a symbol of a simple, alternative lifestyle for the numerous artists who visited it, including Hitchens, Paul Nash and Christopher Wood, the latter supplying it with the designation 'painters' place'.[88] The Nicholsons' aesthetic and lifestyle of rural simplicity was indebted to the Arts and Crafts notion of the 'simple life' advocated by socialist reformers William Morris and Charles Robert Ashbee, but also to the purified spaces envisioned by modernist architects such as Le Corbusier. For Winifred Nicholson the 'modern' represented a social and aesthetic vision, it meant the clearing out of 'Victorian, Edwardian, Old Theology, Old Tory views', and a movement from 'false ornament' toward 'clarity, white walls, and simplicity'.[89] It was also 'informed by a shared interest in new forms of spirituality' – Christian Science – and 'a new way of living'.[90] The Nicholsons fashioned a space in which the everyday was given renewed attention and their still life paintings of the period reflected this commitment. Winifred Nicholson typically painted wild flowers that were handpicked from the local countryside or grew in pots, while Ben Nicholson chose earthenware jugs, mugs and goblets, rather than the sophisticated Edwardian tableware favoured by his father, the painter William Nicholson.

Hitchens experienced the Nicholsons' 'new way of living' in 1925 when he spent the spring at Bankshead, staying on to continue painting after they had departed. He had been attracted to Ben Nicholson's work after seeing it exhibited at Herbert Furst's Adelphi gallery in 1924, and the same year he put him forward for membership of the Seven and Five.[91] Hitchens's response to the uncluttered interiors at Bankshead has been seen as a turning point in his work and it suggests a point of departure from which to consider his evolving interpretation of still life over the subsequent decade. Prior to this he had painted landscapes, but his visit prompted a series of paintings which operate simultaneously as interiors-containing-still-lifes and interiors *as* still lifes.[92] They also suggest ways in which we might revisit still life as a less isolated, purely aesthetic genre and rather as a more conversational, communal art form.

Hitchens recorded the sense of clarity he experienced at Bankshead in a series of paintings flooded by light and amplified space through framing and reflective devices such as mirrors, doorways and windows with exterior views. In *A Border Day (Morning, Bankshead)* (1925) the windowpane appears to dissolve into the outdoor scene, while the cloud formation and light reflecting upon the window edge and interior wall are both rendered in luminous white paint.[93] The painting evokes a sense of the concentrated quietude of a room evacuated of human presence. As Judith Collins points out, however, the Nicholsons have an 'implied presence' in other compositions of Bankshead interiors through the textiles, furniture and colour combinations that characterised their domestic space.[94] Perhaps the work that emblematises the composite influences on Hitchens at this time is *Still Life with Potted Geraniums and a Pencil, Bankshead* (1925) (plate 12). The bold palette and suggestion of patterned textiles seem to pay tribute to several paintings of geraniums by Matisse made between 1906 and 1912, but the subject of potted flowers (with the suggestion of a window) and use of luminous white tones strongly aligns the work with Winifred Nicholson. Hitchens's treatment of the subject is already more abstract and experimental however, and anticipates the development of his vivid chromatic idiom. He layers flat, interlocking segments of red, yellow and grey so that all but the flowers and pencil are virtually unrecognisable as material objects, the artist's tools and inspiration framed together under what might be an undulating cloudscape flowing into the interior.

The practice of painting outdoors and by open windows which was encouraged by Winifred Nicholson, may have contributed to the emergence of the flower piece at a window theme in different permutations in the work of all three painters around this time.[95] As we have seen, the window could function as a formal device through which to enlarge and reinvigorate the space of still life. It was also a visual metaphor for movement between the material and the immaterial, between inner and outer worlds. Photographs of Bankshead interiors during this period reveal ready-made still lifes and flower pieces integrated into the domestic environment as part of its lived architecture. As Jake Nicholson recalled of his parents' home, '[e]ach window of the house was like a picture frame holding the view beyond. [. . .] The old stone walls made deep sills, on which jugs of flowers could stand and relate to the landscape.'[96]

Hitchens took up the theme of potted flowers at a window from 1925 onwards in a series of paintings of cyclamen and hyacinths that reveal affinities with Winifred Nicholson's compositions. However, he was interested in experimenting with the relationship between the flowers and the geometry of the window as well as its illusory reflective possibilities. In *Flowers in a Window* (plate 13), he demonstrates to striking effect what Winifred Nicholson described as the use of harmonious colours that 'make luminosity in the even light of an interior'.[97] The lamp-like flowers reassuringly illuminate the darkened window, conveying a poetic symbol of domestic well-being enhanced by the balanced composition with its half-closed curtains framing the flowers. The yellow-white tones pulse with visible lines of thin vibrating brush strokes creating a glowing interior in which the flowers are the luminous focal point. At this stage, Hitchens was already drawing the light and colour of the outer world inside.

*

In the decade following his visit to Bankshead, still life – and particularly flower painting – became central to Hitchens's art. The following statement from the artist goes some way to elucidating this:

> I love flowers for painting [. . .] not a carefully arranged bunch such as people ought *not* to do – but doing a mixed bunch in a *natural* way. One can read into a good flower picture the same problems that one faces with a landscape, near and far, meanings and movements of shapes and brush strokes.[98]

Hitchens alerts us to the dynamic interplay between flower and landscape painting, and to the 'naturalness' and immediacy he sought in both. While exhibitions and critical commentary have mostly focused on his landscapes, T. G. Rosenthal has rightly declared the artist an 'absolute master' of flower painting, 'rarely conventional' in a genre for which he is 'relatively unknown'.[99] However, Rosenthal identifies the flower paintings as 'temporary excursions from the permanently obsessing landscapes', finding that 'associations with one microcosmic aspect of nature turn the painting into another landscape'.[100] But were they in fact 'temporary excursions', with the insignificance and transience this implies? Here I make the case for Hitchens's ongoing commitment to flower painting – perhaps the most animate form of still life – alongside and as intimately connected to his landscapes.

Hitchens's Hampstead studio with an adjoining garden courtyard, which he occupied through the 1930s, stimulated mediations between nature and culture. 'The whitewashed walls reflected every scrap of light on to the jugs and jars and patterned cloths that appear and reappear in the pictures of the next few years, and there would always be growing things: plants and flowers and two small chestnut trees in pots', the art historian and friend of the painter Peter Khoroche recalls, evoking the vibrant, microcosmic landscape contained within the studio.[101] Hitchens underscores the fundamental link between the studio and nature in his painting *The Blackbird Adelaide Road* (1937) (plate 14). Vibrant plant life takes centre stage in this horizontal format composition divided into five sections. The rhythmic patterns of foliage and numerous darkening spatial recessions distort perspective, rendering the studio somewhat mysterious and untamed in its impenetrability, yet full of life and colour.

Hitchens was one of a 'nest of gentle artists', as Herbert Read characterised the group of Hampstead-based artists and intellectuals of the period, which included Jim Ede, Adrian Stokes and Ben Nicholson following his separation from Winifred Nicholson in 1931.[102] Read's term resonates with Hitchens, but his inclination was to retreat away from group affiliations dictated by the urban art world. When his studio was bombed in the early raids of the Second World War, he purchased six acres of woodland at Lavington Common in West Sussex where a gypsy caravan functioned as a studio and home until he built his house, 'Greenleaves' (a much more solitary, rural 'gentle nest'). If Winifred Nicholson had nurtured his early attraction to painting flowers that were relatively contained in domestic settings, then the 1930s revealed a painter more interested in nature unsevered from its environment. Hitchens's flower paintings became increasingly unanchored and abstracted with flat, fluid mosaics of colour that anticipate and are strongly connected to the colour fantasias of the Sussex landscapes with their ribbons of white canvas showing through. *Autumn Composition, Flowers on a Table* (1932) (plate 15), is pivotal in the transition from what the painter described as his 'urban life', 'before the full impact of nature and country living' that had followed his move to Sussex. [103] We see the artist expressing the chromatic exuberance of a 'mixed bunch' painted in a 'natural way'. The flowers appear as flattened patches of colour but the coordinates of an interior and table are still just visible, with the different textures and intersecting outlines of forms rendered in a manner comparable to Braque's still lifes of the same period.

Hitchens's sensuous unanchored use of colour could be deployed to numinous effect, as another great colourist, Patrick Heron, suggested by calling attention to his 'floating flower-haloes, in which depth is again a *tangible* element'.[104] The spiritual connotations of 'flower haloes' suggest Hitchens's continuing sympathy with Winifred Nicholson's use of colour as a manifestation of the immaterial, an effect which is evident in *Autumn Composition*, where several of the red and white flower heads appear detached or suspended above the fluid patchwork interior.

'Spring in Eden'

That particular forms and motifs in still life could act as a conduit for metaphysical investigations in a quite different way from landscape is suggested by a series of Hitchens's still lifes of the late 1920s and early '30s, in which a sculpted female torso is rendered in various states of solidity alongside a flower piece. These works hint at a dialogue between the everyday and the world of classical art and myth. They also seem to anticipate the artist's later interest in 'Erda'. Khoroche suggests that Hitchens identified Erda – the notion of the Earth Goddess known to the ancient Greeks as 'Rhea' or 'Gaia' – more expansively as 'the totality of the spiritual universe'.[105] He notes that the artist recorded being haunted by the notion of 'Erda' during the 1970s, prompted by listening to Wagner's *The Ring Cycle*, and he translated the idea in terms of 'a female figure sculpted in stone, surrounded by a complex abstract pattern of colour shapes', within which the figure appears spectral and mysterious.[106]

Spring in Eden (1925) (plate 16), which Hitchens painted on his return to London from Bankshead, represents an early exploration of this composition and a variation on the 'still life at a window' motif. He depicts a female sculpted torso placed on a table top alongside a vase with a single delicate flower, a bowl of fruit and a mirror, all of which are positioned at what seems to be an open window with a view onto a garden but is in fact a visual quote from the painted 'garden of Eden' in his large canvas *Forest Scene with Animals* (1920).[107] *Spring in Eden* presents a gathering of objects, which we read as a summation of the painter's youthful creativity at Bankshead – revisited and expressed in the title. Positioned at the window, the sculpted torso invites the viewer's gaze into the garden, which seems barely separated from the interior, while the mirror reflection of the interior serves to blur this separation further. This circular visual journey and the airy, light tones of the composition balance a mood of peaceful reflection with a sense of movement and life: the white flowers and the torso feed each other's luminosity, and on closer looking the gleaming torso reveals fine rippling brushwork that renders its texture almost fleshly. Hitchens painted variations on this theme over the following years, as in *Primrose 2* (1926), where the sculpted torso is mirrored by a flat white spectral version framed between flowing curtains, an apparition-like figure amidst washes of ethereal colour.[108] By subtly interweaving this ambiguous, 'numinous' presence into the domestic order of still life, Hitchens kindles a sense of mystery in the everyday.

'The Musical Appearance of Things'

Hitchens's deeply felt intuitions about the spirituality of nature underpinned his approach to flower painting. As he made clear in his 'Notes on Painting' (1956), he conceived of the encounter between the artist and his subject as a vitalist exchange. 'The canvas receives life, becomes alive, gives back life, and finally shows the relativity of Nature', he wrote, comparing the painter to a magician who 'conjures up life *from within the canvas*'.[109] His sense of the vital relationship between colour and nature in painting is elucidated in a letter of 1940 to John Maynard Keynes, who collected several of his paintings. 'The colour note of an object is essentially Itself', Hitchens explains, 'The representation of objects by their colour notation is one (only one) method of painting nature, but it is essentially a visual thing and appeals most to me.'[110] Finding the 'colour note' was therefore fundamental in translating the life of an object to the canvas. It did not necessarily signify the object's naturalistic or local colour, but rather the frequency at which its 'essential' self vibrates. For the viewer, this involves reading colour notes as a complex of radiating vibrations. 'As the eye naturally moves most readily from side to side,' Hitchens explains, 'these colour notes grow in interest and complexity.'[111] This effect was amplified in the double square canvases he began to use in the mid-1930s, as in *The Blackbird Adelaide Road*. The horizontal format enabled him to structure the canvas into what he described as different 'movements', inducing repetition and opposition into the reading of the painting and disrupting the 'condition of now' which he felt limited the conventional square canvas (and by implication the 'static' nature of painting).[112]

In *Colour and Form* (1937), Adrian Stokes had challenged Fry's early denigration of colour and responded to a younger generation of modern painters by valorising the 'living' quality of colour. It is 'the vitality that shows upon the surface of an object, tinging it as does the life-blood our skins', he argues. It is through the use of colour that the 'true colourist' recreates the '"other", "out-there" vitality he attributes to the surface of the canvas'.[113] Stokes's vision of colour as rooted in sensuous, physical reality yet enigmatic in its 'otherness' is evocative of Hitchens's flower paintings and may have informed – or been informed by – his Hampstead neighbour.[114]

What implications might Hitchens's vibrational chromatic aesthetic have for the 'numinous' still life? As early as 1933 the idea of the affective resonance of colour was intimately connected in the artist's mind with what he referred to as 'the musical appearance of things':

> I often find in music a stimulus to creation, and it is the linear, tonal and colour harmony and rhythm of nature which interests me – what I call the 'musical appearance of things' (in a way the reality of their soul-essence, if there is such an unpopular thing in this mechanistic age) – rather than their objective solid externals. I should like to be able to put on canvas this underlying harmony which I first feel rather than see.[115]

What Hitchens articulates here about a practice of attentiveness and attunement which he aligns with musical receptivity has particular implications for still life, given its associations with quietude and silence. It is also relevant to the notion of 'enchantment' that we have been exploring in this chapter. In his association of the 'soul essence of things' with a musical quality, Hitchens joins many artists and theorists of the period who turned to music as a master metaphor for the 'immaterial' as well as a non-referential language of art.[116] We recall, for instance, Fry's speculation on the development of a 'purely abstract language of form – a visual music' in *Vision and Design* (1920), which was an influential text for Hitchens.[117]

Hitchens was mindful of the unstable place spirituality occupied in a 'mechanistic age', but theosophical teachings on the relationship between vision, colour and spiritual vibration may have informed his frequent use of musical analogies since his reading on the supersensory was extensive, and his father was a member of the inner group of the Theosophical Society.[118] There are ready comparisons to be made between his synaesthetic conception of 'musical appearances' and Kandinsky's use of music as a double metaphor for corporeal and spiritual affect in *Concerning the Spiritual in Art*.[119] In practice too there are parallels, particularly in Kandinsky's Murnau Garden paintings (1909–10), where clusters of flower heads are rendered as flat patches of vibrant colour, and diagonal brush strokes express a sense of dynamism and growth.[120]

Hitchens returned to the question of aural attentiveness in the reception of his work in his 'Notes on Painting'. 'My pictures are painted to be "listened" to', he writes, echoing Fry's notion of a direct transmission between artist and viewer: 'the spectator's eye and "aesthetic ear"' should 'receive a clear message, a clear tune'.[121] Herbert Furst was alert to this when he described Hitchens's early painting *Primroses* (1926) as a 'symphony in yellow', offering it as a contemporary example of rhythm and colour in his study of still life.[122] Similarly, the catalogue for Hitchens's first solo exhibition of 1925 drew attention to the painter's 'rare feeling for colour' in his attempt to 'to strip [. . .] the veil of the familiar from the unfamiliar'.[123] The state of listening quietude described by Hitchens underpinned his approach to disclosing the hidden yet 'underlying harmony' which he first felt rather than saw in the natural world, whether in landscape or flower painting. His concept of 'musical appearances' suggests both a temporal unfolding and a mysterious synaesthetic experience, which challenges conventional characterisations of painting as a static art, and by corollary, the silence and stasis ascribed to still life. The stillness in his paintings is a 'living' stillness, found in the 'haloes' of colour and light held in a vase or pot of flowers, or in the luminous green of holloways, ponds and wooded glades.

Ben Nicholson's Goblets

Ben Nicholson's still lifes, to which we now turn, demonstrate a heightened attention to the everyday, which was staged almost exclusively through commonplace vessels rather than natural objects. Still life was the primary vehicle through which he pursued what he called the 'idea' – the immaterial or 'spiritual' aspect of objects – in expressions which became increasingly more abstract throughout his working life.[124] In Herbert Read's words, he was 'something of a mystic', who believed that 'there is a reality underlying appearances' and that his task was 'to express the essential nature of this reality' by giving it material form.[125] Ben Nicholson equated painting and religious experience as 'the same thing',[126] and although he never subscribed unconditionally to Christian Science, he became aware of its teachings in 1918 and it became a more significant influence during his marriage to Winifred Nicholson.[127]

There are parallels with Jones's 'chalice' paintings in Ben Nicholson's still lifes featuring goblets, which invoke mythological, otherworldly connotations despite the artist's insistence that he chose them simply as 'the object with the simplest form'.[128] In *1924 (goblet and two pears)* (plate 17), a vaporous haze of white paint hovers at the mouth of a grey goblet, creating the effect of an evaporating substance. The painter eschews conventional perspective as well as clear distinction between foreground and background so that the pears appear almost to float on the blue tabletop. The pencil outlining around the objects further creates a provisional effect: the goblet appears insubstantial due to the thinner paint used to render its right side, and there are touches of transparency on the two pears. Rather than anchoring the composition in an everyday comestible reality, the painter evokes a luminous object world that exists in ethereal, light-toned space. The following year Nicholson painted *1925 (jar and goblet)* (plate 18), in which the heightened complementary colours (blue and red) and flattened effect of the two isolated objects create the impression of an after-image, as if we are seeing their 'immaterial' aspect. As in the earlier 'goblet' still life, the light pencil tracery of the goblet and faint, luminous glow surrounding the objects invests the composition with a numinous quality and recalls the 'halo' effect that we have encountered in Winifred Nicholson and Hitchens's flower paintings. The painter is as much interested in the 'aura' or glow around the object as the object itself.

Ede and Sutherland both interpreted Nicholson's 'goblet' still lifes as intimations of the numinous. Ede's overtly theological reading of *1924 (goblet and two pears)* finds it 'the equivalent of an annunciation', with 'the pears correspond[ing] to the angel Gabriel while the goblet, with its halo of light, represents the Virgin Mary'.[129] Sutherland bought a similar composition titled *1925 (still life, bottle and goblets)*, and was struck by the 'strange' and 'interesting shadows' behind the objects, finding that the painter's non-representational approach rendered them unfamiliar: he 'seems to be seeing these goblets for the 1st time as if they'd never been seen before'.[130] The same painting prompted her to meditate on the different ways in which painters seek the inner, 'spiritual' life of things through their material appearances: 'the inward idea – life – is big, weighty – tho' it is puzzling to say how or why or what this spiritual thing, life, idea has been & is expressed in 3 goblets & their shadows . . . What this picture says is spiritual & *said* in paint.'[131]

Sutherland conveys the untranslatable, elusive quality of the 'spiritual thing', which she finds in Ben Nicholson's still life. Later in the same notebook entry, she notes that it was Hitchens who had made her see the difference between 'materialistic' and 'spiritual' painting in this work. Hitchens demonstrated to her that Ben Nicholson had painted 'not in a materialistic way to show the very stuff of the glass bottle', but rather 'as a tone & as part of a scheme of a related harmony of tones'. For him, the exploration of tone and tone harmony represented 'an almost musical phase in painting'.[132] Even at this early stage, then, Hitchens was drawing on musical analogies to interpret the expression of 'immaterial' essences in the objects of still life.

If Ben Nicholson suggests unearthly or spiritual 'realities' in his compositions, then these realities are located not beyond, but within the seemingly earth-bound and sometimes austere sphere of the still life of the table. Khoroche describes how the painter would 'set out a simple picnic meal on a low table in the studio so that it looked like a still life', and by his placing of ordinary objects 'make them seem intensely alive'.[133] We might recall, in contrast, Fry's studio still life – the 'eternal' apples and eggs – from Chapter 1, which remained preserved and protected from the contaminating touch of 'life'. Arguably we can read this contrast as indicative of a wider questioning of the formalist separation of art and life promoted by Fry, which was being complicated by a younger generation of British artists in the 1920s, and even by Fry himself. As Ben Nicholson insisted, living and painting must be 'one thing'.[134]

Many of his still lifes seem to 'enchant' or give renewed perception to ordinary objects by depicting alternative 'worlds' literally inside them. Despite its plain, emphatically unliterary title, in *c. 1927 (still life)* we see a mug and jug decorated in the style of storybook illustrations: a house and two trees in a landscape are depicted on the mug, and on the jug a leaping 'nursery' horse.[135] The tail of the horse appears in the intersecting space of the mug handle, hinting at an unfolding narrative as it crosses from one object to the next. In such works, the artist urges us to look at, as well as to dream *through* the external appearances of objects in order to truly perceive them. They reveal his responsiveness to the appeal for child-like vision advocated from John Ruskin's notion of the 'innocent eye', to the Post-Impressionist and Cubist celebration of 'Primitive' art.[136] The painter finds hidden narratives and sublime geographies within ordinary objects. As Ede recalled of Nicholson, 'a jug standing on a table may convey the emotion which others feel in seeing a Cathedral set in its town square, or a mountain rising from a plain'.[137]

Ben Nicholson's playful elision of external/internal binaries anticipates his later composite works where stronger connections are forged between still life and landscape. In the 1960s he acknowledged that his still lifes were 'closely identified with landscape', while the landscapes 'relate perhaps more to "still life"'.[138] The 'still life at a window' was to become a more prominent feature, but porousness to light and space, which was probably encouraged by Winifred Nicholson's preference for painting by windows and outdoors, can already be seen in a work such as *1927 (apples and pears)* (plate 19).[139] Ede purchased the painting in 1928, and identified in it a 'still light' that 'caresses' objects, a light used 'to revitalise the circumambient'.[140] The composition inevitably recalls the 'unsteady' apples of Cézanne, who was a touchstone for Ben Nicholson. He acclaimed the French painter's 'tipping [of] the fruit bowl' for generating 'the whole contemporary movement in painting', and taking the painters who followed in his wake into 'a different world'.[141] However, unlike the solidity and tactility characteristic of Cézanne's still lifes, here the fruits are rendered as delicate floating forms situated within an airy, undefined expanse which barely registers as a table top.

Bridget Alsdorf makes the persuasive suggestion that 'still life humanizes landscape' in Cézanne's work, 'making it over in miniature model form', with 'tensions and slips between inside and out, between perceptual reality and metaphorical nuance'.[142] Ben Nicholson creates similar Cézanne-esque 'slippages' in works such as *c. 1926–7 (still life)* (plate 20), with its subtle suggestions of landscape. Ostensibly a depiction of a mug, plate and three pieces of fruit on a table, the composition is also expressive of the elemental, atmospheric world. The scraped-back surface in the upper half of the painting creates a weathered effect and the dynamic band of grey in the middle ground invites reading as turbulent low cloud or a hedgerow. Viewed with this metamorphic 'model' landscape in mind, the 'table' is evocative of undulating moorlands such is the effect of the shadows on the right-hand side of the composition. The painter had described a similar effect in lyrical terms in his 'Notes on Abstract Art' of 1941, which nevertheless corresponds with these earlier representational images. Through a freedom of expression with colour and viewpoint, the everyday forms of a 'bottle-mug-jug-plate on a table' could be transformed, he suggests, into 'an equivalent of something much more like deer passing through a winter forest, over foothills and mountains, through sunlight and shadows in Arizona, Cornwall or Provence'.[143] This transposition of still life into a shifting, dynamic landscape with its own poetic narrative has affinities with Jones's insistence on the fluid, anthropomorphic quality of objects and their capacity to be signs of something other.

The painter draws the natural world into the domestic space more overtly in a number of still lifes of the late 1920s, which depict flowers with luminescent petals informally arranged in jugs. These paintings suggest the commingling of the intimate and spacious in the simple domestic aesthetic at Bankshead, but without reference to solid furniture or interiors the flowers hover in blue-grey space and areas of bare canvas draw attention to the illusory, painted reality of the objects in a manner that is markedly different to Winifred Nicholson. However, the symbolic potential and spiritual value of flower painting intensified and gained a personal meaning for both painters at this time. Winifred Nicholson produced a series of contemplative works featuring clusters of living plants in pots on tabletops, which had been given to her during her convalescence after a fall while pregnant in 1927. Flowers can be invoked as motifs of *vanitas*, but they also signify vitality and new life. In a letter recording her gratitude for the 'flower tables', Winifred Nicholson implicitly links them to the healing system of Christian Science, to which she attributed her recovery and the safe birth of her son.[144] *Flower Table* (1928–9) (plate 21), which she painted at Bankshead, invites reading as a meditation on this theme. The objects are bathed in an otherworldly, silvery light and the flowers wrapped in bright white tissue are set against a pulsating background, flecked with silver paint. The light-filled flowers placed on the plain table register as a votive offering, rather like Jones's Eucharistic compositions of the same period.[145] Fulfilling a familiar function in Winifred Nicholson's work, the flowers provide a symbolic bridge or 'ladder' between the metaphysical world and daily life; they draw the 'transfiguring light' celebrated by Sutherland into the home.

'The Fusing of Art and Daily Living': Kettle's Yard as Still Life

For Ede and Sutherland, a defining – and compelling – feature of the Nicholsons' art and lifestyle was their capacity to 'transfigure' the everyday. As we have seen, this capacity was emblematised in their treatment of still life. The attention that both painters gave to the genre implicitly valorised the commonplace world of objects and the associated sphere of domesticity. As such, they represent an alternative to what Christopher Reed identifies as '[t]he tendency for avant-garde artists and architects, along with their promoters, to assert their accomplishments through contrast with domesticity'.[146] In contrast to this 'suppression of domesticity', Sutherland celebrated Bankshead as a place where 'the world of imagination really reaches & touches & lights up & enfranchises the ordinary human life', while Ede observed that he had learnt much 'about the fusing of art and daily living' from Winifred Nicholson.[147] By way of concluding this chapter, we make an imagined visit to Kettle's Yard, Ede's Cambridge home from 1958–73 (and now a gallery), in which he fashioned an aesthetic that I suggest coincides with – and extends – the notion of still life and its relationship with everyday objects that we have considered so far.

Ede envisioned Kettle's Yard as 'a living place where works of art would be enjoyed, inherent to the domestic setting', and he located the germ of his inspiration in his meeting with the Nicholsons in 1924.[148] Still lifes by the Nicholsons and their circle are a prominent feature of his collection, but his aesthetics of display could also be characterised as emergent from a 'still life sensibility'.[149] In his interiors Ede arranged what we might call still life compositions: 'stray objects, stones, glass, pictures, sculpture, in light and space', which he intended would 'make manifest the underlying stability' (see plate 22).[150] The mandate of careful preservation at Kettle's Yard means that the contemporary visitor finds these compositions exactly as Ede had originally arranged them, as if frozen in time. Does the display create a *nature morte*, or a still life? As if to anticipate such questions, the visitor finds their attention subtly directed to encounters between art and nature, which unsettle these apparent oppositions. In the ground-floor sitting room a lemon placed on a pewter dish is linked through colour rhymes with the yellow circle in Joan Miró's painting, *Tic-Tac* (1927), which hangs nearby. Such arrangements are touched by the irony of *nature morte* – the lemon requires replacement when it begins to rot. The ephemerality and 'evanescence' of plant life was also a feature of Kettle's Yard, experienced in the same room in which fresh flowers are placed as if in dialogue with a small flower painting of 1930 by Christopher Wood.[151] *Flowers* depicts a mixed bunch in discoloured water surrounded by soft grey shadow; one of the two daffodils droops slightly while the other is more perkily upright and a jaunty yellow, as if to show the passage of time, or still life's dual temporality.[152]

Ede was implicitly destabilising the very notion of 'rhopography' by creating dialogues between different hierarchies of objects and blurring the borders between art, nature and the utilitarian object world. An arrangement of black Cretan bowls below Ben Nicholson's *1924 (goblet and two pears)* initiates a conversation of form and colour (see plate 23); while the placement of a glass candlestick directly below David Jones's *Flora in Calix-Light* (1950) introduces formal correspondences with the stems of the 'chalices' in the painting.[153] This gesture registers as both aesthetic and votive (Ede interpreted the painting as Eucharistic), and the candlestick forges a participatory connection between the 'real' object world and the illusory but sacramental space of the painting. For Ede the candlestick was 'almost part of the painting, an echo of the artist's vision'.[154]

Ede's book of reflections, *A Way of Life: Kettle's Yard* (1984), constitutes a poetics of this aestheticised domestic space and the life of its objects.[155] Close-up black and white photographs of the collection are juxtaposed with extracts of poetry and prose, many of which are religious or contemplative in character. Ede takes us from St Augustine to the twentieth-century philosopher-mystic Simone Weil, demonstrating his affinity with different forms of spirituality that celebrate the sacred within the everyday. Similarly, at Kettle's Yard, objects from different spiritual traditions co-exist, from a fourteenth-century Khmer Buddha to Winifred Nicholson's evocation of an altar offering, *Daffodils and Hyacinths in a Norman Window* (c. 1950–55).

In *A Way of Life* the verbal meditations on objects 'poised in stillness' operate as prose still lifes that illuminate their visual counterparts.[156] 'It is exciting to be brought so near,' Ede writes of an arrangement of pebbles, shells and glasses depicted in one photograph, 'almost to touch each object, lift it up and feel its so close vibration.'[157] The invocation of vibration, a figure that has become familiar in this discussion of still life, conveys the intimate embodied experience of objects and the impression of their sentience.

Ede repeatedly invoked stillness and silence as revered qualities that hint at an undefined, numinous quality in the domestic environment. Stillness was a 'strange' and elastic concept for Ede, signifying a sort of 'harmony'. To be still meant 'to be attentive, to take in, to search' and yet to exist in a sort of negative state of pure knowledge.[158] In the interiors at Kettle's Yard he experienced a sense of time 'held suspended in silence':

> I like to keep very quiet in a room, and to have it always still. [. . .] it is to me as if it were a pool of silence, and just as a pool when stirred loses its transparency, so a room is stirred by movement. Sometimes I find that if I don't go into a room for a week, and then gently open the door and look in, I am instead invaded by its stillness; and if I tip-toe into it, that stillness stays about me for some moments.[159]

This lyrical rendering of the domestic-interior-as-still life extends the permutations of the genre and suggests an understanding of stillness as an active agent, a penetrating quality – and a state of being. Ede's attraction toward the quality of stillness that inheres in a room has affinities with Virginia Woolf's fascination with interiors from which human life is evacuated, where meaning gathers around seemingly insignificant objects. In her last novel *Between the Acts* – unfinished at her death but written during the Second World War – she employs the shell as a metaphor for the room as a vessel echoing with the lives of those who pass through it. Like Ede, it is the charged emptiness of the room that Woolf explores in incantatory prose that evokes the reverberating melancholy of sounds heard through a shell: 'Empty, empty, empty; silent, silent silent. The room was a shell, singing of what was before time was; a vase stood in the heart of the house, alabaster, smooth, cold, holding the still, distilled essence of emptiness, silence.'[160] Woolf's vase is characteristically paradoxical: cold and silent yet it stands at the beating heart of the house. It functions as another kind of shell, empty yet echoing with allusions to other literary vases and urns: we might think of the stillness of Keats's Grecian Urn, 'that cold pastoral', or Wallace Stevens's 'jar in Tennessee', which 'took dominion everywhere' (and with which we will be concerned in the next chapter).[161]

If we return to the visual world of Ede's home, we find that like many of the still life painters whose work he collected, he was attentive to the conversation between objects on window sills and the elemental world outside. He filled the window in the small 'bridge' between his cottages with an abundance of shells, potted plants, stones and a collection of suspended glass spheres, transparent and translucent, which play with light and shadow. With a view onto the 'outer world', Ede found in this space 'a transparent stillness through which to find and hold a sense of peace amidst "the manifold changes of this world"'.[162] In his conception, the room is an Eliotic 'still point' within the flux of modern life. His affinity with Eliot's assessment of the modern spiritual condition is evident in *A Way of Life*, where he places a photograph of one of his own 'still life at a window' arrangements next to an excerpt from Eliot's *Ash Wednesday* (1930): 'Against the Word the unstilled world still whirled/ About the centre of the silent Word'.[163] Ede's passionate interest in creating tranquillity and stability in the spaces of Kettle's Yard has been linked to his experience of combat in the First World War and the desire in its aftermath to create a still space of peace and harmony. In a recent documentary film *The Secret of Kettle's Yard* (2018), Cary Parker makes such connections more evident by cutting between old film footage of the battlefield and the quietude of contemporary Kettle's Yard interiors. The implication is that underlying such spaces is an unresolved trauma or hauntedness. As with Jones's still lifes, however, one might equally find in them the transformation of conflict.

The atmosphere of contemplative 'still life' Ede sought to create at Kettle's Yard is in many ways consonant with the model of still life expressed by the painters in his circle. Despite their varying spiritual commitments, Winifred Nicholson, Ben Nicholson, Hitchens and Jones sought to renew a sense of enchantment in the object world and to reveal the 'inner life' they sensed animating material appearances. They can be seen as part of a long tradition in contemplative still life painting which operates as an exercise in spiritual discipline through which 'attention itself gains the power to transfigure the commonplace'.[164] For the painters and collectors explored in this chapter, still life delimited a space of intensified and sometimes visionary experience: a way of realising, in Ede's words, that the 'material' world is 'threaded by this need to adjust the "inanimate" to the animate, to fuse them into one'.[165]

Notes

1. The quotation is from Winifred Nicholson, 'Liberation of Colour', in Andrew Nicholson, ed., *Unknown Colour: Paintings, Letters, Writings by Winifred Nicholson* (London: Faber & Faber, 1987), pp. 124–9 (p. 126).
2. I use the term 'group' not to suggest a formal constellation of artists but to point to a shifting circle with overlapping networks of display and reception as well as social relations. Hitchens became a member of the Society in 1920, Ben Nicholson in 1924, followed by Winifred Nicholson a year later, and Jones was elected to join in 1928.
3. Still life was also important to other painters in their circle, notably Christopher Wood and Frances Hodgkins. The Nicholsons' friendship and creative exchange with Wood is well-documented in Christopher Wood, *Dear Winifred: Letters to Winifred and Ben Nicholson, 1926–1930*, ed. Anne Goodchild (Bristol: Sansom & Company,

2013). For a detailed account of the Nicholsons' circle see Jovan Nicholson, ed., *Art and Life 1920–1931: Ben Nicholson, Winifred Nicholson, Christopher Wood, Alfred Wallis, William Staite Murray* (London: Philip Wilson, 2013).

4. 'numinous, *adj.*' in *OED*, http://www.oed.com/view/Entry/129141?.
5. As we have seen in earlier chapters, many modern artists were drawn to investigating the spiritual in art and their spiritualties took diverse and often unorthodox forms particularly in the aftermath of the First World War. For an overview of this tendency see Charlene Spretnak, *The Spiritual Dynamic in Modern Art: Art History Reconsidered, 1800 to the Present* (New York: Palgrave, 2014).
6. Herbert Furst, *The Art of Still-Life Painting* (London: Chapman and Hall, 1927), p. ix.
7. Ibid., pp. 170–1.
8. Charles Harrison, *English Art and Modernism 1900–1939* (London: Penguin, 1981), p. 168.
9. Furst, *The Art of Still-Life Painting*, p. 174.
10. Bennett, *The Enchantment of Modern Life*, p. 4.
11. Winifred Nicholson, 'Liberation of Colour', p. 126.
12. Ibid.
13. Winifred Nicholson, 'Unknown Colour', repr. in *Unknown Colour*, pp. 99–103. Here, as in 'Liberation of Colour', she published under the name 'Winifred Dacre'. The Nicholsons understood constructivism as an expression of spiritual ideas, but the anthology, with its mixed sources in contemporary technology, science and spirituality, did not present a cohesive or coherent aesthetic.
14. Ibid., p. 102.
15. Ibid., p. 101.
16. By foregrounding Winifred Nicholson's work in this chapter, I do not wish to posit her as the dominant painter of the group, but to re-balance the weight of critical discussions of British modernism in which her visual art as well as her contribution to colour theory has been understudied. Valuable attempts to correct this in recent years include Christopher Andreae, *Winifred Nicholson* (Farnham: Lund Humphries, 2009); Elizabeth Fisher, *Winifred Nicholson: Music of Colour* (Cambridge: Kettle's Yard Gallery, University of Cambridge, 2012); and Jovan Nicholson, *Winifred Nicholson: Liberation of Colour* (London: Philip Wilson, 2016), as well as the collection of her numerous writings in *Unknown Colour*.
17. Henri Matisse, 'The Role and Modalities of Colour' (1945), in Batchelor, ed., *Colour: Documents of Contemporary Art,* pp. 98–100 (p. 98).
18. Matisse, 'Notes on a Painter' (1908), in *Colour: Documents*, p. 53.
19. See her recollections on this subject in 'Blinks' (1979), in *Unknown Colour*, pp. 23–4.
20. See Peter Khoroche's discussion of Fry's influence, in *Ben Nicholson: Drawings and Painted Reliefs* (Hampshire: Lund Humphries, 2002), p. 23.
21. See for instance Christopher Neve, 'The Points of View of Winifred Nicholson' (1979), in *Unknown Colour*, pp. 14–20 (p. 15).
22. In 1922 Ben Nicholson noted: 'She has taught me a great deal in the course of learning herself, more especially about colour.' Quoted in Jeremy Lewison, *Ben Nicholson* (London: Tate Gallery, 1993), p. 21.

23. In the mid-1920s the writer Margaret Nash (wife of Paul Nash) introduced Winifred Nicholson to Christian Science and she first mentions it in a letter to E. J. Jenkinson, dated 24 October 1921. However, she was well acquainted with other religious traditions, having read the Vedas in India and studied Hindu and Buddhist writers in the early 1920s (see *Unknown Colour*, p. 39).
24. The entry on Christian Science from the 1984 edition of the Encyclopaedia Britannica, quoted by Judith Collins, in *Winifred Nicholson* (London: Tate Gallery, 1987), p. 18.
25. Winifred Nicholson's correspondence and transcribed conversations show her to have been a close reader of this text. See Collins, *Winifred Nicholson*, p. 18.
26. Mary Baker Eddy, *Science and Health with Key to the Scriptures* (213: 6–9), Project Gutenberg E-book 3458, 11th edn, http://www.gutenberg.org/cache/epub/3458/pg3458.txt.
27. Collins affirms the importance of Christian Science for Winifred Nicholson, linking it directly to her deep interest in 'testing the limits of human perception' (*Winifred Nicholson*, p. 18). Christopher Andreae is more cautious, noting that this belief system 'never prevented her being open to new ideas from other philosophies and religions, yet it gradually became central to her thinking and to her art' (*Winifred Nicholson*, p. 66).
28. Eddy, *Science and Health* (214: 10–17).
29. Helen Sutherland, quoted by Val Corbett, *A Rhythm, a Rite and a Ceremony: Helen Sutherland at Cockley Moor 1939–1965* (Penrith: Midnight Oil, 1996), p. 34.
30. Nick Jones observes of Sutherland's circle that they all shared a yearning for the 'numinous' world and its expression in their work: 'Winifred Nicholson saw the essence of that mysterious life force in colour and flowers [. . .]; Ben Nicholson through form and cleaner geometry; David Jones through language and history and Kathleen Raine through poetry.' Introduction to Corbett, *A Rhythm, a Rite and a Ceremony*, p. 6.
31. See Tate Gallery Archive (hereafter TGA) 958.1, 'Writings by E. C. Hodgkin', pp. 31–4. See also Nicolete Gray, *Helen Sutherland Collection: A Pioneer Collection of the 1930s*, exh. cat. (London: Lund Humphries, 1970–71), p. 24.
32. Frances Spalding, 'Helen Sutherland, Patron, Collector and Friend of Ben Nicholson', *Burlington Magazine*, CLV (July 2013), 480–8 (p. 482).
33. Letter to Winifred Nicholson, April 1927, quoted by Andreae, *Winifred Nicholson*, p. 70.
34. *The Sunday Times*, 8 May 1927, review of *Paintings by Winifred Nicholson* at the Beaux Arts Gallery, April 1927. Excerpt in J. Nicholson, ed., *Art and Life*, p. 80.
35. Winifred Nicholson, 'Moments of Light', one of a series of undated recollections, in *Unknown Colour*, pp. 25–54 (p. 37).
36. The Nicholsons worked closely until their separation in 1931. Studies of the relationship between their works in these years are limited because Ben Nicholson destroyed most of his work from this early period. See Sebastiano Barassi, 'The Allure of the South: The Nicholsons in Italy and Switzerland, 1920–23', in J. Nicholson, ed., *Art and Life*, pp. 9–17 (p. 16).
37. W. Nicholson, 'Moments of Light', p. 37.

38. In 1923, Frank Rutter was one of the first to claim that she had 'invented a new sort of flower piece' through this compositional structure. Quoted in Collins, *Winifred Nicholson*, pp. 15–16. However, a photograph c. 1921–3 of the window and view toward Lake Lugano at Villa Capriccio (TGA 8717 repr. in Lewison, *Ben Nicholson* (1993), p. 17) reveals a single sheet of undivided glass, which may also explain the absence of glazing bars in the Lugano paintings.
39. Kandinsky made additions to the text of the second German edition of 1912, and this text is followed in the *Complete Writings on Art*, ed. Kenneth C. Lindsay and Peter Vergo (New York: Da Capo Press, 1982), I, pp. 181–2, from which these extracts are taken. They are reproduced by John Gage, in *Colour and Meaning: Art, Science and Symbolism* (London: Thames and Hudson, 1999), p. 192.
40. Kandinsky, quoted in ibid.
41. Kandinsky, quoted in ibid.
42. Notes on the envelope of a letter to her daughter Kate, 30 August 1951, repr. in Fisher, *Winifred Nicholson: Music of Colour*, p. 36.
43. W. Nicholson, 'Villa Capriccio, Lugano', in *Unknown Colour*, pp. 33–40 (p. 34).
44. W. Nicholson, 'Moments of Light', p. 31.
45. Jim Ede, *Way of Life* (Cambridge: Cambridge University Press, 1984), p. 221. Ede refers to this painting as 'Flowers in Paper'.
46. Ede, quoted in Fisher, *Winifred Nicholson: Music of Colour*, p. 22.
47. Eddy, *Science and Health with Key to the Scriptures* (247: 19–27).
48. 'In the simplicity of the great white light all colour lives', she writes in 'Unknown Colour', p. 101.
49. Letter to Prof. Glen Schaefer, August 1980, in *Unknown Colour*, p. 256.
50. W. Nicholson, 'Liberation of Colour', p. 126.
51. Quoted by Collins, *Winifred Nicholson*, pp. 18–19.
52. Undated letter to Jake Nicholson, in *Unknown Colour*, p. 223.
53. See 'Abstract Sequence', in *Temenos*, 8 (1987), 163–73 (pp. 174–6).
54. The painting was reproduced in black and white in J. L. Martin, Ben Nicholson and N. Gabo, eds, *Circle: International Survey of Constructive Art* (London: Faber & Faber, 1937) (n.p.). It is in the Tate Gallery collection.
55. Letter to Ben Nicholson, 1950s, in *Unknown Colour*, p. 174.
56. W. Nicholson, 'Unknown Colour', p. 101; 'I Like to have a Picture in My Room', repr. in *Unknown Colour*, pp. 234–5.
57. Ibid., p. 234. She records finding 'still order' in a painting by Mondrian which hung on her wall.
58. Woolf, *A Writer's Diary*, p. 143.
59. Woolf, *The Waves*, pp. 63–4.
60. Kathleen Raine, 'Winifred Nicholson's Flowers', *Temenos*, 8 (1987), 168. Raine and Nicholson became acquainted in 1948 at Helen Sutherland's home in Cockley Moor and remained close friends.
61. Kathleen Raine, *The Land Unknown* (London: Hamish Hamilton, 1975), p. 119.
62. Ibid.
63. Raine, 'Winifred Nicholson's Flowers', p. 164.
64. Winifred Nicholson, quoted from an unpublished article in Collins, *Winifred Nicholson*, p. 142.

65. W. Nicholson, 'Unknown Colour', p. 103.
66. David Jones, writing in 1971, quoted by Paul Hills, in 'The Art of David Jones', in *David Jones* (London: Tate Gallery, 1981), pp. 19–71 (pp. 34–5).
67. David Jones, quoted in ibid., pp. 34–5.
68. Bennett, *The Enchantment of Modern Life*, pp. 4–5.
69. For a revisionary reading of still life in relation to the cultural construction of gender, see Bryson, *Looking at the Overlooked*, pp. 136–78.
70. Fry, in *Nation*, 3 December 1910. Quoted by Spalding, *Roger Fry: Art and Life*, p. 204.
71. Collins, *Winifred Nicholson*, p. 18.
72. For further discussion in the context of gender, see Diane F. Gillespie's introduction to the writings of six female modern painters, which highlights Winifred Nicholson's flower paintings: 'The Gender of Modern/ist Painting', in Bonnie Kime Scott, ed., *Gender in Modernism* (Chicago: University of Illinois Press, 2007), pp. 765–808 (p. 772). During the inter-war period women artists employed still life in ways that often subvert expectations of the genre and its associations with domestic warmth. Frances Hodgkins, who was also a member of the Seven and Five, painted the moonlit still life *Wings over Water* (1930, Tate), in which three shells take centre stage positioned at a window ledge overlooking a shining Cornish seascape. The shells evoke an empty home within a home, marking the absence of the sea creatures who once inhabited them.
73. 'Ede's notes on Jones and on Anathemata (1975)', in Cambridge, Kettle's Yard Archive (hereafter KY): KY/EDE/4/2/4/8, p. 3.
74. David Jones, 'Art and Sacrament', in Harman Grisewood, ed., *Epoch and Artist* (London: Faber & Faber, 1959), pp. 143–79 (p. 150). According to David Blamires, in *David Jones: Artist and Writer* (Manchester: Manchester University Press, 1971), Jones became acquainted with Maritain's writings from 1922 onwards, through the Catholic artist Eric Gill (p. 17). For a detailed account of Maritain's theology in relation to Jones, see Philip Irving Mitchell, '"Recession and Thickness Through": The Debate over Nature and Grace in David Jones's Roman Poetry and Painting', *Logos: A Journal of Catholic Thought and Culture*, 15 (2012), 60–89.
75. See, for instance, the letter from Jones to Ede, 3 May 1943, repr. in Sebastiano Barassi, ed., *Kettle's Yard and its Artists: An Anthology* (Cambridge: Kettle's Yard Publications, 2011), p. 37.
76. Ibid.
77. Fry, *Vision and Design*, p. 157.
78. KY/EDE/4/2/4/8, p. 4.
79. See Jones's friend Kathleen Raine's discussion of the 'creaturely', in *David Jones and the Actually Loved and Known* (Ipswich: Golgonooza Press, 1978), p. 23.
80. David Jones, 'Notes on the 1930s', first published in the *London Magazine*, 5:1 (April 1965), repr. in *The Dying Gaul and Other Writings*, ed. Harman Grisewood (London: Faber, 1978), pp. 41–9 (p. 48).
81. The painting is in the collection at Pallant House Gallery, Chichester.
82. David Jones, Preface to *In Parenthesis* (London: Faber & Faber, 1937), p. xv. All further references are to this edition and are cited in the text.
83. In *The Dying Gaul*, pp. 123–66 (pp. 140–1).

84. Ibid., pp. 137–8.
85. Excerpt from David Jones, 'Life', repr. in John Matthias, 'David Jones: Letters to H. S. Ede', *Notre Dame English Journal*, 14 (1982), 129–44 (p. 132).
86. Jones, quoted by Merlin James, in *David Jones 1895–1974: A Map of the Artist's Mind* (London: Lund Humphries, 1995), p. 18.
87. KY/EDE/4/2/4/8, p. 3.
88. For further discussion of Bankshead as a creative site for these painters see catalogue essays in Judith Collins, *A Painters' Place: Banks Head, Cumberland, 1924–31* (Kendal: Abbot Hall Art Gallery, 1991).
89. Winifred Nicholson, 'New Day', in *Unknown Colour*, pp. 40–1 (p. 41).
90. Chris Stephens, 'Beginnings', in Stephens, ed., *A Continuous Line: Ben Nicholson in England* (London: Tate Publishing, 2008), pp. 15–16 (p. 16).
91. Peter Khoroche, *Ivon Hitchens* (London: Andre Deutsch, 1990), p. 22. Furst set up 'The Little Art Rooms', on Duke Street, Adelphi in 1918.
92. According to Collins 'five interiors and two landscapes' were 'executed at Bankshead or inspired by it', and they comprised almost half of the works displayed at his first solo exhibition at the Mayor Gallery, London, in December 1925 ('Introduction' to *A Painters' Place*, p. 6).
93. The painting is in the Ashmolean Museum, Oxford.
94. Collins, 'Introduction' to *A Painters' Place*, p. 6.
95. The motif appears in Ben Nicholson's pencil drawing, *Window at Banks Head* (date unknown, Fine Art Society, London), and in numerous works by Winifred, including *Flower Piece* (c. 1927, Government Art Collection).
96. Jake Nicholson, 'What Does an Artist look for in a Painting Place?', in Collins, *A Painters' Place*, p. 10.
97. W. Nicholson, 'I Like to Have a Picture in My Room', p. 234. *Flowers in a Window* is undated, but its stylistic and compositional similarities to Hitchens' Bankshead paintings suggest that it was painted during the same period.
98. Ivon Hitchens, quoted in T. G. Rosenthal, 'Ivon Hitchens', in Alan Bowness, ed., *Ivon Hitchens* (London: Lund Humphries, 1973), pp. 7–19 (p. 13).
99. Ibid., p. 12.
100. Ibid., p. 13.
101. Khoroche, *Ivon Hitchens*, p. 27.
102. Herbert Read, 'A Nest of Gentle Artists', *Apollo*, 77 (September 1962), 536–42.
103. Hitchens, Letter to Tate Gallery compiler, 3 July 1978, quoted in Tate online catalogue entry, https://www.tate.org.uk/art/artworks/hitchens-autumn-composition-flowers-on-a-table-t02215.
104. Patrick Heron, *Ivon Hitchens* (London: Penguin, 1955), pp. 11–12.
105. Khoroche, *Ivon Hitchens*, pp. 111–12.
106. Ibid., p. 111. The examples Khoroche gives of this theme, both from 1974, are *Hope* and *A Sibylline Courtyard* (Courtauld Institute Gallery).
107. The painting was propped up against the studio wall while Hitchens was painting *Spring in Eden*. See Khoroche's note in the revised edition of *Ivon Hitchens* (Farnham: Lund Humprhies, 2014), p. 181.
108. *Primrose 2* is in the UK Government Art Collection.

109. Ivon Hitchens, 'Notes on Painting' (1956), first published in *Ark*, the journal of the Royal College of Art, but according to Khoroche 'based entirely on notes made ten years earlier'. Repr. in Khoroche, *Ivon Hitchens*, pp. 54–9 (p. 57).
110. 'A Theoretical Letter from Ivon Hitchens to Maynard Keynes, 27 November 1940', introduced by David Scrase, in *Burlington Magazine*, 125 (1983), 420–3 (p. 422).
111. Ibid., p. 422.
112. Hitchens, quoted by Khoroche, *Ivon Hitchens*, p. 57.
113. Adrian Stokes, *Colour and Form* (1937), in Lawrence Gowing, ed., *The Critical Writings of Adrian Stokes*, 3 vols (London: Thames and Hudson, 1978), II, p. 17. For Fry's demotion of colour see *Vision and Design*, p. 23.
114. On the possible connection with Stokes see David Gervais, 'Ivon Hitchens and the Harmony of Colour', *The Cambridge Quarterly*, 38 (2009), 87–94 (pp. 89–90).
115. Hitchens' statement about the aim and nature of his painting, repr. in Khoroche, *Ivon Hitchens*, p. 109.
116. Musical motifs had also become an important part of Cubist iconography in the early twentieth century. Winifred Nicholson experiments with the inclusion of a lute in *Paris Day or Night* (1933–6); and Ben Nicholson depicts a toy mandolin in a series of still lifes mentioned in the Nicholsons' correspondence of the 1920s.
117. Fry, *Vision and Design*, p. 157. Khoroche suggests that Fry's ideas were a likely topic of discussion during Hitchens' visit to Bankshead, and the work of Cézanne and Braque was of particular importance to both Hitchens and Ben Nicholson before their creative paths diverged in the 1930s. See Peter Khoroche, *Ben Nicholson: Drawings and Painted Reliefs* (Hampshire: Lund Humphries, 2002), pp. 23–4.
118. Khoroche, *Ivon Hitchens*, p. 8.
119. Simon Shaw-Miller notes that 'theosophists saw music as engendering higher consciousness through its perceived immateriality' and they took up the idea that 'just as the spiritual realm could be "seen" by the initiated, so could music be "clearly visible and intelligible to those who have eyes to see"'. *Visible Deeds of Music*, pp. 60, 133–4.
120. Rosenthal affirms Hitchens' interest in Kandinsky during the 1930s ('Ivon Hitchens', p. 12), but Khoroche records that although the painter was acquainted with his theories he showed antipathy when questioned about their possible influence on his work (*Ivon Hitchens*, p. 109).
121. Hitchens, 'Notes on Painting', in Khoroche, *Ivon Hitchens*, pp. 54–5.
122. Furst, *The Art of Still-Life Painting*, p. 258.
123. W. G. Constable, foreword to the catalogue for Hitchens' exhibition at the Mayor Gallery, London, 2–19 December 1925, quoted by Khoroche, *Ivon Hitchens*, p. 25.
124. Lewison points out that, 'For Nicholson, who referred to his works as "ideas", in other words not as depictions of physical objects but the spirit which lay within them, the writings of Mary Baker Eddy [. . .] would have provided some kind of encouragement.' *Ben Nicholson: The Years of Experiment*, p. 26.
125. Herbert Read, 'Ben Nicholson', in *A Coat of Many Colours: Occasional Essays* (London: Routledge, 1945), pp. 79–87 (p. 82).
126. Ben Nicholson, 'Quotations', in Martin, Nicholson and Gabo, eds, *Circle: International Survey of Constructive Art*, p. 37.

127. The period following Ben Nicholson's meeting with the sculptor Barbara Hepworth in 1931 is beyond the scope of this inquiry, but there are suggestive avenues to consider in relation to her creative exchange with his work, especially with regards to the 'still life portrait'.
128. Letter to John Summerson, 25 April 1944, quoted by Jeremy Lewison, in *Ben Nicholson: The Years of Experiment, 1919–39* (Cambridge: Kettle's Yard, 1983), p. 57.
129. Ede, in conversation with Lewison, quoted in *Ben Nicholson* (1993), p. 27.
130. Helen Sutherland, extract from a notebook entry, July 1926, reproduced in *Helen Sutherland Collection*, p. 16.
131. Sutherland, extract from a notebook entry, 7 December 1926, quoted in Khoroche, *Ben Nicholson*, p. 20.
132. Sutherland, extract from a notebook entry, 7 December 1926, quoted in ibid., pp. 20–1.
133. Khoroche, *Ben Nicholson*, p. 43.
134. Helen Sutherland recalling Ben Nicholson, quoted by Spalding, in 'Helen Sutherland', p. 481.
135. This work is in a private collection.
136. In his thesis on the inter-war career of Ben Nicholson, '"Modernist Cell" or "Gentle Nest": Ben Nicholson, Art, Design and the Modern Interior 1924–39' (unpublished PhD thesis, Courtauld Institute, University of London, 2003), Lee Beard describes this 'fantasy world' as a sign of modernity and suggests that the painter may have been influenced by 'the naïve representations of animals found in provincial pottery and Chinaware', which he included in his still lifes of the late 1920s (pp. 52–5).
137. 'Annotated typescript on Ben Nicholson, 1940s', KY/EDE/4/2/4/12 (p. 1).
138. 'Statement', quoted in Maurice De Sausmarez, ed., *Ben Nicholson* (London: Studio International, 1969), p. 40.
139. Ben Nicholson's *Porthmeor – Window Looking Out to Sea* (1930) is perhaps most reminiscent of Winifred Nicholson and Hitchens' Bankshead paintings in its representation of a view framed within the solid horizontals and diagonals of a half-open window. Two flower stems peep out from behind the curtains like a visual quote from Winifred Nicholson's flower paintings.
140. Ede, *A Way of Life*, p. 41.
141. Letter to Winifred Nicholson, 11 March 1967, repr. in *Unknown Colour*, p. 183. The letter includes Ben Nicholson's drawing of the 'tipping' fruit bowl, and urges Winifred that following this example would 'merely increase' the expression of her flower paintings.
142. Alsdorf, 'Interior Landscapes', pp. 314–18.
143. Originally printed in *Horizon*, vol. 4 (1941), an extract is reproduced in J. Nicholson, ed., *Art and Life*, p. 82.
144. See TGA, Edith Jenkinson 9323, Letter to Edith Jenkinson, May 1927.
145. According to the Tate Gallery online catalogue entry for this work, she 'executed six paintings between the years 1926 and 1930 on the theme of potted plants set on a table top', https://www.tate.org.uk/art/artworks/nicholson-flower-table-t03960. The painting invites comparisons with David Jones's *Chrysanthemums* (1930) and *Flowers and Tea-Cup* (1930).

146. Christopher Reed, *Not at Home: The Suppression of Domesticity in Modern Art and Architecture* (London: Thames and Hudson, 1996), pp. 7–8. Beard takes up Reed's re-evaluation of this attitude toward domesticity in his thesis to argue for Ben Nicholson's 'direct engagement with the "home" as a valid site of modernist expression' ('"Modernist Cell" or "Gentle Nest"', p. 17).
147. Letter from Helen Sutherland to Ben Nicholson, undated, TGA 8717/1/2/4712; Ede, *Way of Life,* p. 15.
148. Ibid., p. 17. Ede kept an 'open house' every afternoon so that students could visit Kettle's Yard. He gave the house and contents to the University of Cambridge in 1966.
149. Ede collected work by many of the Seven and Five artists, including Christopher Wood, David Jones, Henry Moore, Barbara Hepworth and the Nicholsons. A cast of *The Dancer*, which we encountered poised on the brink of movement in Chapter 2, is also part of Ede's Gaudier-Brzeska collection.
150. Ede, *A Way of Life*, p. 18.
151. Stephen Bann recalls how plant life was a valued if 'evanescent' part of Kettle's Yard for Ede, in 'Oral History Archive', https://www.kettlesyard.co.uk/collection/recollection/audio/plants-valued-part-kettles-yard-jim.
152. My thanks to the Director of Kettle's Yard, Andrew Nairne, who drew my attention to this painting.
153. The first group of objects is located on the ground floor of the extension; Jones's *Flora in Calix-Light* can be seen in the first-floor sitting room.
154. Ede, *A Way of Life*, p. 72.
155. *A Way of Life* is appositely described in the Publisher's Note as a 'visual equivalent of going inside the door and moving through the house' (n.p.).
156. Ede, *A Way of Life*, p. 80.
157. Ibid., p. 74.
158. Ede in conversation with John Goto, Artist in Residence at Kettle's Yard in 1988–89, in 'The Atomic Yard: Reflections on Childhood, Culture and Kettle's Yard c. 1957', http://www.johngoto.org.uk/atom-yrd/convers.htm. Goto notes that during the residency he began to see the collection as a 'succession of still lives'.
159. Ede, *A Way of Life*, p. 60.
160. Virginia Woolf, *Between the Acts*, pp. 36–7.
161. Stevens, 'Anecdote of the Jar', *Collected Poetry and Prose*, pp. 60–1. Further references to Stevens's poetry will be to this edition, abbreviated to CPP where necessary and given after quotations in the text.
162. Ede, *A Way of Life*, pp. 92–3.
163. Eliot quoted in ibid., p. 94.
164. Bryson, *Looking at the Overlooked*, p. 64.
165. Ede, *A Way of Life*, p. 55.

4

'INACTIVE CONTEMPLATION': WALLACE STEVENS AND CHARLES MAURON

> The first words the artist seems to say to us are: 'Look, listen, but don't move.'
>
> Charles Mauron[1]

> [A] work of art is inaction.
>
> Wallace Stevens[2]

The epigraphs above gesture toward a model of creative attention predicated on the opposition of stillness and movement. The French aesthetician, Charles Mauron (1899–1966), developed his theory of 'inactive' and 'active' contemplation in *Aesthetics and Psychology*, which was translated into English by Roger Fry, his friend and mentor, and published by Virginia and Leonard Woolf's Hogarth Press in 1935. Mauron's central concept in this text is the 'aesthetic attitude', which comes to signify an immobile state of suspended response and heightened receptivity.[3] As the first epigraph from Mauron instructs us: 'Look, listen, but don't move.' The 'aesthetic attitude' offers a paradigm for thinking about the art of still life and is a touchstone for this chapter. Mauron also provides an unexpected but suggestive nexus between the artists and writers of Bloomsbury and Wallace Stevens,[4] who had been reading *Aesthetics and Psychology* in the mid-1930s.[5] In this final chapter, I cross the Atlantic to explore the transmission of his ideas to the American poet.

Stevens made the inscription 'a work of art is inaction', at the beginning of the fifth chapter in his personal, annotated copy of *Aesthetics and Psychology*. It registers a symptomatic instance in which the poet echoes and compresses Mauron's appeal for an aesthetic of contemplative stillness. My inquiry departs from such fertile textual conjunctions to explore the ways in which the art of stillness and the (disputed) stillness of art, emerge as shared aesthetic and ontological concerns for the aesthetician and poet.

Stevens's library copy of *Aesthetics and Psychology*, which is now in the collection of the Huntington Library, California, offers a unique site through which to trace his encounter, or what is effectively a silent dialogue, with Mauron's theory of contemplative attention. From one's first contact with the worn paper cover, the book attests to thorough and responsive reading. The poet made frequent marginal annotations, underlined and marked out passages, and created a personal index on the flyleaf, signalling particular sections of interest. His personal copy affords a tactile and visual experience of the text as material object whilst also creating a sense of proximity with the poet as reader: one reads 'through' Stevens in an experience mediated by his paratexts. It is here that the correlation between the ideas of aesthetician and poet are revealed most vividly, and, for the most part, my readings of Mauron track Stevens's reading by drawing attention to his annotated text.[6]

'The Stillness of the Mind'

Stevens's interest in a mode of attentiveness aligned with 'the stillness of the mind', as he described it in a late poem, invites comparison with Mauron's particular mode of contemplative practice.[7] B. J. Leggett was the first to alert scholars of Stevens to the significance of Mauron's theory of contemplation for the poet. In *Wallace Stevens and Poetic Theory: Conceiving the Supreme Fiction* (1987), he drew attention to a period in the late 1930s and early '40s when *Aesthetics and Psychology* was 'infused into Stevens's imagination'.[8] Leggett's investigation of the shaping influence of this text on Stevens's poetics concludes that Mauron's theory underpins the poet's assumption that poetry is the '"triumph of contemplation"'.[9] Critics have noted the contemplative attention exercised by the poet during the 1930s, but Mauron's contribution in shaping it is almost entirely overlooked in recent scholarship.[10] In *Mind of Winter: Wallace Stevens, Meditation, and Literature* (1988), William Bevis explores the poet's 'meditatively detached point of view toward his own imagination', through the paradigm of non-Western meditative practice, particularly Buddhism.[11] He identifies the late 1930s as a crucial period in Stevens's journey to becoming a 'master of meditative detachment'.[12] The problematic ethical undertow in the relationship between detachment and stillness, which we have encountered in previous chapters, is fundamental to this discussion.

Bonnie Costello is a critic attentive to the political and ethical implications of still life. She similarly locates Stevens's interest in the genre in the 1930s, a period of political and social disruption during which he produced his fourth volume, *Parts of a World* (1942). She makes a case for the poet's 'turn in this stormy time to the art of still life', which she argues was 'less [. . .] a retreat from the storm than a means of contemplating and resisting it'.[13] The still life composition is permeable; or, as Costello eloquently puts it in her study of American still life, '[t]he vibrations of history are transported into the meditative space'.[14] In what follows I argue that the significance of still life to an aesthetic of attentiveness in Stevens's lyric poetry and criticism gains illumination when read in conjunction with the theory of contemplation offered by Mauron (a figure not considered by Costello). I focus on *Parts of a World*, since the composition of this volume coincides with the poet's reading of Mauron. However, I aim to show that what one might call the 'still life impulse' was not restricted to this volume of poetry; it remains important in his later work and criticism.

The temporal congruity between Stevens's composition of *Parts of a World* and an exhibition titled 'The Painters of Still Life', held at the Wadsworth Atheneum in Hartford from 25 January to 15 February 1938, also provides a historical marker for the poet's emergent still life aesthetic. It is likely that Stevens, who had moved to Hartford in 1916, visited the exhibition. Glen MacLeod persuasively traces the still life as a 'poetic idea' for Stevens in the late 1930s to this 'specific event in the contemporary art world', showing how the opposing theories of Surrealism and abstraction which framed the exhibition had significance for Stevens's poetics.[15] The exhibition offered a survey of the genre from the seventeenth century to the present and featured works by masters of still life, Cézanne and Braque, who were among Stevens's favourite painters, and whose specific relation to his aesthetics and taste as a collector will be explored later.[16] The Foreword to the exhibition catalogue is worth noting because it links historical Dutch still lifes to the modern reinvigoration of the genre through the trope of animation, comparing the way in which the insects, shells and hams depicted in these works 'seem to live with something of the mysterious double-life to which the Surrealists have called our attention'.[17] The 'mysterious double-life' of still life has been a theme throughout this book and it remains central in reading Stevens's poetic encounters.

While these historical and material connections go some way to substantiating Stevens's attraction toward still life, Costello rightly cautions against matching the poet to particular artists or movements, noting that he 'does not abandon poetic genres for painterly ones [. . .] but borrows their associations'.[18] I examine the poet's (sometimes ekphrastic) gravitation toward the iconography of still life painting, but rather than focus solely on locating material counterparts or sources for his poems, I am interested in addressing his more elusive and expansive interest in an associated 'stillness of the mind' and the particular way in which still life exerts and focuses attention.

I suggest that reading Stevens's poetry in the light of *Aesthetics and Psychology* provides a new and suggestive framework within which to examine the dichotomies associated with still life and the precarious balances and shuttling between abstention and indulgence in Stevens's object-centred poems. For the link between Mauron's theory of contemplation and still life has not yet been explored, but he addresses the apparent oppositions between activity and passivity, absorption and detachment often associated with the genre, to present a more complex spectrum of 'attitudes' or models of sympathetic being. Such a theory was significant, I argue, to Stevens in the process of developing his 'still life aesthetic' during the 1930s and early '40s and to a poetics of spatial and temporal transitions in which, as Helen Vendler has described, 'local objects, become not things alone but moments as well'.[19]

In 'The Noble Rider and the Sound of Words' (1941), a lecture composed during the same period as *Parts of a World*, Stevens summarises the most salient points of Mauron's argument in relation to the role of poetry:

> That the artist transforms us into epicures; that he has to discover the possible work of art in the real world, then to extract it, when he does not himself compose it entirely; that he is *un amoureux perpétuel* of the world that he contemplates and thereby enriches; that art sets out to express the human soul; and finally that everything like a firm grasp of reality is eliminated from the aesthetic field.[20]

It is amid this cluster of ideas that I consider still life in this chapter. Retracing these threads in Mauron's *Aesthetics and Psychology* allows us to examine the interconnections between notions of epicureanism, the aesthetic and the everyday, the 'active' and the 'inactive'; and the ways in which such ideas might be contested by modes of attentiveness enacted in Stevens's poetics.

'A Curious Mixture': Charles Mauron and the 'Aesthetic Attitude'

> When the whole world is crying *Forward*, he stands still.
>
> Charles Mauron[21]

We have set the stage for Stevens's encounter with Mauron's text, and the cultural and historical context for his proclivity toward still life. Let us now examine Mauron's psychology of creativity a little more closely. The 'aesthetic attitude' is the touchstone for his lexicon of attention and affect in art experience. 'Attitude' emerged from 'aptitude' as a technical term in seventeenth-century discourses of the fine arts, denoting the 'posture or action in which a statue or painted figure is placed'. This sense of human imposition upon an inanimate object shifted in later significations toward the autonomous self-directed gesture: 'A posture of the body proper to, or implying, some action or mental state' or a 'deliberately adopted [. . .] mode of regarding the object of thought'.[22] The term's etymology captures the dialectics of Mauron's theory as it moves between subject and object, active and passive, mind and body. Yet the 'aesthetic attitude' can be shared by both artist and audience. Mauron argues that '[t]he same oddly fascinating glance which the creator makes us cast on his work, he must himself have cast [. . .] on the world around', therefore 'there is no essential difference between the two attitudes' (AP, p. 39). The 'aesthetic attitude' is therefore an especially useful lens through which to re-evaluate still life as a condition as well as a product of aesthetic experience.

At the heart of Mauron's account is his distinction between the 'two attitudes of mind, the active and the contemplative'. He claims that the 'former never ceases to think of a future more or less near at hand, whereas the latter is absorbed in the present' (AP, p. 29). While the contemplative attitude is reminiscent of meditation practices in which the mind and motionless body are quietened, what Mauron envisages is by no means a passive or unfeeling state. The fundamental character of the 'aesthetic attitude' sustains the tension between motion and stasis and between heightened sensation and forestalled movement. It is, he says '[a] curious mixture of sensation and inhibition – the first depending on the second for its keenness, richness and duration' (AP, p. 33).

Mauron's creative psychology is therefore underpinned by something more complex than a simple paradox of motion and rest. He does not entirely polarise the 'active from the contemplative spirit'; rather, the contrasting properties of the 'aesthetic attitude' intermingle and enrich each other to engender a more acutely sensing subject (AP, p. 28). The importance of this 'doubleness' and its implications for still life will unfold further when I examine Stevens's poetry.

In *Aesthetics and Psychology*, Mauron diagnosed modern life as riddled by the rhythms of distraction and the claims of action: 'in life we scarcely look or listen at all, except in view of some future activity' (p. 31). This was the human constant that T. S. Eliot had memorably encapsulated as: '[d]istracted from distraction by distraction', in 'Burnt Norton' (1935), written the same year that Mauron's text was published and concurrent with Stevens's composition of *Parts of a World*.[23] As exemplars of the 'aesthetic attitude', Mauron's ideal artist or audience would represent a counter-current to the distracted modern persona by cultivating an attentive state of mind and body. The 'aesthetic attitude' therefore presents a challenge to a particular strand of future-orientated modernism preoccupied with motion and speed, and indeed with 'struggle' and 'combat', which Mauron claims are antithetical to the artist (an idea Stevens notes on the cover leaf of his book) (AP p. 70). We recollect Mauron's appeal in the epigraph to this section, 'When the whole world is crying *Forward*' the artist 'stands still' (p. 70).

In 'The Noble Rider', Stevens expressed his concern regarding a similar incarnation of modernity, what he referred to as the 'pressure of reality', by which he meant 'the pressure of an external event or events on the consciousness to the exclusion of any power of contemplation', which is exacerbated in the context of a 'world at war' (p. 654). For Stevens, 'resistance' to, or 'evasion' of, this pressure is an act of 'extraordinary imagination' with the power to 'cancel' the pressure (p. 656).[24] He had made a similar point in his essay 'The Irrational Element in Poetry' (1936), with striking resonance for the object world of still life: 'Both the poet and the mystic may establish themselves on herrings and apples. The painter may establish himself on a guitar, a copy of *Figaro* and a dish of melons. [. . .] The only possible resistance to the pressure of the contemporaneous is a matter of herrings and apples.'[25] By considering the art of still life as a mode of resistance to ominous historical events and to the distractions of modern life, one can identify further affinities between the poet and aesthetician. The genre of still life and the 'aesthetic attitude' arguably offer comparable ways of orientating oneself with greater concentration, receptivity and indeed humility toward the world. Nevertheless, the question of inaction was particularly charged in the turbulent political and social climate of the 1930s, and its ethical implications would trouble Stevens.

Leggett makes an important argument for Stevens's reception of Mauron's 'systematic framework for describing the artist's attitude toward the world and the consequences of that attitude', but he is primarily concerned with the ramifications of his theory in relation to poetics rather than aesthetics and he largely overlooks the inter-arts basis of *Aesthetics and Psychology*.[26] The intermedial implications of Mauron's theory are however important to the model of attentiveness developed by both poet and aesthetician, as complementary ways of (re)thinking still life, and as exercises or 'attitudes' through which to approach the world. Mauron typically substantiates his argument with examples from poetry, painting and music, showing a migration of the 'aesthetic attitude' across different art forms and indeed between artist and audience. This comparative, inter-medial approach would have appealed to Stevens who, as we have seen, frequently employed inter-arts analogies in his criticism and was highly engaged in contemporary developments in the arts (as a subscriber to continental reviews and journals and a correspondent with international artists and critics). It is also worth noting that comparisons between poetry and still life had a claim on Mauron's thinking at this time. In his commentary on Roger Fry's translation of Mallarmé's poems, published the year after *Aesthetics and Psychology*, Mauron follows his friend in comparing the poems to still lifes, with one described as 'a kind of triptych of still lives'.[27] Later he compares Mallarmé's belief that 'any spectacle can, under the poet's eye, become [. . .] the subject of a poem', to those painters who find a subject to paint in any group of objects – if they look at it long enough.[28] He seems to indicate here ideas about the transformative and democratising potential of contemplation, which gain further elaboration in *Aesthetics and Psychology*.

Mauron's distinction between immobility and action was informed by a broader concern with the relationship between art and life, which he inherited from Fry. The art critic's profound influence is prominent in the third chapter of *Aesthetics and Psychology*, which is devoted to Fry, and it is here that Mauron reworks his formalist theory toward a more fluid negotiation between the fields of the 'ordinary' and the 'aesthetic'. Fry's distinction between 'art and life' is reconceived with the 'notion of another boundary' which 'distinguishes two attitudes of mind, the active and contemplative' (AP, p. 28). Stevens underscored these propositions in his copy, but he had considered Fry's formalist theory as well as the writings of fellow Bloomsbury critic Clive Bell and his discourses on Cézanne as early as 1919.[29] Fry's transatlantic profile would have been raised by his position as Director of the Metropolitan Museum in New York from 1905 to 1910, and even if Stevens did not subscribe to Fry's formalism he recognised the significance of his ideas. Fry remained a key point of reference decades later when Stevens began his lecture (published as an essay in 1951) for the Museum of Modern Art, New York, 'The Relations between Poetry and Painting', with a quotation from the art critic drawing together the poet Virgil and the painter Claude.[30] From this 'analogy between two different forms of poetry', he develops the inter-arts analogies that cross-pollinate the lecture, advocating flexible 'frontiers' between the arts, and concluding in the third section that there is 'the same interchange' between the world about us and within us 'that there is between one art and another, migratory passings to and fro, quickenings, Promethean liberations and discoveries' (p. 747). Stevens's model of interdependence, like Mauron's 'curious mixture', establishes itself on a series of animating passages, or 'quickenings', between poetry and painting, artist and audience, art and life.

'Unstable Equilibrium' and 'Unalterable Vibration'

Stevens's poetic eye typically exerts a metamorphic pressure on the objects of contemplation in his poetry and prose. 'This object is merely a state/ One of many, between two poles', he writes in 'The Glass of Water', published in *Parts of a World* (CPP, pp. 181–2). The poem considers the migration of the object through solid and fluid states: the glass melting in heat and the water freezing in the cold.[31] The following decade Stevens observed, 'it is commonly said that a still life is a problem in the painting of solids'.[32] His poetry reveals a fascination with transitions between solid and liquid, stillness and motion, and a commitment to developing a poetics for the spectrum of states in between, which we also recognise in Mauron's theory. To this end, both poet and aesthetician employ vibration as a critical tool through which to conceive of the 'migratory passings to and fro' between the inanimate and animate, and as a signifier for a heightened mode of attentiveness.

In 'The Noble Rider', the poet teases out the unsettling proximity between movement and stability with two references to early twentieth-century philosophy. Firstly, he paraphrases Henri Bergson describing 'the visual perception of a motionless object as the most stable of internal states', but this is complicated by his subsequent direct invocation of Bergson's idea that one's vision of a contemplated object differs from one instant to the next, due to '"[m]emory [. . .] which conveys something of the past into the present"'. [33] Stevens continues this intertextual dialogue with an observation from the English philosopher, C. E. M. Joad, which extends the comparison to 'external things':

> Every body, every quality of body resolves itself into an enormous number of vibrations, movements, changes. What is it that vibrates, moves, is changed? There is no answer [. . .] How, then, does the world come to appear to us as a collection of solid, static objects extended in space? (Joad quoted in NR, p. 658)

Joad concludes that the intellect 'presents us with a false view' (NR, p. 658). For Stevens, poetic reality emphasises emergence; the subject of poetry is 'the life that is lived in the scene that it composes', the implication being that it uncovers the shifting, vibrating life veiled by our conventional vision of 'solid, static objects' (p. 658). If vibration functions in the passage from Joad as a somewhat disconcerting process by which the appearance of an object and its utilitarian function can be radically altered and shown to be animate, Stevens takes up this thread later in his essay to affirm his vision of nobility as almost an ethical conviction: 'As in the case of an external thing, nobility resolves itself into an enormous number of vibrations, movements, changes. To fix it is to put an end to it' (p. 664). The poet upholds a vibratory aesthetic, which mediates between the polarities of 'stillness' or fixity, and 'life' in its 'vibrations, movements, changes'.

The domain of inanimate objects associated with still life might appear to represent a tranquil, quiet space in which to attend to the overlooked, but for Stevens it also provides an opportunity to perceive the minute sounds and vibrations of the world through localised auditory attention. Vibration provides the poet with an inter-sensory figure, one that conceptualises the heightened sensitivity and straining of the senses beyond their everyday capacities, which his poetry demands. As he writes in 'The Noble Rider', our 'deepening need for words' to express ourselves, 'makes us listen to words when we hear them, loving them and feeling them, makes us search the sound of them, for a finality, a perfection, an unalterable vibration' (pp. 662–3).

Stevens invites us to listen to the world with searching intensity, but also with sympathy. Similarly, in *Aesthetics of Psychology*, Mauron frequently invokes an auditory element through figures of acute receptivity. He reminds us, and Stevens underscores these lines in his copy of the text: 'In active life we pay little attention to these resonances [past impressions and desires] [. . .] preoccupied as we are with the *next step*, we are not listening. But the artist listens' (AP, p. 41). Listening is equally requisite for the auditor: 'before a work of art, we listen to the repercussions within us, passing from one nerve-centre to the next' (p. 32).[34] Auditory attention is therefore associated with 'inactive contemplation' and yet it evokes a state of vibrational responsiveness between object and subject, which points to a broader, relational model of sympathy. It has affinities with Fry's auditory-vibrational conception of transmission and, further, with his appraisal of poetry as the site wherein 'the complex of word images and their associations [. . .] set up vibrations which continue in the mind', as exemplified by Mallarmé who gave 'to the words for common objects so rich a poetical vibration'.[35] In Mauron's account the 'aesthetic attitude' engenders a pleasurable encounter, located at 'the instant of intense vibration' (AP, p. 63). The moment of prolonged contemplative suspension potentially affords 'ecstasis' or a state of intensified sensitivity, which is accentuated by the connotations of (eroticised) pleasure in vibration.

Earlier in his account, Mauron gives a visceral description of this pleasurable expansion of being: 'Through our very immobility, the excitement is multiplied. From nerve-centre to never-centre it rolls, re-echoing. Thus we learn ourselves to be more profoundly and subtly sensitive than we had imagined. The artist transforms us, willy-nilly, into epicures' (pp. 37–8). Mauron seems to gesture here to another epicurean, Walter Pater, whose influential 'Conclusion' to *The Renaissance* (1873) proposed a transition of the 'quickened multiplied consciousness' stimulated in aesthetic experience, into the experience of daily life.[36] There is an ethical inflection too, in Mauron's vivid physiological descriptions, which express the affective potential of 'inactive contemplation'. The radiating moment of intense sensation, or 'intense vibration', simultaneously removes the artist or audience from the everyday world and reconnects them more intimately and sensitively with it. We are reminded too, that Stevens's desire to achieve 'unalterable vibration' in the medium of language was born out of 'loving' and 'feeling' the sounds of words.

The relationship between sympathetic affect and detached attention underlies many of Stevens's poems, but they receive perhaps their most lengthy 'playing out' in his long poem, *The Man with the Blue Guitar* (1937). Stevens encourages the reader to listen more intently to the sounds and rhythms of the world and thus to discover its unexpected patterns. William Fitzgerald puts this well when he suggests that 'Listening itself, in which our bodies are tuned like instruments, is a kind of music', and music, therefore, 'is the sound of attentiveness'.[37] The 'tune' might be a little hard to hear in *The Man with the Blue Guitar*, as the 'buzzing' and 'chattering' of the guitar evokes tuning up rather than a distinct melody. Nevertheless, the modulating refrain of 'things as they are' and 'the blue guitar' keeps these objects in view, and creates the effect of a constant musical vibration (CPP, IV–V, pp. 136–7).

Picasso's *The Old Guitarist* (1903), painted during his so-called 'blue period', is often suggested as the visual source for Stevens's poem,[38] partly due to the poet's reference to 'this picture of Picasso's, this "hoard/ Of destructions"', which is evocative of Cubism's deconstruction of forms (CPP, XV, p. 141).[39] However, Stevens wrote that he had 'no particular painting of Picasso's in mind' when writing the poem.[40] Given the poet's overlooked but self-confessed 'taste' for Georges Braque, Picasso's fellow Cubist, I propose that the poem can equally fruitfully be read in the light of Braque's still lifes, which sometimes combine musical iconography with the human figure.[41] This is not necessarily to suggest that Stevens sets up a direct ekphrastic relationship with Braque's still lifes or his treatment of musical instruments, but rather that he reveals affinities with the concerns they raise. In particular, about the attention instruments draw to touch and animation, to sound and silence, and indeed to lyric poetry. As Braque reminds us, 'the distinctive feature of the musical instrument as an object is that it comes alive to the touch'.[42]

Braque was a trained musician and his 'musical' still lifes typically deconstruct the forms of inanimate instruments while also evoking sound through painted vibrations across pictorial space. Stevens would have been familiar with these depictions from regular trips to museums and galleries in New York in the early 1910s, but also through visits to the apartment of his Harvard classmate, the art collector Walter Conrad Arensberg, whose walls were adorned with paintings including Braque's *Musical Forms* (1913) and *Musical Forms (Guitar and Clarinet)* (1918).[43] Stevens's familiarity with Braque in museum and domestic settings makes a painting such as *Man with a Guitar* (1911–12) (plate 24) seem a suggestive touchstone for his own *Man with the Blue Guitar*. Where Picasso's more figurative rendering of the *Old Guitarist* speaks to Stevens's 'hunched' musician, Braque's *Man with a Guitar* breaks down the two subjects into barely identifiable forms, merging man and instrument. In this characteristic work of his analytic Cubist phase, there is a sense of constant transformation in the jostling geometric shapes and shimmering silver-blue and brown tones of the painting, while dynamic brush strokes create a palpitating, visually 'sonorous' background.[44]

The 'musical still life', as it were, becomes a symbol of the metamorphic imagination in Stevens's *Man with the Blue Guitar*. He is similarly concerned with the process that takes place when the imagination and reality interact, when 'Things as they are/ Are changed upon the blue guitar' (CPP, I, p. 143). Braque's aphorism – 'The senses deform, the mind forms' – which the poet invokes in 'The Relations between Poetry and Painting' as pertinent for artists across different media, is especially consonant with the metamorphosis promised by his poem (CPP, p. 741).

In the seventh canto, touch, or lack of touch, prompts Stevens to question the implications of the artist's detached stance through the figure of the musician:

> Detached from us, from things as they are?
> Not to be part of the sun? To stand
>
> Remote and call it merciful?
> The strings are cold on the blue guitar. (CPP, p. 138)

The detached 'attitude' – aligned with lunar remoteness – is implicitly critiqued for its separation from 'things as they are' and for a lack of feeling, which could be (mis)read as merciful. The remote position taken by the lyric 'I' accentuates this reading but it is also reflected in the cool irresponsiveness of the instrument, which remains at this point unanimated by human touch, and is described a few stanzas later, with 'arrowy, still strings' (CPP, IX, p. 138).[45]

In *Aesthetics and Psychology* Mauron had been sure to discriminate between the 'active' yet 'cold disinterestedness' of the scientist, and the 'inactive' yet 'almost absolute detachment' of the artist. The artist is defined by his capacity to find pleasure and sympathy in the '[t]he joy of contemplating something other than himself', by which he 'gives us the completest of lessons in altruism' (AP, pp. 49–50). The artist's 'amused detachment' or 'amused acceptance' leads him, Mauron argues, to cultivate 'a sympathy full of delicate reserves' and a mode of 'contemplation, [. . .] balanced quiveringly on the edge of laughter, pity, tenderness and gratitude' (AP, pp. 49–50).[46] Mauron's theory of contemplation acknowledges the shades of meaning between detachment and absorption, and complicates associations with inaction and action. The 'aesthetic attitude' ideally situates the artist/audience 'quiveringly' poised between detached attention and intense affect, a position reminiscent of Woolf's evocation of Fry as a humming-bird hawk-moth 'quivering yet still'.

Mauron elaborates the challenges of this attitude a little later in his study: 'the artist must be double-minded; one side of him seethes with echoes, impulses, desires, emotions; the other, unmoved, savours and appreciates. Now this doubleness is hard to manage; one cannot hold one's soul at arm's length as easily as a piece of china' (AP, pp. 60–1). The notion of 'doubleness' implicitly seeks to elide the tension between the opposing 'sides' by holding them together in simultaneity. Nevertheless, these opposing temporalities and competing rhythms present significant challenges. One questions the human capacity to dissociate desire from such encounters: to 'savour' and 'appreciate' and yet to remain unmoved. Mauron is aware, however, of the demands that 'doubleness' places on the artist and indeed on his audience. It is, he goes on to say, a 'sort of unstable equilibrium, very near a contradiction' (AP, pp. 61–2). We have arrived, then, at another paradoxical state, which speaks to the nature of still life and the potency of creative instability explored in different permutations in this study.[47]

Lurking on the margins of Mauron's description is a 'piece of china', a characteristic object in still life compositions, and a little later he elaborates: 'Most artists [. . .] remain voluntarily on the edge of the great human emotions. And those who, like Chardin, pass their lives in the loving portrayal of pots and pans, are only pushing to the extreme an attitude which appears normal' (AP, p. 69). Mauron's allusion to the celebrated seventeenth-century still life painter implies that the state of 'unstable equilibrium' is intensified in this threshold genre. This clearly caught Stevens's interest, indicated by his markings and marginal notations in his copy of the book. As we look more closely at his poems in the next section we shall see that similar attitudes of precarious balance and vibratory suspension are demonstrated in his meditations on 'still life' objects.[48]

An 'Anxious Polarity': The Still Life of the Table

> We want forms more succulent than dihedral angles [. . .]. We require richness; we demand, in fact, that a work of art should nourish us as real things do, and that we can have the divine experience of it as we have of the actual world.
>
> Charles Mauron[49]

At this juncture, I would like to harness the notion of 'doubleness' that we have encountered in Mauron's theory of contemplation, in order to negotiate between two contrasting traditions in the representation of still life, which will frame our readings of Stevens's still life poems. In one manifestation of the tradition of still life of the table, the invitation to indulgence is stimulated by sensuous and abundant arrangements of food, while in its more ascetic counterpart, pared down compositions signify the will – or indeed the moral obligation – to abstain. Stevens's enthusiasm for tracing his Dutch ancestry led him to engage with Dutch painting and his attraction to still life may partly originate from this interest.[50] In his study of still life, Bryson locates the tension between depictions of abundance and frugality as emergent from interpretations of the genre by Dutch painters of the seventeenth century.[51] We might think of works by Jan Davidsz. de Heem, which encode the economic prosperity of the era in depictions of tables laden with succulent fruits, meats, wine and glowing table and glassware, inviting the gustatory pleasure of the viewer. Yet, as we have seen, displays of material bounty could also remind the viewer of the transience and vanity of worldly goods through *vanitas* and *memento mori* motifs.[52] At the other end of the spectrum, we find the sobriety and modest tables of the sixteenth-century painter Juan Sánchez Cotán, whose works evoke a humbling of the ego and form of spiritual discipline that Bryson sees as rooted in Carthusian monasticism and its commitments to solitude and abstinence.[53] The still life of the table is structured around this 'anxious polarity, with vice and pleasure beckoning at one end, virtue and abstention admonishing at the other'.[54] From the genre's characteristic display of the matter of the table, there emerges a drama of the will with moral implications.

Stevens's still life meditations register the aesthetic and ethical tensions associated with these competing impulses and iconographic codes, yet he rarely presents them as dichotomous. Many of his poems compose aesthetic spaces in which to relish the sensory pleasures of the table and its promise of colour, texture and taste, yet he is also drawn to compositions of commonplace objects, seemingly evacuated of life and sensory invitation.[55] Mauron's theory of contemplation offers a striking parallel since sensory delight underpins the 'aesthetic attitude' as much as the abstemious counter-current demonstrated by suspension and restraint. We recall the gustatory metaphors that sensitise Mauron's prose as he encourages us to relish exquisite sensations: to become 'epicures'. If we examine the meaning of 'epicurean' a little more closely we find that it has special significance for the 'anxious polarity' of the still life of the table. According to Guy Davenport, 'epicurean' 'has its own history as a kind of table fare', and historically the term should refer to 'the simple meal of a philosopher of admirable restraint', but it 'turned into the sense the Arabic word from which his name derives still has, *bikouros* [. . .], high living and rich eating'.[56] The unstable meaning of the term can be seen to play out in Stevens's still life poems, which often compress the provocations of luxuriance and frugality into a single poem.

Indeed, if still life accommodates Stevens's relish of materiality, then it also reveals his taste for the 'immaterial', or for 'spiritual epicureanism'. During the 1930s he was committed to what he called the 'spiritual role of the poet', and the year before publishing *Parts of a World* he concluded a letter describing the pleasures of eating persimmon fruits and the visions they conjured up of antique Japanese prints 'in which monkeys are eating persimmons in bare trees': 'As you see, there is such a thing as being a spiritual epicure'.[57] Such combinations of art, taste, and spiritual nourishment were consonant with Mauron's philosophy that 'richness' in a work of art 'should nourish us as real things do' and even enable 'divine experience', as he had written in an earlier study also owned by Stevens, *The Nature of Beauty in Art and Literature* (1927).[58]

I would like to pick up on the metaphysical implications of aesthetic nourishment as a foil to the materiality of the still life of the table. As we have seen, the metaphysical and material were intertwined in Stevens's imagination, often 'quickening' each other's passage. Visual art provided imaginative sustenance and his private collection included some thirty-six paintings and prints, numbering among them still lifes by Pierre Tal Coat, Raoul Dufy, Jean Jules Cavaillès and Braque.[59] His primary instinct in selecting a work for his collection was to locate something he could 'feed on' and 'live with [. . .] a long time', as he advised the Paris-based art dealer and bookseller Paule Vidal in the spring of 1947.[60] That pleasure and nourishment were essential criteria is apparent in the terms of his approval of Cavaillès' *Interior with Still Life* (1935), which Vidal had purchased for him. He pronounced it 'one of the pleasantest things' in the house, by a painter who 'seeks to give pleasure'.[61] Elsewhere he records finding a fruit shop window as appealing as his visit to the Museum of Modern Art. In a still life 'vision' which blurs art and life, he transforms an everyday scene into an erotic and sumptuous gastronomic composition, 'filled with the most extraordinary things: beauteous plums, peaches like Swedish blondes, pears that made you think of Rubens and the first grapes pungent through the glass'.[62]

Edward Ragg's study of Stevensian abstraction draws attention to the poet's 'abstract appetites', proposing that his 'aesthetic pleasures constitute gastronomic, painterly and literary complexes'.[63] The genre of still life is, I suggest, one such complex for Stevens, and it is rooted in the sensory and close at hand. The culture of the table, so often depicted in still life paintings, was surely a gift for the gastronomic poet who described poetry as 'a health' and conceived of the poet's contribution to the world as 'giving life whatever savor it possesses'.[64] Still life is the site in which we can best observe his encounter with 'contemplative epicureanism' – a phrase he had picked out from the conclusion to Mauron's text (AP, p. 105) – in poetic form.[65]

As we now turn directly to the poems in which Stevens gathers the fruits and flowers familiar to this genre of painting, it will be useful to loosely define the different modes in which he invokes and employs still life, since one or all of the following might be found combined in a single poem. Firstly, the iconographic still life, in which he presents subject matter associated with the genre (such as rhopography), and in which ekphrasis, or 'notional ekphrasis', is occasionally employed.[66] Secondly, the poetic meditation upon everyday objects, by which Stevens evokes the practice of contemplative attention without subscribing to a particular practice. Finally, in the most capacious and abstract application, the still life 'condition' or mood, as an orientation of concentrated and sometimes ambivalent attention.

*

Stevens's addition of his poem 'In the Clear Season of Grapes' to the 1931 reprint of his first volume of poetry, *Harmonium* (1923), means that it forms a connecting link between his early work and his still life poetry of the 1930s. The poem presents an image 'complex' that persists through his later volumes: the still life of fruit that functions as a nostalgic site and symbol of home. It is a meditation on remote domesticity through a simple yet enticing arrangement of fruit, which comes to embody the abstract idea of national identity:

> When I think of our lands I think of the house
> And the table that holds a platter of pears,
> Vermillion smeared over green, arranged for show. (CPP, p. 92)

The poem teases out the relationship between distance and intimacy in a way that resonates with, but also complicates, one of Braque's aphorisms from his notebooks: 'A still life is no longer a still life when it is no longer within arm's reach.'[67] The aesthetic space of still life was tactile as well as visual for Braque, and he suggests that proximity is essential for the genre to function. I would like to keep his aphorism in mind as we consider the ways in which the invitation to touch is encouraged and also thwarted in Stevens's still life poems.

The neutral tone of the poem and disembodied speaker flattens any impression of emotional attachment while the 'smeared' image evokes the blurred pictures of memory. The speaker's attention lingers over local colour, transforming the 'platter of pears' into a 'notional ekphrasis' of a still life painting through the language of pigment and brush strokes. However, the third stanza diminishes the still life objects as it pivots into a larger, more dynamic landscape of 'gross blue' (mountains or sea) which,

> Belittles those carefully chosen daubs.
> Flashier fruits! A flip for the sun and moon,
>
> If they mean no more than that. But they do. (CPP, p. 92)

In this teasing association between the spheres of the fruits and the planets, the 'flashier fruits' point disparagingly, perhaps, to the artifice of bourgeois domesticity, its mere 'show' in contrast to the scale and gravity of the cosmos. The 'gross blue' challenges the self-conscious sophistication of things 'carefully chosen'. Stevens employs the vocabulary of painting – or rather of bad painting ('daubs') – not necessarily to critique the capacities of visual art, but to convey the clumsiness and imprecision of any human re-arrangement or representation of the world. The shifting, uneasy relation between the order of objects (still life) and a less comprehensible, untamed outdoors (landscape), also reflects another dialectic between European refinement and a brash new-world aesthetic, which had preoccupied the poet in *Harmonium*. '[F]lip', with its colloquial, disruptive tone, playfully upturns these aesthetic tensions and undercuts the romantic imagery of sun and moon (are they in fact the brilliant, 'flashier fruits'?). The poem's images are thrown into the air together in an irreverent poetic juggling act that re-orders the object world. Nevertheless, 'flip' is not altogether flippant;

the affirmative diction and repetition of 'do' in the poem's final lines proclaims a subtle modulation of tone and an open-ended potential for 'our lands' to signify 'much more than that'. The poem's defence of meaning ('more than that') sets up a tension between the excess and the evacuation of sense, which would become ever more central in Stevens's later poetry.[68]

In *Parts of a World*, still life becomes a still more unstable site for domestic disruption as well as contentment. Stevens draws on connotations of sensory pleasure and domestic ease evoked by arrangements of fruit, but like many modern still life painters, his compositions also challenge and re-evaluate the genre's fundamental characteristics. Perhaps the most emblematic example is his poem 'A Dish of Peaches in Russia', in which the fruits are brought to our immediate attention in the first lines through a sensory investigation in which the act of looking becomes a form of address, a form of touch:

> With my whole body I taste these peaches,
> I touch them and smell them. Who speaks?
>
> I absorb them as the Angevine
> Absorbs Anjou. I see them as a lover sees. (CPP, p. 206)

The poem enacts an immersion in the 'otherness' of its subject, as local and physical immediacy dilates into figures of elemental absorption and intermingling (the rivers Angevine and Anjou). The speaker's voluptuous attention and the tenderness evoked by 'I see them as a lover sees' recalls Stevens's amorous elaboration of sympathetic attention, the 'loving and feeling' of words, which we observed in 'The Noble Rider'. A passage from Mauron's *Aesthetics and Psychology*, which Stevens underlined, also reveals affinities. Writing of 'the great contemplatives', Mauron argues that they

> contrive to maintain their equilibrium and to love in every manner possible the universe before their eyes. That they have reached this point of detachment and tenderness through pure sensibility [. . .] seems to be unquestionable. I have only to see the way in which Cervantes and Rembrandt *caress* details, to be sure of it. (AP, pp. 50–1)

As if in a memo to his poetic self, Stevens compressed the sense of this passage into a note in the margins of his copy. He reveals his attraction toward the idea of the artist whose detached contemplation engenders, in Stevens's words, 'a tenderness for the thing contemplated' (AP, p. 51). Mauron reiterates this point in the next paragraph with a quotation from the French painter, Auguste Bréal: '*L'artiste est un amoureux perpétuel*', a constant or eternal lover (AP, p. 51). The phrase captures the sensuous contemplation of the speaker in 'A Dish of

Peaches in Russia', and it clearly struck a chord with Stevens as he copied it out by hand in the margins of his text, and re-invoked it in 'The Noble Rider'.[69]

The tender tone of Stevens's poem, its 'caress' of every aspect of the peach with the 'whole body' (CPP, p. 206) of the speaker, reflects an amorous desire to achieve Mauron's notion of 'pure sensibility'.[70] However, while Mauron's text refuses to make any connection between the artist's approach and libido (which he says 'has nothing to do with it', AP, p. 51), Stevens's poem exudes an ambiguous eroticism. It enacts a salivating address or 'caress' of the peaches as a kind of sublimated love object. As we reach the middle point of the poem, we discover that they are 'large and round': 'Ah! and red; and they have peach fuzz, ah!/ They are full of juice and the skin is soft' (CPP, p. 206).

The speaker's enjoyment and plenitude becomes palpable as his discovery of the peaches works through the poem from the gustatory and visual to the olfactory and haptic, reaching the ecstatic exclamation that suggests biting open the fruit. Here we witness Mauron's psychology of pleasure in the practice of poetry: the warm eroticism of these lines gestures toward the 'tenderness to objects' that Stevens had approved in his reading. They become what Meyer Schapiro has identified in Cézanne's depictions of apples, pears and peaches, as 'the objects of a caressing vision' – objects of sublimated eroticism standing in for a woman's body.[71] The caesura following the ecstatic 'ah' prolongs the moment of pleasure in a suspension that embraces the poetic line as the first exhalation meets the second in redoubled delight. We are reminded of Mauron's direction, 'but do not react', and of his epicurean who savours a mouthful of wine, his 'attention concentrated wholly on the delicate black savour', and finds his 'excitement is multiplied' (AP, pp. 38, 32). In Stevens's poem, the still life is consumed by the poet's visceral imagination; the speaker's 'whole body' is invested in the act of attention.

This sensuous approach is widespread in *Parts of a World*, where contact – achieved or attempted – between body, mind and object often forms the crux of the poem. 'Study of Two Pears' describes 'curves/Bulging' and 'touched red' in another composition of fruit in which visual allusions to the female form are implicit even in the punning title (CPP, p. 180). 'Poem Written at Morning' also picks up the pervasive fruit motif (a pineapple) to parade the epicurean contemplative at his most sensorily alert, finding a juice 'fragranter/ Than wettest cinnamon' (CPP, p. 198). The poetic line salivates and consumes in a 'caress' that, like 'A Dish of Peaches in Russia', celebrates multisensory encounter but also, when read cumulatively, reveals in Stevens's appetite (for peach fuzz, bulging curves and 'wettest cinnamon') a somewhat uncomfortable elision between, and consumption of, fruit and the female body.[72]

'Contemplative epicureanism' is not, then, without conflict. While the opening lines of 'A Dish of Peaches in Russia' are predicated on a synaesthetic immersion of the senses, this state is contested by the insistent presence of the lyric 'I': the disembodied voice which repeatedly interjects, 'Who speaks?' (CPP, p. 206). Whether the voice registers the involuntary dawning of self-consciousness into meditative experience or the manifestation of a divided inner self, it is a disorientating mechanism, which eventually dissolves the sense of intimacy. We discover that the questioning voice belongs to a submerged part of the speaker's identity, 'that I/ That animal, that Russian, that exile' (CPP, p. 206). The poem telescopes from a local appreciation of the texture, colour and taste of 'these' peaches, to a vignette of a remote topography: a village (presumably in Russia) where there is 'fair weather, summer, dew, peace', and indeterminate temporality: 'The room is quiet where they are' (CPP, p. 206).

The substance and tangible presence of the peaches recedes and we wonder whether they represent real objects retrieved by nostalgic memory, or objects created and contemplated by the imagination. Arguably, we might read here an expression of detached yet tender contemplation, but it is also an elegiac expression of distance and forced displacement. The speaker is prompted to an act of attention and imaginative border crossing, which strains the lyric's intimacy and almost collapses Braque's condition that still life must remain 'within arm's reach'. If the painter alerts us to the importance of physical immediacy and touch, then this heightens the affective power of Stevens's still life poems in which spatial dimensions take on an ethical and human psychological resonance.

The shift from sensory interaction to imaginative projection in 'A Dish of Peaches in Russia' gains greater significance when we recognise the poem's geographical specificity and historical moment. The image cluster of an idyllic village, peaceful home and ripe fruit could register as propagandist or blindly idealistic in the context of Stalinist Russia in the 1930s, as a brutal politics invaded the homes of ordinary people. In the poem's final lines, the speaker is disturbed even by the 'drifting' curtains and Stevens dramatises the self-dividing internal rhythms and external distractions that threaten to disintegrate epicurean absorption and contemplative stillness:

> [. . .] I did not know
>
> That such ferocities could tear
> One self from another, as these peaches do. (CPP, p. 206)

The peaches remain at the composition's centre but they metamorphose from a site of pleasure and plenty to that of intense and even pernicious affect. They are the objects on which the speaker attempts to stabilise his attention (for which the 'drifting' curtains are a correlative), and yet onto which the trauma of displacement is mapped. The exertion of meditative attention goes beyond its aesthetic function here as the final lines register the vulnerability of the speaker's alert and hypersensitised state: the physicality of 'tear[ing]' selves is made all the more visceral, all the more ferocious, in suggestive proximity to the peaches (a soft fruit easily halved and exposed).

In Costello's reading, the 'spell' of the 'utopia of the still life' is shattered by this 'story of exile'.[73] The context of war is indeed crucial; it unsettles the notion of 'inactive contemplation', and we detect Stevens's underlying concern as to whether this 'attitude' can contend with modern displacement.[74] Nevertheless, a more optimistic reading is possible. The serenity of still life is challenged, but it retains utopian potency as a 'supreme fiction', an idea articulated by the poet in his long poem *Notes Toward a Supreme Fiction*. Still life is understood not as a consolation but as a mode of resistance: a symbol of pleasure, plenty and imaginative sustenance within the rupture of exile, springing from Stevens's affirmative belief in poetry and painting as 'supports of a kind of life, which it seems to be worth living' (RPP, p. 751).

Nevertheless, *Parts of a World* is charged with Stevens's increasing consciousness of the ethical perils of 'contemplative epicureanism'. A sceptical but perhaps superficial reading of Mauron's *Aesthetics and Psychology* might interpret the inaction of the 'aesthetic attitude' as solipsistic or indulgent in the context of the 1930s, in which social and political events demanded not only serious attention but also action. Stevens had faced charges of solipsism and escapism in the critical response to his early volumes, and Leggett suggests that he was attracted to Mauron's theory 'partly because it reinforced a view of art's lack of utility that he had maintained in the thirties against the pressures of the social critics and Marxist-inspired reviewers such as Stanley Burnshaw, who had attacked *Ideas of Order* for its social irresponsibility'.[75] It is striking therefore, that Braque's still lifes of the same period faced critique on similar grounds. For certain critics they 'appeared to be at odds with historical events', while for others their 'spatial and material ambiguity' provided 'a realm free from ideology', and in a further alternative interpretation the still object was 'a reflection, if in reverse, of the violent times'.[76] The latter is an argument that can be made for Stevens's still life poems.

Mauron offers a possible answer to such critiques in evincing a subtle yet urgent sense that cultivating the contemplative spirit leads one to engage with the world with greater sensitivity and attention. The 'aesthetic attitude' is not removed from quotidian experience but deeply imbricated in it, as his democratising vision makes clear:

> In ordinary life we sometimes pause in this way before a tree, a landscape, a piece of furniture, a sentence, or the face of a friend – or at table even, with a mouthful of wine, our attention concentrated wholly on the delicate black savour which we are rolling between the palate and the tongue. In such moments, I think, we are all like artists, because instead of putting an end to the stimulus by a prompt reaction, we keep it in suspense. (AP, pp. 32–3)

The sense of suspending action as a kind of wine-tasting exercise might be difficult for some readers to swallow, but the apparently opposing claims of action and contemplation were urgent and personal to Mauron who had become politically active in the 1930s – a context that would have coloured his writing of *Aesthetics and Psychology*. In the mid 1930s he acted as a representative of the Vigilance Française and supported the resistance movement in Spain, and during the Second World War he became active in the French Resistance.[77] In 'The Noble Rider' Stevens endorses Mauron's vision of enriched engagement and uses it to anticipate and reframe potential charges of 'escapism' (p. 662).[78] Could apparent inaction in fact be an act of resistance, offering a deeper re-engagement with the momentary and local, a celebration of the 'ordinary' in the face of troubled times? A little later Mauron seems to affirm this by concluding that cultivating the contemplative spirit can reveal an 'aesthetic universe' made 'at once richer and stranger' (AP, p. 40). However, Stevens's poems question the possibility of actually achieving the undistracted, pleasurable contemplation of the 'aesthetic attitude' or indeed the 'still life'. If Mauron's 'pause' and the suspension embodied in still life was significant to the poet's savouring of 'ordinary life', it offered unstable sustenance for uneasy times. Nevertheless, it was part of what Siobhan Phillips describes as Stevens's 'mode of the ordinary', the complexities and limitations of which we investigate further as our attention shifts from the culinary to the floral still life.[79]

The Floral Still Life and the Bouquet Poem

The floral still life inhabits a liminal territory between nature and culture, the ordinary and the spectacular, the posed and the natural. The motif of the bouquet of flowers lent itself to Stevens's pictorial experiments in form and colour, as it did for modern painters, but it also functioned as a metaphor for art. Elaine Scarry suggests that flowers provoke 'highly charged' 'aesthetic conversations' in which 'the very precision required to find the exquisitely poised actuality of the flower's "vague sentience" manifests itself as a form of acuity'.[80] This 'form of acuity', which we have witnessed in Ivon Hitchens's and Winifred Nicholson's flower paintings in Chapter 3, seems consonant with the heightened state of attention in Stevens's vivid 'aesthetic conversations' with flowers, in what I call his 'bouquet' poems.

In 'The Noble Rider', Stevens calls attention to a series of flower paintings exhibited in London by the sculptor and painter Jacob Epstein (1880–1959), as an exemplar of the 'unfixed' quality he seeks in the imaginative life. Epstein produced several hundred paintings of flowers during the 1930s in what he later recalled as 'a frenzy of painting' in which he 'lived and painted flowers'.[81] His disregard for the constraining structures of a domestic interior or vase is evident in works such as *Dahlias and Sunflowers* (c. 1936) (plate 25), in which the full-blown heads of the flowers are painted with urgent, expressive brushwork, as if seen from above in a vibrant unruly flower-bed. His energetic reappropriation of this conventional subject seems to have appealed to Stevens, as he quotes the following commentary on the flower paintings from *Apollo* magazine: 'His make no pretence to fragility. They shout, explode all over the picture space and generally oppose the rage of the world with such a rage of form and colour as no flower in nature or pigment has done since Van Gogh' (NR, p. 664). This mode of flower painting, as a 'rage' that explodes the myth of floral (and implicitly female) fragility as well as the domestic calm associated with still life, also functions as a challenge to the 'rage' and disorder of the world.[82] It seems to demonstrate the argument Stevens articulates earlier in this essay, of the imagination as a counterforce 'pressing back against the pressure of reality' (p. 665).

Epstein's barely contained portraits of flowers offer a striking visual correlative for a number of Stevens's verbal floral arrangements, which simultaneously represent and reflect upon the art and artifice embodied in the bouquet. 'You arrange, the thing is posed,/ What in nature merely grows', he writes in his poem 'Add this to Rhetoric', and we might keep in mind this cautionary half-rhyme of 'pose' and 'grows', as we explore his colourful rhetorical bouquets (CPP, p. 182). The image of the bouquet was replete with negative as well as positive connotations for Stevens. In 'Examination of the Hero in a Time of War', published in *Parts of a World*, it is a signal that 'Each false thing ends. The bouquet of summer/ Turns blue and on its empty table/ It is stale and the water is discolored' (CPP, XVI, p. 250). On the other hand, in the later poem, 'Conversation with Three Women of New England', it functions as an expansive metaphor signifying the infinite variety and rich sensory experience of life: the 'bouquet of being' (CPP, p. 470). We can see the seeds of these ongoing debates as early as Stevens's stage play *Bowl, Cat and Broomstick* of 1917, where the subject of critique is 'Le Bouquet', a poem consisting entirely of colour names attempted by a young 'poetess' aspiring to produce a 'visual impression like that produced by the actual sight of dahlias' (CPP, p. 630). The poem prompts one persona in the dialogue to reflect on the 'extraordinary effect one gets from seeing things as they are [. . .] from looking at ordinary things intensely!', while the next rejoins, 'But to look at ordinary things intensely, is not to see things as they are' (CPP, p. 629).

The problem of what it means to look at 'ordinary things intensely' compels Stevens in 'Woman Looking at a Vase of Flowers', a variation on the 'bouquet poem' in *Parts of a World*. The hybrid composition suggested by the poem's title is a familiar one in visual art, aligning the feminine and the flower as objects of beauty and inaction. Yet if we read the female figure introduced in the title of Stevens's poem through Mauron's 'aesthetic attitude' the poem quickly becomes charged by the competing impulses of action and inaction. The mood of ambivalent pleasure, and its volatility, centres on the balance between the female figure and the flower arrangement, between portrait and still life. The poem begins not with the quietude and aesthetic languor hinted at by the title, nor the silence associated with still life, but with a dramatic elemental soundscape: 'It was as if thunder took form upon/ The piano, that time' (CPP, p. 223). In a performance of creative composition, the poem recovers meditative stillness through the taming of the 'crude/ And jealous grandeurs' of the elemental world – the sun and sky – which have 'scattered themselves' in the garden (CPP, p. 223). Modulating from chaos and noise into form and quietude, it invites comparison with the controlled 'rage' that Stevens detected in Epstein's flower paintings. But it is the woman's form-making gaze that gives aesthetic shape to the dispersed elements, domesticating them indoors (flowers in a vase, a tune upon the piano). The vase at once contains and shapes the elemental flux, recalling Stevens's early poem, 'Anecdote of the Jar', in which the jar organised the 'slovenly wilderness' and 'took dominion everywhere' (CPP, p. 60–1). Once again, an aphorism from Braque offers a lens on the way in which things 'take form' in the poem: 'The vase gives a form to the void, and music gives a form to silence.'[83] With this observation, Braque brings visual art and music into close relationship, as acts of shape making and shape taking that can order and animate the world.

In 'Woman Looking at a Vase of Flowers', colour and sound become figures of sensuous attention and compositional process, modes through which to 'caress each detail' (to adopt Mauron's phrase). The reader must attune his ears and eyes, as Stevens's contemplative woman is entreated upon to voice chromatic melodies in the second stanza:

> Hoot, little owl within her, how
> High blue became particular
> In the leaf and bud [. . .]. (CPP, p. 223)

The peculiar inner voice associated with the owl's 'hoot' supplies a mode of communication beyond or perhaps below human language in order to respond to the prism of the bouquet. The linguistic fusion of sound and colour created by 'high blue' is reminiscent of experiments in synaesthesia and 'colour music', which we have seen were popular among artists and composers in the early twentieth century. Each 'hoot' articulates an act of attentive observation, and at the same time registers the untranslatable, subjective nature of colour experience, and the limited human vocabulary with which to express it. The trajectory in this stanza, from the abstract to the particular, and from non-mimetic colour into representational form, is also directed by the intensification of the woman's contemplation, the stress of 'becoming' emphasised by the three-fold repetition of 'became' through the stanza. Although Stevens's poem does not allude to a specific painting, the dynamic chromatics he introduces – from 'high blue' to 'red,/ Flicked into pieces, points of air' in the lines that follow – bring to mind the explosive use of colour and hallucinatory intensity of Epstein's flower paintings. Yet by the end of the stanza the dispersed, abstracted colours have condensed into the focused image of 'the sides of peaches, of dusky pears', returning us to the voluptuous visions of 'A Dish of Peaches in Russia' (CPP, p. 223).

We witness here the strained relations of distance and proximity, of intimacy and detachment, which characterise Stevens's still life poems. However, in the final stanza, the floral still life appears to make closer contact with the human:

> Hoot how the inhuman colors fell
> Into place beside her, where she was,
> Like human conciliations, more like
> A profounder reconciling, an act[.] (CPP, p. 224)

The 'inhuman colors' associated with non- (and therefore in-) human nature and simultaneously with art, are accommodated into the domestic environment and even appear sympathetic to it. But if order is achieved here, it is not because nature has been circumscribed by art. The colours fall 'into place' but they do not appear subject to human arrangement: the composition appears to structure itself autonomously as the 'crude and jealous' elements of the first stanza find an internal order. Tamed and 'fragrant', conciliatory and comforting, 'Nature' nestles 'close' to the human, and yet retains its peculiar separateness.[84]

A fundamental question unsettles and complicates these readings. Is the female figure the author of the arrangement, a part of it, a witness to it, or all three? Depending on how we read the poem, we might question how far her passivity, which has positive as well as negative connotations, removes her from the scene, limiting her engagement in its 'profounder reconciling'. Rather like Fergusson's portraits of Margaret Morris, she is more aligned with the condition of still life and its world of inanimate objects, than an active subject or force in its creation.[85] Alternatively, we might experience Stevens's elusive 'woman' as the subtle architect of the scene's intimacy, emblematised by stillness and quiet intervention. Costello points out that she 'has none of that Sunday morning complacency; her human arrangement of the flowers has the force of epiphany'.[86] The scene certainly has epiphanic force, and it is given weight in the closing lines by the religious inflection of 'profounder reconciling' and 'affirmation free from doubt' (CPP, p. 224). However, the energy or 'force' of the epiphany resides not in any direct action or ownership on the woman's part (it never in fact becomes *her* arrangement), but rather in her suspension from action. As the poem concludes with the floral still life 'close to her', the physical distance announced in the title has been overcome by the intimacy of sustained contemplation 'without clairvoyance', which would, Stevens implies, have meant looking through or beyond the subject (CPP, p. 224). We might detect here the poet's affirmation of 'inactive contemplation', as we witness the creation of form in an attenuated, domestic 'epiphany'.

Stevens continues to probe the question of distance and detachment in 'Bouquet of Belle Scavoir', which also appears in *Parts of a World*. The old French, 'scavoir' (for *savoir*, to know), sets a tone of frustrated and faintly comic *romance* as the speaker searches to give substance to his absent lover through an associated but inevitably inadequate object (the bouquet), rather like a painter searching for beauty and knowledge ('Belle Scavoir') through the elusive and traditionally feminised subject of Nature. The 'freshness of the leaves, the burn/ Of the colors' make the bouquet a vivid, tangible presence, yet it is also an emblem of absence and change (CPP, p. 211). At first it seems to symbolise the consolations of art: the bouquet is metonymically associated with the woman who 'made it', a portrait-of-the-artist in which '[e]verything in it is herself', but its metaphoric richness and ekphrastic presence disperses and he finds only 'reflection', 'shadow' and 'evasion' (CPP, p. 211–12). This unfulfilled yearning for sensuous presence propels the poem to its final lamentation: 'It is she that he wants, to look at directly,/ Someone before him to see and to know' (CPP, p. 212). It seems significant that the woman is summoned not into direct physical contact but into proximate distance, to be looked at. She remains a suspended, shadowy figure, imagined 'before him'. Stevens retains a subtle tension as the speaker expresses a desire for knowledge gained through the intimacy of close looking, rather than the erotic absorption we have encountered in 'A Dish of Peaches in Russia'. Despite the urgency of the impulse for 'direct' perception, the poem paradoxically operates as an exercise in indirect looking and displacement. The speaker looks *through* (and therefore marginalises) the bouquet in order to find his lover in the larger spaces of the world, but '[t]he sky is too blue, the earth too wide' and the poem instead creates a vanishing portrait of a woman who eludes the desire to be seen or known (CPP, p. 212).

Stevens's penultimate volume of poetry, *The Auroras of Autumn* (1950) sees the poet adapting this motif as he ventured further into abstraction. The reflective mood and spare style of the two 'bouquet' poems in this volume invite comparison with the quietude and meditative quality evoked by certain still life paintings. They are, in Bevis's lyrical phrase, 'saturated with patient intensity'.[87] In 'Bouquet of Roses in Sunlight', Stevens presents a floral still life with 'a crude effect' that looks back to the 'crude and jealous formlessness' of 'Woman Looking at a Vase of Flowers'. In this poem colour and form remain in an untamed, raw state, resistant to circumscription of the subject through mimetic representation. The opening lines present a series of discordant colour configurations that seize our attention and defamiliarise the somewhat tired literary conceit of the rose:

> Say that it is a crude effect, black reds,
> Pink yellows, orange whites, too much as they are
> To be anything else in the sunlight of the room. (CPP, p. 370)

The affective pressure of 'too much' and (in the following line) 'too actual' punctuates the litany of colours and subjective sense impressions. As Jane Wilson, a young painter and correspondent with Stevens, observed, 'The rhythm of the poem and the way the mentioning of the colour is used is very like the rhythm of looking intensely.'[88] The roses swell with the excess of significance in their everyday actuality – 'as they are' – generating a trance-like intensity and suspension of the metaphor-making imagination: the 'imaginings' which would make 'lesser things' (CPP, p. 370). The poet valorises 'sense' in this poem since it 'exceeds all metaphor' and produces a generative 'flow of meanings', while also operating as a fluid and receptive approach, demonstrated by the poem's hypothetical lexicon ('Say that [. . .]'). It is this flexible, shifting encounter that makes the roses 'seem/ So far beyond the rhetorician's touch', Stevens writes, concluding the poem (CPP, p. 371). Once again, suspension – even from figurative 'touch' – is crucial: it allows the composition to remain a celebration of 'crude effect' rather than a fixed 'pose'. The movement of 'sense' in this poem arguably goes beyond the 'touch' of Mauron's 'aesthetic attitude' or indeed Braque's insistence on the tactile, toward a more complicated, self-reflexive model of attention. It simultaneously affirms the provisional, unpolished technique explored in earlier still life poems and invokes a more vigorous abstraction, which from the outset resists the attempt to find correspondences to the 'real'.

Stevens continues to unfix the poses of his floral still lifes in 'The Bouquet', positioned a little later in the same volume. Costello reads this poem as a sequel to 'Woman Looking at a Vase of Flowers', but it is also conversant with the critique of metaphor expressed in 'Bouquet of Roses in Sunlight'.[89] Stevens embraces the fiction of representation as he constructs a busy world of 'meta-men' and 'para-things' in which the still life is isolated through its epiphanic simplicity: 'The bouquet stands in a jar, as metaphor/ As lightning itself' (CPP, I, p. 384). However, it metamorphoses and migrates as the poem enacts its performance of attention (or 'inactive contemplation'), in which things are 'transfixed, transpierced and well/ Perceived' (II, p. 385). We follow a trajectory in which the 'eccentric twistings of the rapt bouquet/ Exacted attention with attentive force'; so that after reaching the third lyric through the 'migratory daze' of chromatics, we arrive at: '[t]he infinite of the actual perceived,/ A freedom revealed, a realization touched' (III, p. 386). The floral still life operates, perhaps, as an embodiment of this process of perception, which is simultaneously a creative composition. In the penultimate lyric it achieves an affirmative yet shifting stability: 'The bouquet is part of a dithering:/ Cloud's gold, of a whole appearance that stands and is' (IV, p. 387). Like fool's gold, 'cloud's gold' hints at the ephemeral, possibly deceptive, and ultimately unknowable – the realm of the imagined but affirmative 'supreme fiction'.

In the final stark sequence of the poem, however, a soldier enters the domestic scene and knocks over the bouquet. We witness its anthropomorphised demise as it 'falls on its side' and lies 'slopped over' as if wounded; its semantic vitality and epiphanic register drain away, gesturing toward the condition of *nature morte* (V, p. 387). In Costello's reading, the poet 'abandons' the bouquet and the final canto 'marks the end of the performance', reminding us that 'the world of meditation can never contain the historical world'.[90] One might question Costello's morally inflected 'abandons', and the sense that the exercise is simply a 'performance', but it is clear that the shift from contemplative 'inaction' to violent action transmits a shock, which is registered by – and indeed shatters – the still life, as well as the speaker's contemplative attention. Like Epstein's floral still lifes, Stevens's volatile flower compositions untether the genre from complacent associations with bourgeois comfort and repose, and assert models of encounter, which increasingly turn in on themselves and fracture, or expose desires and instabilities that threaten the domestic order without entirely undermining its power. The bouquet poem can be seen, then, to occupy what Bryson describes as the 'middle zone of the still life spectrum', where we find 'the still life of disorder, poised between harmony and catastrophe'.[91]

'The Day Itself is Simplified': The Ascetic Impulse

What happens when we turn from the colour and sensory exuberance of Stevens's 'bouquet' poems and the 'epicurean' pleasures of his gastronomic meditations to consider the 'ascetic still life'? Stevens's poetry reveals a spectrum of asceticism with which he expresses varying degrees of affinity. Here I want to suggest that his meditative temperament urged him to value the humble everyday object associated with the 'ascetic still life' and to develop a corresponding aesthetic of simplicity, which at times recalls the attentive restraint proposed by Mauron's 'aesthetic attitude'.

Toward the end of 'The Noble Rider', Stevens returns to Joad's description of 'solid, static objects extended in space' to speculate that the space is 'blank space, nowhere, without color, and that the objects, though solid, have no shadows and, though static, exert a mournful power' (NR, p. 662). This 'complete poverty', as Stevens describes it, seems at first glance to express a kind of detachment from reality – a shadowless timeless vacuum – which he critiqued and rigorously attempted to counteract in his poetry (p. 662). In the same year that Stevens published *Parts of a World*, Giorgio de Chirico wrote of a similar kind of poverty manifest in modern painting. He argued that artists were fulfilling the latent 'prophecy' in the term *natura morta* (still life) by painting objects 'portrayed as flat, non-existent and without air, [. . .] "truly dead"'.[92] In contrast he appealed for the realisation of the *vita silenziosa*, 'the silent life of objects and things, a calm life'.[93]

Stevens's argument in 'The Noble Rider' is perhaps more nuanced. He suggests that the poet could transform this colourless vision and reframe 'complete poverty' as a positive choice, a liberating abstention and relinquishment, which would reveal the 'world of poetry indistinguishable from the world in which we live' (NR, p. 662). His vision has affinities with the kinds of negations and purged spaces evoked in the ascetic still lifes of the metaphysical school of Italian painters (led by de Chirico) whose work he followed. We might think of the 'mournful power' of Giorgio Morandi's rows of colourless bottles, his tirelessly repeated subject; or the comestible objects mysteriously enlarged and displaced in the eerie urban 'nowhere[s]' of de Chirico's pre- and inter-war paintings.

The poet implicitly valorised the 'ascetic still life' for the focus it gives to 'things as they are': to the sustained and contemplative study of humble objects in quietude. As we have seen, this impulse was shared by his contemporaries. The refrain from *The Man with the Blue Guitar* chimes with a still life meditation in *The Waves*: 'Let me sit here for ever with bare things, this coffee-cup, this knife, this fork, things in themselves, myself being myself.'[94] Woolf's cadence echoes the sing-song quality of Stevens's refrain, equating the bareness of things with a mode of being that allows the self to recover equilibrium in the solitude of everyday objects. 'To discover a thing is to lay it bare', Braque wrote as one of his aphorisms.[95] For Stevens, it was in the slow revelations prompted by acts of attention toward commonplace objects, in that flicker of animation between stillness and life, that he located the 'quickening' between 'reality' and the 'imagination'. In 'The Relations Between Poetry and Painting' he seems to endorse a practice of patient looking by quoting an account by Leo Stein, the modern art collector (notably of Cézanne), in which he attempts to 'see' as a painter. Stein relates how he experimented in looking at 'an earthenware plate' on a table for 'minutes or for hours' everyday. It prompts what we might call a 'still life vision':

> I had in mind to see it as a picture, and waited for it to become one. In time it did. The change came suddenly when the plate as an inventorial object [. . .] went over into a composition to which all these elements were merely contributory. [. . .] I had made a beginning to seeing pictorially.[96]

Stein's recollection of this exercise in intense looking evokes a trajectory typically accorded to meditative experience. He reaches the kind of 'still life moment' we have encountered widely in art and discourses on the genre but it is also reminiscent of the 'inactive contemplation' advocated by Mauron. The notion of 'seeing pictorially' would have appealed to Stevens since it un-fixes the object from its utilitarian ('inventorial') sphere, enabling it to become fluid and migratory – to become material for the imagination. Indeed, Stein's description leads to the curious, epiphanic moment when a shift takes place and the object metamorphoses ('the change came suddenly'), from the 'ordinary' plane of rhopography to a site of aesthetic vision. Yet he never entirely departs from the grounded 'earthenware' object: what he describes is an example of uncovering, as Stevens has it, the 'world of poetry indistinguishable from the world in which we live' (NR, p. 662). Stein's disciplined model of attention similarly accords with Stevens's description later in 'The Relations between Poetry and Painting', of the poet's 'effort of the mind' and the 'laborious element', which both poetry and painting share, and which, he implies, enable new modes of perception (RPP, p. 744).

In Ragg's reading of Stevens, the poet 'aestheticize[s] a domestic existence where "less is more", his self-denials *and* acquisitions becoming fecund flirtations with ascetic experience'.[97] 'Flirtations' implies a casual, irreverent acquaintance with the ascetic, and as Stevens's asceticism often takes gastronomic form, this is often lightly expressed. 'I indulge in abstemious spells,' he confessed on one occasion, 'merely to keep my balance.'[98] Another teasing gourmet analogy expresses his preference for the wholesome ('ordinary') over the sophisticated and indulgent ('extraordinary'): 'the bread of life is better than any soufflé'.[99] However, the playfulness of such comments in his letters belies his serious engagement with a demanding poetics of attentiveness, 'the laborious element', which directs itself toward the simple objects of everyday life. As we have witnessed, the poet's interest in meditative detachment went beyond a superficial 'flirtation', and he carefully digested Mauron's theory of contemplation, which instructed restraint and prolonged suspension before consumption.[100]

Stevens's taste in works of art for his domestic environment was similarly governed by a frugal aesthetic. He relished what Ragg describes as the 'modest' and 'second rate';[101] but he made an exception in purchasing one of Braque's first colour lithographs, *Nature Morte III, Verre et Fruit* (1921).[102] Alongside a large goblet the composition cradles an apple and pear at its centre, with the fruits lightly touched green with roughened contours. Stevens yoked Braque to the 'ascetic' when he remarked in 1947, 'There is a siccity and an ascetic quality about his color that is very much to my liking. Some of his greens and browns are almost disciplinary. [. . .] one can be as much ravished by severity as by indulgence.'[103] As we return to *Parts of a World*, we find that for Stevens, the 'siccity' and 'severity' of a loaf of bread could be as affecting as the ferocities of peaches.

The poet's competing appetites are inscribed in this volume of poetry. If our reading follows the published order of poems, then we must meditate upon the bare necessities of 'The Glass of Water', and inhabit the 'tragic land' of 'Dry Loaf' before feasting on the succulent 'Dish of Peaches'. 'Dry Loaf' brings the still life's local, domestic focus into contact with the distant international landscape of 'burning countries' (CPP, p. 183). By transposing hardship into gastronomic terms, the title obliquely invokes the political upheavals of the 1930s, which led to the Spanish Civil War and the Second World War.[104] The nominal association of bread with basic nourishment and well-being is counteracted by its dryness and singularity and the brown monochrome landscape in which it exists. If the poem is an expression of the ascetic, if it has 'siccity' and 'severity', to adopt Stevens's critical lexicon for Braque, then this is not as a gastronomic or aesthetic choice but as the signifier of a 'tragic land' (CPP, p. 183).

In the first stanza of the poem, our attention is immediately directed away from the loaf by the measured, pedagogic tone of the artist-speaker who repeatedly instructs us to 'Regard' what was 'painted behind the loaf' (CPP, p. 183). Harold Bloom has noted the nuanced use of this verb in Stevens's poetry: 'To "regard" is a warier and more passive verb. It is to look at something attentively or closely, but with a touch of looking back at [. . .] to watch out for something.'[105] This specificity of attention is prescient in the poem, since the local, still life object is entirely displaced in the following stanzas by a threatening, and disturbingly animate landscape. Birds threaten to engulf the foreground as they arrive 'spreading [. . .] as waves', and the rhythms of war, the 'battering of drums' and marching soldiers, assert an insistent auditory presence (p. 183).[106]

The artist-speaker 'regards', but he also listens. He is a witness to the 'hungry' in the fourth stanza: 'It was hunger, it was the hungry that cried' (p. 183). The biblical parable of the dividing loaves seems implicit here, yet in the absence of a miraculous response the cry also functions as a lamentation of aesthetic famine. It signals a question about the capacity of this meagre still life, which has by this point receded from the foreground of the poem, and of art in general, to assert a nourishing presence in the world. David Jones had raised a similar question in his essay 'Art in Relation to War', observing that the artist is 'not always convinced that the "bread" available today is "valid matter", because it has itself been emptied of creatureliness on the one hand and is alien to "sign" (or is patient only of being a sign of itself, that is of material-as-power) on the other'.[107]

If Jones is concerned with a more specific form of spiritual nourishment and 'sign making', Stevens's poem nevertheless articulates that the question of what makes 'valid matter' was ever more crucial in a 'tragic time'. We remember that a few years after publishing this poem, he observed that his generation was 'experiencing essential poverty in spite of fortune', even as he remained convinced that the arts could offer 'supports' (RPP, pp. 748, 751). 'Dry Loaf', the most humble of comestibles – the 'ascetic' still life – prompts searching reflections, but if the poet makes a social or ethical point in taking up this subject, it cannot easily be aligned with the moral imperatives of the still life tradition, where material indulgence contests with spiritual asceticism, nor with Jones's theologically grounded analogy.

The ascetic still life finds perhaps its 'purest' form but also its most rigorous critique in Stevens's canonical poem, 'The Poems of Our Climate'. Although it was published in *Parts of a World*, it can be associated with the 'mind of winter' and 'bare place[s]' of early poems such as 'The Snow Man' (CPP, p. 8), and the pared down subject matter of 'Anecdote of the Jar'. 'The Poems of Our Climate' adapts the 'bouquet' motif, giving the containing vessel as much significance as the flowers themselves. Established in a hypothetical, metaphysical space in which detached attention might be achieved and the self purified, the poem can be read as a thought experiment in the aesthetic experience of ascetic still life (whether in visual or verbal art).

The simplicity of the composition dazzles in the opening lines of the poem through the contrast of primary colours and the language of light: 'Clear water in a brilliant bowl,/ Pink and white carnations' (CPP, p. 178). The objects inhabit a space of almost inhuman clarity far removed from the chromaticism and sensory invitation of Stevens's arrangements of fruits and bouquets. Within this space, which occupies a threshold between the domestic and the elemental (the room's light is like 'snowy air'), the still life exerts a centripetal force and yet its effect ripples outwards to contain and, like the jar in Tennessee, take 'dominion'. By the end of the first stanza, '[t]he day itself/ Is simplified: a bowl of white', and the composition appears bare and isolated with: 'nothing more than the carnations there' (p. 178). In contrast to the affective excesses (the 'too much') of other compositions, these pared down images, almost purged of emotional or associative resonance, can be seen as the result of exercising contemplative attention. The negative poetics of 'The Poems of our Climate' are arguably expressive of Stevens's 'ascetic' impulse. Bevis makes the important point that although critical interpretations of 'nothingness' in Stevens's poetry largely characterise it as a nihilistic state (especially in poems such as 'The Snow Man'), in the context of the psychology and practices of Eastern meditation 'nothingness' can be valorised as a positive quality or 'positive negative'.[108] Indeed, the 'cold porcelain' of the bowl repels human touch, yet it intimates the promise of ritualistic cleansing and even rebirth: the 'complete simplicity' which we encounter in the second stanza (pp. 178–9).

Stevens's poem reverses the contemplative trajectory of a still life poem by Rainer Maria Rilke, which addresses a similar subject, 'The Bowl of Roses' (1907). In this poem discordant images of human passion and violence at the outset are gradually dispelled by the sheer haecceity of 'a bowl that's filled with roses', which is offered as the focus of an intense meditation that unfolds through the poem. Presented to the reader with almost votive appeal, the bowl of roses becomes a way of rediscovering the senses and at the same time subsuming the impurities of human existence. Part of the promise of this 'still life' is a 'stasis that might be ours'.[109] Three decades later, the climate of Stevens's poem is disillusioned of such a possibility. Seeds of discontent and distraction are already manifest in the sixth line: 'Pink and white carnations – one desires/ So much more than that' (CPP, p. 178). The disruption of contemplative observation is indicated on the local level of the line with a dash that severs the contemplative mind from its no-longer satisfying object. The poem simultaneously proposes and undermines the validity of 'complete simplicity' in still life meditation. It not only questions how far the (ascetic) still life can satisfy and nourish as an aesthetic composition and a mode of attention, but also troubles the human capacity to cultivate a corresponding state of purified attentiveness. These deliberations intensify in the second stanza:

> Say even that this complete simplicity
> Stripped one of all one's torments, concealed
> The evilly compounded, vital I
> And made it fresh in a world of white (CPP, p. 179)

Here the poet suggests that the human element is never entirely evacuated from still life; nor is it comfortably accommodated. In fact the 'evilly compounded, vital I' lurks at the centre of the poem, concealed within a world of purified inanimate objects. Stevens questions, moreover, whether this complete purification would in fact be a desirable state to achieve. If the 'brilliant-edged' whiteness, the 'snowy' coolness, of this aesthetic space functions as a site for 'cleansed' vision, it also expresses an uncanny remoteness from the colourful animations that we have seen signify the fertility of human imagination in other poems. With a reversal of the syntax of denial and negation, the 'vital I' demands more as this stanza concludes: 'Still one would want more, one would need more' (p. 179). The pun on 'still' unsettles the composition's atemporal tranquillity as the poem becomes increasingly charged by the tension between stillness and motion and between 'less' and 'more'.

In *The World as Will and Representation* (1818), Arthur Schopenhauer brought his conception of 'pure contemplation' into contact with the Dutch still life in a way that is pertinent to thinking through the conflicted motions of Stevens's poem.[110] If we turn back to the passage from Schopenhauer that I examined in the Introduction to this study, we recall that he identified Dutch still life painters as the masters of 'pure contemplation'.[111] He asserts that from their work one obtains a reflected sense of 'the profound spiritual peace' and 'complete silence of the will' which they required in 'plunging so deeply into those inanimate objects', and 'comprehending them with such affection'.[112] There are parallels here with the 'tenderness' and sympathy toward commonplace subjects advocated by Mauron's 'aesthetic attitude', but Schopenhauer also draws notice to the contrasting internal states experienced by the viewer. He argues that because the viewer is invited to participate in this tranquil state, 'his emotion is often enhanced by the contrast between it and his own restless state of mind, disturbed by vehement willing'.[113] The final stanza of 'The Poems of Our Climate' dramatises a similar friction between Schopenhauer's 'restless state' and the tranquillity of the still life composition (with the internal dynamics highlighted by my italics):

> There would *still remain* the *never-resting* mind,
> So that one would want to *escape*, *come back*
> To what had been so *long composed*. (CPP, p. 179)

The 'never-resting mind' (or 'vehement' will) increasingly disturbs but also reinvigorates 'what had been so long composed'. Between remaining and restlessness, this oscillating state recalls the creative instability that Mauron had conceived as 'unstable equilibrium'. Nevertheless, the poem concludes in celebration of what Stevens calls, a few lines later, the 'imperfect [. . .] so hot in us' (p. 179). This is his affirmation of human vitality but also fallibility, and of the unruly body which injects a range of feeling, from 'bitterness' to 'delight', into the 'cold' condition of still life (p. 179).

*

Over the course of this chapter we have witnessed Stevens's attraction to still life as a genre that pays intensified attention to everyday objects and partakes in their transformative, shape-shifting potential. The poet expands the conceptual and metaphysical value of 'still life', developing a poetic mode which is illuminated by but also departs from Mauron's theory of contemplation. The intersection of the aesthetic, ethic and gastronomic in his still life poems exposes man's 'evilly compounded' nature. Indeed, we sense the conflicting vibrations of his restless speakers in even the 'purest' and most ascetic of his compositions. The poems I have discussed ask difficult questions about the (im)possibility of immobility, and about different forms of sympathy and detachment. They reveal an affective spectrum and lexicon that invites comparison with the shades of attentive being outlined in Mauron's theory of contemplation, and a shared attempt to comprehend 'lifeless objects' with 'tenderness'. However, as we have found, to approach an object 'as a lover sees' is a fraught matter that leads to responsive excess as much as to a measured state of restraint or attentive stillness. The colour and activity of the imagination and the 'never-resting' nature of the 'vital I' unsettles and animates static compositions, giving full play to the paradox of 'still life'. For Stevens, still life creates 'unstable equilibrium', or to invoke the terms of his poetics, it encompasses 'an enormous number of vibrations' yet seeks 'unalterable vibration'.

Coda

At this juncture we might pause to recall that Mauron's *Aesthetics and Psychology* arrived at Stevens's desk via his subscription to Virginia and Leonard Woolf's Hogarth Press. Woolf, Fry, Mauron and Stevens therefore form an intertextual nexus, associated not so much by channels of direct influence as through a collage of reverberating texts in which metaphors and ideas overlap. We have already had cause to notice resonances and correspondences between Woolf's and Stevens's approach to still life and the 'ordinary'; in this Coda, we return to the Bloomsbury artists of the first chapter to consider where Woolf might be positioned in relation to Mauron's theory of inactive contemplation.

As Mauron's publisher, Woolf would have had an intimate acquaintance with *Aesthetics and Psychology* and *The Nature of Beauty in Art and Literature*, and she expressed admiration for his translations of her own work. Their relationship strengthened while they were both grieving Roger Fry's death in 1934, and while Woolf was writing Fry's biography she and Mauron corresponded and met on numerous occasions.[114] By 1940 she found him 'so fine a thinker' that she wrote, 'I feel I could learn more from you about writing than from any English critic.'[115]

The French aesthetician presents a theoretical lexicon and a dialectic between 'inactive' and 'active' contemplation that has a particular affinity with and may have informed Woolf's aesthetics of attention. She formulated her 'philosophy' of 'being' and 'non-being' during the 1930s, the same period in which her relationship with Mauron was consolidated, and in which she was perhaps most receptive to his ideas. Despite this, *Aesthetics and Psychology* has been almost entirely overlooked in studies of her work.[116] We might consider that the 'aesthetic attitude' offers a way of re-reading the rhythms of dulled and heightened attention that characterise 'non-being' and 'being', and the tension between ec-stasis and rapture in Woolf's 'exceptional moments'. In fact, Lorraine Sim's reading of these states as 'two attitudes', which we encountered in Chapter 1, seems all the more pertinent in the light of Mauron's concept of 'two attitudes of mind' (AP, p. 28).

Mauron adapted Fry's early formalist theory in ways that would seem to answer elements of Woolf's critique of the art critic, notably in revising his separation between 'art' and 'life'. For the artist to fulfil the 'aesthetic attitude', we remember, he must be 'double-minded'. He must be acutely receptive to his personal emotions and desires (and therefore somewhat distracted by 'life'), and at the same time cultivate 'unmoved' appreciation: a 'quiveringly' balanced mode of contemplation. There are striking affinities between Mauron's notion of 'unstable equilibrium, very near a contradiction', and Woolf's reading of Fry's 'two rhythms' in her biography, where 'the distracted' and 'still' are held 'in being simultaneously'. In reading Fry in this way, was she thinking, one wonders, of Mauron's double-minded artist?

We might also consider a different direction of intertextual exchange by looking back to the previous decade when Woolf can arguably be seen to anticipate a nascent version of Mauron's 'inactive contemplation' in *To the Lighthouse*, the novel in which 'standing still' becomes a refrain. In the celebrated supper party scene in 'The Window' section of the novel, Woolf portrays Mrs Ramsay in an attitude with which we have become familiar: hovering 'like a hawk suspended' over the table, as she contemplates her friends and family 'rising in this profound stillness' (pp. 120–1). As she assumes this attitude of suspended yet finely tuned receptivity she experiences a visionary 'still life' moment: the feeling 'of peace, of rest', becomes entwined with the materiality of domestic objects: 'here, she felt, putting the spoon down, was the stillness that lies about the heart of things; where one could move or rest; could wait now [. . .] listening' (p. 121). The correlation between Mrs Ramsay's meditative suspension and the compound of sensory attention and physical immobility advocated by Mauron becomes even more compelling when we read a little later: 'whereas in active life she would be netting and separating one thing from another [. . .] urging herself forward; now she said nothing. For the moment she hung suspended' (p. 123).

Woolf's model of acutely receptive attention appears to exemplify what Mauron describes in *Aesthetics and Psychology* as 'the luminous focus of an attention no longer distracted' (p. 59). However, as we have seen, she constructs a vibrational aesthetic in which the still and the contemplative are necessarily charged and disrupted by the 'distracted life'. If in the supper party scene Mrs Ramsay anticipates Mauron's 'contemplative epicure', then Woolf, like Stevens, makes us all the more aware of the inevitable transience of such acts of contemplation. Before long, desire intervenes, and as the scene unfolds 'a hand reached out, took a pear, and spoilt the whole thing' (p. 125). This irreverent gesture disorders the still life, dissolves the intensity of Mrs Ramsay's attention, and brings into play the forward-urging temporality critiqued by Mauron.

Both Stevens and Woolf examine such forms of attention in which the relationship between absorbed participation and detached contemplation is endorsed as well as critiqued. Mauron's 'contemplative epicureanism' strains under the 'restless I' of Stevens's poetic imagination, even as his speakers appear to enact the 'aesthetic attitude'. The poet interrogates the formalist rhetoric of detachment, yet the tension between the artist who engages and he who 'stands/ remote' and refuses the invitation to touch remains unresolved in his work. The haptic is also significant in Woolf's writing of Fry's studio: the forbidding placard which guards his still arrangement – 'Do not touch' – makes a larger point about the art critic's construction of borders between art and life. In Woolf's work a different although similarly contested model of detached attentiveness emerges through the hovering suspendedness of insects. In *Roger Fry*, her implicit critique of the art critic's aesthetic theory simultaneously becomes a celebration of his embodied practice. To be 'quivering yet still', like a humming-bird hawk-moth, represents an intensely sensitised, vibrational model of aesthetic experience, which she develops throughout her writings. In so doing, she constructs a physiologically and psychologically demanding 'still life', which redefines the binaries of passivity and activity.

However, when Stevens and Woolf create textual still lifes, their model of attention to everyday 'things' reveals considerable differences that go beyond their obvious differences as a poet and prose writer. In *Parts of a World* Stevens typically evacuates his compositions of human presence or contact, dwelling on inanimate objects, which become increasingly destabilised under the lyric 'eye'. Woolf's commitment is to things that 'quiver into being'.[117] As she vigorously – if rather disingenuously – expresses the distinction in her essay 'The Leaning Tower' (1940), the writer takes '[n]othing so simple as a painter's model; it is not a bowl of flowers, a naked figure, or a dish of apples and onions', rather, he must 'keep his eye upon a model that moves'. His subject is 'human life'.[118]

Notes

1. Charles Mauron, *Aesthetics and Psychology*, trans. Roger Fry and Katherine John (London: Hogarth Press, 1935), p. 31. The edition to which I refer was Stevens's personal copy of the text: WAS 440369, Wallace Stevens Library, Huntington Library, San Marino, California. Further references to this edition are abbreviated to AP, where necessary, and given after quotations in the text.
2. Marginal inscription alongside Mauron's text in Stevens's personal copy of *Aesthetics and Psychology*, p. 31.
3. Like Fry, Mauron initially trained as a scientist and he attempted to integrate the fields of science and aesthetics in his writings. See Linda Hutcheon, *Formalism and the Freudian Aesthetic: The Example of Charles Mauron* (Cambridge: Cambridge University Press, 1984), for a comprehensive account of Mauron's work in relation to psychology, and on his close relationship to Fry.
4. Stevens is rarely read in relation to Bloomsbury aesthetics, and I return to this in the Coda to this chapter, but his personal library includes all of Woolf's major works, and many publications by the Hogarth Press, to which he had a subscription.
5. It is not possible to determine the exact date by which Stevens had read *Aesthetics and Psychology*; however, in *Wallace Stevens and Poetic Theory: Conceiving the Supreme Fiction* (Chapel Hill: University of North Carolina Press, 1987), B. J. Leggett notes that '[b]its and pieces of Mauron's discussion begin to appear in his poetry and prose in 1936', from which he infers that this was when Stevens first read the work (p. 73).
6. Stevens's thoroughgoing acquaintance with the text is especially significant given that few of his library books in the Huntington collection bear evidence of annotative reading.

7. 'The Novel' was published in *The Auroras of Autumn* (1950), repr. in CPP, pp. 391–2.
8. Leggett, *Wallace Stevens and Poetic Theory*, pp. 73–4.
9. Ibid., p. 84. Stevens borrows this phrase from Benedetto Croce in his essay 'The Noble Rider and the Sound of Words'. Leggett's interest is in 'describing the impact of Mauron's writing on Stevens's conception of poetry, rather than in finding echoes in scattered passages of verse' (ibid., p. 74). He considers how Mauron's ideas shaped Stevens's 'psychology of pleasure' in *Notes Toward a Supreme Fiction* (1942) in Chapter 4 of his study, and explores their 'parallel notions of obscurity in poetry' (p. 72) in Chapter 5.
10. There has been no extensive exploration (of which I am aware) of the connection between Stevens and Mauron since Leggett's study. However, in *Wallace Stevens and the Aesthetics of Abstraction* (Cambridge: Cambridge University Press, 2010), Edward Ragg draws attention to Stevens's reading of Mauron in his chapter on 'Abstract Appetites', pp. 136–65 (which I discuss later), but his primary interest differs from mine in considering how Mauron's theory bolsters Stevensian abstraction.
11. William W. Bevis, *Mind of Winter: Wallace Stevens, Meditation, and Literature* (Pittsburgh: University of Pittsburgh Press, 1988), p. 5.
12. Ibid., pp. 104, 9.
13. Bonnie Costello, 'Planets on Tables: Still Life and War in the Poetry of Wallace Stevens', *Modernism/Modernity*, 12 (2005), 443–58 (p. 444). Costello builds on this article in Chapter 1 of her book, *Planets on Tables*, which focuses on Stevens and 'Local Objects and Distant Wars'.
14. Costello, *Planets on Tables*, p. 35.
15. Glen MacLeod, *Wallace Stevens and Modern Art: From the Armory Show to Abstract Expressionism* (New Haven: Yale University Press, 1993). MacLeod cites a letter of 21 January 1938, in which Stevens had yet to decide upon an idea for his next volume; 'only eight days later, in a letter of 29 January he was able to write: "I am beginning to feel that I know what I want to do next."' MacLeod concludes that '[w]hat occurred between these two letters was the opening of an [the still life] exhibition' (p. 83). Mauron is absent from MacLeod's insightful study of the influences at work on Stevens in the sphere of the visual arts.
16. I shall have more to say later about Stevens's connection to Braque, which is little remarked upon, while his affinity with Cézanne is frequently observed. Wilson E. Taylor recorded that his interest in painting 'centered on the works of Cézanne'; and in a letter of 31 March 1938 Stevens describes the painter as 'the source of all painting of any interest during the last 20 years'. In Frank and Robert Buttel, eds, *Wallace Stevens: A Celebration* (Princeton: Princeton University Press, 1980), p. 101. For further discussion see Betty Buchsbaum, 'Contours of Desire: The Place of Cézanne in Wallace Stevens's Poetics and Late Practice', *Criticism*, 30 (1988), 303–24. Stevens's library includes the *Selected Letters of Rainer Maria Rilke 1902–1926* (London: Macmillan, 1946), WAS 491462, in which the German poet offers his lyrical response to Cézanne's still lifes. Perhaps Stevens identified with the following assessment of Rilke in a review from the *New Statesman and Nation*, 9 March 1946, a clipping of which he enclosed inside his personal copy (now in the Huntington collection): 'a rather rare

but genuine type of artist who is primarily interested in the sensations aroused in him by the objects, animate as well as inanimate, which surround him'.

17. Foreword, signed J. R. S., *The Painters of Still Life* (Hartford, CT: Wadsworth Atheneum, 1938), n.p. See MacLeod on the case the exhibition catalogue makes for the relationship between Dutch painting and Surrealism and its opposition to abstraction (*Wallace Stevens and Modern Art*, pp. 89–90).
18. Bonnie Costello, 'Effects of an Analogy: Wallace Stevens and Painting', in Albert Gelpi, ed., *Wallace Stevens: The Poetics of Modernism* (Cambridge: Cambridge University Press, 1985), pp. 65–85 (pp. 65–6).
19. Helen Vendler, *Wallace Stevens: Words Chosen Out of Desire* (Knoxville: University of Tennessee Press, 1984), p. 8.
20. Wallace Stevens, 'The Noble Rider and the Sound of Words', in CPP, pp. 643–65 (p. 661); first delivered as a lecture at Princeton University and published in 1942. All further references to this essay are to this edition and will be abbreviated to 'NR' and given after quotations in the text.
21. AP, p. 70.
22. 'Attitude, *n.*', in *OED*, http://www.oed.com/view/Entry/12876.
23. Eliot, 'Burnt Norton', in *Four Quartets*, p. 174.
24. Leggett sees Mauron as a direct influence on Stevens's definition of nobility in 'The Noble Rider', claiming that it 'is, in fact, his own version of Mauron's theory of "inactive" contemplation' (*Wallace Stevens and Poetic Theory*, p. 83).
25. Stevens, 'The Irrational Element in Poetry', CPP, pp. 781–92 (pp. 788–9).
26. Leggett, *Wallace Stevens and Poetic Theory*, p. 109.
27. See Mauron's commentary on 'Does All Pride Smoke out Evening', in Stéphane Mallarmé, *Poems*, trans. Roger Fry (London: Chatto & Windus, 1936), p. 248.
28. Ibid., p. 250.
29. Stevens's library includes Clive Bell's *Pot Boilers* (London, Chatto & Windus, 1918), WAS 49144. This diverse collection of essays includes 'The English Salon' and 'English Post-Impressionists' (at which point a bookmark is placed in Stevens's copy). During my research on Stevens's library, I found two newspaper clippings, placed inside his copy of *Pot Boilers*, which indicate an early interest in Cézanne and in Clive Bell. One clipping is of Bell's review of *Paul Cézanne* by Ambroise Vollard, titled 'Cézanne', from the *Athenaeum*, 16 May 1919. The article evidently interested Stevens as he made another related clipping (date unknown), titled 'Cézanne: *To the Editor of* The Athenaeum', signed Clive Bell. These material details offer another point of contact between Stevens and Bloomsbury.
30. The essay begins: 'Roger Fry concluded a note on Claude by saying that "few of us live so strenuously as never to feel a sense of nostalgia for that Saturnian reign to which Virgil and Claude can waft us"' (RPP, p. 740).
31. The desire for a stabilising centre or fixed point does, however, become pronounced in Stevens's late poem, 'The Ultimate Poem Is Abstract', where the speaker yearns to be 'just once, at the middle, fixed/ In This Beautiful World Of Ours' (CPP, p. 376).
32. Letter to Paule Vidal, 31 October 1949, *Letters of Wallace Stevens*, ed. Holly Stevens (Berkeley: University of California Press, 1996), p. 655.
33. Bergson, quoted by Stevens, in NR, p. 658. Stevens's source is Bergson's *Creative Evolution*.

34. In 1940 Mauron became blind as a result of a worsening eye condition, which may have heightened his non-visual senses and his interest in memory.
35. 'An Early Introduction' (written 1921), repr. from *The Poems of Mallarmé* (1936), in *A Roger Fry Reader*, pp. 297–304 (pp. 300, 303).
36. Walter Pater, *Studies in the History of the Renaissance* (Oxford: Oxford University Press, 2010), p. 121.
37. William Fitzgerald, discussing another 'musical' poem, 'Peter Quince at the Clavier', in '"Music is Feeling, Then, Not Sound": Wallace Stevens and the Body of Music', *SubStance*, 21 (1992), 44–60 (pp. 50–1).
38. Stevens would have seen this painting at the first Picasso retrospective at the Atheneum, Hartford in 1934. Numerous critics have speculated over the poem's relationship to Picasso and Cubism, including Daniel R. Schwarz, '"The Serenade of a Man Who Plays a Blue Guitar": The Presence of Modern Painting in Stevens's Poetry', *Journal of Narrative Technique*, 22 (1992), 65–83; and Judith Rhine Sheridan, 'The Picasso Connection: Wallace Stevens's "The Man with the Blue Guitar"', *Arizona Quarterly*, 35 (1979), 77–89. David Hockney offers a wry commentary on the poem in his etching, *A Moving Still Life (from Blue Guitar)*, from the series *The Blue Guitar, etchings by David Hockney who was inspired by Wallace Stevens who was inspired by Pablo Picasso* (1976–77).
39. MacLeod suggests that we look for Stevens's inspiration in a special Picasso issue of *Cahiers d'art* (1935), which is the source for the 'hoard of destructions' quotation, and which he argues demonstrates Picasso's Surrealism rather than Cubism as significant for the poem's context (*Wallace Stevens and Modern Art*, pp. 63–78).
40. *Letters*, to Renato Poggioli, 1 July 1953, p. 786.
41. On 23 January 1947, Stevens wrote to Paule Vidal: 'The truth is that I have a taste for Braque and a purse for Bombois.' *Letters*, p. 545. Critics rarely consider Stevens's affinity with Braque but Monroe Wheeler recalled that he was the poet's 'favourite painter': 'we talked a lot about him. It was the style that suited him. He simply took pleasure in him; he didn't analyse.' Quoted in Peter Brazeau, *Parts of a World: Wallace Stevens Remembered. An Oral Biography* (New York: Random House, 1977), p. 191.
42. Braque, quoted by Alex Danchev, *Georges Braque: A Life* (London: Penguin, 2005), p. 135.
43. See MacLeod, *Wallace Stevens and Modern Art*, pp. 10–15, for an illustrated discussion of Arensberg's apartment and collection, which also included Cézanne's *Still Life with Apples* (c.1880–85) among other works by the painter.
44. For further discussion see Sophie Bowness, 'Braque and Music', in John Golding, ed., *Braque: Still Lifes and Interiors* (London: A South Bank Centre Touring Exhibition, 1990), pp. 57–67.
45. The mood and subject of the still life motif shifts subtly throughout the poem, however, and stanza XIV illuminates a scene of contentment: 'the fruit and wine,/ The book and bread, things as they are' (CPP, p. 141).
46. If Mauron's expression of faith in the artist's capacities for altruism seems too easily achieved, or the curious neologism 'amused detachment' rather vulnerable as a concept, there is nevertheless a logic at work here. To be amused is to become diverted (and thus detached) from oneself and therefore to move towards sympathetic contact

and pleasurable communion with 'otherness'. 'Amused detachment' may seem an unfamiliar, even peculiar expression, but this may be the result of awkward translation from the French. To my knowledge no copy of a French language text exists, which prevents a more detailed comparison.

47. 'Unstable equilibrium' recalls, for instance, D. H. Lawrence's descriptions of Cézanne paintings.
48. Stevens underlines Mauron's phrase: 'Expressive art . . . flourishes most happily apart from or rather on the edge of the great eddies of the human soul' (AP, p. 68), and draws attention to the passage up to Mauron's mention of Chardin with three dashes. He also made notations in the margins of this passage.
49. Charles Mauron, *The Nature of Beauty in Art and Literature*, trans. Roger Fry (London: Hogarth Press, 1927), p. 19.
50. See MacLeod on the link between Stevens's Dutch ancestry and his interest in still life, *Wallace Stevens and Modern Art*, pp. 51, 86.
51. Bryson, *Looking at the Overlooked*, pp. 112–16.
52. See Brysons's chapter on 'Abundance', which offers a nuanced discussion of the sometimes contradictory messages encoded in such paintings (ibid., pp. 96–136).
53. Ibid., p. 66.
54. Ibid., p. 112.
55. The spectrum of feeling prompted by these compositions in *Parts of a World* is well observed by Douglas Mao, who notes that the volume 'pursues every imaginable variation on the Stevensian ur-tableau of subject confronting discrete solid object across a divide of nonknowing and desire'. In *Solid Objects: Modernism and the Test of Production* (Princeton: Princeton University Press, 1998), pp. 222–3.
56. Davenport, *Objects on a Table*, p. 5.
57. *Letters*, to Henry Church, 1 June 1939, p. 340; and to C. L. Daughtry, 24 November 1941, p. 394. Another incarnation of the 'spiritual epicure' can be identified in the poet's description of the artist or 'man of imagination' who 'becomes the ethereal compounder' (*Letters*, to Hi Simons, 28 August 1940, p. 372).
58. Mauron, *The Nature of Beauty in Art and Literature*, p. 19. In many ways this text anticipates his argument in *Aesthetics and Psychology*.
59. For a list of works in the poet's private art collection see photographic prints in the Wallace Stevens Papers, Huntington Library, California. Originals are in the Watkinson Library, Trinity College, Hartford, CT.
60. *Letters*, to Paule Vidal, 6 March 1947, p. 548. Paule Vidal and her father Anatole purchased art works for Stevens from the mid-1930s, as well as publications on modern art. His correspondence with the Vidals over the period 1935–55 reveals much about his aesthetic preferences.
61. *Letters*, 6 March 1947, p. 548; and 13 May 1954, p. 834.
62. *Letters*, 9 September 1949, p. 647.
63. Ragg, *Wallace Stevens and the Aesthetics of Abstraction*, pp. 136, 215, in reference to the 'bourgeois abstraction' of late Stevens. The gastronomic expression of aesthetic values in Mauron's work is where my interest coincides with Ragg's; however, my reading centres on still life as a framework for epicureanism in Stevens's poetry while Ragg is concerned with where Mauron's theory supports Stevensian abstraction.

64. Wallace Stevens, from *Adagia*, in *Opus Posthumous*, ed. Samuel French Morse (New York: Vintage, 1982; repr. of Alfred A. Knopf, 1957), p. 176; and NR, p. 661.
65. The poet marked out the concluding passage of Mauron's final chapter from which this phrase is taken.
66. 'Angel Surrounded by Paysans' is a salient example, as one of the few still life poems that can be identified with a still life painting by Pierre Tal Coat. Its connections with the poem are made explicit in Stevens's correspondence. For a persuasive account see Alan Filreis, 'Still Life without Substance: Wallace Stevens and the Language of Agency', *Poetics Today*, 10 (1989), 345–72.
67. Georges Braque, *Illustrated Notebooks (1917–1955)*, trans. Stanley Appelbaum (New York: Dover Publications, 1971), p. 77. This aphorism is not directly invoked by Stevens but he evidently had a taste for Braque's aphorisms, inscribing the following in his own notebook of aphorisms: 'Usage is everything ("*Les idées sont destinées à être deformée à l'usage. Reconnaître ce fait est une prevue de désintéressement.*" Georges Braque. *Verve* No. 2)', in *Adagia*, *Opus Posthumous*, p. 159. The Spring 1938 issue of *Verve*, from which this quotation is taken, featured a long article about Braque illustrated with works including a still life, *Woman with a Mandolin*, and the painter's 'Reflections'.
68. The poem's insistence on meaning 'much more than that' anticipates 'Study of Two Pears', published in *Parts of a World*, in which the fruits are similarly abbreviated (to 'yellow forms' and 'blobs'), but the effect is to emphasise the way in which they exceed the perceiver's capacity to express the experience: 'The pears are not seen/ As the observer wills' (CPP, p. 172).
69. Stevens employs the phrase in direct reference to Mauron's ideas in the passage from NR, p. 661, cited at the beginning of this chapter.
70. Stevens anticipated the amorous approach of 'A Dish of Peaches in Russia' in 'Evening without Angels', published in *Ideas of Order* (1936), for which the epigraph from Mario Rossi describes '*the joy of having a body, the voluptuousness of looking*' (CPP, p. 111).
71. Schapiro, 'The Apples of Cézanne', p. 27.
72. For further discussion of the gender politics of Stevens's appetites see Melita Schaum, ed., *Wallace Stevens and the Feminine* (London: University of Alabama Press, 1993).
73. Costello, *Planets on Tables*, p. 34.
74. For further exploration of Stevens in the historical framework of the 1930s see Alan Filreis, *Wallace Stevens and the Actual World* (Princeton: Princeton University Press, 1991).
75. Leggett, *Wallace Stevens and Poetic Theory*, pp. 82–3.
76. Karen K. Butler, 'The Known and Unknown Worlds', in Karen K. Butler and Renée Maurer, eds, *Georges Braque and the Cubist Still Life, 1928–1945* (London: DelMonico Books, 2013), p. 9.
77. See Hutcheon, *Formalism and the Freudian Aesthetic*, pp. 30–1.
78. Ragg draws on this aspect of Mauron's theory to suggest that Stevensian abstraction offered an enriched connection with the everyday.

79. See Siobhan Phillips, 'Wallace Stevens and the Mode of the Ordinary', *Twentieth Century Literature*, 54 (2008), 1–30, and her chapter on Stevens in *The Poetics of the Everyday: Creative Repetition in Modern American Verse* (New York: Columbia University Press, 2010), pp. 71–111. The last two decades have seen increasing critical attention to the role of the 'commonplace' in Stevens and in modernism more widely. In *Modernism and the Ordinary*, Liesl Olson finds Stevens's notion of the commonplace to be grounded in pragmatist philosophy and expressive of 'a satisfaction with the material rather than the spiritual, the local rather than the exotic' (p. 116); James Longenbach explores the co-existence of poetry, politics and economics in the poet's 'ordinary' life in *Wallace Stevens: The Plain Sense of Things* (Oxford: Oxford University Press, 1991).
80. Elaine Scarry, 'Imagining Flowers: Perceptual Mimesis (Particularly Delphinium)', *Representations*, 57 (1997), 90–115 (pp. 93, 107).
81. Epstein, quoted by Jacky Klein (March 2002), Tate, http://www.tate.org.uk/art/artworks/epstein-dahlias-and-sunflower-t05759/text-summary.
82. The poet's taste for works in his own home was less experimental as is reflected by his choice of a conventional floral still life *Blue Bowl of Red Flowers*, by Eric Detthow, which is listed as part of his collection of paintings.
83. Braque, *Illustrated Notebooks*, p. 48.
84. Stevens similarly sought to 'tame' the paintings in his private collection. In a letter to Paule Vidal on 5 October 1949, he describes his new still life by Pierre Tal Coat as becoming 'almost domesticated. Tal Coat is supposed to be a man of violence but one soon becomes accustomed to the present picture'. He goes on to claim that the title he gives to the picture, 'Angel Surrounded by Peasants', 'tames it as a lump of sugar might tame a lion' (*Letters*, pp. 649–50).
85. Stevens's approach to the 'feminine' has proved difficult to characterise. Lisa M. Steinman traces some of the 'conflicting views of what is implied by the poems that represent female figures as passive or silent', in 'The Feminine', in Glen Macleod, ed., *Wallace Stevens in Context* (Cambridge: Cambridge University Press, 2017), pp. 344–52 (p. 349).
86. Costello, 'Planets on Tables', p. 454.
87. Bevis, *Mind of Winter*, p. 112.
88. Quoted in Sandra Kraskin and Glen MacLeod, eds, *Painting in Poetry, Poetry in Painting: Wallace Stevens and Modern Art* (New York: Baruch College, Sidney Mishkin Gallery, 1995), p. 28.
89. Costello, 'Planets on Tables', p. 456.
90. Ibid., p. 456.
91. Bryson, *Looking at the Overlooked*, p. 121.
92. Giorgio de Chirico, *Le Nature Morte*, in 'L'Illustrazione Italiana', 24 May 1942, p. 500, repr. in *Metaphysical Art,* 14/16 (2016), 116–17 (p. 117).
93. Ibid., p. 117.
94. Woolf, *The Waves*, p. 254.
95. Braque, *Illustrated Notebooks*, p. 26.
96. Leo Stein, 'On Reading Poetry and Seeing Pictures', in *Appreciation: Painting, Poetry, and Prose* (New York: Crown Publishers, 1947), pp. 93–138 (p. 103). Quoted by Stevens in RPP, pp. 741–2.

97. Ragg, *Wallace Stevens and the Aesthetics of Abstraction*, p. 223.
98. *Letters*, to C. L. Daughtry, 24 November 1941, p. 394.
99. *Letters*, to Jose Rodriguez Feo, 19 February 1952, p. 741.
100. Bevis demonstrates this in his study, noting that 'A number of Stevens's poems seem not only to use meditative issues and points of view, but also to imitate the structure of meditative experience, an advanced, sensate, meditative experience.' *Mind of Winter*, p. 104.
101. Ragg, *Wallace Stevens and the Aesthetics of Abstraction*, pp. 211–12.
102. There is no evidence of the date on which Stevens purchased this work.
103. *Letters*, to Paule Vidal, 6 March 1947, p. 548.
104. For a reading of the poem in the context of the Spanish Civil War, see MacLeod, who suggests that its inspirations sprung from an article on 'Miro and the Spanish Civil War' published in the *Partisan Review* (*Wallace Stevens and Modern Art*, pp. 84–5).
105. Harold Bloom, *Wallace Stevens: The Poems of Our Climate* (Ithaca: Cornell University Press, 1977), p. 57.
106. Costello reads 'the presentation of a fixed object in the foreground' as 'an orientation, a sense of arrangement and form, and a local and individual connection to the flux of history' ('Planets on Tables', p. 452), but the stability of the 'dry loaf' is in question as it recedes from view in the 'waves' of other images through the poem.
107. Jones, *The Dying Gaul*, pp. 136–7.
108. Bevis, *Mind of Winter*, pp. 28–9; for his reading of 'The Poems of our Climate', see pp. 146–7.
109. Rainer Maria Rilke, 'The Bowl of Roses', in *New Poems*, trans. Len Krisak (London: Boydell & Brewer, 2015), pp. 167–70.
110. Schopenhauer, *The World as Will and Representation*, I, p. 196. In 'Wallace Stevens and Schopenhauer's *The World as Will and Idea*', *Tulane Studies in English*, 20 (1972), 135–68, Richard P. Adams claims that 'Stevens read at least some parts of *The World as Will and Idea* [an alternative translation of *The World as Will and Representation*], probably in the translation of Haldane and Kemp, and probably before 1914', and cites this text as 'one of the philosophical works from which he borrowed ideas for his poetry' (p. 137). Although there is no surviving copy of this work in Stevens's library, it does include Schopenhauer's *The Wisdom of Life*, trans. T. Bailey Saunders (London: George Allen & Unwin, 1923), WAS 491237. See also Bart Eeckhout on the 'intertextual relevance' of Schopenhauer's text in his reading of the second half of 'The Snow Man', in *Stevens and the Limits of Reading and Writing* (Missouri: University of Missouri Press, 2003), p. 83.
111. Schopenhauer, *The World as Will and Representation*, I, pp. 196–7.
112. Ibid., p. 219.
113. Ibid., p. 197.
114. Mauron's translations included an early version of the 'Time Passes' section of *To the Lighthouse* in 1926, followed by *Orlando* and *Flush*. Woolf's letters and diaries of this decade testify to their continuing intellectual exchange and her regard for Mauron. See esp. Letter to Julian Bell, 14 November 1936, *Letters of Virginia*

Woolf, VI, p. 84; and to E. M. Forster, 19 January 1936, *Letters*, VI, p. 7. For a more detailed discussion see Claudia Tobin, '"The Active and the Contemplative": Charles Mauron, Virginia Woolf, and Roger Fry', in Nicola Wilson and Claire Battershill, eds, *Virginia Woolf and the World of Books* (Clemson: Clemson University Press, 2018).

115. Letter to Mauron, 28 April 1940, quoted by Mary Ann Caws and Sarah Bird Wright, in *Bloomsbury and France: Art and Friends* (Oxford: Oxford University Press, 1999), p. 281. For a discussion of Mauron's role as Bloomsbury's conduit to French culture, see esp. pp. 267–89.
116. Kimberly Engdahl Coates is the notable exception with her perceptive reading of Woolf's essay 'On Being Ill' in relation to Mauron's text, in 'Exposing the Nerves of Language: Virginia Woolf, Charles Mauron and the Affinity Between Aesthetics and Illness', *Literature and Medicine*, 21 (2002), 242–63. Allen McLaurin and Ann Banfield both identify Mauron's concept of 'psychological volumes', which he developed in *The Nature of Beauty*, as an influence on Woolf in writing *To the Lighthouse*, but they do not examine *Aesthetics and Psychology*.
117. Woolf, 'Donne after Three Centuries', p. 32. Douglas Mao is one of the few critics to note Stevens's 'theoretical connection to Woolf's circle' through his receptivity to Mauron. However, for Mao 'The Noble Rider' 'illuminates a vast gap between Bloomsbury solicitousness about violence against the object and Stevensian anxiety on behalf of the human [. . .] to present contemplation not as a relaxation from action but as a different kind of force' (*Solid Objects*, p. 240). As I have argued, however, in different ways Woolf and Fry are also engaged in recasting contemplation as a 'kind of force'.
118. Woolf, 'The Leaning Tower', in *The Moment*, pp. 105–25 (p. 105).

CONCLUSION: 'ON THE VERY BRINK OF UTTERANCE': ALDOUS HUXLEY, MARK GERTLER AND TRANSFIGURED THINGS

In his review of Mark Gertler's 1922 exhibition, Huxley appends the subtitle, 'A Painter Who Knows How to Record the Qualities of Things'.[1] Huxley's analysis of Gertler returns this inquiry, by way of a conclusion, to those questions about the eloquent yet disquieting life of objects with which we began. What happens when still life permeates other genres, for instance when portraits or landscapes become still lifes? What happens when the living animates the still? What is the difference between 'material' and 'spiritual' comprehension of everyday objects? In Huxley's early poetry, still life is a symbol of modern instability and an object of parody, but it also functions as a metaphor for ways of seeing and interpreting the world in his art criticism, which gain validation decades later in his meditation on visionary experience under the influence of mescaline, *The Doors of Perception* (1954).

What particularly attracts Huxley to Gertler's work is the 'wonderfully satisfying sense of mass and solidity' in his still lives' (p. 69).[2] Identifying qualities that his friend D. H. Lawrence and many others had admired in Cézanne, Huxley observes the way Gertler paints the solidity and texture of objects with 'a strange intensity of vision' that gives them 'extraordinary significance' and seems to penetrate their 'material essence' (p. 68). It is this capacity to communicate on the level of physical response that Huxley emphasises in Gertler's rendering of bottles, china figures and draperies which 'produce an almost tactile impression' on the viewer and enable them to 'share his feeling for the material essence of things' (p. 69). A painting by

Gertler titled *Meditation* illustrates Huxley's article, depicting a languid nude in an armchair, her limbs hanging heavily, one hand loosely holding a book. For Huxley, this is not a portrait but rather the painter's 'application of the still life method to a study of the nude' (p. 69).

Gertler's paintings of the early 1920s can be situated in the tradition of the sensuous, luxuriant still life. Fruit, drapery and voluptuous human flesh are brought into close relationship in *The Queen of Sheba* (1922) (plate 26), a painting which was exhibited with the London Group the same year. The nude woman is enfolded by flesh-like drapery as she lies propped suggestively but with a rather vacant expression alongside a bowl of fruits and scattered cherries – glowing, warm-toned objects arranged together for the viewer's delectation. Whereas in Ben Nicholson's still lifes of the same period we find the ascetic, pared down forms of an earthenware jar or goblet, in Gertler's increasingly congested and luxuriant compositions the invitation is to touch and consume. Like his Bloomsbury contemporaries, he was fascinated by Cézanne's apples. His letters record admiration for the 'great man', and for the 'plasticity and construction' of the still life of apples owned by Keynes and lauded by Bloomsbury.[3] Gertler painted still lifes of apples and pears with bold black outlines and shifting contours, which take their reference from the French painter, and his compositions frequently incorporated familiar elements such as drapery and compotiers.[4] In the spring of 1924, however, Gertler would write of his attempt to move away from the 'tastiness' of another tutelary French still life painter, Renoir. He is 'exquisite – delicious', writes Gertler, but 'He is really too "tasty". It is too refined for us – too sweet.' His consciousness of the brutality of his moment in post-war culture complicates any simplified notion of the still life as an arena of luxuriance and pleasure, and he concludes: 'We must have something more brutal today.'[5]

As we have seen throughout this book, still life is a permeable, even a leaky genre. It absorbs and spills across boundaries, sometimes eliding landscape or portrait with still life. Huxley's observation of a 'vision and attitude of mind' associated with still life in Gertler's work anticipates and in some ways extends the interpretation we have seen Lawrence make of the inter-relationship between different genres in Cézanne (p. 69). If Gertler's portraits capture the 'material essence' and 'solid form' of his sitters, it is – in Huxley's assessment – because he makes them into 'still lives [. . .] studies of the matter out of which their faces and bodies are made'. The 'strange intensity' of these works emerges out of the painter's 'complete material comprehension rather than a spiritual comprehension' of his sitters. Huxley implies that something is lacking in Gertler's portraits, they are 'not complete', limited by his preoccupation with 'tangible qualities of matter' (p. 69). Seeking the 'spiritual' as well as 'material comprehension' of inanimate things would increasingly preoccupy Huxley in his own work.

The year following his review of Gertler, Huxley pursued the still life theme in another article for *Vogue*, 'Dead Nature or Life: Certain Theories of the Dead Nature School'.[6] It finds him weary of the ubiquity of compositions such as 'the plate of apples, the crumpled napkin, the black quart bottle', in the exhibitions of young modern painters. They are filled with 'pure artistic turpentine' rather than the 'heady and illicit wine of life'.[7] In critiquing these works he exploits the transcultural slippage of meaning in the term 'still life', reaching for the *nature morte*, 'Dead Nature', as more appropriate due to its pejorative connotations. 'Still Life', on the other hand, 'for all the delicious quietism of the first word, suggests in the second a notion of rude energy and vitality'.[8] Huxley's complaint is levelled at painters of the 'Dead Nature School', but it is with formalist theories of aesthetics that he is ultimately concerned. 'A work of art should concern itself only with aesthetics – with the relation of planes and masses and so on – not at all with life', he writes in parody, as if anticipating Lawrence's attack on Bloomsbury's preoccupation with 'Pure Form', and he goes on to bemoan the young painters influenced by such theories who 'disinfect and sterilize their pictures of every germ of passion or external life'.[9]

When Huxley arrives at Wyndham Lewis, however, it is to single out a painter not 'led astray by the Dead Nature theories of aesthetics'. His art 'feeds on life' and is 'passionately living'.[10] We remember that Lewis himself had used *nature morte* as a term to critique Ezra Pound and James Joyce, and as early as the first issue of *Blast* in 1914, Picasso had received Lewis's blasting for becoming 'a miniature naturalistic sculptor of the vast natures-morte of modern life'.[11] Lewis draws attention to the painter's recently exhibited small sculptures – 'structures in cardboard, wood, zinc, glass string, etc' – which experiment with the limits of naturalism by reproducing the surface and texture of real objects. 'Should a human form be included he would hardly be content until he could include in his work a plot of human flesh', Lewis can't resist quipping.[12] If, for Huxley, it is 'life' that is the defining absence in the 'Dead Nature School', for Lewis what is at stake is the lack of transformation from 'life' into 'art'. Picasso's objects not only lack 'the necessary physical stamina to survive', but also, by attending to things of 'inferior significance' – the machinery of everyday life (a kettle or plate for instance) – he strays too far from the work of interpretation and makes only 'dead nature'.[13] The terms of still life are ever more embattled.

In an early poem published in Huxley's *Defeat of Youth* collection of 1918, titled 'Crapulous Impression', he presents a still life vision of material overindulgence as a prompt to parody contemporary modes of perception and moral or religious codes. The still life is seen through an alcohol blurred (crapulous) haze which pits an impressionist flux of light against an unnaturally solid composition: 'the high-lights shine/ Hard and sharp on the bottles: the wine/ Stands firmly solid' and '[t]he fruits metallically gleam'.[14] Human life is marginalised and the faces that hover on the periphery of the scene are disembodied and become absorbed into the composition by the end of the first stanza: 'Part of this still, still life . . . they've lost their soul'. Soulnessness and the inertia of still life are coupled in a leap from the material to the metaphysical, as the second stanza demands 'What about God?', and the answer, when it comes, is that He's found in all objects. The poem concludes with a game of chess as 'God-in-the-bottle' is checkmated by 'God-in-the-salt'. Jane Goldman has commented on the poem's skewing of literary and artistic impressionism but perhaps more pertinent here is her suggestion that the poem anticipates 'in compressed form' the dinner party scene in Woolf's *To the Lighthouse*, in which the painter Lily Briscoe uses the salt cellar to map out her composition and by corollary to oppose the idea of marriage by absorbing herself in creative problems.[15] In different ways, still life is co-opted to make radical points about aesthetic practice and metaphysics.

If Huxley's early poems parody still life, and his novels of the 1920s such as *Crome Yellow* paint ambivalent portraits of artists (such as Gombauld, modelled on Gertler), by the time he was writing *The Doors of Perception* (1954), still life had been recast as a laboratory for heightened vision. The vase of flowers is a constant subject in the still life tradition and Huxley's extended meditation on this subject is one of the most striking examples in this text that can be placed in this tradition. He attempts to recount, both empirically and lyrically, the effects of 'looking intently' at an arrangement containing a rose, carnation and an iris, after taking a dose of mescaline.[16] His description of natural appearances shifts toward the revelatory as he perceives not simply an 'unusual flower arrangement' with dissonant colours but, 'what Adam had seen on the morning of his creation – the miracle, moment by moment, of naked existence' (p. 7). His imagery of radiant 'living' light and cleansed spiritual perception is reminiscent of Winifred Nicholson's writings on flower painting. We read of 'a bunch of flowers shining with their own inner light' and 'all but quivering under the pressure of the significance with which they were charged'. The rose, iris and carnation signify the paradox of still life: 'a transience that was yet eternal life, a perpetual perishing that was at the same time pure Being' (p. 7). Was Huxley reaching for the capacities he recognised in Lawrence, the 'mystical materialist', as he described his friend, for whom 'the mystery was always [. . .] a *numen*, divine'?[17] Huxley's contemplative vision is sustained to the point at which he attests to the sentient quality of the flowers, detecting what seems to be 'the qualitative equivalent of breathing' (p. 7). Like Mauron's contemplative epicure, the percipient becomes aware of 'fine shades of difference', alert to the texture and hues of each flower, their 'feathery incandescence' and 'sentient amethyst' (pp. 14, 7). The trajectory he articulates from the commonplace to the sublime circumvents or overcomes the weary irony of his early poetry and criticism, and he grasps for a language of mystical experience across different spiritual traditions: for 'Grace' and 'Transfiguration', *Sat Chit Ananda* or 'Being-Awareness-Bliss' (pp. 7–8).

In Woolf's essay 'Pictures and Portraits', we witnessed ekphrastic intoxication over a still life of 'red-hot pokers', which revealed to the writers a sharpened perception of colour. When Huxley examines the same subject, a clump of red-hot poker flowers, he finds them 'so passionately alive that they seemed to be standing on the very brink of utterance' (p. 36). This urgent sense of revelation and non-verbal communication echoes, indeed seems directly to borrow from, Lawrence's description of Cézanne's compositions of 'apples and kitchen pots' which allowed intuitive consciousness to triumph and 'broke into utterance'. The superlative nature of still life is registered in Huxley's account: he describes 'the excessive, the too obvious glory of the flowers', which even as the effects of the drug recede 'still trembled on the brink of being supernatural' (pp. 36–7).

When Huxley's attention turns toward the furniture in his room (a typing-table, wicker chair and desk), he finds these objects also transformed into a pattern or composition, for which his analogy is a Braque or Juan Gris still life. How can we define this kind of perception? Huxley's assessment is that it is neither utilitarian, nor that of the scientist, but rather that of a 'pure aesthete' with a 'Cubist's-eye view'. It is not static, however, and evolves into what he calls a 'sacramental vision of reality', as if fulfilling the transition from the 'material comprehension' of objects which he had intuited in Gertler's paintings, to 'the spiritual' (p. 10).

Whether Huxley's still life meditations are 'sacramental visions' or hallucinations, they demonstrate a dynamic we have repeatedly encountered in the artists and writers I have explored. That is, a tension between the ascetic and the sensuous, the active and the passive, and related ethical concerns that still life may be charged with indulgence, passivity or quietism. The problem, as Huxley frames it in *The Doors of Perception*, is how to reconcile 'this timeless bliss of seeing' with 'temporal duties'; how 'cleansed perception' could be sustained alongside 'a proper concern with human relations, with the necessary chores and duties, to say nothing of charity and practical compassion' (pp. 19, 23). The danger or seduction of seeing 'how things really are', in Huxley's account, is that 'just looking, just being the divine Not-self of flower, of book, of chair [. . .] would be enough'. With more than a trace of the Stevensian restless 'I', Huxley is troubled by the way in which this contemplative state involves an apparent withdrawal from the social and human, indeed from 'ethical values' (a familiar critique of still life) (pp. 19, 25). The paradox he experiences is that 'participation in the manifest glory of things' exceeds and thereby occludes 'the ordinary, the necessary concerns of human existence' (p. 19).

We return, then, to the question of the active/contemplative, that 'age-old debate' as Huxley describes it (p. 23). The kind of contemplation accessed under the influence of mescaline is limited, he concludes, 'incompatible with action and even with the will to action' (pp. 23–4). Huxley draws together the 'quietist, the *arhat*' but also 'the landscape painter and the painter of human still lives' in this shared ethical impasse (p. 24). As if to test this hypothesis, his own meditation on 'real-life' still life compositions in *The Doors of Perception* is followed by readings of still life painters from Vermeer to Cézanne. If Cézanne is the key to radically renewed vision for Lawrence, Vermeer performs the same role for Huxley. Both writers find the crux of the matter in their interrogation of the exchange between the genres of portraiture and still life in these artists. Huxley seems to write back to Lawrence's account of Cézanne by glancing over the painter's 'pippin-like women' – his portraits of people as apples – to pronounce Vermeer 'the greatest painter of human still lives' (pp. 21–2). In his analysis, it was only in the untroubled condition of physical and mental 'repose' that Vermeer could perceive the 'divine essential Not self' in human beings and render it in 'a subtle and sumptuous still life' (p. 22). Still life becomes a condition necessary to sense the divine in the object world but also in the human.

*

Reflecting on the peculiar power and critical value of still life uncovers intertextual dialogue between Huxley and Lawrence, but it also uncovers unexpected interconnections, imagery and a shared web of concerns between artists rarely juxtaposed in studies of modernism (as we have seen in drawing together Woolf and Stevens). At the outset of *Modernism and Still Life*, I drew attention to the potent paradox, the 'doubleness', encapsulated in the genre's terminology and inscribed in its etymology across different languages. We have seen this revealed in far-reaching permutations across the chapters of this book, in prose, painting, dance, sculpture, poetry and in hybrid, inter-medial forms. As we draw toward a conclusion, we might turn to Giorgio de Chirico's article 'On Metaphysical Art' (1919), in which his understanding of still life unfolds in an evocative passage that has been a touchstone for my inquiry and offers a way of consolidating some of its themes. De Chirico elucidates two kinds of solitude contained in every profound work of art, one of which is 'plastic loneliness', meaning:

> the beatitude of contemplation produced by the ingenious construction and combination of forms, whether they be still lifes come alive or figures become still – the double life of a still life, not as a pictorial subject, but in its supersensory aspect, so that even a supposedly living figure might be included.[18]

We have found De Chirico's 'double life of a still life' expressed variously across the preceding chapters. The artists I have explored re-imagine but also re-assert the binaries associated with the genre, between animate and inanimate, vital and morbid, public and private, uncanny and human. We trace still life's 'double life' in Lawrence's intuition of the 'mobile but come to rest' in Cézanne's paintings; in Fry's 'two rhythms' and permutations of the 'quivering yet still' across Woolf's writings; in the 'still lifes come alive or figures become still' of movement practices in Chapter 2; in the 'earthly and unearthly' evoked in still-lifes-as-landscapes of Chapter 3; in Mauron's 'double-minded' artist and the negotiations between the ascetic and epicurean in Stevens's textual still lifes; and finally, in Huxley's 'material' and 'spiritual' comprehension of objects. Mysterious double lives are part of the fabric of still life across the textual, visual and cultural range of this book. Taken collectively, its chapters reveal that ideas about stillness and the meaning of 'still life' were at the heart of modern practice, and inflected urgent questions about what modern art could mean and do.

This study makes manifest a constellation of tropes associated with still life, one of the most potent of which is its connection with meditative or spiritual practice. This can be identified in Winifred Nicholson's experience of the sacred in flower painting; in the more ambivalent epiphanies of Woolf's 'moments of being'; and in the intersections between unorthodox spirituality and body movement in Morris's and Steiner's practices. Whether underpinned by a certain theology or by less orthodox spiritual or secular notions of 'enchantment', we have seen that still life as transformation or transfiguration haunts discourses as well as cultural products associated with the genre. Bryson's proposal that still life can 'transfigure' the commonplace by bestowing attention on what is usually disregarded and considered lowly is widely exemplified in the different practices I have considered.[19] Flowers, to take one example, are far from representing the tired or feminised subject of a minor genre. They generate profound meditations and experimentation in the vastly different spheres of Stevens's bouquet poems, Hitchens's and Winifred Nicholson's flower paintings, and Huxley's hallucinatory visions. Yet we have also seen that even the humblest everyday object could become the subject of a mode of attentiveness through which the object world could be defamiliarised and re-enchanted.

Modern artists and their auditors bestow multisensory attention on the object world: they look, but they also touch, taste and listen to the 'overlooked'. The modern still life plays upon the close relationship between the silent and the still. We recall the notion of 'visual music' conceived by Fry, to which Hitchens's conception of the 'musical appearance of things' is indebted, and Winifred Nicholson's notion of the 'music of colour'. Elsewhere, the vibrations that govern the eurythmic gesture are felt rather than heard, and the phenomenon of vibrating stillness identified as the hallmark of modern dance is exemplified in the 'active stillness' of Morris's repertoire. These examples alert us to the ways in which modern still life subtly expounds a mode of experiencing the world, which stimulates an expansion and intermingling of the senses, and sometimes reaches toward its 'supersensory aspect'.

When Woolf identifies a 'mysterious quality of potation' in her contemplation of Cézanne's *Still Life with Apples*, she evokes an experience which simultaneously registers still life's vaguely unsettling, uncanny sentience and also the creative sustenance it provides her as a writer. The theme of nourishment – aesthetic, physical and spiritual – underwrites still life. The journey of this inquiry from Cézanne's apples through the visceral absorption and 'feeding' on visual art represented variously through the chapters highlights the tension between sensual pleasure and ascetic simplicity – a 'dish of peaches' or a 'bowl of white' – such as we find in Stevens's poetic encounters.

To consider certain cultural and artistic experiments of the first half of the twentieth century through the paradigm of still life, or indeed *as* still life, is therefore to reveal a range of ideas and projects, aesthetic, ethic and spiritual, which have at times been overlooked or marginalised in narratives of modern art, but which were in fact fundamental to it. The chapters of this book can be seen to chart the fundamental stages in a narrative about modernism and still life, which reveals that far from representing an inert group of objects or a 'minor' genre, the meaning and significance of still life expanded and intensified in vital ways over the first half of the twentieth century. In the examples we have considered, still life becomes not only an important aesthetic category but also a condition which was necessary – if not entirely satisfactory or achievable – to contend with modernity; an 'attitude of mind' or orientation which is not circumscribed by medium. Of course still life manifests itself in diverse ways and with different priorities in the work of different artists, but those considered in this book are representative of a significant strand in modernism that finds stillness at the heart of motion, and animate energy at the heart of stillness.

Paying attention to the modern still life unsettles narratives of modernism as predominantly preoccupied with notions of speed and movement. If still life encourages us to look at the overlooked, and to attend to the slow, the silent and the still, then it also functions as a useful critical tool. For instance, close examination of Woolf's insect analogy prompts us to consider the peculiar ways in which she embodies aesthetic experience, and it simultaneously cultivates a critical attentiveness to the overlooked temporalities and small-scale in her work. Still life invites us to consider a more nuanced spectrum of motion between the apparent polarities of stillness and movement, from which a broader sense of the interactions between the static and the mobile emerges, revealing a picture of vibratory and rhythmic modernism.

We have witnessed, then, the elasticity of still life – the 'latitude' observed by Charles Sterling. The boundaries of the genre stretch from the still life in painting, through various compound forms, including the domestic-interior-as-still-life at

Kettle's Yard and the biography-as-still-life in *Roger Fry*, but the parameters and definitions of this capacious genre remain open and resist definitive characterisation, enabling a rethinking of the inter-disciplinary and geographical boundaries of modern art. Indeed, the potency of the term 'still life' derives to a large extent from its semantic flexibility and capacity for the proliferation of meaning as the 'too much' of Stevens's bouquet poems so vividly expresses.

To conclude, if I have argued that still life gained a new acuity in the late nineteenth and early twentieth centuries, then the poetics of stillness that unfolds in this book is protean and complex. Its aesthetic, physiological and even 'spiritual' potency was a shared concern for artists as they confronted the new temporalities of emerging technologies and the claims of a seemingly accelerating world. Even as still life sought to anchor the wandering, unfocused attention or 'distracted' rhythms of modern life, the relationship between the 'still' and 'distracted' continued to permeate the art forms and discourses I have discussed. Modern art and artists articulate a relationship toward the 'still' which reveals unease as well as fascination, and an often unresolved but energising tension between the still and the moving. Many were ambivalent about what 'stillness' might mean: 'stillness' and 'still life' were not coherent or stable terms, and they suggested connotations both pejorative and positive. Woolf, we remember, was troubled by the desire to 'fix' or silence life. In *Roger Fry*, she sought to keep her subject quiveringly, reverberatingly alive lest the biography become a wax 'effigy', or a *nature morte*. Other artists craved 'stillness' in the sense of prolonged contemplation and close attention; or, as we saw in Chapter 2, they sought to express through the body the 'inner rhythms' of the natural world and the animate stillness of sculpture.

That modern art charged the 'still' with animation, vibration and 'inner rhythm' has become palpably evident. While rhythm and vibration meant different things to different artists, their appeal serves to underline that there was a widely shared impulse to re-animate – to inject life and rhythm into stillness – which we recognise in the semantic shift from *nature morte* to still life. I have situated my claim for this dynamic resuscitation of still life in the context of a new consciousness of the world as animate, rather than consisting of 'dead' or inert matter, which was shaped by various philosophical, scientific and cultural developments, and interweaving currents of metaphysical and spiritual research. What emerges is that movement and stasis were intertwined and often complementary in the imaginations of modern artists, and that 'life' was as much the subject of still life as 'stillness'. Reading modernism in the light of still life therefore allows us to see what is often occluded in accounts of this period: that transformation and movement live at the heart of stillness and the ordinary.

'So we come to the end of this journey of initiation into the unknown life within the still life', Proust writes in a lyrical early essay on 'Chardin and

Rembrandt'.[20] It is his suggestion that in taking Chardin as our contemplative guide, we might learn to see the everyday world of objects afresh: 'Still life will become, above all else, alive. Like life itself, it will always have something new to tell you, some marvel to highlight, some mystery to reveal.'[21] We have taken Cézanne as our guide, but the same claim is articulated in various forms throughout this book. That still life asserts the animate in all things at the same time as it expresses the desire to 'still' or 'fix' life. For the artists I have explored, a poetics of stillness is necessarily – if paradoxically – a poetics of life. Indeed, if there is still life, it is by nature a 'double life': 'quivering yet still' and 'never *statically* at rest'.

Notes

1. 'Mark Gertler', *Vogue*, 59:4 (Late February 1922), 68–9 (all further references are given in the text). James Sexton makes a convincing case for the attribution to Huxley of over sixty anonymous essays (including this one) published in *Vogue* and *House and Garden* in the early 1920s. He contends that 'all, or at least most of them' were authored by him, and points to Huxley's critique of the modern still life painter as a 'linguistic fingerprint' in several essays, including 'Mark Gertler'. See 'Aldous Huxley *aka* Condé Nast's "Staff of Experts", Part 1', in Jerome Meckier and Bernfried Nugel, eds, *Aldous Huxley Annual: A Journal of Twentieth-Century Thought and Beyond*, 5 (2005), 1–10 (p. 3). Thirteen of the essays are reprinted in this volume; 'Mark Gertler' is repr. pp. 19–21.
2. Huxley's correspondence shows that he supported Gertler by buying his work in 1923, and he wrote an introduction to his exhibition catalogue in 1937. See letter to Suzanne Nys, 9 February 1923, in *Letters of Aldous Huxley*, ed. Grover Smith (London: Chatto & Windus, 1969), p. 211.
3. *Mark Gertler: Selected Letters*, ed. Noel Carrington (London: Rupert Hart-Davis, 1965), to Dorothy Brett, September 1913, p. 55; to Carrington, 5 January 1919, p. 169.
4. See in particular *Still Life with Bowl, Spoon, Apples* (1913, Hatton Gallery), *Apples in a Bag* (Ashmolean) and *Fruit* (1922, Manchester Art Gallery)
5. *Mark Gertler: Selected Letters*, to Valentine Dobree, 6 April 1924, pp. 210–11.
6. This article was signed by Huxley, 'Dead Nature or Life', *Vogue*, 61:11 (Early June 1923), 44–5, repr. in the *Aldous Huxley Annual*, 5 (2005), 62–4 (p. 62).
7. Ibid., p. 62.
8. Ibid.
9. Ibid.
10. Ibid., p. 63.
11. Wyndham Lewis, 'Relativism and Picasso's Latest Work', in Lewis, ed., *Blast*, 1 (June 1914), 139–40 (p. 139).
12. Ibid., p. 139.
13. Ibid., p. 140.
14. Aldous Huxley, *The Defeat of Youth and Other Poems* (Oxford: Blackwell, 1918), p. 36.

15. Jane Goldman, *Modernism, 1910–1945: Image to Apocalypse* (New York: Palgrave, 2004), pp. 115–17.
16. Aldous Huxley, *The Doors of Perception* (1954) (London: Vintage, 2004), p. 6 (all further references are cited in the text).
17. Aldous Huxley, 'D. H. Lawrence' (1932), in *Stories, Essays & Poems* (London: J. M. Dent & Sons, 1937), pp. 331–52 (pp. 341, 333).
18. Quoted by Soby, *Giorgio de Chirico*, p. 66.
19. Bryson, *Looking at the Overlooked*, p. 64.
20. Marcel Proust, *Chardin and Rembrandt*, trans. Jennie Feldman (New York: David Zwirner Books, 2016), p. 21. The essay was written c. 1895 but left unfinished and untitled and published posthumously in 1954.
21. Ibid., p. 14.

BIBLIOGRAPHY

ARCHIVE SOURCES

California, San Marino, Huntington Library:
Wallace Stevens Papers and Library (WAS)

Cambridge, Kettle's Yard (KY):
Writings on Artists: KY/EDE/4/2/4

London, Royal Borough of Kensington and Chelsea, Central Library:
Chelsea Miscellany (CM)

London, Rudolf Steiner House Archive:
Performing Arts, Eurythmy

London, Tate Gallery Archive (TGA):
Ben Nicholson, 8717/1/2/4695–4924
Edith Jenkinson, 9323 [uncatalogued]

Perth, The Fergusson Gallery:
Margaret Morris Collection (MMC)

Other Sources

Adams, Richard P., 'Wallace Stevens and Schopenhauer's *The World as Will and Idea*', *Tulane Studies in English*, 20 (1972), 135–68.

Alsdorf, Bridget, 'Interior Landscapes: Metaphor and Meaning in Cézanne's Late Still Lifes', *Word & Image*, 26 (2010), 314–23.

Alt, Christina, *Virginia Woolf and the Study of Nature* (Cambridge: Cambridge University Press, 2010).

Alter, Judith, *Dancing and Mixed Media* (New York: Peter Lang, 1996).

Anderson, Neil, 'On Rudolf Steiner's Impact on the Training of the Actor', *Literature & Aesthetics*, 21:1 (June 2011), 158–74.

Andreae, Christopher, *Winifred Nicholson* (London: Lund Humphries, 2009).

Antliff, Mark, *Inventing Bergson: Cultural Politics and the Parisian Avant-Garde* (Princeton: Princeton University Press, 1993).

Ardis, Ann L., *Modernism and Cultural Conflict 1880–1922* (Cambridge: Cambridge University Press, 2002).

Armstrong, Tim, *Modernism, Technology, and the Body: A Cultural Study* (Cambridge: Cambridge University Press, 1998).

Armstrong, Tim, *Modernism: A Cultural History* (Cambridge: Polity Press, 2005).

Arrowsmith, Rupert, *Modernism and the Museum* (Oxford: Oxford University Press, 2011).

Bacci, Francesca and David Melcher, eds, *Art and the Senses* (Oxford: Oxford University Press, 2011).

Baird, James, *The Dome and the Rock: Structure in the Poetry of Wallace Stevens* (Baltimore: Johns Hopkins University Press, 1968).

Banfield, Ann, *The Phantom Table: Woolf, Fry, Russell and the Epistemology of Modernism* (Cambridge: Cambridge University Press, 1998).

Barassi, Sebastiano, ed., *Kettle's Yard and its Artists: An Anthology* (Cambridge: Kettle's Yard Publications, 2011).

Batchelor, David, ed., *Colour: Documents of Contemporary Art* (London: Whitechapel, 2008).

Batchelor, Tim, ed., *Dead Standing Things: Still Life Painting in Britain 1660–1740* (London: Tate Gallery, 2012).

Bates, Milton J., *Sur Plusieurs Beaux Sujets: Wallace Stevens' Commonplace Book* (Stanford: Stanford University Press, 1989).

Beale, Helen and Angela Smith, *Outsiders in Paris: John Duncan Fergusson, Katherine Mansfield and their Circles*, No. 9 (Stirling: Stirling French Publications, 2000).

Beard, Lee, '"Modernist Cell" or "Gentle Nest": Ben Nicholson, Art, Design and the Modern Interior 1924–39', unpublished doctoral thesis, University of London, Courtauld Institute, 2003.

Beer, Gillian, *Virginia Woolf: The Common Ground* (Edinburgh: Edinburgh University Press, 1996).

Beer, Gillian, '"Wireless": Popular Physics, Radio and Modernism', in Francis Spufford and Jenny Uglow, eds, *Cultural Babbage: Technology, Time and Invention* (London: Faber & Faber, 1996), pp. 149–66.

Bell, Ian F. A., 'Ezra Pound and the Materiality of the Fourth Dimension', in John Holmes, ed., *Science in Modern Poetry: New Directions* (Liverpool: Liverpool University Press, 2012), pp. 130–50.

Bell, Vanessa, *Selected Letters of Vanessa Bell*, ed. Regina Marler (London: Bloomsbury, 1993).

Benjamin, Walter, 'The Image of Proust', in *Illuminations*, trans. Harry Zohn, ed. Hannah Arendt (New York: Shocken Books, 1968), pp. 201–15.

Bennett, Jane, *The Enchantment of Modern Life* (Princeton: Princeton University Press, 2001).

Bergson, Henri, *Creative Evolution* [1911 in translation], trans. Arthur Mitchell (Lanham: University Press of America, 1983).

Bergson, Henri, *Time and Free Will: An Essay on the Immediate Data of Consciousness* [1889], 3rd edn (New York: Dover Publications, 2001).

Besant, Annie and C. W. Leadbeater, *Thought Forms* [1901] (London: Theosophical Publishing House, 1925).

Bevis, William W., *Mind of Winter: Wallace Stevens, Meditation, and Literature* (Pittsburgh: University of Pittsburgh Press, 1988).

Binckes, Faith, *Modernism, Magazines, and the British Avant-Garde* (Oxford: Oxford University Press, 2010).

Bissell, David and Gillian Fuller, eds, *Stillness in a Mobile World* (London: Routledge, 2011).

Blackwood, Jonathan, 'Sculpture with a Scots Brogue: John Duncan Fergusson, c. 1916–24', in David J. Getsy, ed., *Sculpture and the Pursuit of a Modern Ideal in Britain c. 1880–1920* (Farnham: Ashgate, 2004), pp. 245–66.

Blamires, David, *David Jones: Artist and Writer* (Manchester: Manchester University Press, 1971).

Blanchard, Marc Eli, 'On Still Life', *Yale French Studies*, 61 (1981), 276–98.

Bloom, Harold, *Wallace Stevens: The Poems of Our Climate* (Ithaca: Cornell University Press, 1977).

Bowness, Alan, ed., *Ivon Hitchens* (London: Lund Humphries, 1973).

Bowness, Sophie, 'Braque and Music', in John Golding, ed., *Braque: Still Lifes and Interiors* (London: A South Bank Centre Touring Exhibition, 1990).

Brandstetter, Gabriele, *Poetics of Dance: Body, Image, and Space in the Historical Avant-Gardes*, trans. Elena Polzer with Mark Franko (New York: Oxford University Press, 2015).

Braque, Georges, *Illustrated Notebooks (1917–1955)*, trans. Stanley Appelbaum (New York: Dover Publications, 1971).

Brazeau, Peter, *Parts of a World: Wallace Stevens Remembered* (New York: Random House, 1977).
Briggs, Julia, *Reading Virginia Woolf* (Edinburgh: Edinburgh University Press, 2006).
Brockington, Grace, *Above the Battlefield: Modernism and the Peace Movement in Britain* (New Haven: Yale University Press, 2010).
Brockington, Grace and Claudia Tobin, 'London's Little Theatres', *British Art Studies*, 11, https://doi.org/10.17658/issn.2058–5462/issue-11/theatres.
Brooker, Peter and Andrew Thacker, eds, *The Oxford Critical and Cultural History of Modernist Magazines*, 3 vols (Oxford: Oxford University Press, 2009), I.
Brüderlin, Markus and Ulrike Groos, eds, *Rudolf Steiner and Contemporary Art* (Wolfsburg: Kunstmuseum, 2010).
Bryson, Norman, *Looking at the Overlooked: Four Essays on Still Life Painting* (London: Reaktion Books, 1990).
Buchsbaum, Betty, 'Contours of Desire: The Place of Cézanne in Wallace Stevens' Poetics and Late Practice', *Criticism*, 30 (1988), 303–24.
Bullen, J. B., ed., *Post-Impressionists in England: The Critical Reception* (London: Routledge, 1988).
Butler, Karen K. and Renée Maurer, eds, *Georges Braque and the Cubist Still Life, 1928–1945* (London: DelMonico Books, 2013).
Carden-Coyne, Ana, *Reconstructing the Body: Classicism, Modernism, and the First World War* (Oxford: Oxford University Press, 2009).
Carrell, Christopher, ed., *Winifred Nicholson: Paintings 1900–1978* (Glasgow: The Third Eye Centre, 1979).
Casson, Stanley, *Some Modern Sculptors* (Oxford: Oxford University Press, 1929).
Caws, Mary Ann and Sarah Bird Wright, *Bloomsbury and France: Art and Friends* (Oxford: Oxford University Press, 1999).
Chase, Cleveland B., 'Mrs. Woolf Explores the "Time" Element in Human Relationships', *New York Times*, 21 October 1928, http://www.nytimes.com/books/97/06/08/reviews/woolf-orlando.html.
Cheeke, Stephen, *Writing for Art* (Manchester: Manchester University Press, 2008).
Clarke, Bruce and Linda Dalrymple Henderson, eds, *From Energy to Information: Representation in Science and Technology, Art, and Literature* (Stanford: Stanford University Press, 2002).
Coates, Kimberly Engdahl, 'Exposing the Nerves of Language: Virginia Woolf, Charles Mauron and the Affinity Between Aesthetics and Illness', *Literature and Medicine*, 21 (2002), 242–63.
Collins, Judith, *Winifred Nicholson* (London: Tate Gallery, 1987).
Collins, Judith, *A Painters' Place: Banks Head, Cumberland, 1924–31* (Kendal: Abbot Hall Art Gallery, 1991).

Connor, Steven, *Beckett, Modernism and the Material Imagination* (Cambridge: Cambridge University Press, 2014).

Connor, Steven, *Beyond Words: Sobs, Hums, Stutters and Other Vocalizations* (London: Reaktion, 2014).

Corbett, Val, *A Rhythm, a Rite and a Ceremony: Helen Sutherland at Cockley Moor 1939–1965* (Penrith: Midnight Oil, 1996).

Costello, Bonnie, 'Effects of an Analogy: Wallace Stevens and Painting', in Albert Gelpi, ed., *Wallace Stevens: The Poetics of Modernism* (Cambridge: Cambridge University Press, 1985), pp. 65–85.

Costello, Bonnie, 'Planets on Tables: Still Life and War in the Poetry of Wallace Stevens', *Modernism/Modernity*, 12 (2005), 443–58.

Costello, Bonnie, *Planets on Tables: Poetry, Still Life, and the Turning World* (Ithaca: Cornell University Press, 2008).

Cowan, Michael, *Technology's Pulse: Essays on Rhythm in German Modernism* (London: Institute of Germanic & Romance Studies, University of London, 2012).

Crary, Jonathan, *Suspensions of Perception: Attention, Spectacle, and Modern Culture* (Cambridge, MA: MIT Press, 1999).

Cumming, Elizabeth, ed., *Colour, Rhythm and Dance: Paintings and Drawings by J. D. Fergusson and his Circle in Paris* (Edinburgh: Scottish Arts Council, 1985).

Curtis, Penelope, 'How Direct Carving Stole the Idea of Modern British Sculpture', in David J. Getsy, ed., *Sculpture and the Pursuit of a Modern Ideal in Britain c. 1880–1920* (Farnham: Ashgate, 2004), pp. 290–318.

Danchev, Alex, *Georges Braque: A Life* (London: Penguin, 2005).

Danius, Sara, *The Senses of Modernism: Technology, Perception, and Aesthetics* (Ithaca: Cornell University Press, 2002).

Dann, Kevin T., *Bright Colors Falsely Seen: Synaesthesia and the Search for Transcendental Knowledge* (New Haven: Yale University Press, 1998).

Davenport, Guy, *Objects on a Table: Harmonious Disarray in Art and Literature* (Washington DC: Counterpoint, 1998).

De Chirico, Giorgio, *Le Nature Morte*, in 'L'Illustrazione Italiana', 24 May 1942, repr. in *Metaphysical Art*, 14/16 (2016), 116–17.

De Sausmarez, Maurice, ed., *Ben Nicholson* (London: Studio International, 1969).

Doran, Michael, ed., *Conversations with Cézanne*, trans. Julie Lawrence Cochran (Berkeley: University of California Press, 2001).

Duffy, Enda, *The Speed Handbook: Velocity, Pleasure, Modernism* (Durham, NC: Duke University Press, 2009).

Eddy, Arthur Jerome, *Cubists and Post-Impressionism* (Chicago: A. C. McClurg, 1914).

Eddy, Mary Baker, *Science and Health with Key to the Scriptures*, Project Gutenberg e-book 3458, 11th edn, http://www.gutenberg.org/cache/epub/3458/pg3458.txt.

Ede, Jim, *A Way of Life: Kettle's Yard* (Cambridge: Cambridge University Press, 1984).

Edwards, Jason, ed., 'In Focus: *The Singer* Exhibited 1888 and *Applause* 1893 by Edward Onslow Ford' (April 2013), http://www.tate.org.uk/art/research-publications/edward-onslow-ford.

Eeckhout, Bart, *Wallace Stevens and the Limits of Reading and Writing* (Missouri: University of Missouri Press, 2003).

Elbert-Schifferer, Sybille, *Still Life: A History*, trans. Russell Stockman (New York: Harry N. Abrams, 1999).

Elder, Bruce, *Harmony and Dissent: Film and Avant-Garde Art Movements in the Early Twentieth Century* (Waterloo: Wilfrid Laurier University Press, 2008).

Elder, Eleanor, *Dance: A National Art* (London: Theosophical Publishing House, 1918).

Elder, Eleanor, 'Movement, and the Culture of Expression', *The Theosophist*, ed. Annie Besant, 39:1 (March 1918), 616–31.

Eliot, T. S., *The Complete Poems and Plays* (London: Faber & Faber, 1969).

Eltringham, H., *The Senses of Insects* (London: Methuen, 1933).

Emerson, Richard, *Rhythm and Colour* (Edinburgh: Golden Hare, 2018).

Enns, Anthony and Shelley Trower, eds, *Vibratory Modernism* (Basingstoke: Palgrave Macmillan, 2013).

Fergusson, J. D., *Painting and Sculpture by J. D. Fergusson* (London: Lefevre Galleries, 1928).

Fernihough, Anne, *D. H. Lawrence: Aesthetics and Ideology* (Oxford: Clarendon Press, 1993).

Fernihough, Anne, *Freewomen and Supermen: Edwardian Radicals and Literary Modernism* (Oxford: Oxford University Press, 2013).

Filreis, Alan, 'Still Life without Substance: Wallace Stevens and the Language of Agency', *Poetics Today*, 10 (1989), 345–72.

Filreis, Alan, *Wallace Stevens and the Actual World* (Princeton: Princeton University Press, 1991).

Fisher, Elizabeth, *Winifred Nicholson: Music of Colour* (Cambridge: Kettle's Yard, University of Cambridge, 2012).

Fisher, Philip, *Wonder, the Rainbow, and the Aesthetics of Rare Experiences* (Cambridge, MA: Harvard University Press, 1998).

Fitzgerald, William, '"Music is Feeling, Then, Not Sound": Wallace Stevens and the Body of Music', *SubStance*, 21 (1992), 44–60.

Flink, Hilary L., *Bergson and Russian Modernism, 1900–1930* (Evanston: Northwestern University Press, 1999).

Flitch, J. E. Crawford, *Modern Dancing and Dancers* (London: Grant Richards, 1912).

Forel, Auguste, *The Senses of Insects*, trans. Macleod Yearsley (London: Methuen, 1908).

Frank, Joseph, 'Spatial Form in Modern Literature: An Essay in Three Parts', *The Sewanee Review*, 53 (1945), 643–53.

Fry, Roger, *Vision and Design* (London: Chatto & Windus, 1920).

Fry, Roger, *Cézanne: A Study of his Development* (London: Hogarth Press, 1927).

Fry, Roger, *Characteristics of French Art* (London: Chatto and Windus, 1932).

Fry, Roger, *Last Lectures* (Cambridge: Cambridge University Press, 1939).

Fry, Roger, *Letters of Roger Fry*, ed. Denys Sutton, 2 vols (London: Chatto & Windus, 1972).

Fry, Roger, *A Roger Fry Reader*, ed. Christopher Reed (Chicago: University of Chicago Press, 1996).

Furst, Herbert, *The Art of Still-Life Painting* (London: Chapman and Hall, 1927).

Gage, John, *Colour and Meaning: Art, Science and Symbolism* (London: Thames & Hudson, 1999).

Gelpi, Albert, ed., *Wallace Stevens: The Poetics of Modernism* (Cambridge: Cambridge University Press, 1985).

George, W. L., 'The Esperanto of Art', *The Blue Review*, 1 (1913), 28–36.

Gerdts, William H., *Painters of the Humble Truth: Masterpieces of American Still Life, 1801–1939* (Columbia: University of Missouri Press, 1981).

Gertler, Mark, *Mark Gertler: Selected Letters*, ed. Noel Carrington (London: Rupert Hart-Davis, 1965).

Gervais, David, 'Ivon Hitchens and the Harmony of Colour', *The Cambridge Quarterly*, 38 (2009), 87–94.

Getsy, David, 'Punks and Professionals: The Identity of the Sculptor 1900–1925', in Penelope Curtis, ed., *Sculpture in 20th-Century Britain: Identity, Infrastructure, Aesthetics, Display, Reception*, 2 vols (Leeds: Henry Moore Institute, 2003), I, pp. 9–20.

Getsy, David, 'Acts of Stillness: Statues, Performativity, and Passive Resistance', *Criticism*, 56 (2014), 1–20.

Gilbert, David, David Matless and Brian Short, eds, *Geographies of British Modernity* (Oxford: Blackwell, 2003).

Gillespie, Diane, *The Sisters' Arts: The Writing and Painting of Virginia Woolf and Vanessa Bell* (New York: Syracuse University Press, 1988).

Gillespie, Diane F., 'The Texture of the Text: Editing Roger Fry: A Biography', in James M. Haule and J. H. Stape, eds, *Editing Virginia Woolf: Interpreting the Modernist Text* (Basingstoke: Palgrave, 2001), pp. 91–113.

Gillespie, Diane F., 'The Gender of Modern/ist Painting', in Bonnie Kime Scott, ed., *Gender in Modernism* (Chicago: University of Illinois Press, 2007), pp. 765–808.

Gillies, Mary Ann, *Henri Bergson and British Modernism* (Montreal and Kingston: McGill-Queen's University Press, 1996).

Ginner, Ruby, *The Revived Greek Dance* (London: Methuen, 1933).

Golding, Martin, 'An Echo in the Body: Painting, Experience and Still Life', *Modern New York Painters*, 11 (1998), 110–13.

Goldman, Jane, *The Feminist Aesthetics of Virginia Woolf: Modernism, Post-Impressionism and the Politics of the Visual* (Cambridge: Cambridge University Press, 1998).

Goldman, Jane, *Modernism, 1910–1945: Image to Apocalypse* (New York: Palgrave, 2004).

Goossens, Eugene, *Overture and Beginners: A Musical Autobiography* (London: Methuen, 1951).

Gorringe, T. J., *Earthly Visions* (New Haven: Yale University Press, 2011).

Gosetti-Ferencei, Jennifer Anna, *Ecstatic Quotidian: Phenomenological Sightings in Modern Art and Literature* (University Park: Pennsylvania State University Press, 2007).

Goto, John, 'The Atomic Yard: Reflections on Childhood, Culture and Kettle's Yard c. 1957', http://www.johngoto.org.uk/atom-yrd/convers.htm.

Gray, Nicolete, ed., *Helen Sutherland Collection: A Pioneer Collection of the 1930s* (London: Arts Council of Great Britain, 1971).

Green, Christopher, ed., *Art Made Modern: Roger Fry's Vision of Art* (London: Merrell Holberton, 1999).

Guido, Laurent and Olivier Lugon, eds, *Between Still and Moving Images* (Eastleigh: John Libbey, 2012).

Harris, Alexandra, *Romantic Moderns* (London: Thames & Hudson, 2010).

Harris, Alexandra, *Virginia Woolf* (London: Thames & Hudson, 2011).

Harrison, Charles, *English Art and Modernism 1900–1939* (London: Penguin, 1981).

Harvey, Benjamin, 'The Rest is Silence: The Senses of Roger Fry's Endings', *Journal of Art Historiography*, 9 (December 2013), https://arthistoriography.files.wordpress.com/2013/12/harvey.pdf.

Haule, James M., Virginia Woolf and Charles Mauron, '"Le Temps Passe" and the Original Typescript: An Early Version of the "Time Passes" Section of *To the Lighthouse*', *Twentieth Century Literature*, 29 (1983), 267–311.

Henderson, Linda Dalrymple, *The Fourth Dimension and Non-Euclidean Geometry in Modern Art* (Princeton: Princeton University Press, 1983).

Henry, Holly, *Virginia Woolf and the Discourse of Science: The Aesthetics of Astronomy* (Cambridge: Cambridge University Press, 2003).

Herbert, Zbigniew, *Still Life with a Bridle: Essays and Apocryphas*, trans. John and Bogdana Carpenter (London: Cape, 1993).

Heron, Patrick, *Ivon Hitchens* (London: Penguin, 1955).

Hickman, Miranda, 'The Gender of Vorticism: Jessie Dismorr, Helen Saunders, and Vorticist Feminism', in Mark Antliff and Scott W. Klein, eds, *Vorticism: New Perspectives* (Oxford: Oxford University Press, 2013), pp. 119–36.

Hills, Paul, 'The Art of David Jones', in *David Jones* (London: Tate Gallery, 1981), pp. 19–71.

Hills, Paul, ed., *David Jones, Artist and Poet* (Aldershot: Scholar Press, 1997).

Hitchens, Ivon, 'A Theoretical Letter from Ivon Hitchens to Maynard Keynes, 27 November, 1940', introduced by David Scrase, *Burlington Magazine*, 125 (1983), 420–23.

Hoberman, Ruth, *Modernizing Lives: Experiments in English Biography, 1918–1939* (Carbondale and Edwardsville: Southern Illinois Press, 1987).

Hoberman, Ruth, *Museum Trouble: Edwardian Fiction and the Emergence of Modernism* (Charlottesville: University of Virginia Press, 2011).

Holden, Cliff, 'Meeting Bomberg: Tradition and the Dancing Muse' (2004), http://www.cliffholden.co.uk/documents_2004_30.shtml.

Hollander, John, *The Gazer's Spirit* (Chicago: University of Chicago Press, 1995).

Hornby, Louise, *Still Modernism: Photography, Literature, Film* (Oxford: Oxford University Press, 2017).

Humm, Maggie, *Modernist Women and Visual Cultures: Virginia Woolf, Vanessa Bell, Photography, and Cinema* (Edinburgh: Edinburgh University Press, 2002).

Humm, Maggie, ed., *The Edinburgh Companion to Virginia Woolf and the Arts* (Edinburgh: Edinburgh University Press, 2010).

Hutcheon, Linda, *Formalism and the Freudian Aesthetic: The Example of Charles Mauron* (Cambridge: Cambridge University Press, 1984).

Huxley, Aldous, *The Defeat of Youth and Other Poems* (Oxford: Blackwell, 1918).

Huxley, Aldous (attributed to), 'Mark Gertler', *Vogue*, 59:4 (Late February 1922), 68–9.

Huxley, Aldous, 'Dead Nature or Life', *Vogue*, 61:11 (Early June 1923), 44–5, repr. in the *Aldous Huxley Annual*, 5 (2005), 62–4.

Huxley, Aldous, *Letters of Aldous Huxley*, ed. Grover Smith (London: Chatto & Windus, 1969).

Huxley, Aldous, *The Doors of Perception* (1954) (London: Vintage, 2004).

J. R. S., ed., *The Painters of Still Life* (Hartford, CT: Wadsworth Atheneum, 1938).

Jacobs, Karen, *The Eye's Mind: Literary Modernism and Visual Culture* (Ithaca: Cornell University Press, 2001).

James, Merlin, *David Jones 1895–1974: A Map of the Artist's Mind* (London: Lund Humphries, 1995).

Jarraway, David R., *Wallace Stevens and the Question of Belief: Metaphysician in the Dark* (Baton Rouge: Louisiana State University Press, 1993).

Jewell, Edward Alden, 'Virginia Woolf's Life of Roger Fry', *New York Times*, 15 December 1940, http://www.nytimes.com/books/00/12/17/specials/woolf-fry.html.

Johnson, Galen A. and Michael B. Smith, eds, *The Merleau-Ponty Aesthetics Reader: Philosophy and Painting* (Evanston: Northwestern University Press, 1993).

Jones, David, *In Parenthesis* (London: Faber & Faber, 1937).

Jones, David, *Epoch and Artist*, ed. Harman Grisewood (London: Faber & Faber, 1959).

Jones, David, *The Dying Gaul and Other Writings*, ed. Harman Grisewood (London: Faber & Faber, 1978).

Jones, David, 'Life', repr. in John Matthias, 'David Jones: Letters to H. S. Ede', *Notre Dame English Journal*, 14 (1982), 129–44.

Jones, Susan, '"At the still point": T. S. Eliot, Dance, and Modernism', *Dance Research Journal*, 41 (2009), 31–51.

Jones, Susan, *Literature, Modernism and Dance* (Oxford: Oxford University Press, 2013).

Kandinsky, Wassily, *Concerning the Spiritual in Art*, trans. M. T. H. Sadler (New York: Dover Publications, 1977, repr. of London: Constable and Company, 1914).

Kandinsky, Wassily, *Arnold Schoenberg and Wassily Kandinsky: Letters, Pictures, and Documents*, trans. John C. Crawford (London: Faber & Faber, 1984).

Kaplan, Sydney, *Circulating Genius: John Middleton Murry, Katherine Mansfield and D. H. Lawrence* (Edinburgh: Edinburgh University Press, 2010).

Khoroche, Peter, *Ivon Hitchens: Forty-Five Paintings* (London: Serpentine Gallery, 1989).

Khoroche, Peter, *Ivon Hitchens* (London: Andre Deutsch, 1990).

Khoroche, Peter, *Ben Nicholson: Drawings and Painted Reliefs* (London: Lund Humphries, 2002).

Kiely, Robert, '*Jacob's Room* and *Roger Fry*: Two Studies in Still Life', in Robert Kiely, ed., *Modernism Reconsidered* (Cambridge, MA: Harvard University Press, 1983), pp. 147–66.

Kolocotroni, Vassiliki, 'Still Life: Modernism's Turn to Greece', *Journal of Modern Literature*, 25 (2012), 1–24.

Kraskin, Sandra and Glen MacLeod, eds, *Painting in Poetry, Poetry in Painting: Wallace Stevens and Modern Art* (New York: Baruch College, Sidney Mishkin Gallery, 1995).

Krieger, Murry, *Ekphrasis: The Illusion of the Natural Sign* (Baltimore: John Hopkins University Press, 1992).

Lallemand, Henri, *Cézanne: Visions of a Great Painter* (New York: Todtri, 1994)

Landauer, Susan, William H. Gerdts and Patricia Trenton, eds, *The Not-So-Still Life: A Century of California Painting and Sculpture* (Berkeley: University of California Press, 2003).

Lawrence, D. H., 'Introduction to his Paintings', in *Selected Essays* (Harmondsworth: Penguin, 1950; repr. from *The Paintings of D. H. Lawrence*, Mandrake Press, 1929), pp. 307–46.

Lawrence, D. H., 'Art and Morality', in *Study of Thomas Hardy and other Essays*, ed. Bruce Steele (Cambridge: Cambridge University Press, 1985), pp. 161–8.

Lazenby, Donna J., *A Mystical Philosophy: Transcendence and Immanence in the Works of Virginia Woolf and Iris Murdoch* (London: Bloomsbury, 2014).

Leca, Benedict, ed., *The World is an Apple: The Still Lifes of Paul Cézanne* (London: Giles, 2014).

Lee, Hermione, *The Novels of Virginia Woolf* (London: Methuen, 1977).

Lee, Hermione, *Virginia Woolf* (London: Vintage, 1997).

Leggett, B. J., *Wallace Stevens and Poetic Theory: Conceiving the Supreme Fiction* (Chapel Hill: University of North Carolina Press, 1987).

Leighton, Angela, *On Form: Poetry, Aestheticism, and the Legacy of a Word* (Oxford: Oxford University Press, 2007).

Lepecki, André, 'Still: On the Vibratile Microscopy of Dance', in Gabriele Brandstetter and Hortensia Volckers, eds, *Remembering the Body* (Ostfildern-Ruit: Hatje Cantz, 2000), pp. 334–64.

Lessing, Gotthold, *Laocoön: An Essay on the Limits of Painting and Poetry*, trans. Edward Allen McCormick (London: Johns Hopkins University Press, 1984).

Lewis, Cara, 'Still Life in Motion: Mortal Form in Woolf's *To the Lighthouse*', *Twentieth Century Literature*, 60:4 (Winter 2014), 423–54.

Lewis, Wyndham, 'Our Vortex', *Blast*, 1 (1914), 147–9.

Lewis, Wyndham, 'Relativism and Picasso's Latest Work', *Blast*, 1 (1914), 139–40.

Lewis, Wyndham, *Time and Western Man* (London: Chatto & Windus, 1927).

Lewison, Jeremy, *Ben Nicholson: The Years of Experiment, 1919–39* (Cambridge: Kettle's Yard, 1983).

Lewison, Jeremy, *Ben Nicholson* (London: Tate Gallery, 1993).

Lloyd, Rosemary, *Shimmering in a Transformed Light* (Ithaca: Cornell University Press, 2005).

Longenbach, James, *Wallace Stevens: The Plain Sense of Things* (Oxford: Oxford University Press, 1991).

Lowenthal, Anne W., ed., *The Object as Subject: Studies in the Interpretation of Still Life* (Princeton: Princeton University Press, 1996).
McCarren, Felicia, *Dancing Machines: Choreographies of the Age of Mechanical Reproduction* (Stanford: Stanford University Press, 2003).
McGregor, Sheila, 'L'Esprit Gaulois: Fergusson's Celtic Nationalism', in Alice Strange, Elizabeth Cumming and Sheila McGregor, eds, *J. D. Fergusson* (Edinburgh: National Galleries of Scotland, 2013), pp. 91–102.
Macintosh, Fiona, 'Dancing Maenads in Early Twentieth-Century Britain', in Fiona Macintosh, ed., *The Ancient Dancer in the Modern World* (Oxford: Oxford University Press, 2010), pp. 188–208.
Macintosh, Fiona, 'The Ancient Greeks and the "Natural"', in Alexandra Carter and Rachel Fensham, eds, *Dancing Naturally: Nature, Neo-classicism and Modernity in Early Twentieth-Century Dance* (Basingstoke: Palgrave Macmillan, 2011), pp. 43–57.
McLaurin, Allen, *Virginia Woolf: The Echoes Enslaved* (Cambridge: Cambridge University Press, 1973).
Maclean, Caroline, *The Vogue for Russia: Modernism and the Unseen in Britain 1900–1930* (Edinburgh: Edinburgh University Press, 2015).
Macleod, Glen, *Wallace Stevens and Modern Art: From the Armory Show to Abstract Expressionism* (New Haven: Yale University Press, 1993).
Macleod, Glen, ed., *Wallace Stevens in Context* (Cambridge: Cambridge University Press, 2017).
Mallarmé, Stéphane, *Poems*, trans. Roger Fry (London: Chatto & Windus, 1936).
Mao, Douglas, *Solid Objects: Modernism and the Test of Production* (Princeton: Princeton University Press, 1998).
Martin, J. L., Ben Nicholson and N. Gabo, eds, *Circle: International Survey of Constructive Art* (London: Faber & Faber, 1937).
Martin, Kirsty, *Modernism and the Rhythms of Sympathy: Vernon Lee, Virginia Woolf, D. H. Lawrence* (Oxford: Oxford University Press, 2013).
Materer, Timothy, *Modernist Alchemy: Poetry and the Occult* (Ithaca: Cornell University Press, 1995).
Mauclair, Camille, 'Psychologie de la nature morte', in *Trois Crises de l'Art Actuel* (Paris: Bibliothèque Charpentier, 1906), pp. 16–194.
Maude, Ulrika, 'Modernist Bodies: Coming to our Senses', in Corinne Saunders, Ulrika Maude and Jane Macnaughton, eds, *The Body and the Arts* (Basingstoke: Macmillan, 2009), pp. 116–30.
Mauron, Charles, *The Nature of Beauty in Art and Literature*, trans. Roger Fry (London: Hogarth Press, 1927).
Mauron, Charles, *Aesthetics and Psychology*, trans. Roger Fry and Katherine John (London: Hogarth Press, 1935).
Merleau-Ponty, Maurice, *Phenomenology of Perception*, trans. Colin Smith (London: Routledge & Kegan Paul, 1962).

Merleau-Ponty, Maurice, *The Merleau-Ponty Aesthetics Reader: Philosophy and Painting*, ed. Galen A. Johnson and Michael B. Smith (Evanston: Northwestern University Press, 1993).

Mester, Terri A., *Movement and Modernism* (Fayetteville: University of Arkansas Press, 1997).

Mitchell, Philip Irving, '"Recession and Thickness Through": The Debate over Nature and Grace in David Jones's Roman Poetry and Painting', *Logos: A Journal of Catholic Thought and Culture*, 15 (2012), 60–89.

Mitchell, W. J. T., *Picture Theory: Essays on Verbal and Visual Representation* (Chicago: University of Chicago Press, 1999).

Moore, Madeline, *The Short Season Between Two Silences: The Mystical and the Political in the Novels of Virginia Woolf* (London: George Allen & Unwin, 1984).

Morris, Frances, *A Natural History of British Moths*, 4 vols (London: Henry Edward Knox, 1871), I.

Morris, Margaret and Fred Daniels, *Margaret Morris Dancing: A Book of Pictures* (London: Kegan Paul, 1926).

Morris, Margaret, *The Notation of Movement: Text, Drawings and Diagrams* (London: Kegan Paul, 1928).

Morris, Margaret, Letter dated 25 July 1964, repr. in 'Oak Rhythm', J. D. Fergusson: Catalogue entry, Tate, http://www.tate.org.uk/art/artworks/fergusson-oak-rhythm-t00668/text-catalogue-entry.

Morris, Margaret, *My Life in Movement* (London: Peter Owen, 1969).

Morris, Margaret, *The Art of J. D. Fergusson: A Biased Biography* (Glasgow: Blackie, 1974).

Morris, Margaret, *Margaret Morris: Modern Dance Pioneer, A Resource Pack for Teachers and Students of Dance History*, ed. Bev Trewhitt and Jim Hastie (Biggin Hill: International Association of Margaret Morris Movement, 1997).

Mulvey, Laura, *Death 24x a Second: Stillness and the Moving Image* (London: Reaktion Books, 2006).

Murry, John Middleton, 'Art and Philosophy', *Rhythm*, 1:1 (1911), 9–12.

Murry, John Middleton, ed., *The Blue Review*, 1 (1913).

Murry, John, *Still Life* (New York: E. P. Dutton, 1916).

Murry, John Middleton, *Between Two Worlds: An Autobiography* (London: Jonathan Cape, 1935).

Nakano, Eiko, 'Katherine Mansfield, *Rhythm* and Henri Bergson', in Janet Wilson, Susan Reid and Gerri Kimber, eds, *Katherine Mansfield and Literary Modernism* (London: Continuum, 2011), pp. 30–41.

Nead, Lynda, *The Haunted Gallery: Painting, Photography, Film c. 1900* (New Haven: Yale University Press, 2007).

Neri, Janice, *The Insect and the Image: Visualizing Nature in Early Modern Europe, 1500–1700* (Minneapolis: University of Minnesota Press, 2011).
Neve, Christopher, *Unquiet Landscape* (London: Faber & Faber, 1990).
Nicholson, Jovan, ed., *Art and Life: Ben Nicholson, Winifred Nicholson, Christopher Wood, Alfred Wallis, William Staite Murray, 1920–1931* (London: Philip Wilson, 2013).
Nicholson, Winifred, *An Unknown Aspect of Winifred Nicholson: Abstract Paintings 1920–1930* (London: Crane Kalman Gallery, 1975).
Nicholson, Winifred, *Flower Tales* (Carlisle: LYC Press, 1976).
Nicholson, Winifred, *Unknown Colour: Paintings, Letters, Writings by Winifred Nicholson*, ed. Andrew Nicholson (London: Faber & Faber, 1987).
Olson, Liesl, *Modernism and the Ordinary* (Oxford: Oxford University Press, 2009).
Owen, Alex, *The Place of Enchantment: British Occultism and the Culture of the Modern* (Chicago: University of Chicago Press, 2004).
Papapetros, Spyros, *On the Animation of the Inorganic: Art, Architecture, and the Extension of Life* (Chicago: University of Chicago Press, 2012).
Parkes, Adam, *A Sense of Shock: The Impact of Impressionism on Modern British and Irish Writing* (Oxford: Oxford University Press, 2011).
Pater, Walter, *Studies in the History of the Renaissance* (Oxford: Oxford University Press, 2010).
Peucker, Brigitte, *The Material Image: Art and the Real in Film* (Stanford: Stanford University Press, 2007).
Phillips, Siobhan, 'Wallace Stevens and the Mode of the Ordinary', *Twentieth Century Literature*, 54 (2008), 1–30.
Phillips, Siobhan, *The Poetics of the Everyday: Creative Repetition in Modern American Verse* (New York: Columbia University Press, 2010).
Potts, Alex, *Flesh and the Ideal: Winckelmann and the Origins of Art History* (New Haven: Yale University Press, 1994).
Powell, Jennifer, ed., *NEW RHYTHMS. Henri Gaudier-Brzeska: Art, Dance and Movement in London 1911–15* (Cambridge: Kettle's Yard, 2015).
Preston, Carrie J., *Modernism's Mythic Pose: Gender, Genre, Solo Performance* (Oxford: Oxford University Press, 2011).
Prettejohn, Elizabeth, *Beauty and Art 1750–2000* (Oxford: Oxford University Press, 2005).
Prettejohn, Elizabeth, *The Modernity of Ancient Sculpture: Greek Sculpture and Modern Art from Winckelmann to Picasso* (London: I. B. Tauris, 2012).
Proust, Marcel, *Chardin and Rembrandt*, trans. Jennie Feldman (New York: David Zwirner Books, 2016).
Punter, David, *Rapture: Literature, Addiction, Secrecy* (Brighton: Sussex Academic Press, 2009).

Ragg, Edward, *Wallace Stevens and the Aesthetics of Abstraction* (Cambridge: Cambridge University Press, 2010).
Raine, Kathleen, *The Land Unknown* (London: Hamish Hamilton, 1975).
Raine, Kathleen, *David Jones and the Actually Loved and Known* (Ipswich: Golgonooza Press, 1978).
Raine, Kathleen, 'Winifred Nicholson's Flowers', *Temenos*, 8 (1987), 163–73.
Read, Herbert, *A Coat of Many Colours: Occasional Essays* (London: Routledge, 1945).
Read, Herbert, 'A Nest of Gentle Artists', *Apollo*, 77 (September 1962), 536–42.
Reed, Christopher, 'Through Formalism: Feminism and Virginia Woolf's Relation to Bloomsbury Aesthetics', *Twentieth Century Literature*, 38 (1992), 20–43.
Reed, Christopher, ed., *Not at Home: The Suppression of Domesticity in Modern Art and Architecture* (London: Thames & Hudson, 1996).
Resh, Vincent H. and Ring T. Cardé, eds, *Encyclopaedia of Insects*, 2nd edn (London: Academic Press, 2009).
Rice, Anne Estelle, 'Les Ballets Russes', *Rhythm*, 2:7 (1912), 106–10.
Rilke, Rainer Maria, *Letters on Cézanne*, ed. Clara Rilke, trans. Joel Agee (London: Vintage, 1991).
Rilke, Rainer Maria, 'The Bowl of Roses', in *New Poems*, trans. Len Krisak (London: Boydell & Brewer, 2015), pp. 167–70.
Ringbom, Sixteen, *The Sounding Cosmos: A Study in the Spiritualism of Kandinsky and the Genesis of Abstract Painting* (Abo: Abo Akademi, 1970).
Rodker, John, 'The Choric School', *The Drama*, 23 (1916), 436–46.
Rodker, John, *Poems and Adolphe 1920*, ed. Andrew Crozier (London: Carcanet, 1996).
Rose, Sam, 'The Significance of Form', *Nonsite*, 20 (January 2017), http://nonsite.org/feature/the-significance-of-form#foot_src_12–9852.
Royle, Nicholas, *Telepathy and Literature: Essays on the Reading Mind* (Oxford: Basil Blackwell, 1991).
Rubin, Adrianne, *Roger Fry's 'Difficult and Uncertain Science': The Interpretation of Aesthetic Perception* (Oxford: Peter Lang, 2013).
Rubin, James Henry, *Manet's Silence and the Poetics of Bouquets* (London: Reaktion Books, 1994).
Ruprecht, Lucia, 'Gesture, Interruption, Vibration: Rethinking Early Twentieth-Century Gestural Theory and Practice in Walter Benjamin, Rudolf von Laban, and Mary Wigman', *Dance Research Journal*, 47:2 (2015), 23–41.
Sadler, Michael, 'Fauvism and a Fauve', *Rhythm*, 1:1 (1911), 14–18.
Salmon, Michael A., *The Aurelian Legacy: British Butterflies and their Collectors* (Berkeley: University of California Press, 2000).
Sander, Jochen, ed., *The Magic of Things: Still Life Painting 1500–1800* (Frankfurt: Städel Museum, 2008).

Scarry, Elaine, 'Imagining Flowers: Perceptual Mimesis (Particularly Delphinium)', *Representations* (1997), 90–115.

Schapiro, Meyer, *Paul Cézanne* (New York: Harry N. Abrams, 1962).

Schapiro, Meyer, *Modern Art: 19th and 20th Centuries* (London: Chatto & Windus, 1978).

Schneider, Norbert, *Still Life* (Cologne: Taschen, 2003).

Schopenhauer, Arthur, *The World as Will and Representation*, trans. E. F. J. Payne, 2 vols (New York: Dover Publications, 1969), I.

Schwartz, Hillel, 'Torque: The New Kinaesthetic of the Twentieth Century', in Jonathan Crary and Stanford Kwinter, eds, *Incorporations* (New York: Urzone, 1992), pp. 71–126.

Schwarz, Daniel, '"The Serenade of a Man Who Plays a Blue Guitar": The Presence of Modern Painting in Stevens's Poetry', *Journal of Narrative Technique*, 22 (1992), 65–83.

Scott, Bonnie Kime, ed., *Gender in Modernism* (Chicago: University of Illinois Press, 2007).

Scott, Bonnie Kime, *In the Hollow of the Wave: Virginia Woolf and Modernist Uses of Nature* (Charlottesville: University of Virginia Press, 2012).

Sexton, James, 'Aldous Huxley *aka* Conde Nast's "Staff of Experts", Part 1', in Jerome Meckier and Bernfried Nugel, eds, *Aldous Huxley Annual: A Journal of Twentieth-Century Thought and Beyond*, 5 (2005), 1–10.

Shattuck, Roger, *The Banquet Years: The Origins of the Avant-garde in France, 1885 to World War I*, rev. edn (London: Jonathan Cape, 1969 [1958]).

Shaw-Miller, Simon, *Visible Deeds of Music: Art and Music from Wagner to Cage* (New Haven: Yale University Press, 2002).

Shepherd-Barr, Kirsten, 'Modernism and Theatrical Performance', *Modernist Cultures*, 1 (2009), 59–68

Sheridan, Judith Rhine, 'The Picasso Connection: Wallace Stevens's "The Man with the Blue Guitar"', *Arizona Quarterly*, 35 (1979), 77–89.

Siegloch, Magdalene, *How the New Art of Eurythmy Began: Lory Maier-Smits, the First Eurythmist* (London: Temple Lodge Publishing, 1997).

Sim, Lorraine, *Virginia Woolf: The Patterns of Ordinary Experience* (Farnham: Ashgate, 2010).

Simister, Kirsten, *Living Paint: J. D. Fergusson 1874–1961* (London: Mainstream Publishing, 2001).

Smith, Paul, 'Cézanne's Color Lab: Not-So-Still Life', in Benedict Leca, ed., *The World is an Apple: The Still Lifes of Paul Cézanne* (London: Giles, 2014), pp. 91–143.

Soby, James Thrall, *Giorgio de Chirico* (New York: Museum of Modern Art, 1966).

Spalding, Frances, *Roger Fry: Art and Life* (Berkeley: University of California Press, 1980).

Spalding, Frances, 'Helen Sutherland, Patron, Collector and Friend of Ben Nicholson', *Burlington Magazine* (July 2013), CLV, 480–8.

Spalding, Frances, *Vanessa Bell: Portrait of the Bloomsbury Artist* (1983) (London: I. B. Tauris, 2016).

Spock, Marjorie, *Eurythmy* (New York: Anthroposophic Press, 1980).

Spretnak, Charlene, *The Spiritual Dynamic in Modern Art: Art History Reconsidered, 1800 to the Present* (New York: Palgrave, 2014).

Steiner, Rudolf, 'The Inner Nature of Music and the Experience of Tone', 12 November 1906, Rudolf Steiner Archive and e.Lib, http://wn.rsarchive.org/Lectures/GA283/English/AP1983/19061112p01.html.

Steiner, Rudolf, 'Lecture 1: "The Creative World of Colour"', 26 July 1914, in *The Creative World of Colour: Four Lectures at Dornach*, Rudolf Steiner Archive and e.Lib, http://wn.rsarchive.org/Lectures/GA/GA0291/19140726p01.html.

Steiner, Rudolf, 'Eurythmy', Introductory words by Dr Rudolf Steiner at a performance of Eurhythmy, given at Dornach, 12 December 1920, unknown translator, in Rudolf Steiner Archive and e.Lib, http://wn.rsarchive.org/Lectures/EU4313_index.html.

Steiner, Rudolf, 'Anthroposophy and the Visual Arts', 9 April 1922, Lecture trans. from unrevised notes by V. C. Bennie, in Rudolf Steiner Archive and e.Lib, http://wn.rsarchive.org/Lectures/19220409p01.html.

Steiner, Rudolf, *A Lecture on Eurythmy: Given at Penmaenmawr on 26th August, 1923* (London: Rudolf Steiner Press, 1967, repr. 1st edn 1926).

Steiner, Rudolf, 'Supersensible Knowledge: Anthroposophy as a Demand of the Age', Lecture I, 26 September 1923, Rudolf Steiner Archive and e.Lib, http://wn.rsarchive.org/Lectures/GA084/English/AP1943/19230926p02.html.

Steiner, Rudolf, *Eurythmy as Visible Speech* (1931), trans. and rev. by V. and J. Compton-Burnett and S. and C. Dubrovik (London: Anthroposophical Publishing Co., 1956).

Steiner, Rudolf, *Eurythmy as Visible Song*, trans. V. and J. Compton-Burnett (London: Anthroposophical Publishing Co., 1932).

Steiner, Rudolf, *Colour* (London: Rudolf Steiner Press, 1935).

Steiner, Rudolf, *A Lecture on Eurythmy*, 1926 (London: Rudolf Steiner Press, 1967).

Steiner, Rudolf, *Knowledge of the Higher Worlds* (London: Rudolf Steiner Press, 1969).

Steiner, Rudolf, *An Introduction to Eurythmy: Talks Given before Sixteen Eurythmy Performances*, trans. Gladys Hahn (New York: Anthroposophic Press, 1984).

Steiner, Rudolf, *Philosophy, Cosmology, and Religion: Ten Lectures* (1922) (London: Anthroposophic Press, 1984).

Steiner, Rudolf, *Eurythmy: An Introductory Reader*, original texts compiled and introduced by Beth Usher, translations rev. by Christian von Arnim (Forest Row: Sophia Books, 2006).

Stephens, Chris, ed., *A Continuous Line: Ben Nicholson in England* (London: Tate Publishing, 2008).

Sterling, Charles, *Still Life Painting from Antiquity to the Twentieth Century*, 2nd rev. edn, trans. James Emmons (New York: Harper & Row, 1981 [1959]).

Stevens, Wallace, *The Necessary Angel: Essays on Reality and the Imagination* (New York: Alfred A. Knopf, 1951).

Stevens, Wallace, *Opus Posthumous*, ed. Samuel French Morse (New York: Vintage, 1982; repr. Alfred A. Knopf, 1957).

Stevens, Wallace, *Sur Plusieurs Beaux Sujets: Wallace Stevens' Commonplace Book*, ed. Milton J. Bates (Stanford: Stanford University Press, 1989).

Stevens, Wallace, *Letters of Wallace Stevens*, ed. Holly Stevens (Berkeley: University of California Press, 1996).

Stevens, Wallace, *Collected Poetry and Prose*, ed. Frank Kermode and Joan Richardson (New York: Library of America, 1997).

Stoichita, Victor, *The Pygmalion Effect: From Ovid to Hitchcock*, trans. A. Anderson (Chicago: Chicago University Press, 2009).

Stokes, Adrian, *Colour and Form* (1937), in Lawrence Gowing, ed., *The Critical Writings of Adrian Stokes*, 3 vols (London: Thames & Hudson, 1978), II.

Taxidou, Olga, '"Do Not Call Me a Dancer" (Isadora Duncan, 1929): Dance and Modernist Experimentation', in David Bradshaw, Laura Marcus and Rebecca Roach, eds, *Moving Modernisms: Motion, Technology, and Modernity* (Oxford: Oxford University Press, 2016).

Teukolsky, Rachel, *The Literate Eye* (Oxford: Oxford University Press, 2009).

Thacker, Andrew, *Moving through Modernity: Space and Geography in Modernism* (Manchester: Manchester University Press, 2003).

Thurschwell, Pamela, *Literature, Technology and Magical Thinking, 1880–1920* (Cambridge: Cambridge University Press, 2001).

Tickner, Lisa, *Modern Life and Modern Subjects* (New Haven: Yale University Press, 2000).

Tillyard, S. K., *The Impact of Modernism 1900–1920* (London: Routledge, 1988).

Tobin, Claudia, '"The active and the contemplative": Charles Mauron, Virginia Woolf, and Roger Fry', in Nicola Wilson and Claire Battershill, eds, *Virginia Woolf and the World of Books* (Clemson: Clemson University Press, 2018).

Tobin, Claudia, 'Virginia Woolf, Still Life and Transformation', in Laura Smith, Enrico Tassi and Eloise Bennett, eds, *Virginia Woolf: An Exhibition Inspired by Her Writings*, (London: Tate, 2018).

Torgovnick, Marianna, *The Visual Arts, Pictorialism, and the Novel: James, Lawrence, and Woolf* (Princeton: Princeton University Press, 1985).

Trotter, David, *Cooking with Mud: The Idea of Mess in Nineteenth-Century Art and Fiction* (Oxford: Oxford University Press, 2000).

Trower, Shelley, *Senses of Vibration: A History of the Pleasure and Pain of Sound* (London: Continuum, 2012).

Turner, Sarah Victoria, '"Spiritual Rhythm" and "Material Things": Art, Cultural Networks and Modernity in Britain, c. 1900–1914', unpublished doctoral thesis, University of London, Courtauld Institute, 2009.

Turner, Sarah Victoria, 'Ezra Pound's New Order of Artists: "The New Sculpture" and the Critical Formation of a Sculptural Avant-garde in Early Twentieth-Century Britain', *Sculpture Journal*, 21:2 (2012), pp. 9–22.

Uhlmann, Anthony, 'Virginia Woolf and Bloomsbury Aesthetics', in Maggie Humm, ed., *The Edinburgh Companion to Virginia Woolf and the Arts* (Edinburgh: Edinburgh University Press, 2010), pp. 58–73.

Van Campen, Cretien, *The Hidden Sense: Synesthesia in Art and Science* (Cambridge, MA: MIT Press, 2008).

Van den Beuckel, Karlien, 'Torque: Dancers and Sappers in Some Early Bomberg Sketches', exhibition text for *David Bomberg: Objects of Collection*, Borough Road Gallery, London (2014).

Van Eck, Caroline, *Art, Agency and Living Presence: From the Animated Image to the Excessive Object* (Boston: De Gruyter, 2015).

Varga, Adriana L., ed., *Virginia Woolf and Music* (Bloomington: Indiana University Press, 2014).

Vendler, Helen Hennessy, *Wallace Stevens: Words Chosen Out of Desire* (Knoxville: University of Tennessee Press, 1984).

Villeneuve, Crispian, *Rudolf Steiner in Britain: A Documentation of his Ten Visits*, 2 vols (London: Temple Lodge, 2011), I.

Von der Ruhr, Mario, *Simone Weil: An Apprenticeship in Attention* (London: Continuum Books, 2006).

Von Goethe, Johann Wolfgang, *Goethe's Colour Theory*, trans. Herb Ach (London: Studio Vista Limited, 1971).

Wilson, Leigh, *Modernism and Magic: Experiments with Spiritualism, Theosophy and the Occult* (Edinburgh: Edinburgh University Press, 2012).

Winckelmann, Johann Joachim, *History of the Art of Antiquity*, trans. Harry Francis Mallgrave (Los Angeles: Getty Publications, 2006).

Wood, Christopher, *Dear Winifred: Letters to Winifred and Ben Nicholson, 1926–1930*, ed. Anne Goodchild (Bristol: Sansom & Company, 2013).

Woolf, Virginia, *The Moment and other Essays*, ed. Leonard Woolf (London: Hogarth Press, 1947).

Woolf, Virginia, *A Writer's Diary: Being Extracts from the Diary of Virginia Woolf*, ed. Leonard Woolf (London: Hogarth Press, 1953).

Woolf, Virginia, *Granite and Rainbow* (New York: Harcourt Brace, 1958).
Woolf, Virginia, *The Death of the Moth and Other Essays* (1942), ed. Leonard Woolf (London: Penguin, 1961).
Woolf, Virginia, *The Waves*, new edn (London: Penguin, 1964).
Woolf, Virginia, *To the Lighthouse* (1927) (Harmondsworth: Penguin, 1964).
Woolf, Virginia, *Collected Essays*, ed. Leonard Woolf, 4 vols (London: Hogarth Press, 1966–67).
Woolf, Virginia, *Between the Acts* (1941) (New York: Harcourt Brace, 1969).
Woolf, Virginia, *The Letters of Virginia Woolf*, ed. Nigel Nicholson and Joanne Trautmann, 6 vols (London: Hogarth Press, 1975–80).
Woolf, Virginia, *The Diary of Virginia Woolf*, ed. Anne Olivier Bell, assisted by Andrew McNeillie, 5 vols (London: Hogarth Press, 1977–84).
Woolf, Virginia, *The Complete Shorter Fiction of Virginia Woolf*, ed. Susan Dick, rev. edn (London: Hogarth Press, 1989).
Woolf, Virginia, *Roger Fry: A Biography* (1940) (London: Hogarth Press, 1991).
Woolf, Virginia, *Moments of Being: Autobiographical Writings*, ed. Jeanne Schulkind, rev. Hermione Lee (London: Pimlico, 2002)
Woolf, Virginia, *Congenial Spirits: The Selected Letters of Virginia Woolf*, ed. Joanne Trautmann Banks (London: Pimlico, 2003).
Woolf, Virginia, *The Essays of Virginia Woolf*, Vols 1–4, ed. Andrew McNeillie, Vols 5–6, ed. Stuart N. Clarke (London: Hogarth Press, 1986–2011).

INDEX

CPSIA information can be obtained
at www.ICGtesting.com
Printed in the USA
JSHW022022140522
25872JS00009B/29

9 781474 455145